The Triumph of Hate

The Political Theology of the Hitler Movement

Christopher Vasillopulos

For Fitc ,

Best wishes ,

UNIVERSITY PRESS OF AMERICA,® INC.
Lanham · Boulder · New York · Toronto · Plymouth, UK

Copyright © 2012 by
University Press of America,® Inc.
4501 Forbes Boulevard
Suite 200
Lanham, Maryland 20706
UPA Acquisitions Department (301) 459-3366

Estover Road
Plymouth PL6 7PY
United Kingdom

Library of Congress Control Number: 2011935392
ISBN: 978-0-7618-5670-2 (clothbound : alk. paper)
ISBN: 978-0-7618-5671-9 (paperback : alk. paper)
eISBN: 978-0-7618-5672-6

For Lara

THE WIDOW'S MITE

Too soon she came, too soon conceived, too soon
Except for her whose time reserved by God.
So small is she yet so fine and elegant
Prehensile hands and feet and mouth clamped tight
Around the engorged teat. So small is she
My heart can break upon her body slight.
If she be the price of sin, what God would so
Exact this due? If it be just for me
To die for sin remit, please God, take me.
Immersed in sin, I plead, take me as though
I were the sweetest lamb and more, the Christ
Of your own loins. No bargains this, I know,
So sweet a child for worthless wretch exchange,
And yet accept this widow's mite, my life.
—*Christopher Vasillopulos*

Incidentally, the entire problem of the *Jews* only exists within national states. Their energy and higher intelligence, and the capital of will and spirit that they have accumulated in their long ordeal over the generations, have made them successful to the point that they now arouse envy and hatred, so much so that in almost every nation the vulgar journalistic practice of leading the Jews to the slaughter as scapegoats for every imaginable public or private misfortune is gaining ground—more so in the more nationalistic countries. As soon as it is no longer a question of conserving the nation but of producing the strongest possible mixed race, the Jews will be as usable and desirable an ingredient in the mix as any other national residue. Every nation, every man, has unpleasant, even dangerous characteristics; it is cruel to demand that the Jews should constitute an exception. Even if the characteristics of the Jews are particularly dangerous and repulsive and even if the young Jew of the stock exchange is the most disgusting specimen of the entire human race, nonetheless, I would like to know how much in general accounting, we will have to forgive a people, and here we are very much to blame, who have had the most tragic history and who we owe the most noble man (Christ), the purest wise man, (Spinoza) and the mightiest book and the most effective moral code in the world.

—Nietzsche, *Human, All Too Human,* 1878, section 475

Contents

Acknowledgments

Even for those with a better memory and a deeper sense of gratitude than I possess, it is difficult to thank adequately those who have helped me through a long life. Nevertheless, I cannot avoid trying. First, I wish to thank my father, whose life of unrelenting toil in a business far beneath his abilities and against his natural aptitudes, led him to an early grave. My brother, Michael George, the world famous floral designer, and I have lived long enough to appreciate our father's sacrifice and in some small measure to validate his hopes for us. Then, I wish to acknowledge my teachers: Maynard Smith and Irving Louis Horowitz of Hobart College, who encouraged me beyond the evidence and their better judgment; and Martin Shapiro, of Berkeley, who gave me the confidence to complete a dissertation which no one else could warrant or classify; the late Norman Jacobson, for demonstrating that there was more than one way to be a great teacher, Sheldon Wolin, and Ernst Haas, who exemplified the value of scholarship. Among my colleagues and friends, I must acknowledge first Hope Fitz of Eastern Connecticut State University, who has supported me professionally and personally beyond all measure. I must also thank David Carter, now Chancellor of Connecticut State University, for hiring me when no one else would. Leon Sarin, John Dierst, Mizan Kahn, Branko Carvakapa, and Pat Terry, all of ECSU, and Norton Mezvinsky and Taso Papathasis of Central Connecticut State University, all of whom have played important roles in my life. Grant Havers of Trinity Western University has been a valuable friend and colleague from British Columbia. From the University of Athens, Panos Eliopoulos has become my second brother. I should also acknowledge several students, now friends, who supported me in ways that only teachers can appreciate: Ben Kelmendi, Blerim Rexhaj; Frank Robacker, Tom Zinza, among many, many others. And finally, some lifelong friends, without whom life would have lost its savor: Rick Weissmann, who knew how to take life as it came and went. Larry Stone, who kept me sane in the Army; Joe DeCelles, my favorite quarterback; Gordon Carlisle, my nemesis and advocate; Peter Haley, who, despite being a lawyer, has been an intellectual stimulus for thirty years; James Penna, who defines friendship. And Victoria Sheldon, who, despite mountains of contrary evidence, believed that I might amount to something. Finally, to Sema, whose devotion to Lara helped me to complete this book.

Chapter One

Paul and the Foundations of Anti-Judaism

PROLOGUE

A scrawny runt of a man scuttled along the rock-hard desert road, needing a destination. Why couldn't he forget the execution? By offending important people, by offending the Law, he invited it. Only the rabble remained loyal. Still the crucifixion stayed with him. He would escape, to Damascus, to anywhere. Bent to his journey, he quickened his pace. He would work to become the best Jew ever, driving this image from his mind. Every *iota* of the Law would be fulfilled. He had been too much Tarsus, not enough Jerusalem. The acid righteousness of the Law would sear away his Greekness. The ancient wisdom of observance would banish all his questions, easing his troubled mind. He would observe the Law, the self-justifying Law. God's ordinances demanded obedience, not inquiry. Pure and simple. Questions, justifications, reasons, all these were hopelessly Greek, defiled, pagan.

Staring into the relentless sun, hoping it would burn out his doubts, his need to question, his need to understand, he prayed: 'O God, give me the strength to obey with all my soul. Help me follow the paths of righteousness.' Scorching his twisted body, the sun drove him to his knees and then onto his face. Then the Voice, as much within as without, enveloped him. 'Saul, Saul.'

His ears ringing with soundless agony, naked before the enemy within, dumbfounded, Saul asked, 'Who are you? What are you?'

'I am Love. And you are loved.'

'What?'

'I am Love and you are loved.' Before the bewildered man could respond, the Voice said, 'Arise, my beloved son.'

It was dark before Saul could shake the dust from his clothes and resume his journey. The Voice, he would strive to reach the Voice. He would spend

his life in the effort to hear the Voice again. Before, he had a thousand answers and a troubled mind. Now, he had a thousand questions and his mind
was free. He wanted to know why. Did it have something to do with the crucified man? 'God is Love. To love one another is to love God, for God loves
you as he loves all His Creation.' He would find out what this simple man had
to do with this message of love. Had this itinerant, down at the heels prophet
discovered something profound about the living God, the God of Wrath and
Righteousness? Was the living God the God of Love and Forgiveness? Was
this the answer to all his questions? Could it be that God loved his Creation?
And that we acknowledge His love by loving each other? Surely there must
be more to it than that. 'Is that all?' he wanted to ask the Voice.

Other questions tumbled in his mind. If the Law was not the way, why had
the Voice spoken to him? Or, did the Voice speak to all men, but only some
heard? Why did so many fail to hear it? Perhaps this was his new work, his
mission. Could he help people hear it, heed it? 'Won't you participate in the
love feast?' it seemed to say. He would explain this invitation to those who
did not hear the Voice. Is this why he heard it? Could he use reason to convince all who needed reasons to heed the message: Love one another, for God
is Love? No prophet, no singer of songs, not anointed, he was only a man.
Loved him as he was, the Voice said, 'Arise, my beloved.' Me, whom no one
has ever loved? Me, a bundle of torments? 'Arise, my beloved.' Was this the
message: if I can be loved, then all can be loved? And if I can be loved, cannot I love all? Well, then, I will use myself up.

Joyfully, Paul walked to Damascus. Loved, knowing he could love, his
'cup runneth over.' Having a mission, whether it lasted a day, a decade or a
hundred years, he knew: 'Surely goodness and mercy would follow him all
the days of his life.' Never again would he be afraid, never again would he
be alone, for the Voice was with him.

> In the belief and thought of Paul it is just the *identity* of the heavenly Messiah,
> on whom he the Jew had fixed his faith, with the crucified Jesus who walked the
> earth in human form, obedient to God, humble, selfless, suffering, that stands as
> the adorable wonder at the center from which all rays emerge. Johannes Weiss[1]

AN APPROACH TO PAUL'S THEOLOGY

Paul's version of what happened to him outside Damascus differs from the
prologue. Paul had his reasons and I have mine for our accounts: first, mine,
then my suggestions regarding Paul's version. The prologue captures Paul's
understanding of Jesus' most profound insight: God loves Creation. Every
creature, including men and women, is part of God's expression of love and,

therefore, part of God. This is the essence of Pauline Christianity, that is, the essence of Paul's appreciation of Jesus as the Christ, the proclaimer of the *Gospel*. Nearly every Pauline insight, argument, or assertion stems from the core idea that the universe expresses divine love. John would say: 'God is Love.' Love not only governs the universe, it is the universe. Paul would try to live accordingly and try to convince others to do likewise. If they listened to him, if they heard the Voice of God, they would be saved, Here and Now and for all Eternity.

Why did Paul render his account in *Acts* of his experience on the road to Damascus in these terms? He heard a voice saying, 'Saul, Saul, why do you persecute me?' He asked, 'who are you, Lord?' The reply came, 'I am Jesus.' There are two interrelated reasons. First, Paul was too good a Jew to equate himself with Abraham or Moses and claim that God spoke to him. Second, when he believed that Creation was the expression of the Loving and Living God, he reevaluated his understanding of Jesus. Not only did he cease persecuting his followers, he inferred that Jesus was the Messiah, the Christ.

Lacking a proper background in Jewish learning, Jesus spoke of God so simply, so directly, so authoritatively that he seemed to have a personal relationship with Him. Only the Christ could have understood that God is Love. Note, it was not that Paul determined that Jesus was the Christ and, therefore, His message was God's Word. Paul believed the message was God's Word, therefore, Jesus had to be the Christ. Only Christ, only the offshoot of God, could know Him so intimately. Only Christ could speak with such assurance that the core of Judaism was the command to love one another as God loves His Creation. To love one's neighbor is to love God. The very transformation of these ideas into a tripartite universal principle, which dwarfed all the other values, concepts, rites, practices, and values of Judaism, required far more than a gifted rabbi. Paul believed that only the Christ could know the Word of God this profoundly, this simply, this directly. Only the Christ could proclaim it, as Jesus did, to all who would listen, to all as creations of divine Love. In this light Paul's version and mine of his epiphany converge. Christ proclaims the Word of God. He proclaims the truth of God's Love, even if He must suffer for it. We must do likewise. From this epiphany Paul inferred his life's mission: to proclaim the Word of God as expressed by Christ Jesus. The Good News.

I have already suggested two of the many difficulties which beset the interpretation of Pauline Christianity. Paul had an agenda which he saw as far more important than theological exposition. He would do and say almost anything to deliver the message that God is Love. For Paul, the end not only justified the means; it subsumed them. In an important sense the very distinction of means and ends in Paul's writing is problematic. The End, the *Eschaton*, as we shall see, is all. And it includes the Beginning, the moment of Creation. Beginning and End are one, one with God. Some of the difficulties of Pauline interpretation are generic. He dealt with questions which still vex philosophers and theologians. Moreover, he did so in the form of letters, making systematic presentation virtually impossible. Consider by contrast the multi-volume works of Aristotle or Kant, philosophers who took pains to be understood. Yet, after centuries of extraordinary scholarship, many of their ideas remain disputed. Other difficulties are peculiar to Paul. No philosopher, notwithstanding the profundity of his thought, Paul wished only to proclaim the message of the Christ. Although he was brought up in Tarsus, a Hellenistic city rich in philosophy, although he used Greek as his primary language and was familiar with the main currents of Greek thought, Paul remained a Jew in the deepest structure of soul, no matter how familiar he was with Greek, its locutions, its concepts, or its rationality. In at least one important respect, however, Paul was deeply influenced by his Greek surroundings. He needed reasons for his beliefs, reasons to know what his beliefs were. He did not have a set of convictions which he then supported with arguments. Not assertions, Paul's doctrines were products of his experiences, values, and mode of thinking. By assuring himself of their truth, Paul would then search for ways to convince others.

The failure to appreciate the distinction between Paul's reasons or the reasoning process intrinsic to his pattern of belief acquisition, on the one hand, and the reasons adduced to present his beliefs to others, on the other, has led to many interpretive confusions. Many of the contradictions, inconsistencies, or paradoxes imputed to Paul result from not keeping the mode of discovery and the mode of persuasion distinct. In other words, he was a much more coherent thinker than he has been given credit for, more at home with dialectical reasoning than with undifferentiated feeling, more Apollonian than Dionysian, to use Nietzschean concepts. Although it is impossible to reconcile Paul's writings, his most important ideas, nonetheless, follow logically from his understanding of the Christ.

There remains a further difficulty with my reading of Paul, one intrinsic to this work. Although I studied him long before I conceived of this book, my understanding of him may have been colored by this project. I may have read back into Paul the profound estrangement of Jews and Christians. Though he believed to his death that he was advocating the true version of Judaism, he provided a theological foundation for anti-Judaism. Hardening their doctrines, faces, and hearts one to the other, Jewish-Christian antagonism became much more acrimonious, unrelenting, and violent. I realize that anti-Judaism was reciprocated by virulent anti-Christianity, yet the power differentials between the two peoples became so one-sided, as Christianity spread to the far reaches of the Roman Empire, becoming its official religion, that to treat them as equivalents courts distortion. The consequences for European Jewry have been catastrophic. It is inconceivable that anti-Semitism would have developed so murderously, absent millennia of anti-Jewish teaching and theology.[2] This development to a great extent began with Paul. Therefore, it is important to know how Paul's revised understanding of Judaism widened, if it did not create, the chasm between Christians and Jews. Before we undertake this task, one more qualification needs to be made. Although I believe my interpretation of Paul is valid in its own terms, one valid account among many, the argument of this book requires only that Paul's thought can be interpreted as part of the foundation of anti-Judaism. If this be true, it matters little what Paul intended. Of course, it matters a great deal to Jewish-Christian relations in the twenty-first century to appreciate that Paul's conviction that God's Creation is Love, so profound, so powerful, so pervasive that it leaves no room for hate.

> Judaism might have endured a Messianic sect in its midst, but could not tolerate the abrogation of the Mosaic Law of holiness, on which in the last resort its own consciousness of the Covenant was based. H.J. Schoeps[3]
>
> [Paul] thought backward from solution to plight and his thinking…was governed by the overriding conception that salvation is through Christ. E.P. Sanders[4]

THE THEOLOGY OF THE CHRIST-EVENT

As understood by Paul, the death and resurrection of Jesus Christ changed everything. Signaling more than a new path to redemption or a new way to understand Creation, the Christ-Event signified a new way, the only way, to understand Judaism. The Messiah has come, been crucified, and resurrected. For Paul the Christ-Event, far from denying the truth of Judaism, fulfilled it. The Christ-Event implied that traditional Judaism had to be modified. While Jesus was not the kind of Messiah for whom the Jews yearned or Judaism had prophesied, He had come. It seemed to Paul that traditional Judaism could not take 'Yes' for an answer. Perversely preferring to cling to traditional concepts of the Covenant, the Law, and the Messiah, all in the face of the Christ-Event, Judaism undermined God's purpose. If traditional Judaism, largely reduced the Mosaic Law in Paul's writings, could have played the role ascribed to it, then the Christ-Event would not have been necessary. It occurred, because Judaism needed to be brought into line with Christ, rightwised with God, if it were to remain Judaism at all, just as every individual needed to be rightwised with God by faith. Through the concept of Christ, Paul believed he understood Judaism better than anyone else. Of course, Christ was no mere concept for him but the human expression or offshoot of the living God.

There are of course many points of difference between Paul's version of Judaism and the traditional mainstream. Let us begin with the Law, as Sanders understands Paul:

> Paul's 'not by works of law' shows that he had come to hold a different view of God's plan for salvation form that of non-Christian Judaism. It was never... God's intention that one should accept the Law to become one of the elect. Though fully evident now that Christ has come, God's intention to save on the basis of faith was previously announced in Scripture. The case is made above all by Abraham, who was chosen without accepting the Law. *This is, in effect an attack on the traditional understanding of the Covenant and election,* according to which accepting the Law signified acceptance of the Covenant.[5]

By denying that the Law could provide righteousness, Paul did far more than narrow the Law to a set of legalisms or empty rituals. He 'disconnected and isolated the Law from the controlling reality of the Covenant.'[6] By desacralizing the *Torah* in this way, Paul convinced himself that Jews have perceived the Law as a path to salvation in and of itself. By observing the Law, Jews became righteous in the sight of God and, therefore, believed they could expect God to reward them. Many Christian theologians have echoed Paul: 'By offering it [the Covenant] to the people, God had entered into mutual obligations with them.'[7] Disagreeing, Jewish theologians have criticized Paul for grossly distorting the nature and function of the Law: 'Every child of the Jews...knows that the Law had no other purpose than that of being given by God in order to be kept and not transgressed, in order increase the resistance to sin and not augment sin.... But the most essential point in the Jewish understanding of the Law is that God gave it to the people of His choice, in order to bind Israel closely with God, because the holy God through the Law wishes to render His people holy.'[8] Moreover, Schoeps claims that Paul did not understand the most basic elements of Judaism:

> Paul did not perceive...that the *Biblical* view of the Law is integral to the Covenant; in modern terms it was the constitutive act by which the Sinai Covenant was ratified, the basic ordinance which God laid down for His 'house of Israel.' In the first place it was given in order to bind the Israelite people to its Covenant God as His peculiar possession.... Now when Paul speaks of the Jewish *nomos* he implies a twofold curtailment; in the first place he has reduced the *Torah,* which means for the Jews both Law and teaching, to the ethical (and ritual) Law; secondly, he has wrested and isolated the Law from the controlling context of God's Covenant with Israel.[9]

And further: 'Because Paul had lost all understanding of the characteristics of the Hebraic *berith* as a partnership involving *mutual obligations*, he failed to grasp the inner meaning of the Mosaic Law, namely, that it is an instrument by which the Covenant is realized.'[10]

There can be little doubt that Paul did understand the relationship of the Law to the Covenant and other fundamental principles of Judaism, notwithstanding his disagreement with them. The very idea of the inherent interdependence of the Law and the Covenant is precisely what Paul saw as misconceived. It was traditional Judaism which misunderstood the Law, not him, and did so in two interlocking ways: first, that the Law obligated God in any way; second, that it made a particular people His 'peculiar possession,' to use Schoeps's words, leaving all others, by implication, outside God's plans for salvation. Paul over-legalized the Law for two reasons: (1) in order to attack the concept of the Chosen People, that is, to reformulate the concept the Children of Abraham, at least as it had evolved under the influence of the Mosaic Law and (2) to deny that God could be obligated. Paul believed that 'the new Christian community is the Israel of God, the old Israel has been rejected by God.'[11] To see how he arrived at this breathtaking reversal, we must consider the Christ-Event in greater detail.

Finite spirit—individual and social—is seen [by Hegel] as an aspect of infinite or absolute Spirit; without which the suffering a loss of its real finitude, it is a phase in the self-realization of the divine Spirit. Emil Fackenheim[12]

TWO KINDS OF SPIRIT

Let me begin with the crux of the Christ-Event. According to Schoeps, '[Christ's "pneumatic existence"] removes Him from the sphere of the human, from the aeon of the fleshly, for His *phusis* is filled with the working of the Holy Spirit with divine *dynamis* and has become *theia phusis....* '[13] Much more than the idea that the Creator is manifest in Creation is meant by *theia phusis*, something which Schoeps emphasizes by quoting E. Lohmeyer: 'for to be *kyrios* means nothing else than to be equal to God—and that in full humanity.'[14] Paul was too Jewish to have uttered so bald a statement—God, despite many anthropomorphic attributes, was still too awesome, too righteous, and too wrathful to be conjoined to humanity.

Resisting mystical explanations, Paul tried to understand the Christ-Event rationally, however, imperfectly. The term 'rationalist' must be used advisedly. Paul did not believe that the world was Reason or that it can be comprehended by the use of Reason. God and His Creation are fundamentally beyond man's intellectual capacity. While Paul did not have faith in Reason *per se*, he believed Reason could help man understand the implications Creation, if not its Why. A consequence of faith in God's Creation, Reason, better Right Reason, could avoid the snares consequent to having faith only in itself. Incapable of ascertaining truth, Reason was not, as it was for the Greeks, a mode of under-standing truth, much less generating it. Reason can only elaborate truth *already* given or revealed. Nevertheless, it was not enough for Paul to have an insight, a revelation, or an intuition. Needing to make his insights coherent, not only to convey them to others, but to verify them, Reason had an important role to play. In this limited sense, Paul was a rationalist. Weiss's explains: 'With all his soul and with all the power of his will he belongs among those who can really re-joice in an experience only when they have found for it a satisfying theoretical formula for its expression, and for whom, on the other hand, a consistent logical sequence of thought produces not only intellectual peace and satisfaction but indeed, and especially, a religious inspiration.'[15]

Applying Pauline rationality, what then can be made of Schoeps's concept of a divine body? First, note the distinction between flesh and *phusis,* then note the synthesis of the divine and the material, *theia phusis*, which indicates that God is as much implicated in humanity as humanity is in God's Creation. The lordship, the *kyrios*, of Christ is not merely an expression of the power, *dynamis*, of the Holy Spirit. It is not merely, or perhaps at all, a statement of divine rule over Creation, not an assertion of the Will of God, a reiteration of the basis of His right to command obedience. If it were, it would be consistent with much of traditional Judaism. God did not choose a good man to be in-fused divine powers to impress skeptical men and women. The Christ-Event demonstrated that Christ always existed, existed before Creation, before Time and Space. Christ was not, strictly speaking, an event or an existent but an expression or offshoot of God. *The Christ-Event was this expression, as it took place in Time, in an aeon, but not the aeon of the flesh.*

Hence the significance of distinction of flesh and matter, *phusis*. The world of the flesh is that part of existence that has somehow become estranged from Creation. It is without Spirit or *pneuma*. How Paul dealt with this troubling concept is an extraordinarily important topic. Not wishing to consign the world entire to sin, Paul distinguished between flesh and the body and flesh and matter. God created the world and it was good, good, that is, so long as human beings were infused with the Holy Spirit. That this infusion could take place so completely as to become a *theia phusis* is central to Pauline Chris-tianity, for it established that God was implicated in humans and not merely a transcendent omnipotent and omniscient power. Christ is God-Matter. Equally important and equally derivative of the Christ-Event is that Matter, far from beyond reconciliation with God, is capable of being filled with the Holy Spirit to the extent that the aeon of the flesh is no more, notwithstanding human existence in Time and Space. This is not to say that matter becomes spiritualized, but that its Spirit-Nature is now beyond doubt in the wake of the Christ-Event. The Christ-Event made manifest what has always been true: God did not and cannot abandon Creation without denying Himself. Humans through Christ are God-Matter. This realization provides the joy of Pauline Christianity.

Perhaps Paul's most difficult concept: that humans can to die to the flesh and live in Christ. Although the limits of language suggest a sequence, first die, then live, this is not Paul's meaning. To live in Christ is to die in the flesh. Two expressions of one event, they signify the acceptance of God's Love. To die in the flesh means that the flesh, that is, the material devoid of Spirit, no longer dominates human existence. Living in Christ means that the material world is suffused with Spirit-Existence or, in Paul's terms, living in the body (*soma*) of Christ. By living in Christ salvation is already achieved as much as is possible while existing in Time as Spirit-Existence. This is the realized *Eschaton*, the salvation achieved by living in Christ and by acknowledging the Word of God. The Final *Eschaton* is reached at the End of Days, that is, at the end of Time, when God no longer expresses Himself in Creation but only as the Eternal Spirit-God.

The question remained for Paul: how can God's goodness and the goodness of His Creation be squared with the sins of the flesh or, more precisely, with human susceptibility to sins of the flesh? If existence entails sin, as it did for Paul, the question is not only *why* God would bother with fallen or Adamic man, but *how* He would do so? This question was so troubling that the Pharisee Saul could not ask it. The solution in this respect, as in so many others preceded the question: the Christ-Event. Now that God has demonstrated His connection to the world, His implication in it, Paul was able to ask this question or, rather, explain why Christ must be the answer. No longer was it proper to conceive of God or the Holy Spirit as perfectly transcendent, as something outside of Creation, neither touching it or touched by it. The Christ-Event allows men and women to realize that they, like Abraham, could be saved, despite being immersed in existence and separated from God, because existence does not imply separation from all forms of the Spirit. Matter, including human beings, can be spiritualized, or rather that Spirit-Matter can be recognized by humans, by accepting God's gift of faith. Faith in Christ proves that the Spirit of God has infused human matter. Humans are no longer *of* existence, for existence is now seen as imbued with the Spirit. Although Spirit-Existence is not the Spirit of God, for the same reason that Time is not and cannot be part of Eternity, nevertheless, Spirit-Existence signifies that God remains part of the world, that He is in Time *and* Eternal.

It was an open question for Paul whether our knowledge of God, because it, too, is in Time, distorts the true or Eternal essence of God. But, this does not really matter, for not only will our faith in Christ save us, it will bring us

into the Eternal realm at the End of Days, when we will be reconciled with
God, becoming one with Him, as Christ has always been one with Him. This
is possible; nay, it is undeniable, because the separation from God implied by
existence was never as humans conceived it before the Christ-Event taught
them better. Existence has always been an expression of God. How could
Creation be otherwise? Before the Christ-Event, however, it was possible
in the manner of traditional Judaism to misconstrue Creation as a testing
ground, which assumed that humans could make themselves worthy of God
by obedience to His Will, the Law. This conception assumed that God threw
off the world in some sort of inexplicable spasm, resulting in sinful Adamic
man. The Covenant was accordingly a sort of divine reconsideration, which
gives the Chosen People a second chance through adherence to the Law, becoming perhaps acceptable to God's Awe-filled Presence.

The Christ-Event made nonsense of this conception. Everything has been
ordained. By creating the world in Time and Space, God did not throw off
human existence. Creation, as an expression of God, entails transcending its
existence in Time and Space and its reconciliation with Eternity. The throw-
ing off of the world by God was merely a human misconception born of
despair, loneliness, and death, a consequence of man's inability to appreciate God's Love, God's Grace and God's Goodness in the face of existence.
Abraham knew this. Now the children of Abraham, redefined as those who
accept the Christ-Event in all its power and glory, know it too. Existence is
but an expression of God which humans see as a sojourn, because they cannot
think in the light of the Eternal. Faith, however, Abrahamic faith, now made
undeniable by the Christ–Event, enables us to glimpse the Eternal. Faith in
Christ allows the Holy Spirit to enter us, making sin impossible, by destroying the power of the flesh. Faith in Christ enables humans to partake of the
divine. The gift of Christ shows us that God partakes of the human. God is
part of Time and Space; the things of Time and Space are part of God. For
Paul, the two kinds of Spirit, the Spirit of God and Spirit-Existence, indicate
that God is both transcendent *and* immanent and that humans are born to die
and born to live forever. The Christ-Event demonstrated that they can live
in Eternity as they live in Time. All they need to do is to die to sin and be
born again in Christ. Anticipating my discussion of Heidegger, God dwells
in Creation and it in Him.

While Paul did not deal directly with the problem of evil, his theology suggests an approach to this vexing issue. Simply put, if God is Love, if God is
Goodness Absolute, why does He allow human beings to sin? Why does He
allow them to feel estranged or to damned? Why were they not imbued with
faith sufficient to the temptations of the existence He has imposed on them?
Does God need to sacrifice the Christ to be reconciled to humans to cure its

injustice? Does God forgive to be forgiven, love to be loved? Is Creation at best a graded exercise with God as a humorless schoolmaster? Related issues deal with the existence and the power of evil spirits, demons, and Satanic forces. If God be all-powerful, whence these creatures or forces? Must they be part of Creation? What would this say regarding God's Absolute Power or Goodness?

Paul's theology renders most of these questions and issues irrelevant, if not absurd, and this is its strength. Otherwise, almost all of these questions would have to be unasked, evaded, or dealt with by explanatory wild cards like paradox or mystery. Given Paul's central proposition that Creation is an expression of God's absolute Love, evil is impossible. At most, evil could refer to the limitations of Spirit-Existence, which allows man to feel estranged from God. For evil to exist as something more than a human misconception, it would have to dwell in Creation and thereby dwell in God. If this were true, then God's Absolute Goodness would vanish, which for Paul was absurd. Unlike traditional Judaism and like Jesus, Paul came close to asserting that there is no such thing as an intrinsically sinful act, except for the sin of allowing a mispremised sense of estrangement to determine human life, a life in and of the flesh. Humans see God as not merely angry with man for sinning but as wrathful in His nature, because He allows them, even tempts them to sin. Paul believed, however, that the sense of estrangement has not been ordained by God. Estrangement is rooted in the limitations of Spirit-Existence which cannot be identical with Spirit-God, because it exists in Time and Space. To appreciate this error one need only to credit God's ability to infuse existence with his Spirit. While Spirit-Existence is not identical with Spirit-God, it enables humans to realize they are not estranged from God by virtue of Creation. Moreover, their faith in the Christ-Event saves them from sin in the Here and Now. The *theia phusis* invites humans to believe that God is Love and that Creation expresses Love. Furthermore, the *theia phusis* implies that the Spirit-God dwells in Spirit-Existence, thereby enabling humans to dwell in the Spirit-God within the limits of Time and Space. This understanding also illumines the reality of the Final *Eschaton*: Eternal Oneness with the God-Spirit.

> We find in Paul's positive teaching about God…unmistakable traces of his acquaintance with widespread Greek ideas which to be sure may have come to him through Jewish sources. Especially is this true of the statement, 'that the invisible things of him since the Creation of the world are clearly seen, being perceived through the things that are made, even his everlasting power and divinity; that they be without excuse.' In this terse and comprehensive sentence, almost every word and the whole train of thought can be demonstrated from Hellenistic sources.[16] J. Weiss

THE TRANSVALUATION OF CONCEPTS

Paul's conception of the Christ-Event radically altered traditional Jewish beliefs regarding the Law, the Covenant, and the Chosen People. By themselves, Paul's reformulations made any accommodation between him and traditional Judaism impossible. Pauline theology implied a new religion, not a new doctrine within Judaism. Less obviously, he changed many Jewish concepts too radically to be accommodated in mainstream Christianity. In other words, most Christian confessions have retained notions more acceptable to traditional Judaism than to Pauline theology, making him well honored in the breach. Generally speaking, Paul has been credited with making the message of Jesus more amenable to institutionalization, to church building, to congregation molding, and to proselytizing. Undoubtedly true, but, to the extent that it suggests that Paul watered down the more radical Jesus, it is misleading. His theology, for all its differences with Jesus of the *Gospels*, is much closer to the Word of Jesus than is often acknowledged. He deepened the central teaching of Jesus that God is the loving Creator, by drawing the inference that God's Love of Creation subsumes all other loves, including the love of one's neighbor or even the love of God by men and women. Paul's theology has been too much for traditional Judaism, then and now, and too much for traditional Christianity, primitive or contemporary and everything in between, because they, unlike Paul, have not been able to do without the God of Wrath.

Paul's transmutation of wrath from a property derived from God as Judge to an imputation by humans to God, falsely believing that God abandoned them to the forces of evil, has been anticipated in this analysis. Evil ceases to be independent of human fear that God threw him out of the Eternal Realm. It is impossible for me to believe that Paul saw evil spirits as demons hiding under bridges or in haunted houses. It is equally difficult to believe that God's Love of Creation, allows it to cabin malevolence. There are ambiguities and inconsistencies in Paul, but they do not add up to the contradiction that the God of Love could coexist with evil in Creation.

Similar transvaluations have occurred in almost every important concept in Judeo- Christian thought. Although space allows me the opportunity to discuss only a few these, they are sufficient to suggest why Paul has proved as difficult for Christian theology to accommodate as first century Judaism. This discussion also serves the more narrow concerns of this book, underscoring how different his understanding of God was from the rabbis of his time, a difference which accounts for the mutual hostility of Christians and Jews. Second, it indicates that the unwillingness of Christianity to appreciate the Christ-Event undermines its claim to embody the teachings of Jesus. By believing in the *Hebrew Bible's* conceptions of sin, death, redemption, and repentance, Christianity, in most of its confessions, retained much of its wrath. For these concepts, if understood in a pre-Pauline way, imply a Righteous God, who punishes His creatures, who demands unquestioned and absolute obedience, who answers anguished questions with, I Am who I Am. Traditional Judaism cannot see that God is Love, the Creator who loves His Creation, including humans, no matter what, and, what's more, who cannot fail to love them. Pre-Pauline God remains just another father, *albeit* more powerful, who loves according to their deserts and who punishes accordingly: Creation as God's Tribunal, not the fount of His Love. Fearing eternal damnation, humans strive to ascertain the Will of God and to comply with it. Humans do not love because they are unconditionally loved; they love because God *commanded* them to love their neighbors. Humans love, not because they are suffused with God's Love, but to avoid transgressing a divine commandment. Whatever merits this theology, in either its Judaic or Christian forms, may possess, it is certainly not Pauline.

It might have been expected that by moving Christianity closer to traditional Judaism than Paul's theology allowed, Christian-Jewish antagonism would have abated. By retaining the God of Wrath and other Jewish concepts, Christianity took pains to distinguish itself from Judaism. The new religion did not wish to be seen by potential converts as Judaism light or as a Jesus-cult version of Judaism. Christianity became increasingly hostile to Judaism, as it shed more and more of the radical elements of Pauline theology. As the official religion of the Roman Empire, Christianity's dominance of Judaism was assured. Christians were the chosen of God and Jews the rejected.

THE PROBLEM OF DEATH

Many anthropologists believe that the naturalistic impulse to religion originates in the human desire to account for death. One response has been to locate it in the natural order. Another response conceives death as unnatural, a curse or a judgment by a divinity for some human transgression. If death results from sin, then perpetual life must have been possible, even more, intended by God for his creatures. While it is possible to read Paul this way, it is better to read him in a much more Greek, more naturalistic way. Not a curse, not the product of sin, at least not in the simple-minded sense of traditional Judaism and Christianity, death is part of the process of living. Eternal life for any of God's creatures is not only materially impossible but conceptually absurd. What then did Paul mean by death? If it be not a curse, what is it? If it be part of nature, inextricably connected to Creation, then why has it seemed problematic?

An answer lies in another of his most memorable phrases: 'Where, O Death, is your victory? /Where, O Death, is your sting' [I *Cor.* 55]. Of course this could be read as the promise of everlasting life in the next world, as has been done through the centuries. Paul, however, did not deny physical death. He did not say, 'Goodbye, Death, you had a nice run, since Adam fell for Eve. Too bad it's over. Now all of God's creatures will live forever, if they acknowledge the Christ.' Eternal life in Pauline thought is quite consistently reserved to the Eternal realm, beyond Space and Time. But if death were indeed a curse in Paul's mind, an aberration from the intended nature of things, brought about by sin, then why did not the Christ redeem the sin and abolish death in the material world, restoring God's intention?

One answer might be that Adam offended God so profoundly that even He found it beyond His power to forgive him completely, so He gave Adam and his descendents life in the next world as a second prize to perpetual life in this world. The reader should realize how Paul would have responded to an answer which limits God. Saul, however, generally agreed with the following line of reasoning: Feeling abandoned, humans began to rely on their own resources to deal with the trials of material existence which they saw in the light of his unwarranted separation from the Eternal realm of the Spirit-God. These trials, chief of which was mortality, the curse of death, the sickness unto death, were seen as punishments for being unworthy of God's presence. Perhaps humans were thrown into existence because they were unworthy even in God's mind before the Creation: Humanity as a sinful thought! Was Creation the sin of God? Did God long for Creation, long for another expression of Himself? Was He in this sense incomplete? Was not human sinfulness the product of the proto-sin of God? In any event, it has been difficult for humans to conceive of life as self-justifying, so they tried to justify themselves by atoning for the sin of existence. To put it this way, however, would judge God, so humans took the blame, not for Creation, which was impossible, but for what they did after Creation. Somehow Creation became an arena for evil spirits, which befell humans due their devices and desires. If humans, however, learned to overcome these forces of evil, if they could learn to behave righteously, they might win back the favor of God.

There is little question that Saul the Pharisee believed in this sort of explanation. There is equally little question that Christian churches, purporting to follow Paul, have adhered to the views of Saul rather than Paul of the Christ-Event. It is not, however, necessary to read him, as if he retained his Judaic understanding of the Creation and the Fall. He appreciated, perhaps more than most men, that human beings have felt estranged from Creation, the mistake which made the Christ-Event necessary. Fearing death, men and women have led their lives, as if cursed. More than an error, this fear prevented human beings from living properly as loving and loved creatures. Pious men and women tried to live in accordance with ethical and moral ideals, which they imputed to God's Will, strictures embodied in the Law; they lived anticipating judgment. Having discussed Paul's difficulties with the Law as a way to curry God's mercy, if not demand His Grace, here we need to consider the Law as a pharisaical means of dealing with death: while a righteous life could not guarantee salvation, an unrighteous one guarantees damnation. The Law has been conceived as a way of undoing the worst effects of the curse of death, of undoing the worst consequences of Adam's sin. Paul believed in Adam's sin, but not in the trivial sense of falling for the sexual advances of Eve or the serpent. Adam's sin, by extension, all humanity's, was due to misreading Creation as *separation* from God. Creation could not be separated from God, because it was a manifestation of God. Creation is part of the substance of God, to use Spinoza's terms. Creation dwells in God, to use Heidegger's. If God is Love and Creation is an expression of God, then it has to be conceived as part of God's nature. The death of natural things, like the life of natural beings, is also an expression of God's nature. Human sinfulness should not be perceived as a propensity to bad actions, but a cast of mind which believes that God estranged Himself from His Creation in anticipation of the Fall. This false belief has so distorted human understanding that men and women have lived, as if they were at odds with Creation and therefore subject to the Wrath of God. This sin, not paradoxically, is manifested as much by good actions, obedience to the Law, for example, as by bad actions. *Sin is not in the act but in the reason for the act.* The true substratum of human sin is lack of faith, as Paul said repeatedly. Adherence to the Law is a sign of human estrangement from God. By continuing to bring the sin of the Fall into the present, the Law reinforced the human misconception of Creation. Humans have not had sufficient faith in God's Goodness or Love to believe that Creation was a manifestation of God and so, too, were all its creatures, including themselves. This is the sin, the false belief that the Coming of Christ reveals. All other sins are merely mistakes of flesh, incidents in Time and Space, all of which lose their significance in the presence of Faith.

The coming of Christ proclaims the truth that God is Love. To believe in Christ is to believe that God is Love. To believe that God is Love is to accept unconditionally the goodness of all of Creation, including the inevitability of death. To have such a faith does not deny the physical reality or necessity of death, it denies death its *power* over the living. The faithful are no longer the living dead awaiting burial. They have died in the flesh, that is, they are dead to the power of death to poison their lives by turning Creation into a curse or an arena of degradation. They are alive in Christ, which means that they are already saved, already beyond the sting of death. They are alive to the joy of

Creation, because they see it as the expression of God's Love in Time and Space and as a sign of their Eternal existence with the Spirit-God at the End of Days.

If this interpretation of the Christ-Event is plausible, it implies a reassessment of Paul's impact on the history of the Jewish-Christian relations. To the degree that Paul's concept of the Christ-Event and its implications for Judaism made it impossible for traditional Judaism to accept, he might be said to be anti-Jewish or anti-Judaic, regardless of his contrary claim. However unintentionally, Paul laid the foundations for an intelligent, faith-based alternative to traditional Judaism. It cannot be said, however, that he can be implicated in the persecution of Judaism and Jews by Christians in his time or later. The reason is simple and profound. It is impossible to harm or persecute anyone and be consistent with his understanding of Creation as an expression of the central dictum that God is Love. To hate or harm is blasphemy. To hate denies that God's loves the universe. To hate denies that God is Love. To the extent that Christian churches have encouraged or even allowed for the persecution of Jews, pagans, apostates, or anyone else, these churches have blasphemed God. An appreciation of Paul's idea of the Christ-Event makes this conclusion inescapable.

> By the fulfillment of God's commandment a people must truly become itself...
> In Israel this task was fully experienced and exhibited. The idea of the beginning
> of the people and the idea of God's choice cohered as one.[17] Leo Baeck

LEO BAECK: A RABBI'S ANSWER TO PAUL

Just as there are many versions of Christianity or Pauline Christianity, there is no single form of Judaism or Orthodox Judaism. Nevertheless, there are fundamental elements in each religion without which the religion would be unrecognizable. Like Christianity without the Christ, Judaism without the Covenant would be incomprehensible. More controversial is the proposition that Pauline Christianity without the Christ-Event, *as outlined in this book*, would make it incoherent. Profoundly rejecting Paul's concept of the Christ-Event, Baeck defends Judaism at the nexus of Paul's attack: the interdependence of Law, the Covenant, and the Chosen People. Unlike many scholars, Christians and Jews alike, Baeck does not rebuke Paul for narrowing the Law to legalistic ritual, but for much more profoundly misunderstanding it. Baeck asserts that the Law has metaphysical *and* divine properties: 'In the *Bible*, the idea of Law, as suggested by the word *berith* [Covenant], encompasses the idea of the living creation through the One, and the living revelation of the One, the idea of the beyond entering the present. Law, Creation, Revelation—all are fused in a single word.'[18] Moreover, Baeck maintains that: 'There is more to the character of this religion than its teaching of the One God and His Law, more than its monotheism and ethics. Rather its uniqueness reveals itself in that the Will of the One God is recognized as the focal point from which the understanding and thinking, acting and hoping, receive their structure.'[19] The Covenant was given to the world, all the Nations, all the generations since Adam, but only Jews appreciated it, through Noah, Abraham, and Moses and their adherence to the Covenant: 'The religion of this people, in which its genius matured, in which alone it could flourish, is marked by a unique concept: human existence elevated into the realm of the task and Chosenness of man. Everything given to man in his existence becomes a commandment; all that he has received means "Thou shalt!"'[20] Grasping this complex idea, Jews were given a dual task: to be a holy People and to save the humanity. Chosenness implied separateness: 'A moral chasm, a spiritual abyss, seemed to have opened up; Israel lived alone. When it looked about, it could not see where humanity dwelt. For the sake of humanity it had to feel separate from the many peoples…. It could only look to its own future. It had no other choice. If it had no future humanity had none.'[21] By remaining holy and separate from the other Nations, Israel could redeem the world. 'Israel is a people of history; and therefore, it is a Messianic people.'[22] In this context 'Messianic people' does not mean a Nation waiting for a worldly Messiah, who will throw off the oppressors of God's people, although this is included. It means that the Jews are chosen by God to redeem the world by making the Covenant real to those who have failed to appreciate it. In other words, Chosenness, despite it implication of separation, means that Jews as a People have a mission to the Nations of the Gentiles. Separation is anything but exclusiveness, although as a holy people a sense of spiritual superiority is virtually inevitable. Rather, it is a condition for the fulfillment of Judaism's profound connection with the world, God's way of fulfilling a divine mission.

Judaism, thus understood, serves the same function as the Christ-Event for Pauline Christianity. It brings the world as close to God as possible, while remaining in the world, while remaining in Time, awaiting only the Final *Eschaton* and union with God in Eternity. In other words, the Covenant is the source of salvation, working in much the same way as the Christ-Event does for Paul. It is a concept that is in Time *and* in Eternity, which functions in individuals and in Nations, with the proviso that Paul's emphasis is on the community of believers, not biological descendants. Redeeming the world in the Here and Now, removing the power of sin, initiated by God, the Covenant has to be received by humans. It signifies that God has not forsaken the world and that He will never forsake it. It is, in Baeck's words, both 'immanent and transcendent.'[23] Thus understood, the Christ-Event becomes a redundancy, if not blasphemy, for all that is necessary for the salvation of Jews and, through them, the salvation of the world, is already at hand in the Covenant, perpetually renewed, conceived as Law-Creation-Revelation. Paul is thereby neatly and completely reversed.

To the extent that Baeck's understanding of Judaism and Paul's understanding Judaism, reformulated through the Christ-Event, remain exclusive doctrines, then the differences between the religions cannot be bridged by ecumenical exegesis, however well-intentioned, and retain their core ideas and ideals. Not all Jews agree with Baeck. Among those who agree with him that Jews are the Chosen People and that only they have been given the Law are Jews like Schoeps, who believe that the Christian Revelation is equally valid: 'Jews and Christians cannot and must not abandon the absolute claim made upon them by their separate witnesses to the truth. Therefore, by the revealed will of divine predestination, they go their separate ways through history, parallel to each other. But as Christians and Jews, they know that in the supernatural future of the Kingdom of God, the parallels will intersect, and the two ways will be but one way....'[24] Neither Paul nor Baeck would agree with Schoeps's ecumenical reading of the faiths. Baeck and Paul cannot be reconciled. However unfortunate or dangerous this conclusion may seem, however much atrocity and hate these unbridgeable differences have already generated, it should not be surprising. For the basis of such profound rejectionism lies in the belief in an absolute God who acts in history through individuals and Nations and who must so act to bring faithful and only faithful human beings back to Him at the End of Days. With stakes so high and so conceived, the wonder is not that millions have died in the name of the One Just and Righteous God, but that we are capable of treating each other across this and other equally deep divides decently at all.

> He [Paul] went to the Greeks and Romans and brought with them his 'Christianity': a 'Christianity' with which all the Roman Empire became unhinged. 'All men are equal! Brotherhood! Pacifism! No more privileges!'And the Jew triumphed. Dietrich Eckart[25]

SO FAR FROM DAMASCUS:
HITLER'S UNDERSTANDING OF PAUL

My discussion of Paul's important role in the increasing estrangement of the early Christian Church from its Jewish sources and the intensifying hostility the divorce provoked may seem greatly removed from modern anti-Semitism and not only in time. What could the often abstruse doctrinal disputes between traditional Jewish scholars and Paul or between Paul and the Disciples have to do with concentration camps in a Nation-State a thousand miles and two thousand years away? The idea that, however deeply rooted anti-Judaism has been in Christianity, theological differences between the two great monotheisms could have spawned anti-Semitism, to say nothing of its most radical expression in Hitler and the Nazis, seems to defy common sense. And not only common sense, for many contemporary scholars have taken pains to distinguish anti-Judaism from anti-Semitism. Many others have simply ignored anti- Judaism in their discussions of the Third Reich, arguing that National Socialism can be explained as a hyper-modern nationalism or industrial tribalism or some such, without reference to anti-Judaism. In general, only Jewish students of the Nazis have been comfortable with linking Hitler to German intellectual history and Christian theology, and only a few of them have paid attention to anti-Judaism prior to the Medieval period. This book follows these Jewish scholars to the extent that it holds that anti-Semitism could not have found its way to Auschwitz without a two thousand year tradition of Christian anti-Judaism. This complex proposition will be argued as the book unfolds. Here, however, I will foreshadow some of the argument by discussing Hitler's view of Paul.

Hitler believed that Paul was intensely and intimately related to the Jewish Question. Second, Hitler had an intuitive sense of what Paul was about, which is closer to my analysis of the Apostle than the received version of Christian churches, Catholic or Protestant. Third, Hitler viewed Paul as his most profound and most deadly enemy, the Jew of Jews, incarnating everything he hated in his portrait of infernal Jewry. Fourth, Hitler's conception of Paul, both when intuitively accurate and when erroneous, illuminates a great deal of the Nazi doctrine. Hitler's hatred of Paul demonstrates why anti-Judaism *cum* anti-Semitism lies at the core of the Nazi movement, providing its purpose and its dynamism. Far more than a bone Hitler threw to the ignorant, superstitious, desperate, and terrified German masses, anti-Semitism was central to the Hitler Movement from *Mein Kampf* to the bunker. Without anti-Judaism, no anti-Semitism. Without anti-Semitism, no Hitler Movement. Of course many other factors need to be taken into account, but all of these without anti-Semitism could not have resulted in the successes or the excesses of the Third Reich. Again, this proposition is the subject of the entire book and cannot be elaborated here. Nor will I criticize Hitler's view of Paul here, except as criticism has been implied by my understanding of Pauline Christianity sketched above.

Given Paul's role in the development of anti-Judaism, it might be thought that Hitler would have given him some respect for what Jews have perceived as his attack on traditional Judaism, if for nothing else. Instead, for Hitler, Paul was the archetype of the eternal and infernal Jew and, therefore, a Bolshevik! Consider how an eminent German scholar explains the National Socialist view:

Until 1945 Germany remained too Christian for even the most powerful man in all of Germany's history to have dared publicly to call the Apostle Paul a Bolshevik.... But the fact that for him the Apostle Paul really did remain...a central figure of Jewish Bolshevism...was finally proved with the publication of *Hitler's Table Talk*. Paul...had taken the idea of the Aryan Christ as a crystallization point for slaves of all kinds against their masters and authority. The religion of Paul of Tarsus, later known as Christianity, was simply the Communism of today. This Christianity was the severest blow mankind had ever suffered. It destroyed the Roman Empire, and the result had been centuries of darkness. Christianity was an early form of Bolshevism, Bolshevism an offspring of Christianity—and both were inventions of the Jew for the purpose of disrupting society. Christianity had destroyed the serene, limpid world of antiquity, Bolshevism was getting ready to destroy the pre-eminence of the white race in the world. Yesterday's agitator was called Sha'ul; today's was called Mordecai.[26]

According to Hitler, echoing Nietzsche, Paul founded a religion of slaves, thereby, undermining the concept of authority, an attack which struck at the foundations of nature, which entailed a steep hierarchy based on Social Darwinian principles of aggressive selection, principles which have produced the rule of the white race with Aryans at its apex. The success of Christianity, a monstrous invention of Paul, in defiance of the Aryan Christ, destroyed the Roman Empire and threatened the very survival of European civilization, in particular its rightful rulers, the Germans. Christianity's earlier appeal to the brotherhood of man and pacifism now perniciously reappears in Bolshevism. Although his understanding of Paul did not explicitly refer to Paul's notions of the unity of Creation, the love of God, and the absence of wrath, Hitler, nevertheless, appreciated that Paul's universalism stuck at the core of the Nazi's conception of a world; a world which belonged to the strong, ruthless, and violent, a world based on a steep race-based hierarchy, ordained by a God of hate and vengeance, a God who delegated enforcement of His judgments to an elite who appreciated his true nature. Again, this is a complex argument which will unfold in the following chapters.

The road from Damascus to Auschwitz was long and tortured. It was paved by hate, fear, and ignorance and by the attribution of these all too human attributes to a God of Wrath. Many of the first stones were laid by Christian anti-Judaism. The Pauline doctrine of Love, twisted out of shape by the struggles of the early Christians and tortured to serve the institutional Church and its Protestant descendents, is perhaps history's cruelest irony. One of the many dreary lessons of the Third Reich is that human beings, no matter what their level of civilization or refinement, still need the God of Wrath, who makes choices among his creatures, ordaining some to be slaves and others to be masters. An even more disheartening lesson is that many intellectuals and others, who should have known better, were willing to lend their support to a movement which they viewed as reprehensible and absurd. There were many paving stones that led to Auschwitz; none should be ignored to placate the sensibilities of anyone. The stakes have always been too high to tolerate evasion or, if you prefer, noble lies.

NOTES

1. Weiss, Johannes: *Earliest Christianity, Vol. I*, translated by Frederick Grant *et.al*, NY, 1959, p. 161.

2. See Isaacs, Jules: *The Teaching of Contempt*, McGraw Hill, NY, 1965.

3. Schoeps, H.J.: *Paul: The Theology of the Apostle in the Light of Jewish Religious History*, translated by Harold Knight, Westminster, Philadelphia, 1959, p. 199.

4. Sanders, E.P.: *Paul, the Law, and the Jewish People*, Philadelphia, 1983, p. 68.

5. *Ibid.*, p. 46, emphasis supplied.

6. *Ibid.*, p. 29.

7. Bultmann, R.: *Primitive Christianity*, translated by R.H. Fuller, Philadelphia, 1980, p. 35.

8. Schoeps, *op. cit.*, pp. 194–5.

9. Schoeps, 'Paul's Misunderstanding of the Law,' Meeks, Wayne, editor: *The Writings of St. Paul*, Norton, NY, 1972, p. 357.

10. *Ibid.*, p. 360, emphasis supplied.

11. *Ibid.*, p. 234.

12. Fackenheim, Emil: *The Religious Dimensions in Hegel's Thought*, Boston, 1970, p. 57, original emphasis.

13. Schoeps, *Paul, op. cit.*, p. 152.

14. *Ibid*, p. 152.

15. Weiss, *Earliest, op. cit., Vol.II*, p. 423.

16. Weiss, *Earliest, Vol.I, op. cit.*, p. 240.

17. Baeck, Leo: *The People of Israel*, Holt, NY, 1964, p. 9.

18. *Ibid.*, p. 13.

19. *Ibid.*, p. 23.

20. *Ibid.*, p. 8.

21. *Ibid.*, p. 11.

22. *Ibid.*, p. 53.

23. *Ibid.*, p. 78.

24. Schoeps, H.J.: *The Jewish-Christian Argument*, Holt, Rinehart, NY, 1963, p. 6.

25. Eckart, Dietrich: *Bolshevism from Moses to Lenin, A Dialogue Between Hitler and Me*, translated by William L. Pierce, National Vanguard Books, 1924, 1966, p. 42.

26. Nolte, Ernst: *Three Faces of Fascism*, translated by Leila Vennewitz, Mentor, NY, 1963, 1969, p. 513.

Chapter Two

Christendom

The Struggle between the
Holy Roman Empire and the Papacy

PROLOGUE

An unusual pulse throbbed in the feudal town, too much activity for midsummer. At the political center of the region was the residence of the Lord. In each direction, down the country roads, meeting at the square, loomed the plain, more a presence than a vista, its sweep truncated haphazardly by buildings. More real than the town, a circus troop transformed the marketplace into a carnival, although few noticed its tawdry, pathetic attractions. On the edges of the square agrarian commerce continued as it had for generations. Nothing unusual in this, nothing to explain the town's strangeness. Fixing attention was a scaffold without a platform, a boom turning in the breeze, its leather straps hanging languidly in the air, waiting.

A perfunctory fanfare stirred the crowd, drawing them close to the gyre. Two men were helped into the straps, their faces grim, but lacking the terror of the sobbing third man, who was dragged by men in uniform. As a clear, potent drink was distributed, they taunted the prisoner. 'You won't last long!' 'Not more than two turns!' One of the strapped men grabbed the terrified victim, locking his arms, which were tied behind his back, in his muscular grasp. The other strapped man, hanging from the end of the boom, grabbed the victim's hair, as a gang of men began to hoist the boom. Absorbing the weight of the screaming prisoner, the strapped men strained, the boom reaching its maximum height, as the gang of men pulled on another series of ropes. The gyre turned slowly then faster, swinging the men out in an increasing arc. While this laborious task was undertaken, men below planted a variety of iron-tipped stakes of various colors in concentric circles around the gyre, as the crowd yelled instructions.

'Put the blue ones here, not so far out.' 'No, not the red ones!'

Amid much wrangling bet were made, the victim's agony ignored. Now and again he lost consciousness, until the gyre slowed sufficiently to decrease the stress on his body. It was early. In the crowd was a face, Germanic like the rest, but sober and detached, a face the color of wheat with eyes the color of a cloudless sky. Accompanied by two friends, urging him away from the gyre, the victim's screams drowned out his friends' injunctions.

'Nothing can be done about it.' 'The Lord owns everything.' 'The Devil has the people by the throat.' 'We must leave.'

Turning faster and faster, its straps carving wider and wider arcs, the strapped men straining, reddened muscle bulging with fatigue, the victim's agony reached its climax. Occasionally, one or the other lost his grip, regaining his hold with a great wrenching effort, intensifying the prisoner's pain. If the victim slipped far enough, his body would graze one or two of the iron stakes, lines of blood etching the ground in scattered and broken threads. Paid according to how long they held the victim, the strapped men kept the gyre turning, until exhaustion overwhelmed their greed. Pierced more and more frequently, losing more and more blood, the victim eventually lost consciousness. Finally, the strapped men lost their grip, impaling the victim. While the bettors counted the bloodied tips and measured the length of the brown-red trails clotting in the thin dust around the gyre, the victim died in his own time.

The young blond man inquired in the tavern. 'What had the prisoner done to warrant so cruel a death?' 'Why did the villagers make a spectacle of the execution?' 'Why did the villagers trade in blood and death?' All the answers were the same, 'the Lord.' Against his friends' protests, the young man repeated his questions in front of the Lord's mansion.

Not received, neither was he ignored. While returning to his lodgings, he was assaulted and told: 'Leave the town while you still can!'

Eager to depart, despite the pain of his cuts and bruises, having no trade, no vocation, no tie to estate or man, he had no reason for staying here or anywhere else. An anomaly in the tightly bound society of the land, he was free to go wherever he chose, driven by the wind, restrained only by his willingness to resist it. A stranger, a wanderer, Ishmael, he was no hero. In his travels he had witnessed cruelty to man and animal, famine, disease and pestilence. All were inevitable, accepted like the bleakness of winter. Resignation marked the land and he was of the land. Anger, depression, fatigue ran hot and cold through his body, pulsing with the seasons. But he was not the same. The gyre changed him. To whom could he protest? Certainly not to those for whom protest itself was a crime. To what end? Certainly not to change what could not be changed. Tyranny lived in the land like the power of spring. Nothing could forestall it, not even the despair of winter. Yet the gyre called for protest, even in this bestial hole. Unlike the unrelenting and harsh cruelty of the earth, universal and inevitable, the gyre was barbaric, making men worse than beasts, agents not only of brutality but of enslavement, self-enslavement. And this unknown son of an unknown father would tell them so. He had power to change them, but neither did they have power to deny him witness. No hope of stopping the executions, but perhaps the sport, if not the horror, could be eliminated. Perhaps the people would cease to watch, cease to revel in the agony of a fellow creature? Perhaps.

In sublime language, as unforeshadowed as his own existence, he spoke to all who would listen. In the taverns, in the streets, on the road, he spoke to them of their humanity, of their duty to be human, of God's love for them, of their reflection of Him. All saw the danger in his quiet words and hastened to leave but were drawn to him, as they had been drawn to the gyre, reluctantly, inevitably. Garbled and confused in the recounting, his words nevertheless retained their meaning, as they reverberated throughout the region. Something had to be done to stifle the growing influence of the fair stranger. A great festival was planned, a pre-harvest celebration, climaxed by a ritual execution. The Lord would demonstrate his munificence by his capacity to forgive. Invited to speak to the Lord directly, he went to town ignoring his friends' warnings. How could he refuse an opportunity to speak with the one man who had the power to breathe life into his message?

By the middle of the great day, no word had come from the Lord's mansion. Patiently the prophet waited for his audience. Food and drink had been lavished upon the revelers. Alive with anticipation, all speculated upon the ritual to come. No one could remember when the Lord had been so generous. Something special must be planned. What would he expect in return? As the men went about their debauches, uneasiness settled among the women. Ever since the announcement, they had campaigned against their men's participation in the festival, only to be dismissed. By late afternoon a well-liquored, ugly, and unruly crowd caused anxiety among the bookmakers, who knew it would be difficult, even dangerous, to collect from losers.

The square was splendid! The buildings had been scrubbed, the gyre freshly stained, flags and banners hung everywhere. Street musicians vied with vendors for the attention of the milling, ominously impatient crowd. All seemed ready. Finally, the Lord summoned the prophet. After a brief exchange of greetings, he suggested that the young man misunderstood the nature of the ritual, which produced many valuable benefits. More than punishing criminals, it supplicated the gods, particularly the gods of the harvest. It taught the people the necessity for order and respect for those in authority, and it provided much needed entertainment for lives, otherwise consumed by dull and arduous labor. Nevertheless, if he could be shown why the ritual was harmful, contrary to nature and God, as he reportedly said, he would discontinue its use. The interview concluded, as the Lord's entourage made its way to the square.

The least surprised man in the crowd smiled as his arms were bound. Feeling their breath and smelling their bodies, the prophet leaned into the strapped men anticipating the warmth and strength of their arms. He did not understand his actions. He did not want to die. He did not feel heroic. Yet he had to do this, to fill his words, so new to him, so alien to his experience, with meaning. Pouring his life into his message, it might live, becoming real to others. Only this mattered. His blue eyes remained serene, as his face twisted with pain. Suffering for many hours, longer than anyone could remember, teams of well-paid strapped men and turners extended his agony with exquisite precision, as the crowd howled its delight. Then, unexpectedly, all became quiet. As the prophet's agony surpassed their capacity to game with his suffering, the people became sullen, inexplicably, instantly, sober. At first, they were pleased to see this man, who made them feel unworthy, suffer. Now, undercurrent to their pleasure, something different surged to the surface: rage.

'I think it is time to go, your Excellency. The end must be near.'

'You would think they would tire of this. How easily they are distracted,' the Lord said draining his goblet. 'I believe, if I could arrange for them to see their own torture, they would not object.'

'They probably would enjoy it,' his advisor suggested tentatively. 'Have you observed the rapture on their faces in the final moments?'

'Rapture is a curious term for the rabble. No matter. Have you the silver?'

'Yes, my Lord,' the advisor replied.

When the Lord moved to the center of the square, showering coins, the crowd did not respond. Tentatively, warily, sensing the strange mood, a few boys and an odd bookmaker picked up coins, only to replace them in the dust, as if it had never been disturbed. Hastening to depart, the Lord called for his guards. He never left the square. For a long time the coins lay in the dirt and the Lord on the iron stakes, as the gyre burned, a pale yellow flame and gray-brown smoke twisting into the solemn sky.

Since the tragic history of Medieval Germany casts its shadow over the larger part of her modern development, the chief reasons for the collapse of the Medieval national State are significant for an understanding of modern German history. Hans Holborn[1]

NO FURTHER THAN THE INQUIRY DEMANDS

Mental constructs, including incoherent or contradictory ideas independent of material facts, can influence and shape events. Leaving aside the possibility that an idea, ideology, or vision can take on event-like characteristics—the *Sermon on the Mount, the Ten Commandments, the Ninety Five Thesis, Pericles' Funeral Oration, the Gettysburg Address*, ideas have mattered. Absent the possibility of empirical verification, following Aristotle, the nature of the subject matter and the nature of the inquiry determine how much certainty can be expected from an inquiry. In human studies, propositions good for the most part define the limit of reasonable expectations. Moreover, appreciating the sensitivity of an issue does not obviate the need to discuss it. Are we to discuss only those matters that have no capacity to injure or offend? We need to try to understand why human beings are capable of torture, mass murder, and countless other expressions of hatred. Such efforts may not explain very much, yet they are needed. Often my inquiries can only reach for coherence, not proof, and in some cases, coherence requires sensitivity to literature rather than to historical narrative or social scientific analysis. For example, the most convincing portraits of Hitler have come from J. P. Stern and George Steiner, rather than historians, social scientists, or psychologists. Of course, this may be a matter of taste, as well as, an unavoidably subjective judgment. Can we abstain simply because the material resists positivistic science or factually pristine sequencing or any other methodologically structured explanation?

These remarks assume that human beings are more than physical/chemical/electrical bundles of potential events which discharge, producing an event or a fact that a given academic discipline can get its method around. For certain inquiries it makes sense to conceive of human beings in one or another reductionist way. Data and evidence must be arrayed. Questions must be manageable according to the canons of the inquiring discipline and the limitations of the researcher. Sometimes, however, it makes more sense to see human actors as value-laden, idea-laden, and occasionally vision-dominated organisms whose decisions and actions are determined, shaped, or conditioned by their construction of reality. In these instances, evidence is always problematic, often contradictory; questions hard to formulate, except provisionally and vaguely. No scholar, no matter how learned or disciplined, can avoid the sense of arbitrariness, a sense that coherence is bought at too high a price, that decisions regarding what to leave in and what to leave out are fraught with preconceptions or prejudice. These limitations, if they do not imply silence, suggest humility. Authors cannot avoid making judgments which, after all, are existential choices no less for being tied to an inquiry. They must, nevertheless, try to avoid being unfair to the material and to the reader.

Keep in mind these general considerations, as we discuss the German emperors, the popes, the rise of the Papal Monarchy, and the other significant developments of the period from the late tenth to the mid-thirteenth centuries, a period which marks the beginning of Europe, the beginning of German history, the development of Nation-States, the rise of the Papal monarchs, and many other social/historical trends. As antiquarian as much of this discussion might seem to contemporary readers, almost all the trends and ideas of this period shaped Europe into the nineteenth century. Many, some of the most troubling, are still present.

Perhaps more than any other age, ideas, especially political/theological ideas, motivated and precipitated events. No small part of the unity of the Middle Ages is reflected by the difficulty of separating ideas and actions, especially when terms like Church and State (or spiritual and secular) are used casually. Anticipating our discussion, the struggle between the Empire and the Papacy was *not* about the separation of Church and State. Both emperor *and* pope believed that religious and secular authority should be subordinate to a divinely ordained order. Both believed in theocracy, that is, a political organization that combines secular and spiritual authority, because that was how they conceived Christendom. They differed regarding the proper leader of this political/spiritual organization, not its purpose, origin, or reason for being.

This conflation of concepts does not imply that the material basis for explaining political/ theological ideas and events can be dispensed with. This study is concerned with ideas, transcendent or supernatural, only insofar as they have impacted events, alert to the difficulty of keeping these cardinal concepts clear and distinct. In this respect the idea that Christ is present in the sacrament of the Lord's Supper has the same logical relation to events as the widespread belief in witches, demons and other supernatural beings. Ideas do not lose importance because they cannot meet scientific standards of analysis or verification. Physical scientists often distinguish the process of discovery, which often defies logical analysis, from the verification of the discovery, which is grounded in it. Rife with beliefs in the reality and importance of ideas which could not be warranted according to modern notions of evidence and validity, which killed, maimed, and tortured innumerable people, the Middle Ages confirmed that ideas, even absurd ones, matter. Complicating analysis further, their notions of proof often differed from ours. In the final analysis, it seems fair to proceed on the assumption that, between the rise of the first German emperors in the tenth century and the death of Frederick II in the thirteenth, ideas, including supernatural ones, shaped the actions of secular and religious officials.

It was just this conflation of secular and religious authority that was at the root of the struggle for European hegemony, the struggle between the Empire and the Papacy. The issue was who would wield political/spiritual authority, who would be sovereign, who would be judge, who would represent, if not incarnate, both the mind and hand of God. This struggle for hegemony was premised on two radically opposed visions of the proper ordering of society

under divine authority, not whether this order was divinely ordained. Virtually every political and theological question passed through this centrifuge:
the place of man in God's plan, the respective roles of kings and popes, the
limits and overlaps of the various sources and forms of authority, and the
validity of sacraments, when performed by priests or bishops considered dubious for one reason or another, by one rival or another. The ensuing discussion would be nothing but a tawdry, dreary story of the struggle for power but
for the sincere and often laudatory convictions which motivated and shaped
its development. While the effort to secure power was the most important
element in the conflict between differing world visions, it was not as a mere
contest for wealth, control over the elements of coercion, for honor, fame,
or for any of the other prizes which have motivated human beings since the
beginning of civilized life. Whatever else can be said of the three centuries
under discussion, it seems beyond dispute that the struggle for power was not,
as it so often is today, for its own sake. It was a reaching, often an overreach-
ing, for the material and spiritual bases of power and authority *in the pursuit
of an ideal.* Fallible men sought power to serve God. This is why one German
king after another took essentially the same approach to the Papacy and why
pope after pope took the same approach toward the Empire. The struggle was
principled and systemic, not opportunistic and personal, although the conflict
was rife with opportunism and personality conflicts.

> The cruel excitement and coarse compassion raised by an execution formed an
> important item in the spiritual food of the common people. They were spectacu-
> lar plays with a moral. For horrible crimes the law invented atrocious punish-
> ments. J. Huizinga[2]

EUROPE AS STATE OF SIEGE

Absent the sympathetic imagination of a poet, it is almost impossible for
one age to appreciate another. Perhaps no period of history seems less intel-
ligible to us than the Middle Ages. Of course there is no such thing as *the*
Medieval worldview, as any detailed historical or philosophical study would
demonstrate. My purpose, however, is merely to distinguish the years roughly
from the middle of the tenth century to the middle of the thirteenth from what
came afterward: what we call modernity. There can be little question that in
general the beginning of this age was vastly different from its end. Some
historians believe that almost all the elements of modernity were in place by
the mid-thirteenth century, and all the elements of Medievalism were already
in decline or obsolete. This is not to say that everything in the world of the
thirteenth century would seem more similar to the twenty-first century than
it was to the tenth.

Though the world had greatly changed in these three centuries, it did not change all at once, or in a straight line. There were periods of economic development and prosperity and periods of calamity. The Church rose to unprecedented heights, only to be subject to near fatal doctrinal and political maladies. So rapid and disruptive was change that those who most benefited from new developments were as anxious as those that did not. Perhaps this tension between objective well-being and subjective malaise provides us with a fruitful point of access to this complex age, for this tension seems normal, not paradoxical. One purpose of this chapter is to provide a background to the modern world; another is to ground the Reformation, which dramatically ended chances for a universally accepted notion of Christendom; and to create the context for an appreciation of the troubled history of Christians and Jews in Europe, which became much crueler in this period. My discussion of Medieval Jewry, like that of the Reformation, is reserved for a later chapter.

The great historian Johan Huizinga opens *The Waning of the Middle Ages*, with a chapter entitled: 'The Violent Tenor of Life.' My prologue indicates how brutal and arbitrary punishments were and worse, how routine. Only the reversal, the crowd turning on the Lord, was unusual, yet uncontrolled and unpredictable violence was ever present by the late Middle Ages, as the particularly hideous fourteenth century came to its close. Although it was better to be rich than poor, the well-off were well aware that their privileges had shallow roots. From our perspective, immersed as we are in the vulnerability of complex interdependency and the dislocations of unprecedented and accelerating change, we see the Middle Ages as calm, unchanging, even serene. This is a false picture. Life was precarious, if not Hobbesian: 'solitary, nasty, brutish and short.'

There are several important points to be made about this core of Europe apart from its birth in desperate military defense: first, after the fall of Rome, Europe ceased to be a Mediterranean culture and civilization. It turned inward, landward. Second, urban centers disappeared. Third, trade and other economic activity dependent upon surplus production, that is, production beyond necessities, virtually ceased. Fourth, violence, brutality, including the celebration, even sanctification, of torture, prevailed. Europe—by this I mean France and Central Europe, largely Germanic—did not develop a siege mentality; it was a siege mentality. This sense of being under attack was not limited to military invasion. Nature itself seemed malevolent. Fuhrmann offers a telling statistic gleaned from a cemetery north of the Alps, which can stand for many: 'The majority of those who died were aged between fourteen and twenty…or between twenty and forty…. Only one in four lived to be over forty.'[3]

Europe is the consequence of the successful resistance to three nearly simultaneous invasions, which followed the dissolution of the Carolingian Empire: the Vikings from the North and West, the Hungarian-Magyars from the East and the Saracens from Mediterranean. Circumstances in Germany differed from the West and were usually worse: 'The eastern border of the kingdom of Germany had a different character; right through the high Middle Ages relations between the Empire and its Eastern neighbors were characterized by more or less permanent warfare.... Until the twelfth century there were invasions and expeditions almost annually, using same tactics each time and almost always the same invasion routes.'[4] In these conditions, survival and stability were coterminous. Correlatively, change and chaos were mutually reinforcing, the work of demonic forces like Jews and other infidels. All the invaders were non-Christians. No one was more afraid of the East than Pope Urban II, the father of the First Crusade. Moreover, 'the passage of time intensified this awareness [Urban's] of the inexhaustible resources of the enemy they had so light-heartedly engaged. To the south and east of the Mediterranean, so far as the mind could reach or report could verify, there were Moslems.'[5] The association of the East with evil was not limited to the fear of Islam: 'Under the shock of crisis Westerners were ready to see their nearest neighbors as the "wicked East" incarnate. This was the French view of the Germans, the German view of the Poles, the Polish view of the Russians, the universal view of the Mongols when they appeared in the early thirteenth century, and later of the Turks.'[6]

With stabilization, always tenuous and greatly differential in degree, Europe began to breathe. Almost immediately, the very security the siege mentality provided Europeans began to undermine its parochial and defensive structures. According to Southern: 'The stabilization of the boundaries of Europe, the slow recovery of political order, and the unprecedented acceleration of economic activity were not only in themselves silent reversals of previous tendencies: they were the conditions which made possible even more secret and momentous changes in thought and feeling, and in the direction of society for both secular and spiritual ends.'[7] It began to make sense to invest; in other words, to anticipate a future where one could enjoy things beyond immediate consumption. Commerce revived, towns developed from trade fairs, river traffic increased, money circulated, including the reintroduction of gold coins. The economic foundations of civilized life were laid. By the middle of the thirteenth century, almost all the elements of the modern world were in play, and Medieval structures, in decline.

Medieval men and women had an almost pathological fear of non-Europeans or non-Christians, especially those from the East and South. This residual fear of the Saracens was reinvigorated by the rise of the Ottoman Turks, who for centuries dominated the Mediterranean and threatened to burst out of the Balkans into Central Europe. The dread of 'Asia' to this day haunts many Europeans. This mentality survived its objective basis in part due to the teachings of the Church militant, the Church of the Crusades; in part due to how Europe was precariously formed and sustained; in part due to the persistence—one might say the need—for casual and not so casual violence and cruelty of the times; in part due to the deep-seated suspicion and the invincible ignorance of the peasant masses. Dreading the foreign or the inexplicable is not a unique attribute of the Middle Ages. What is unique or nearly so was how much the views of the uneducated were also advocated by educated elites. Nowhere can this be better appreciated by the belief in supernatural power of relics and demons, to say nothing of the supernatural core of Christian rituals. 'The majority of people must have been aware of the Christian religion as an intrusion of the supernatural into their lives in the form of miracles and ritual ceremonies.'[8] More than symbols of devotion: 'In the relic collections of the king lay the safety of the kingdom. They compensated for his powerlessness before man and nature.... Relics were the main channel through which supernatural power was available for the needs of ordinary life.... Among all the objects of the visible, malign, unintelligible world, relics alone were both visible and full of beneficent intelligence. For the rest, the visible world was either meaningless or filled with evil.'[9] How easy it was, given this constellation of beliefs virtually common to the entire Christian world, to see all outsiders as evil. How easy to believe that annihilating them was a Christian duty.

Long before nationalism or even truly modern European languages, the commonalities of the European heartland can be discerned: shared history, religion, fears, enemies, agrarian cultures, and economies. Certainly, notwithstanding the variations implied by the localism and isolation of primitive communications and difficult transportation, the Frankish and Germanic lands and peoples had more in common with each other than with the peoples across their borders, Slavs, Nordics, Greeks, Arabs, and Ottoman Turks. Therefore, one might conclude that altercations, including wars, were conflicts between cousins, if not brothers. After a short clash of arms, peace would be re-established, rather an armistice, a pause between hostilities. And so it was.

Although many of these common factors would persist to the present, disintegrative factors, latent in the mid-thirteenth century, by the middle of the fifteenth century began to undermine the European unity. The most important immediate consequence was the development of the modern State, largely modeled on the Roman *imperium*.[10] Although the situation in Germany was much more complex, 'France and England were in their different ways on the way to becoming unified states in 1200....'[11] The all too familiar tax collecting, rationalizing, bureaucratic, gargantuan power State rapidly developed in France and England. Modern national feelings were becoming important features of intra-European economic, social, and political activities. The

Reformation, both as cause and effect of many of these forces, divided Christendom into countless sects, each claiming a monopoly of Truth. The Nation and the State became yoked with a fateful hyphen; seldom has a punctuation mark signified so much death and destruction. Wars, now struggles for survival between peoples, became more deadly and protracted. Yet for all these differences and their countless consequences, it still made sense to speak of a European culture, a people and land substantially distinct from its neighbors. Conceptually, however, there were now two ways of perceiving the French and Germanic Nations: one which emphasized similarities, on a shared history and humanity; the other, differences. Quite naturally, those responsible for physical security, economic and military, tended to focus on differences and their correlative dangers.

THE GERMAN PROBLEMATIC

From the perspective of Western Europe, Germany, things Germanic, history, culture, attitudes, values, people, have always seemed problematic, often qualitatively different from its Western and Eastern neighbors. Although much closer to the West than to the Slavic East—it was part of the Roman world and the principal part of the Carolingian Empire—Germany seemed to grow more distinct from its Western and, especially, its Atlantic neighbors. Into the nineteenth century, despite its enormous and in many ways unparalleled contributions to Western civilization, Germany seemed not quite part of the West, a view shared by non-Germans and Germans alike. Germany seemed to oscillate between the highest refinements, an almost precious sensitivity, empyrean idealism, and self-obliterating romanticism on the one hand and the crudest expressions of power politics, overbearing rudeness and vulgar sentimentality on the other. The German sense of estrangement arose out of a suspicion of things Roman, including the Roman Church, *and* its antithesis, Enlightenment France. Anglo-Saxons fared little better as the incarnation of materialism, individualism, and other manifestations of liberalism. The basis for these perceptions had roots in the Middle Ages. In Fuhrmann's words: 'Towards the end of the eleventh century changes were taking place in Europe and in the Mediterranean region which left Germany and its kingdom remarkably untouched: the first signs of the future development of Germany. Something like a system of States began to come into existence; the reform Papacy helped in the setting up of new states and saw itself as the center of political integration.'[12] The widespread perception that the Germans were different and that they imperiled the security and sensibilities of Western Europe increased over the centuries. In the twentieth century, after more than a generation unified under Prussian domination, Germany precipitated the Great War. Not the causes of German aggression, German unification and its doctrine of 'Blood and Iron' merely expressed an inherently aggressive Teutonic people who resented Western European civilization. By vandalizing the library at Liege Germans proved their 'Otherness,' which uncontained would destroy Europe. The failure to pursue a Carthaginian peace, a kind of Versailles Treaty Plus, would soon have more catastrophic results, as German refinements and sensibilities dissolved in a primal stew of mysticism, spiritual racism, and hyperbolic nationalism, coalescing into total war and death camps.

Students of Germany have offered many explanations for its problematic status. There has been a 'German question' for at least nine hundred years, without there being a 'French question' or an 'English question.' Many reasons focused on what did not happen in Germany or rather among German peoples, parceled out among scores of sovereign or near sovereign entities in central Europe. It did not become a unified State like France or England. Germans did not have the equivalent of the English or the French Revolution. Their middle classes did not develop politically, as they improved economically. There was no hunger for political influence, much less a boiling indignation over oppressive policies. For all their love of vocal music, can one imagine a German *Marseillaise*? They had little or no sense of liberty, to say nothing of the Rights of Man. An otherwise brilliant book by Leonard Krieger, *The German Idea of Freedom,* makes the same claim, one which is demonstrably false, unless limited it to the nineteenth and twentieth centuries *and* on a Natural Rights model of freedom.[13] The absence of German assertions of freedom bespoke not just of a different experience or perhaps a slower rate of development, but of toleration for, or even a love of, tyranny. Burke's criticism of the French Revolution at least treated it seriously, for all its threats to English notions of constitutional liberalism. Without the love of freedom, without respect for individuals, without the institutional and constitutional armor of inalienable rights, Germans seemed to cling to barbaric notions of community, feudal allegiances, and social structures. Unable to develop like France or England, Germans were flawed, their differences in development, economic, social and political, more than variations; they reflected fundamental German inadequacies.

More charitably and less ideologically, German 'Particularism,' a term which partially accounts for the lack of German national unity, seemed to derive from political immaturity. Aside from assuming that West European political development should be the measure of all European peoples, this line of reasoning suggests that only internal factors determined German political experience. Moreover, this appreciation of German history suggests that Europeans have suffered unjustly from German hands, because Germans could not become proper Europeans. All European wars involving German States were caused, not so much by power politics or the perpetual search for security at the expense of neighboring States, but by German deficiencies. There seemed to be something irremediably barbaric about Germans. Civilization, that is, things French, could never be more than an ill-fitting costume of a brute still smelling of the sty, or still blinking as he emerged from the forest gloom into the sun of Versailles. Although this West European portrait of the German problem might seem over-drawn, to any eleventh century observer this portrait would have seemed fantastic. Germany was the best ordered polity in Europe, the most viable claimant of Carolingian authority and wisdom; its kings the most astute and God-fearing.

German history began with the East Frank response to the troubles, which plagued Europe after the death of Charlemagne. Without his genius, political acumen, and prestige, the centrifugal forces of his Empire revealed themselves. Given the vicissitudes of ninth century transportation and communication, and the marginality of its economies, the Empire disintegrated from internal weaknesses and external pressures. Each of the three parts of the Carolingian inheritance responded in different ways to his death. To cope with the new geopolitical realities, feudalism took hold in West Frankish lands, less so in the Middle Kingdom and only sporadically in East Frankish lands. Germany's shallow absorption of feudalism helped forge the thesis of its 'late and incomplete' development, intensifying similar 'inadequacies' regarding the absorption of Roman and Christian values and practices. Yet this 'failure' or series of failures might have proved advantageous, once the more immediate external threats to Germany (East Frankland) were confronted. Germany was divided into seven or eight large pieces, while West Francia (France) was much more fragmented into what would become classic feudal estates, rapidly forming the practices and values of 'feudalism.' Thus, although German borders were more porous than other parts of the Carolingian inheritance and would remain so for a thousand years, the unification of East Frankish lands needed only to amalgamate several large political units, each loosely organized. It did not have to fuse hundreds of feudal estates or solve the more difficult problem of changing a way of life to fit the needs of more centralized political organization. Another ostensible weakness of the lands east of the Rhine was its resistance to Roman culture. Perhaps its best sign was the retention of the German language, while the West Franks developed Latinate French. In addition, for related reasons, the attitudes and organization of the Roman Church were more completely absorbed west of the Rhine than in the East. Nevertheless, under the rule of the Ottos and the Salians, Germany had become the most politically advanced, most centrally organized state in Europe, the proper heir to Charlemagne's Empire, as was nearly universally recognized.

So powerful were these developments that German weaknesses might have been better characterized as strengths. The very openness of its eastern borders, once a threat to Germanic survival as a people and as a political entity, now promised expansion beyond the Elbe to the Oder and further into Slavic lands, into areas which would benefit not only from increased law and order but from a more advanced economy and culture. France, by contrast, seemed less secure than locked in behind its Mediterranean, Atlantic and Alpine borders. Able to expand only eastward, there France faced the Germans. The Middle Kingdom, comprised of present day Alsace, Lorraine, Belgium, the Netherlands and some parts of northwest Germany, into the Alps, was becoming more German every day. Even the Roman Church sensed the implications of this German reality. It cooperated eagerly with the German kings, especially the Salians, who through a mixture of sincere Christianity and prudent policies, realized how useful religious authority could be to a new form of political organization. For its part, the Church (increasingly conceived as the Papacy rather than the aggregate of all Christians or Christian edifices) saw concomitant benefits. Christianity had prospered and spread, its liberty and property guaranteed by the power of the German Empire, which was much more reliable and predictable than the protection offered by the multifarious estates of feudal France. To understand what happened, we need to look more closely at early German history.

> The Ottonian period, which inaugurated German history, set the tone and in some ways acts as a microcosm of all the later vicissitudes of German civilization. In the Ottonian Empire we see that peculiar combination of aggressive, ruthless efficiency and the expression of a childlike, lyrical idealism or, as the German writers call it, that union of *macht* and *Geist* that so often distinguishes the history of the lands between the Rhine and the Elbe. Norman Cantor[14]

FINE BEGINNINGS: OTTONIAN AND SALIAN GERMANY

In the first few years of the tenth century it seemed that ostensible German weaknesses—indefinite and perhaps indefinable borders, hostile neighbors, and inadequate absorption of Carolingian institutions—would prove fatal to the East Frankish domain. According to Barraclough, 'it looked as though the East Frankish kingdom was on the point of splitting like the Lotharingian Middle Kingdom into a number of petty *regna*. The development was furthered by the persistence of deep-seated regional differences.'[15] But when the Saxon Henry I (918–36) took the throne, he attacked these regional differences by his own example, becoming a Frankish king, giving up his Saxon heritage. The three Ottos, succeeding Henry, ruling from 936 to 1002, continued consolidating

German lands and people. Their main adversaries were the regional princes; their main limitation, the lack of material resources necessary to protect and defend all German lands. In this royal effort, which tried to secure the loyalty the people to the Crown and the resources necessary to provide the physical security upon which loyalty depended, the kings' main allies were the bishops and abbots and the imperial German Church. At the end of the tenth century, the royal estates were still located almost exclusively in Saxony and Franconia, and therefore did not immediately strengthen the position of the monarchy in South Germany. 'In order to exercise royal control throughout the duchies, and particularly to strengthen its position in the south, the monarchy needed a less localized instrument. This it found in the Church.'[16] Barraclough explains the interrelationship between the material and spiritual basis of authority, both of which would be necessary to defeat anti-monarchical forces:

> As representatives of Christ...kings were not merely servants and protectors but rulers of the Church.... Because of his position as *rex et sacerdos*, the king could therefore use the Church, not as an uneasy ally or an unwilling tool diverted from its proper function, but as an instrument placed by God in royal hands for the work of civilization and social organization, regarding the objects of which Church and State were still as one. These three reigns [Otto I, Otto II, and Otto III], and that of Henry II (1002–24), saw royal control over churches and abbeys elevated into a principle of government.[17]

In the light of subsequent struggles between the German Empire and the Church, this alliance may seem odd or at best a matter of convenience. In reality, it was anything but.

There were three reasons for the policy of alliance with the bishops and abbots within the royal domains. Few questioned the monarch's right to rule and obligation to protect the Church from all its adversaries, including rapacious princes and barbarians. This was the operational meaning of *rex et sacerdos*. Secondly, the lack of royal resources made an alliance with the Church and its revenue essential. Thirdly, in the royal quest for legitimacy, the Church's spiritual offices, benefices and authority could be enlisted in the king's behalf. Thus close, cooperative, and mutually beneficial relations between German kings and clerical officials were not simply founded on the maxim—the enemy of my enemy is my friend—but on a deep appreciation of the material and spiritual sources of legitimate royal authority. So well did this policy work that

> As they broke the hold of the dukes over the churches and asserted their own ultimate control, the Saxon rulers increasingly gave the Church a share in secular government, at the same time endowing it, building up its landed wealth and favoring it with rights of toll and market, etc.... But the ecclesiastical estates...

were usually scattered far and wide.... Hence in order to strengthen the Church and make it a more effective instrument of government, the Saxon kings increasingly adopted the practice of investing bishops and abbots with the powers of counts, conferring whole counties on them....[18]

Without the accomplishments of Henry I and his successors, German history would perhaps too neatly have conformed to the weakness, incompleteness, backwardness theses which have dominated interpretations of German history. The difficulty is that Ottonian success is inexplicable in these terms. Instead of signifying the demise of the monarchical principle, the many rebellions against his kingship indicated, at least arguably, its strength.[19] Differing with Cantor, whose epigraph opened this section, Barraclough concludes his analysis of Ottonian monarchs: 'Compared with the French under Robert II (992–1025), the second ruler of the new Capetian dynasty, it was a homogeneous land, held together by great and enduring traditions, ruled over by energetic and intelligent sovereigns, who had proved competent to resist and counteract the disintegration of society which accompanied the ravages of invasion from north and east.'[20] Although the German State gained its subjects' allegiance from military victories, German kings were fashioning far more than a security zone between the Rhine and the Elbe. To become more than a policing power, the German monarchy would have had to provide the benefits of a rational/legal political organization, economic development, and cultural enrichment. No betting man in the mid-eleventh century would have favored France over Germany in this competition for the hearts and minds of Europeans.

This portrait of progress seemed likely to be elaborated under the Salians, chiefly Henry III and IV. The relative lack of feudalism offered an opportunity to develop the Germany monarchy on modern lines, because there were fewer aristocratic estates to absorb into the control of the monarch. The main proviso was to ensure bureaucratic dependence, in the persons and functions of the *ministeriales,* a non-aristocratic administrative and military class, on the Crown would result in the same concentration of authority that the long process of overcoming French feudal lords was doing for the Capetians. This proviso was not fulfilled. The effort by the Salians to achieve what would later be called rational/legal authority failed, destroying chances for a unified Germanic State.[21] Self-inflicted wounds contributed to this failure.

With the accession of Henry III (1039–56), following his father, Conrad (1024–39), the future looked bright for Germany and its monarchy. Henry III, perhaps more than any monarch of this period, was profoundly religious and conscientious, deeply committed to an intimate relationship with the imperial Church. Unwilling to separate material from spiritual concerns, his duty was to shepherd the souls of his people, by ensuring that priests and monks were worthy of their spiritual callings. Correlatively, he believed the Papacy needed to be disentangled from the universally acknowledged corrupting influences of Italian politics.

> The authority of the emperor and of the Holy Roman Empire was most effective in the tenth and early eleventh centuries under the rule of the Saxon or Ottonian emperors, who really were the protectors, guardians and leaders of the Church and Christendom. They reformed the Church and the monasteries, made and unmade popes, and intervened decisively in those grave conflicts which had turned the Papacy, politically enfeebled and spiritually degraded, into an object of booty wrangled over by the cliques and clans of the Roman nobility.[22]

Ironically, the reformed Church would prove the German monarchy's most deadly adversary.

To make good his role of *rex et sacerdos*, in defiance of his father's advice, Henry ceased to receive payments for the bestowal of royal lands upon the Church and monasteries, considering these payments simoniac. Although the loss of much needed revenue by the monarchy was significant, Henry reasoned that he could live without tainted money. Controlling the Church, appointing its leaders, would they not support him in every appropriate way? The more faithful he was, the more true to Christian doctrine, he believed, the more the Church would favor his reign. Spiritually and officially dependent upon the Crown, the king would not need to extort revenue from his appointees, much less extort it in exchange for their right to sell benefices to the people. All concerned would see the wisdom and the Christian duty to serve Christ to the best of their abilities, with the king as the leading exemplar. Henry believed that the separation of Church and State entailed sacrilege, and would have an abdication of his duty as *rex et sacerdos*. While the Church's commercial activities created occasions for corruption, would not the vigilance of an honest and pious Christian monarch be the best way to contain this danger? Was not his refusal to receive payments for offices an undeniable sign of his good faith and fitness to rule? Far from endangering the Crown, by keeping its clerical officials both solvent and spiritually clean, the well-served, well-saved, people would reward the king with their devotion.

Henry III was wrong for at least four reasons: (1) The material basis of the Crown was irrevocably weakened by the donations he made to the Church; (2) Royal authority was compromised further by clerics who became more independent of the king; (3) The king would be severed from his spiritual claims by the Investiture Contest; (4) The reformed Papacy, on its way to becoming a monarchy itself, would soon command the loyalty of all its priests, regardless of who appointed them. All of these reasons flowed from the anachronism of Henry's conviction that he ruled a theocratic empire based on the essential unity of Christendom. The regency of his French wife, Agnes of Poitou, merely reinforced the anti-German implications of Henry's mispremised, if well-intentioned, policies. Continuing to make generous contributions of royal lands to the Church, she preferred to look after her soul, ending her days in a monastery under the protection of Hildebrand, who as Gregory VII, would be her son's most determined enemy.[23]

As Henry's view of simony impacted his conception of his role as *rex et sacerdos,* a brief digression is apt. In its purest form simony is the payment for a spiritual blessing of benefice. Presumably, payment would be necessary due to some *defect* in the petitioner's request. In such cases simony would amount to bribery. Few defended this exchange. So universally despised a practice finds its definition easily expanded. As the Church became worldly, the definition of simony became more elastic, more suited to the material or political needs of the Church. Henry III, believed simony included the payment for appointment or investment as bishop or abbot or other officials of the Church, *even if well qualified.* These payments had for centuries been considered compensation for the lands and rights of administration over its subjects bestowed on the rulers of new bishoprics and monasteries. In his role of protector of the Church and ward of his subjects' souls, Henry believed that commerce in benefices, however sanctioned by time or necessity, was blasphemous, an abdication of his spiritual responsibilities. In other words, Henry ignored simony's function as traditionally practiced: 'Simony worked as a kind of equalization fund: the king would be paid a large sum for an office by a rich candidate, a sum which he would then pass on to others, or he would choose a dignitary for a not very well-endowed bishopric who disposed of substantial private means....'[24] This process may seem excessively commercial in the light of the spiritual objectives of both the monarchy and the Church. Human institutions, however, regardless of their objectives, require resources to sustain themselves. Appropriate compensation, even in a rudimentary economy, cannot be forsworn, except by the most austere monks. The people needed the sacraments and other services; the priests needed to eat, be clothed, and housed; the king needed revenues to defend his kingdom, including its people and its institutions; the Church needed to meet the needs of its members, and so the circle of mutual dependence and service revolved around its center: money.

No German king prior to Henry and few clergy objected to the material basis of either the monarchy's or the Church's existence. Hoping to set a spiritual and fiscal example to corrupt Rome, Henry's reform pursued an overly delicate understanding of commerce, wishing to be paid in another coin for his grants of land and rights and his other services to his people and their Church. Wanting their loyalty and their acceptance of his authority as *rex et sacerdos,* he was willing to trade land for spiritual authority. If his attempt to secure the loyalty of his invested clergy had succeeded, he might have made good the loss of revenues (and, the erosion of the material basis of his authority), if it could have been buttressed by the increase in spiritual authority of the Church *with him as its acknowledged head.* Perhaps too idealistic, Henrican reform, given its time and place, might have improved the Church and contributed to the German monarchy. The aversion to simony in any of its many forms, however, served many masters and interests. As it was having its salutary effects on the clergy and extracting the Papacy from Italian corruption, it began to serve another reform movement, this one directed by the Papacy, one which had a very different understanding of the relations between secular rulers and the Church: '[Humbert] took the professional ecclesiastical reformer's term for the sale of spiritual offices and made it a battle cry of a revolution which tore the whole of the Carolingian world to pieces. Simony became the name for the adulterous cohabitation of Empire and Church under the German emperors, simoniac the word for most of the imperial bishops and higher clergy of the old world.'[25] If there can be little question of the spiritual basis of Humbert's reform, there can be equally little question regarding its political implications both for the Papacy and the Empire. The Church did indeed reform itself, turning into the Papal Monarchy. In this revolutionary process, simony became a battle cry to be hurled against all the opponents of the Papacy, clerical or secular, with little regard to the original two meanings of the term.

When Henry IV took control in 1065, he found a deteriorating situation: 'What a difference between the beginning of the reign of Henry III and that of his son! Henry III had had three duchies—Bavaria, Suabia and Carinthia—in his own hand; Henry IV had none.... From about 1068 Henry began an energetic policy of recuperation of Crown lands in Thuringia and eastern Saxony....'[26] This struggle to recoup the material basis of secular authority consumed his energies throughout his reign. If he were to restore royal order, if he were to place Germany, its people and lands, on the path trod by all the kings from Henry I through Henry III, leaving his father's mispremised idealism and spirituality aside (to say nothing of his spectacularly foolish mother), he had to restore royal lands and rights. Henry IV realized that his father's assumption of a divinely ordained harmony under the beneficent German Crown was problematic at best. Not bonding its recipients to the monarchy, the grant of royal lands fed the springs of independence and rebellion, made all the more possible due to the weakened financial position of the monarchy. Conflicting visions, values, and conceptions, among the elites of the tenth and eleventh centuries, in addition to their lust for power, increased resistance to a unified State. How could it have been otherwise?

Pursuing an aggressive, sometimes ruthless, program of restoring what he considered expropriated royal lands and rights, building castles to enforce his claims, Henry IV relied on his own *ministeriales*, royal bureaucrats, in these endeavors. Predictably, the nobles rebelled in 1070 and 1073, joined by wide sections of German society, including 'an extensive class of freemen.'[27] Contrary to twentieth century stereotypes, a sense of liberty has long premised German political organization. Shared by aristocrats and other freemen, this sense of freedom underlay the revolt in Saxony in 1073. Henry defeated these rebels, slaughtering thousands of Saxon footmen, the ensuing peace favoring the nobles over the free peasants. In the light of later successful royal alliances with the people against the nobles, it is possible that Henry made a fatal mistake, losing his last chance to unite Germany under a monarchy. To reach this conclusion fairly would require an assessment of the material resources of the free peasantry. If they could have supplied Henry with the soldiers and money required to defeat the nobles, Henry should have supported the freemen, notwithstanding the hierarchical mentality of the times. In any event, Barraclough concludes he still might have succeeded. To seal his victory he imposed measures, which, though harsh, 'held the promise for the healthy development of the German constitution and of German political life.'[28] It is impossible to say whether these measures, assuming they could have been applied without external interference, would have provided for the basis for the political unification of all Germanic lands and peoples, as would occur to a much greater degree in France and England. It does seem fair to say that German political development made a good start, overcoming many obstacles, toward developing a modern monarchy. Ironically, it was the existence of a class of freemen, who had a marked distaste for feudal vassalage, which had to be overcome, a distaste shared by many aristocrats as well. To this extent the incompleteness thesis might be valid, although not in the way many non-German and anti-German historians have stated it: Germany's 'failure' to feudalize fully left a vibrant and rebellious free peasant class and many aristocrats, who did not wish to trade their independence for the dubious protections of vassalage. Although these forces were defeated by Henry IV, a residue of resentment and anger must have festered, undermining the legitimacy of monarchical authority. Civil strife always leaves open wounds which only time, often a great deal of time, and wise and generous policies aiding the defeated, can close.

For all this, it must have seemed to Henry that he might have succeeded in reinvigorating the German monarchy, at least to the extent of retrieving the losses of Henry III and Agnes. If he had been able to create a unified State, Henry IV would have decisively changed history. Much, if not all, of the resentment of Germans by their neighbors and the resentment by Germans of their neighbors might have been kept at manageable levels. Appreciating the scope and difficulty of his problems, Henry dealt with them aggressively, energetically, and ruthlessly, if unimaginatively. Reasonable bettors could have predicted his success. No betting man, however, could have imagined Gregory VII.

> Sacral kingship at this time enjoyed an undisputedly ecclesiastical function and dignity. Gerd Tellenbach[29]

> The two universal powers of the early Middle Ages, the Papacy and the Empire, succeeded in humiliating each other. The Papacy achieved the degradation of the empire, only to succumb to the power which was formerly its staunchest ally, the French monarchy.... Friedrich Heer[30]

THE INVESTITURE CONTEST: DENOUEMENT

Although scholarly opinion supports the view that the Investiture Contest dealt a severe, perhaps fatal, blow to the Ottonian and Salian efforts to unite the Germanic lands under a theocratic, hereditary state, there is a respected alternative view. According to Tellenbach, 'It has been argued that Henry III's ecclesiastical reforms were a political mistake, on the ground that they strengthened the Church and so helped to weaken the power of the German State. This argument is, however, incorrect ....'[31] Furthermore: 'Henry IV's kingship had long been threatened and weakened from other quarters. The German kingdom had already entered into a crisis before Henry came to the throne, whose origins had nothing to do with the ecclesiastical problems of the time. Henry IV had to defend his position on two fronts, and Gregory VII found himself with allies for whom his ideals and aims were only of secondary importance.'[32] Much turns on the definition of 'ecclesiastical problems.'

In the twenty-first century, it is reasonable to distinguish ecclesiastical problems from the difficulties attendant to founding a hereditary monarchy or any other kind of secular polity. It is possible to analyze the German monarchy and its relationship with the Papacy in secular terms. It is not possible, however, to conclude a study of either the early German monarchy or its relations with the Papacy without dealing with the interaction of spiritual and secular (rational/legal) authority. Moreover, the struggle between the popes and German kings indicates that dichotomizing secular and ecclesiastical problems is eccentric. Gregory VII struck at Henry's power to invest bishops by asserting that laymen, including kings, were inferior to the clergy in spiritual matters. If bishops did not control their territories as princes, Gregory might be understood to have been making an ecclesiastical point. Given the economic realities of the day, spiritual authority of the bishops generated revenue which financed their political control. Henry wished to reform the Church, not only in the name of good government, but for the benefit of the souls of his subjects. Moreover, he wished to become an example of religious and secular probity.

Henry refused payment for investiture, because of an appearance of simony. For his part, did not Gregory attack German monarchs to weaken a rival, using religious means to pursue secular goals? For all these reasons, secular and spiritual matters cannot be distinguished, as Tellenbach admits. According to Southern, 'Church and society were one, and neither could be changed without the other undergoing similar a transformation.'[33] To suggest that the deeply religious Henry III acted independently of ecclesiastical matters borders on the absurd. The other major element of Tellenbach's interpretation deals with the issue of Investiture *per se*. It doubts whether a question of appointing (investing) bishops and abbots or pope for that matter could have had the devastating consequence of keeping Germans disunited for nine hundred years. This interpretation has four key elements: (1) It discounts any Papal intention to weaken the emperor, notwithstanding its denial of his sacerdotal authority. (2) Moreover, it discounts the worldly interests of the Church, except as material concerns are inextricably entwined with the Church's spiritual mission. (3) It doubts the intention to establish the Papal Monarchy, to say nothing of a Papal desire to dominate secular rulers. (4) It depends on the significance and cogency of two ideas: that some Papal *plan* was necessary to destroy the possibility of a hereditary German monarchy and that the Investiture Contest must be defined narrowly, boiling down to the question: who had the right to initiate the appointment of bishops and abbots?

No stalemate, the Investiture Contest was a German defeat, the political consequence of the Western Europe antipathy for Germans. Anti-German policies and attitudes would impact European politics for hundreds of years, poisoning Germany's relations with the West, culminating in the Third Reich. For now let the most famous of these compromises indicate the direction of my analysis: 'The Concordat of Worms brought the system of government known as the imperial Church system of the Ottonians and the Salians to an end. "The immediate control over the imperial Church was transformed into an indirect one through feudal ties on the basis of the Concordat," in the words of H. Mitteis. *The king was excluded from the sacramental aspects of election and ceased to be lord of the imperial bishoprics and monasteries in a proprietary sense....*'[34] Without the imperial Church system, there could be no German monarchy worthy of the name. Henry III's attempt to create a loyal and reformed clergy, under the aegis of a God fearing and God ordained ruler, depended on his ability to invest bishops. This attempt failed when Investiture was taken from his hands, for not only was a loyal clergy made dubious, and his revenue base undermined, his sacerdotal authority was undercut. The German Empire, and with it all hopes of a unified hereditary monarchy, died.

Contrary to Tellenbach, the Investiture Contest was a metaphor for a struggle between two world views, making its importance undeniable. According to Heer:

> The most momentous of all the actions and movements of modern European history was the Gregorian reform. From this reform sprang the curial Papacy and the national states, the reforming nobility, the crusading movement, humane urban civilization, scholasticism, modern European mysticism and the spiritualism, philosophical rationalism and philosophical materialism of the last few centuries. Europe's theology and philosophy of history and all the reformations and revolutions of the thirteenth to the nineteenth centuries were profoundly dependent upon the Gregorian movement.[35]

While Heer does not include the destruction of a hereditary German monarchy in this imposing list, Fuhrmann states the obvious:

> The French and the English had managed to achieve political unity by the time of the High Middle Ages, whereas Germany only became a nation in the nineteenth century, and even then did not include all Germans.... The history of France and England shows a sharp contrast to the German path. The Capetian king rounded off the crown domain just as a lesser noble might have done with his family lands and took care to see that the Crown vassals did not cut him off from the lower classes. An administration with a fixed central point and a royal residence were built up, and the royal income was put on a reliable footing.... Germany became an agglomeration of petty states scarcely ruled by the king.[36]

The Investiture Contest strengthened the authority of German princes, while feudal authority continued to weaken in France. The consequences for kingship in both countries were obvious. Of course, other factors eroded the chances for a unified German hereditary monarchy, but the removal of spiritual authority at this critical time was decisive.

As the author of the assault on royal spiritual authority, Gregory VII was a radical leader, not an original thinker. Dependent not only upon his near contemporary Humbert, Gregory was indebted to a long tradition of clerical restiveness attendant upon imperial rule and its theocratic aspirations. When Constantine the Great co-opted Christianity as the official religion of the Empire, his object was political. 'He saw it [Christianity] as an instrument of cohesion, a pillar of the new imperial structure he was building a state religion to underpin his government....'[37] He was willing to pay for this instrument: 'Constantine himself made grants from the State treasury, and the Church began to accumulate estates and rely more and more on revenues from properties and endowments bestowed by emperors, officials and wealthy individuals, instead of depending for its income on the small, voluntary donations contributed week by week by the rank and file of ordinary Christians.'[38] Barraclough rightly concludes that financial dependence was 'the first obstacle to the rise of Papal power.'[39] To portray it as a struggle for worldly power may seem cynical. But clerics had longed considered power a legitimate tool of the Church, however much it needed fashioning to meet spiritual needs: '[Gelasius I (492–96) told the emperor] contrary to the whole practice of secular government since Constantine—that bishops, not the secular power, should be responsible for the administration of the Church' and laid down...that the world was ruled by two powers, "the sacred authority of the bishops" and the "royal power," adding that of the two, the former were the weightier, since the priests had to render account to God for kings.'[40] Although the basis of conflict inheres in the tension between the imperial and the clerical understanding of the relationship of secular and sacred authority, the conflict was contained until the tenth century within the traditional appreciation of the primacy of the imperial government. Tellenbach admits: 'Until the time of the Investiture Controversy the general conviction prevailed that kings were essentially different from all other laymen. They had a special mission from God and in them God's ruling will was peculiarly active, ennobling their persons.... The king's rule is holy, his person sacred; he is set up and put down by God.'[41] He adds, with a significant qualification: 'All were agreed that the king, who ruled on earth, typified the Savior, who ruled in heaven. It was admitted that he shared the priestly office...yet the opinion was widespread that *the king remained nevertheless inferior to the priest in dignity and was bound like all laymen to obedience in spiritual matters.*'[42]

A great deal turns on the meaning of 'spiritual matters.' If it simply denotes the delivery of the sacraments as a clerical duty, then few sovereigns would have objected. If, however, 'spiritual matters' implies an umbrella over secular authority, then virtually all rulers would have objected. The Church behaved flexibly. When threatened, it pulled back, defining clerical power narrowly: 'The pope [Stephen II (752–57)], on his knees and in tears, besought Pippin's protection [in 754]. Pippin, for his part, promised to defend and protect the rights of St Peter. The connection between the Papacy and the Frankish monarchy, which was so decisively to affect Papal history for the next five hundred years, had been forged.'[43] When popes became more secure physically and financially, a more expansive doctrine of spiritual supremacy came to the surface. The Investiture Contest was the most dramatic illustrations of this tendency of the Papacy to test its muscles.

Under the impetus of Henry III's efforts to reform the Church, reformers within the Church began to feel more confident in their ability to contain secular authorities to their proper inferior zone of activity. Cardinal Humbert was the theoretical mind of Gregory VII, the Marx to his Lenin. According to Heer: 'Humbert and the new Romans wanted to revive golden Rome, the golden St Peter's of the fourth to the eight centuries, and to make it what Leo the Great, the victor over the Huns, had meant when he called the Roman Church "a holy stock, an elect people, a priestly and royal citizenship, raised by the See of Peter to be the head of the world." This golden Rome, pure and holy, had been shamefully degraded, because the barbarians and the German emperors had ruined the liturgy.'[44] Tellenbach adds, 'In his [Cardinal Humbert] epoch-making work, the *Libri adverse simoniacos*…the sacred character of kingship was ignored, and for Humbert the king was a layman pure and simple.'[45] Although Henry III was aware of the tension between ecclesiastical and secular authority, he did not anticipate the revolutionary claim that the king was merely a layman. By eliminating the imperial basis of theocracy, the Papacy monopolized spiritual authority. Before the Papal victory, both Church and State had sacerdotal and secular authority, deployed according to custom; with both kinds of authority interpenetrating and checking each ruler. After the Papal victory, the king was only the bloody and defiled Sword necessary to deal with fallen man, essentially the servant of the Church. Not only did the monarchy lose sacerdotal authority, secular rulers, including kings, would be judged by the pope regarding his suitability for this purely secular role. There was no reciprocal grant coming from the Papacy: 'Nor did Humbert and Gregory envisage that the Church should give up its huge secular possessions. Unity was to be secured by subordinating the laity to the clergy.'[46]

Gregory's specifications of Papal authority were stated with breathtaking sweep and simplicity in his *Dictatus Papae:*

For him and all his successors, the primacy was the gift of Christ himself, and the Papal authority over kings and emperors came from no human transference of imperial authority but from God alone.

The pope can be judged by no one;
The Roman Church has never erred and never will err until the end of time;
The pope alone can depose and restore bishops;
He alone can make new laws, set up new bishoprics, and divide old ones;
He alone can translate bishops;
He alone can call general councils and authorize canon law;
He alone can revise his own judgments;
He alone can use the imperial insignia; he alone can depose emperors;
he can absolve subjects from their allegiance;

all princes should kiss his feet;

his legates, even through in inferior orders, have precedence over all bishops;

an appeal to the Papal court inhibits judgments by all inferior courts;

a duly ordained pope is undoubtedly made a saint by the merits of St. Peter.

Taken as a whole these statements comprise nothing less than a complete program of action. They imply nothing less than a total Papal sovereignty in all the affairs of the Christian community.... With one exception [the last] each one of them became a practical force in European life within an astonishingly short space of time.[47]

In Barraclough's estimation, 'Doctrines such as these fell like a bombshell on the traditional thought of the age. They were poles apart from the aims and endeavors of the earlier reformers.'[48] Not only did these ideas undermine the theocratic claims of the German emperors, they implied the legitimacy of Papal rule over the secular world: 'The vision Gregory and Humbert had had of the right order in the Christian world was magnificent, naïve, and unrealistic. In their view the higher rank assigned in the scheme of salvation by Gelasius I to priestly authority was also valid in secular affairs.'[49] Moreover, 'Characteristic of Gregory's attitude to the world was the argument "if the Apostolic See may decide on and judge spiritual things by virtue of the powers conferred on it by God, how much more may it judge worldly things?"'[50]

Yet, important as these unintended consequences have been for European history, they do not capture Gregory's greatness, for '[it]...lay not in what he achieved, but in the ideals which he passed on to his successors; far more than any of his predecessors, including Nicholas I, he set the Papacy on the road to universal dominion and absolute theocratic power....'[51] In brief Gregory created the conditions for the development of the Papal Monarchy. This is no figure of speech: 'The Medieval Church was a State. It had all the apparatus of the State: laws and law courts, taxes and tax collectors, a great administrative machine, power of life and death over the citizens of Christendom and their enemies within and without.'[52] While it did not achieve Christendom's idealistic aims, perhaps due to its success in the world, 'the Middle Ages may be defined as the period in Western European history when the Church could reasonably claim to be the one true State, and when men (however much they might differ about the nature of ecclesiastical and secular power) acted on the assumption that the Church had overriding political authority.'[53] And it endured: 'From the age of Bede to that of Luther, from the effective replacement of imperial by Papal authority in the West in the eighth century to the fragmentation of authority in the sixteenth, from the cutting of the political ties between Eastern and Western Europe to Europe's breaking out into the wider western world beyond the seas, the Papacy is the dominant institution in

Western Europe.'[54] Gregory set the standard: 'The ideal Church of the twelfth and thirteenth centuries was a society of disciplined and organized clergy directing the thoughts and activities of an obedient and receptive laity—kings, magnates, and peasants alike.'[55]

In the long run, the Investiture Contest began a long of the decline of the Church's claim to ultimate authority, a claim which made secular rulers agents of the Papacy. In other words, no matter how one evaluates the various agreements, resolutions and compromises which tried to reconcile the German Crown with Rome, the temporal power of the Church was undeniably diminished in the following centuries, its spiritual monopoly shaken from internal as well as external forces, resulting in the earthquake of the Reformation. Worse, from the perspective of the Church, the very revolution Gregory desired, the merging of temporal and spiritual authority, was accomplished by the royal State. In other words, the Gregorian plan to subordinate the State to the Church was reversed. Nation-States would effectively assert that spiritual authority resided in the political realm. Beginning in the Middle Ages, monarchs were increasingly able to control unprecedented wealth and power, which in itself combined secular and sacerdotal authority, achieving a near monopoly of force and revenue harvesting. When absolute royal authority was infused with the idea of nationalism, the modern Nation-State could pursue power for its own sake, unhindered by any institutional rival. Churches, especially in Protestant Europe, became cheerleaders for the State and apologists for the sacredness of State power, including the idea that disobedience to State authority was sacrilege. Catholic leaders attempted to assert the independence of Rome from these nationalizing trends, but, nevertheless, accommodated themselves to the realities of absolute secular authority, making due as acolytes to the possessors of real power. Nazi Germany would be the most extreme example of this nearly universal phenomenon: the Nation-State.

Although Gregory did not cause the rise of the absolute monarchs of the West, he all but destroyed the possibilities of similar development in Germanic lands. To the degree that German history has been the consequence of an absence of political unity, incomplete absorption of the Latin European values and institutions, and the lateness of development, the Investiture Contest, affecting these processes, has to be considered decisive. The conflict precipitated by Gregory's assertion of Papal supremacy, triggering the battle between Rome and Germany, has resonated down the centuries, only to be silenced in the din of the Third Reich.

All human activity, political and religious, stems from an undivided root. As a rule, the first impulse for...social action comes from tangible interests, political or economic.... Ideal interests elevate and animate these tangible interests and lend them justification. Man does not live by bread alone; he wants to have a good conscience when he pursues his vital interests; and in pursuing them he develops his powers fully only if he is conscious of simultaneously serving purposes higher than purely egotistical ones. Interests without such spiritual elevation are lame; on the other hand ideas can succeed in history only when and to the extent that they attach themselves to tangible interests. Otto Hintz[56]

THREE KINDS OF AUTHORITY: INVESTITURE REVISITED

This final section argues in more analytical terms that the German monarchy was decisively defeated by Gregory VII in the Investiture Contest. Whatever chances Germany had to develop a hereditary monarchy, which united all Germanic peoples in one realm, were effectively eliminated by loss of the emperor's spiritual authority. This loss could not be compensated, despite competent Hohenstaufen kings, Frederick Barbarossa and Frederick II. While England and France developed hereditary monarchies, Germany lost ground and over the next several centuries becoming more fragmented. Although, there were many differences between Germany and France and Germany and England, which might have prevented Germany hereditary monarchy, there is little doubt that Gregory's revolution and the rise of the Papal Monarchy harmed Germany much more grievously than either of the Atlantic states.

Unless one can afford to have one policeman for every subject and then a policeman for the policeman, effective rule, however coercive, however ruthless, requires large amounts of legitimate authority. 'Who guards the guardians?' has been recognized as a problem since Plato. The only answer, unsatisfactory as it has often proved, has been, 'No one can.' The guardians must restrain themselves. Moreover, the subjects must also restrain themselves, for no regime can afford to police all the subjects all the time. Furthermore, the more expansive the claims of a regime are, the more it wishes to control its subjects, the more it wants to extract from them, the more the citizens must subordinate themselves, by generally accepting commands issues by officials. Hence, the pervasiveness of propaganda in authoritarian regimes. All States, indeed all law, entails coercion, more or less obvious, more or less severe. All States are police States to some degree, the only relevant differences revolving around the limits to police power. Constitutional States, especially those based on Natural Rights, have stronger limits than non-constitutional States, where ordinary legislation can expand police power indefinitely.

Sovereignty relies on legitimacy, that is, the perception that official commands and actions are generally accepted by the vast majority of the regime's constituents with a minimum of resistance. In other words, official commands are considered authoritative.[57] 'Authority' is the term an observer properly applies to a relationship where one party 'commands' another to do something and the second party complies, when it is likely the second party would not have done so on his or her initiative. Then and only then can one say the commander has authority or, more precisely, that the follower has bestowed authority on the command. When someone physically forced to do something, authority does not exist, regardless of the official position of the coercer. Coercion and authority are independent of each other. While compliance often occurs in the light of coercion, nevertheless, for 'authority' to obtain, coercion cannot have *caused* compliance.

According to Weber, there are three sources of public authority: traditional, rational/legal, and charismatic. Rational/legal—'resting on a belief in the legality of patterns of normative rules and the right of those elevated to authority under such rules to issue commands.' Traditional—'resting on an established belief in the sanctity of immemorial traditions and the legitimacy of the status of those exercising authority under them;' Charismatic—'resting on devotion to the specific and exceptional sanctity, heroism or exemplary character of an individual person, and of the normative pattern or order revealed or ordained by him.'[58] Differing slightly with Weber's terms, because his applied to all the societies he studied, from ancient to modern, on nearly every continent, while mine deal with Medieval Europe and German history, and then only as a background to the Third Reich. So instead of 'charismatic' authority, I use 'spiritual' authority. And when I use 'traditional authority,' it should be understood in the context of the 'Good Old Law.' So, too, with 'rational/legal' authority, which should be understood in the context of Christendom's struggle to apply this essentially Roman concept.

For sake of this analysis, let us assume that a viable organization, whether secular or religious, primarily material or spiritual, needs *one unit* of authority. In other words, a legitimate regime needs one unit of authority, day in day out, to conduct its business. It does not matter what portion of this unit is comprised of traditional, rational/legal, or spiritual authority, as long as it totals one unit. This concept of one is not a spurious attempt to quantify the unquantifiable, but an effort to indicate the necessary relationships among the three kinds of authority. In the rare instance when a concept of authority, say, rational/legal, corresponds exactly with reality, this correspondence does not indicate independence from either of the other forms, unless the reality admits of the possibility that rational/legal authority is so pervasive that by itself it created regime legitimacy. I know of no instance where one form of authority sufficed, except in brief periods of emergency. So, as a practical matter, the lessening of the importance of one form of authority implies its compensation by another. The ruler's main objective is to obtain and secure this unit of authority, this unstable and fragile troika, without which uneasy lies the head which wears the Crown. The fragility of this unit of authority makes all new regimes tenuous. Is this not why nearly every revolution makes claims that it is restoring age old liberties or practices, while demolishing everything in its path? Or, why, failing to adhere to tradition, revolutionary leaders appeal to universal human values which are by definition just and applicable at all times? The most ostensibly materialist revolutionaries have made appeals to the transcendent, without any sense of irony or contradiction. Is not Marx's *History* a transcendent force? Is not the appeal to revolutionary justice? Men cannot live by bread alone, revolutionaries least of all. With these ideas in mind, I would like to reconsider the Investiture Contest.

With barbarians invading from three quarters, protecting their lands and people was the priority of the East Franks. In these pressing circumstances, successful military leaders had the best claim to the Throne. Under more adverse conditions than the West Franks faced, Ottonian kings made a good beginning toward achieving a unified rule, despite encountering massive obstacles. Communications and transportation were primitive; the economy produced little more than subsistence, the bureaucratic apparatus, so essential to executive rule, was embryonic, and rivals abounded. Moreover, in their quest to establish their legitimacy, the East Franks could not rely on German traditions, at least not to the same extent as the West Franks. This may seem odd, as the Germans were widely considered less developed or more barbaric than the West, and therefore more bound by tradition. Unlike the Gauls, they were able to defeat Caesar, who was perhaps the first to use the term 'Germans' to designate the fierce peoples east of the Rhine. If 'development' is measured by how much of Rome Germans absorbed, this assessment is largely true. Despite the fact that the Franks, East and West, were of the same stock, they developed differently. The Romans found French lands much more congenial and Gauls easier to subdue than Germans:

> In the West, the Franks inherited a Roman provincial organization of govern-ment...which was already functioning; and it was only necessary at the time of the invasion to introduce Frankish counts into the existing administrative ma-chinery in order to direct government in accordance with the interests of the new Frankish ruling class. In the Eastern or German provinces, on the other hand, there was no suitable administrative machinery in existence which could be taken over and adapted to Frankish needs and interests; here the Frankish counts were themselves the agents through whom a new framework of administration had for the first time to be established, organized and built up. [59]

There were other consequences of the impact of Rome in what would become France. Roman law and the growth of canon law, indispensable to administra-tion, were increasingly important in the West and only indifferently applied in the East. The Latinization of France was reinforced by the development of the French language.

Since Rome had little influence east of the Rhine, it would be reasonable that the Germans would have retained age-old practices, providing rulers with traditional authority. The difficulty was that tradition worked against monarchical authority. As Fritz Kern indicates, German traditions functioned according to the 'Good Old Law.' Its most important provision was that rulers, all rulers, were subordinate to this law: 'No full-blown doctrine of monarchical irresponsibility could be evolved whilst the Law was regarded as sovereign...throughout the early Medieval period. The State existed for the realization of the Law, and therefore the Law was primary, the State only secondary.... The deeply-rooted Germanic idea of law was that of the Good Old Law, unenacted and unwritten, residing in the common sense of justice, the sum total of all the subjective rights of individuals; the king's right to rule was but his private right, a mere parcel of the law itself.'[60] Unable to make or alter it, rulers had the duty to enforce the Good Old Law. If they were derelict, their subjects had the right, virtually the obligation, to disobey the ruler, who by his dereliction became an outlaw: 'A monarch must be obeyed, but not a tyrant. The instant a ruler interferes with the rights of others without their consent, he ceases to be a king and becomes a tyrant and simultaneously loses his claim to obedience, without any necessity for formal legal proceedings on the part of the community.'[61] The power of this check on sovereigns can perhaps best be appreciated when compared to John Locke. Despite Locke's Natural Rights basis of civil society and despite his contempt of Divine Right, he never advocated disobedience. Famously, tyrannized subjects could 'appeal to heaven.' At least in this respect, the barbaric, pre-Christian Germans took limits to State power more seriously than seventeenth century Englishmen. Partly for these reasons, German traditions clung to the idea of royal election for many centuries: 'The early Germanic kings, however, did not come to the throne through a simple personal right of succession. At best they possessed only a "privileged throne-worthiness," in virtue of their descent; election or at least acceptance by the people alone gave them a legal right to the throne.... Kin-right not hereditary right was the Germanic custom....'[62] It seemed clear to them that, if birth determined who would be king, it would be more difficult for mere men to remove him. 'The hereditary succession of the first-born, along with the doctrine of equal birth of princes, created that legitimist mysticism which already in the later Middle Ages prepared the ground for Absolutism.'[63] Thus the Henrican attempt to develop a hereditary monarchy had to overcome German traditions, expressed by the Good Old Law: 'It was inevitable that the right of resistance, now that frequent exercise and theoretical definition gave it an appearance of a permanent element in folk law, should be attacked by the Henricans and by them stripped of its legal character....'[64]

The inability of German monarchs to supplement rational/legal authority with traditional authority gave Rome an opening: 'Gregory VII was the first pope who dared to take extreme measures against a monarch. He could do so because the king in question was already opposed by a great part of his subjects.... To the chaotic vagueness of the Germanic tradition of resistance, he opposed one great even alien principle: the subordination both of princes and of people to the Papal Monarchy, the infallible judgment of a supreme, super-human justice.'[65] Every German ruler appreciated the peril of the principle of the Papal Monarchy and resisted its application to their lands. This resistance necessarily had to rely on spiritual, sometimes mystical, authority: 'The kings of ancient Germania liked to claim descent from the gods.... It was from the mystic virtue with which their persons were imbued that their peoples looked for victory in battle and in time of peace fertility for their fields.... This supernatural quality, of which anointing was the confirmation rather than the origin, was deeply felt in an age accustomed to associate the influences of the Beyond with everyday life; yet a genuinely sacerdotal kingship would have been incompatible with the religion which prevailed throughout Western Europe.'[66]

But what of Eastern Europe? Why could not its theocratic experience be drawn upon? As we have seen, the example of Byzantium was used to justify *rex et sacerdos*, one which served for hundreds of years and one which the Latin Church found distasteful for just as long. At least from the time of Gelasius in the fifth century, 'Clerical theory itself had little doubt of the divine origin and mission of imperial power; anything else would have run counter to the current ideas of Christian theocracy.'[67] When the Church was poor and dependant upon secular authority for protection from its enemies, it bided its time, downplaying the implications of its doctrines. It accepted imperial or royal theocracy, as it existed from Constantine through Charlemagne, and to have Charlemagne's successors reestablish European order. Once these conditions were in force, as the Church became wealthy in the recovering European economy of the tenth and eleventh centuries, the application of *its* theocratic doctrines became a possibility. Standing in its way, was the German (Byzantine) theocratic idea. 'It was because of this theocratic outlook that the rulers of the Germanic states of the Middle Ages intervened in ecclesiastical matters even more than the Christian Roman emperors had done.'[68] The Church had long understood the nature of its authority: 'By the beginning of the eleventh century, therefore, the Papacy had laid up a considerable store of moral [in my terms, "spiritual"] capital. The new Nations, the peoples whom Christianity had brought into the main current of European civilization, looked to Rome for spiritual leadership.... It was no accident that, during Gregory VII's great conflict with the emperor Henry IV, he was able to draw on support from the countries on the periphery of the Empire: Denmark, Poland, Hungary, Bohemia, Croatia.'[69] The time seemed ripe to establish the proper relationship between divine and secular authority. The 'secular control of the Church, [which] had been an accepted fact for genera-tions,' had to end.[70] Hence, the Investiture Contest.

Not content with Byzantine precedents, German monarchs also justified their notion of theocracy by citing Charlemagne's reign:

> The Carolingian concept of a David-like kingship was decisively theocentric....
> Nothing could have been more contrary to the Reichenau painter. His emperor
> is in the place of Christ.... In short, the Ottonian concept of rulership displayed
> by the Reichenau artist was not theocentric: it was decisively Christocentric....
> In fact the unique Reichenau miniature is the most powerful pictorial display of
> what might be called 'liturgical kingship'—kingship centered in the God-Man
> rather than in God the Father. As a result, the Reichenau artist ventured to trans-
> fer to the Ottonian emperor also the God-man's 'two natures in one person.'[71]

Designed to keep the Church at bay, this conception distinguished the king's use of force from other rulers. Facing two powerful enemies, the king's sac-erdotal authority had to be reinforced:

> The position of the count was based on violence.... By contrast the position of
> the king rested on eternal foundations: he was in the strict sense God's anointed,
> endowed by God with powers which combined important aspects of the powers
> of bishops and priests, as well as the sanctions of secular rule. He was anointed
> with the holy oil used in the consecration of priests; he was invested with the ring
> and staff conferred on bishops, with the power to destroy heresies and to unite
> his subjects in the Catholic faith; and he received the sword and scepter with the
> words that gave the highest authority to his use of violence. It was by virtue of
> this consecration that kings could call themselves...*Vicars of Christ*....[72]

But Gregory and his successors claimed sole authority as the Vicars of Christ. Hence, the Investiture Contest was fought on many fronts, but for one goal: supremacy of a theocratic ideal. 'The capacity to offer the sacrifice of Christ was the exclusive guarantee of the power of saving grace, without which the Church of Rome had no claim against the three ancient realms of salvation: Byzantium, the powerful German emperors, and the salvation system of ar-chaic society.'[73] Therefore, the idea of a hereditary German monarchy had to deal with (1) a pre-Christian German tradition that had a duty of resistance to tyrannical authority and which did not accept hereditary kingship; (2) an idea of theocracy, derived from the Eastern Church, which itself was becoming irrelevant in the West; (3) a wealthy, secure, and arrogant Papacy, which saw Germany as its chief rival, if not its enemy; and (4) to secure sufficient resources to finance the rational/legal authority it had to rely on increasingly, as the Investiture Contest took its toll on its claims to spiritual authority; in addition to the geographic vulnerabilities that have marked German history. The only plausible strategy was to seek spiritual authority on the basis of the Carolingian legacy.

Thus, every German king made it a priority to secure their claim to sacerdotal authority, to reinforce their warrant to rule. Until new traditions could be established, perhaps along French lines, perhaps by absorbing Roman ideas of State and citizenship, there was no alternative to the tradition of sacerdotal status of German kings to buttress their rational/legal authority. This accounts for why every German king tried to reform the Church, whether they were personally pious or not. Reform meant, first of all, cleaving the Papacy from its dependence upon the notoriously corrupt realm of Roman politics. Only in this way could the other leg of reform be financed, the purification of the clergy. Reform would make spiritual authority more powerful and useful to the monarchy, because the faithful needed to believe that the delivery of the sacraments came from clean hands, washed by the king!

As the basis of spiritual authority, the sacraments were central to the concerns of both the Papacy and the Empire. Today they are matters of faith. Then, they were perhaps the most important concepts in the struggle for political power between the German monarchs and the Papacy. As signs that secular and religious thought and practice were inextricably bound, both for secular and Church authorities, it is essential to understand their role, especially the Lord's Supper. In the Church's view:

> In Christ, the Son of God took human nature upon Himself, and so united Himself with humanity. As one of us, as the perfect man, the representative of mankind, He propitiated God the Father by His life and His sacrificial death, and won back the Grace which was lost by the Fall of Adam. He left behind Him the sacraments, in which He is always present and is eternally becoming man again within the community of believers, who are united with Him in their belief and in the sacraments in order to become sharers with Him in Grace and co-heirs of the Heavenly Kingdom. The visible Church and all its institutions, as founded by Christ, is His earthly community. Just as once He put on an earthly body, so now the Church is His mystical body which He fills with His Spirit; He is its head, and all believers are its members.[74]

From this conviction, it was easy to infer the superiority of anyone who could call on the power of the sacraments, that is, priests, over those who could not, that is, all lay people, including kings:

The spiritual power, he [Gregory] says, was created by God in His own honor, and was vouchsafed to the world by His mercy. The priests of Christ are the fathers and teachers of all kings and princes. The priest Baptizes men, drawing them out of the Devil's power and strengthening them in their belief by the holy chrism. It is the priest who prepares the Body and Blood of the Lord and who grants absolution from the bondage of sin; to him is given the power to bind and loose on earth and in Heaven. If, therefore, kings have on account of their sins, be judged by priests, by whom can they more rightly be condemned than by the highest of all priests, the Roman bishop?[75]

Many scholars believe that Gregory marked an extreme regarding the Church's claim to spiritual and therefore temporal authority. Tellenbach does not: 'Gregory merely grasped the idea of the Papacy more logically than any of his predecessors and was therefore one of the truest representatives of the spirit of Catholicism *in the whole course of history.*'[76] This is not to say that Gregory did not institute a revolution. He did, by changing the theocratic basis of Imperial rule, as it had existed since Constantine and as modified by Charlemagne. The Church had accepted its subordination as a matter of practical necessity not doctrine. When that necessity no longer obtained at the end of the eleventh century, Gregory seized the opportunity. The Imperial mouse may have been surprised as he left his nest. The patient, lethal Papal cat was not. Although his assertion of Papal supremacy was aimed at Germany, it was not so limited. Nor was Gregory modest regarding the temporal implication of his understanding of the sacraments: 'Gregory VII regarded himself, historically and logically, as the reincarnation of Scipio, Caesar, and Augustus. This "holy Roman father" strove to make Christian kings and princes of Spain and England, Brittany and Denmark, Saxony, Bohemia, Hungary, Dalmatia, Croatia, Serbia and Russia (1075!) his vassals, by subjecting them to the sovereignty of St. Peter.'[77] Not striving to establish the independence of the Church from the Empire and other secular rulers, he tried to establish the Papal Monarchy in the fullest sense of the word: the Pope was to be the Supreme Pontiff in matters spiritual *and* matters secular. All so-called sovereigns were but vassals to him, the Vicar of Christ. Wilks appreciates how far-reaching and influential Gregory's idea has been: 'The modern doctrine of the State, which still retains its fictitious personality, as the embodiment of right living and the supreme power for good, is thus seen to be a direct inheritance from Medieval political thought with its emphasis on the reality of that abstraction, the rightly governed Ecclesia, which embraces all the essentials of the Christian way of life.'[78] Not be confused with the Roman power State of the Caesars, claiming the same absolute authority of Rome, adding to it the concept of goodness, the State has become a moral and a spiritual entity, because it derived from Divine Order and Justice.

In addition to its monopoly of legitimate force and claims of omnicom-petence, the Nation-State provides its citizens with transcendent meaning. Between the contemporary the Papal Monarchy and the Nation-State stood, in logical and historical progression, the concept of the Divine Right of kings: 'By the stress on the divine origins of authority and its necessity to human ends, by the denial that it could be dependent on human consent, and by the assertion that the royal duty to promote the common good could not be lim-ited by any human laws or measured by the judgment of the community, the doctrine of the Divine Right of kings was formed from fragments of the Me-dieval synthesis.'[79] Although wealth was not the principal goal of either the Pope or the Emperor, both understood that economic resources were essential to the successful prosecution of their efforts to achieve sovereignty: 'The richest man in a particular area, i.e. the one with the most land, is as a direct result the most powerful militarily, with the largest retinue; he is at once army leader and ruler.'[80] This primitive link between money and military or police force was soon rationalized in accord with economic development. For the same reasons that legitimate authority is more efficient than coercion, taxing is preferable to theft. 'For the taxation apparatus gave him [the king] a share of the increasing wealth; a part of all the earnings in his area of rule came to him, and his income consequently increased to an extraordinary degree with the growing circulation of money.... As the financial opportunities open to the central function grew, so too did its military potential.'[81] In addition to its monopoly of legitimate force, the State monopolized the taxing power: 'Free use of military weapons is denied the individual and reserved to a central au-thority of whatever kind, and likewise the taxation of the property or income of individuals is concentrated in the hands of a central social authority. The financial means thus flowing into this central authority maintain its monopoly of military force, while this in turn maintains the monopoly of taxation.'[82] Money became the mother's milk of rational/legal authority, as rational/legal authority became the defining characteristic of the modern State.

The analysis thus far has over-dichotomized spiritual and rational/legal authority. In the world of experience, there was no clear separation between the spiritual authority of the Papal Monarchy and the rational/legal authority of the German Empire. As the economy improved in the eleventh century and afterwards, more wealth was available to both the Empire and the Papacy, both institutions realizing how important wealth was to the pursuit of their missions. Not a simple struggle between Church and State: 'The relationship between kingship and priesthood was the dominant problem of Medieval political thought.... It was essentially a question of the mutual adjustment of authority of two sets of offices serving two sets of human purposes.... It was fundamentally not a problem of State versus Church...but of rifts within the single *respublica Christiana*.'[83] Both the Papacy and the Empire realized that victory would go to the institution which controlled enough resources to finance its needs, while denying its adversary of the same capability. Much of the Investiture Contest was about revenue. The bishops, after all, were often local rulers of towns, regions and sometimes of provinces. They taxed the people like any other sovereign authority, the major reason why German monarchs wanted the bishops beholding to them not the Pope. Furthermore, through the administering of the sacraments and other clerical services, for which fees were almost invariably paid, the Church became wealthy in direct proportion as Christians became more prosperous. Because the Empire depended more on rational/legal authority than the Papacy, it had a greater need for money. Nevertheless, appreciating the value of wealth, the Papacy undermined the Empire's ability to secure the resources it needed to achieve a hereditary monarchy. For example, 'In forbidding kings to tax the clergy of their realms without Papal consent, he [Boniface VIII] struck at a power which had become essential to the continued development of the Medieval kingdom, and which was certainly not a self-evident threat to the spiritual independence of the Church.'[84] The interactive effects of spiritual and rational/legal authority can also be seen in the efforts of many of the most dedicated kings tried to at least appear to lead pious lives, and several actually did, most notably, Henry III. The more pious, spiritual, the king was, the more legitimacy his rule would contain, the less his commands would have to be enforced. Spiritual authority was cost-effective to an extent rational/legal authority could only envy. Spiritual authority in the Empire was especially important due to the relative slowness of its economic development and to its relative inability to keep the Church's hands out of German purses.

This attempt both to enhance and sustain spiritual authority was the justification for the grant of royal Germanic lands to found bishoprics and monasteries at a time when royal finances were insufficient to create the infrastructure of rational/legal authority. The sincerity and the importance of this effort were substantiated by Henry III's refusal to take the customary compensation for the bestowal of royal lands, partly in the expectation of increased cooperation with the Church, for the Church's effective bureaucracy performed many administrative and juridical functions. While Henry III was undoubtedly a devout Christian and had a strong aversion to simony in all its manifestations, he was not entirely unrealistic. He knew that he needed to retain Investiture, if his generosity or piety were not to be subject to temptation. His naiveté centered on his belief that the age old practice of allowing kings to invest bishops and abbots would not be questioned and certainly not overcome. As the linchpin of spiritual authority, Investiture was obvious to all rulers: German kings and their adversaries in France and Rome. Gregory

VII launched his attack at precisely this nexus of the German monarchy's claim to spiritual and traditional authority: 'Gregory VII was the first pope who dared to take extreme measures against a monarch. He could do so because the king in question was already opposed by a great part of his subjects.... To the chaotic vagueness of the Germanic tradition of resistance, he opposed one great even alien principle: the subordination both of princes and of people to the Papal Monarchy, the infallible judgment of a supreme, superhuman justice.'[85] His timing was inspired. With the weakness attendant upon Henry III's death, the dramatically negligent regency of Agnes (whose only devotion was to Gregory and the Church), Henry IV's troubled minority, and the lust for power and riches among the princes, secular and ecclesiastical, Gregory saw his chance, seizing it decisively. Thus the Investiture Contest commenced, initiated by the major beneficiary of the reforms of the Church, almost all of which came from north of the Alps. Regardless of his motives, Gregory's intention to remove sacerdotal authority from all kings, but most especially Germans, was patent. The undisputed outcome was that German kings lost the power of investiture at this critical juncture of the development of the monarchy. Never making good this loss, it is doubtful whether any king or any constellation of events could have done so.

Although the Papacy's victory in the Investiture Contest was decisive, because it prevented the development of a unified German hereditary monarchy, the victory did not end the struggle between the Papacy and the Empire. For two hundred years the Papal Monarchy became wealthier and more powerful, while Germany became more politically fragmented. The very success of the Papal Monarchy, however, led to its demise as a secular power and, more importantly, its demise as the spiritual superior to secular rule. By the end of the fifteenth century, calls for fundamental reform in the Church were all but universal, the most successful and the most cataclysmic was Luther's Reformation. Placing the Reformation in a national context Barraclough writes: 'His appeal was to the "German Nation" and to the "Christian Nobility of the German Nation." He planned, of course, to reform the universal Church; but the resistance of Rome threw him back increasingly on German support and gave his propaganda a peculiarly German flavor. "It is for you Germans," he wrote in 1531, "that I seek salvation and sanctity."'[86] Tellenbach emphasizes doctrine: 'The superiority of the Church over the State derives therefore from the Catholic belief in the Church and its vocation.... Hence Protestant Christianity immediately reoriented its attitude towards the State. Protestantism recognizes no visible institution on earth which is infallibly entitled to speak in the name of God, or which possesses an unqualified claim to represent Him. For the Protestant there is consequently no authority which can issue commands to the State, since the dignity of the State in his eyes second to no other community on earth.'[87]

While Luther's Reformation, by attacking the worldliness of the Church, and especially the Papacy, has been widely understood as an effort to undo the Renaissance, less often appreciated is that the Reformation was an attempt to reverse the German defeat in the Investiture Contest. Far from establishing a theocracy, Luther wanted to destroy the basis of all theocracies, which he believed were impediments to salvation, which could be achieved only by submission to God's Will. The Reformation destroyed the Medieval assumption of the inextricable nature of secular and clerical authority. By radically liberating the secular realm from all extra political restraints, moral or spiritual, Luther legitimated unlimited secular power. When the transcendental properties of nationalism were added to the authoritarian State, the Third Reich became possible, revealing in the most horrific manner the catastrophe of the new linkage of spiritual and secular authority.

NOTES

1. Holborn, Hajo: *A Modern History of Germany: the Reformation*, Knopf, NY, 1964, p. 16.

2. Huizinga, J.: *The Waning of the Middle Ages*, Doubleday, NY, 1954, p. 11.

3. Fuhrmann, Horst: *Germany in the High Middle Ages, c.1050–1200*, Cambridge, 1986, p. 10.

4. *Ibid.*, p. 21.

5. Southern, R.W.: *The Making of the Middle Ages*, New Haven, 1953, p. 71.

6. Heer, Friedrich: *The Medieval World: Europe 110–1350*, translated by Janet Sondheimer, NY, 1998, pp. 9–10.

7. Southern, *Making, op. cit.*, p. 13.

8. Southern, R.W.: *Western Society and the Church in the Middle Ages*, Michigan, 1970, p. 29.

9. Southern, *Church, op. cit.*, p. 31.

10. See d'Entreves, A.P.: *The Notion of the State*, Oxford, 1967.

11. Fuhrmann, *op. cit.*, p. 29.

12. *Ibid.*, p. 73.

13. Krieger, Leonard: *The German Idea of Freedom*, Chicago, 1957. I am an advocate of Natural Rights. This conviction, however, cannot warrant ignoring other conceptions of freedom.

14. Cantor, Norman: *The Civilization of the Middle Ages*, Harper, NY, 1993, p. 217.

15. Barraclough, G.: *The Origins of Modern Germany*, NY, 1963, p. 23.

16. *Ibid.*, p. 31.

17. *Ibid.*, p. 33.

18. *Ibid.*, p. 35.

19. *Ibid.*, p. 27.

20. *Ibid.*, p. 72.

21. *Ibid.,* pp. 83–5.
22. Heer, *Medieval, op. cit.,* p. 269.
23. Fuhrmann, *op. cit.,* p. 57.
24. *Ibid.,* p. 40.
25. Heer, *Intellectual, op. cit.,* p. 97.
26. Fuhrmann, *op. cit.,* p. 62.
27. Barraclough, *Origins, op. cit.,* p. 86.
28. *Ibid.,* p. 97.
29. Tellenbach, *Church, op. cit.,* p. 23.
30. Heer, *Medieval, op. cit.,* p. 9.
31. Tellenbach, *Investiture, op. cit.,* p. 97.
32. Tellenbach, *Church, op. cit.,* p. 223.
33. Southern, *Church, op. cit.,* p. 16.
34. Fuhrmann, *op. cit.,* pp. 93–4, emphasis supplied.
35. Heer, *Intellectual, op. cit,* p. 94.
36. Fuhrmann, *op. cit.,* p. 168.
37. Barraclough, Geoffrey: *The Medieval Papacy,* Norton, NY, 1979, p. 21.
38. *Ibid.,* p. 20.
39. *Ibid.,* p. 22.
40. *Ibid.,* p. 28.
41. Tellenbach, *Investiture, op. cit.,* p. 57.
42. *Ibid.,* p. 58, emphasis supplied.
43. Barraclough, *Papacy, op. cit.,* pp. 36–7.
44. Heer, *Intellectual, op. cit.,* p. 101.
45. Tellenbach, *Investiture, op. cit.,* p. 109.
46. Tellenbach, *Church, op. cit.,* p. 265.
47. Quoted in Southern, *Church, op. cit.,* pp. 100–3.
48. Barraclough, *Papacy, op. cit.,* p. 86.
49. Tellenbach, *Church, op. cit.,* p. 265.
50. *Ibid.,* p. 337.
51. Barraclough, *Papacy, op. cit.,* p. 89.
52. Southern, *Church, op. cit.,* p. 18.
53. *Ibid., p. 24.*
54. *Ibid.,* p. 26.
55. *Ibid.,* p. 38.
56. Quoted in Bendix, Reinhard: *Kings or People: Power and the Mandate to Rule,* Berkeley, 1978, p. 17.
57. Barnard, Chester: *Functions of the Executive,* Harvard, Cambridge, 1938.
58. Weber, Max: *The Theory of Social and Economic Organization,* translated by A.M. Henderson & Talcott Parsons, Free Press, NY, 1947, p. 328.
59. Barraclough, *Origins, op. cit.,* pp. 8–9.
60. Kern, Fritz: *Kingship and the Law in the Middle Ages,* translated by S.B. Chrimes, Harper, NY, 1914, 1970, p.xx.
61. *Ibid.,* p. 196.
62. *Ibid.,* p.xix.

63. *Ibid.,* p. 25.

64. *Ibid.,* p. 91.

65. *Ibid.,* p. 108.

66. Bloch, *op. cit.,* p. 380.

67. Tellenbach, *Investiture, op. cit.,* p. 34.

68. *Ibid.,* p. 69.

69. Barraclough, Geoffrey, *Papacy, op. cit.,* p. 51.

70. *Ibid.,* p. 86.

71. Kantorowitz, Ernst: *The King's Two Bodies: a Study in Medieval Political Theology,* Princeton, 1957, 1957, p. 78. 'It remains a fact that the glorification of the emperor as displayed by the miniature of the Aachen Gospels [tenth century Abbey of Reichenau] by far surpasses anything that was customary in Eastern or Western art. The image shows the emperor in the *maiestas* of Christ, on the throne of Christ, holding his open and empty left hand like Christ, with the mandorla of Christ, and with the animal symbols of the four Gospels which are almost inseparable from the images of Christ in Majesty.' *Ibid.,* p. 64.

72. Southern, *Making, op. cit.,* p. 93.

73. Heer, *Intellectual, op. cit.,* p. 99.

74. Tellenbach, *Investitute, op. cit.,* p. 127.

75. *Ibid.,* p. 152.

76. *Ibid.,* p. 160.

77. Heer, *Intellectual, op. cit.,* p. 170.

78. Wilks, Michael: *The Problem of Sovereignty in the Later Middle Ages*, Cambridge, 1964, p. 525.

79. Lewis, Ewart: *Medieval Political Ideas,* Knopf, NY, 1954, p. 164.

80. Elias, Norbert: *Power and Civility,* translated by Edmund Jephcott, Pantheon, NY, 1982, p. 43.

81. *Ibid.,* p. 9.

82. *Ibid.,* p. 104. The significance of a disarmed citizenry will be discussed in chapter VII.

83. Lewis, *op. cit.,* p. 506.

84. *Ibid.,* p. 528.

85. Kern, *op. cit.,* p. 108.

86. Barraclough, *Origins, op. cit.,* p. 369.

87. Tellenbach, *Investiture, op. cit.,* pp. 167–8.

Chapter Three

Revenge of the Spirit
Luther and the Reformation

You must preach as a mother suckles her child. Martin Luther[1]

Luther has been both vilified and sanctified, and both by sincere and proven scholars, who have spent a good portion, if not all, of their lifetimes reconstructing him from the raw data—only to create, whenever they try to encompass him with a formula, a superhuman or superhuman robot, a man who could never have breathed or moved or least of all spoken as Luther spoke. Erik Erikson[2]

PROLOGUE: MARTIN'S GIFT

Beneath the lines on his face shone a kindness which no austerity could efface. 'Yes, Martin,' he said, as the solemn young monk entered, limply slightly.

'My Lord Abbot....'

'Have you been abusing yourself, Martin?'

The monk dropped his head and mumbled, 'I couldn't sleep.'

'Penance is not meant to be a somnolent,' the Abbot said, affecting sternness. 'Nor is it to be done for no reason.'

'But...'

'Martin,' he began to answer in exasperation, then reconsidering, asked calmly, 'Martin, what is it?'

'I request a special confession.'

'I have just left the chapel.'

'Yes, I know, Abbot, but...'

'You may confess tomorrow. I am certain your sins will keep.'

The monk turned toward the door, then stumbled as he reached for the handle.

'Martin,' the Abbot said sharply, now concerned for the young man's health, 'come and sit down. Let's have a talk.'

The Abbot's kindness and compassion shamed the already shamed monk the more. His piety and goodness seemed to the monk as natural as a cat sleeping in the sun, while he tormented himself merely to avoid depravity. He knew he would spend eternity in Hell and was reconciled to all its trials, save one. How would he do without the goodness of Abbot Staupitz? How would he do without the goodness which seemed to flow from Heaven itself?

'Did you dream again, Martin?'

'Yes, my Lord,' he replied dejectedly.

'Do you want to talk about it?'

'I am too ashamed.'

The Abbot smiled at the monk's fastidiousness. He could confess a sin to a priest but not confide it to a friend. 'Dreams can be God's way of speaking to us, when he can be sure we are listening.'

'I know I talk too much,' the monk said abjectly.

'It's worse not to listen,' the Abbot said lightly, and still worse not to laugh.'

The boy's shoulders quaked, as he sobbed.

'Oh, Martin, can it be that bad?'

'Yes, even worse.'

'Then you must tell me, tell me as your friend.'

'I saw my mother naked,' he stammered, 'naked to the waist. At one breast was a child suckling, the milk overflowing his lips and spilling down her body.'

As the Abbot suppressed a smile, the monk continued.

'At her other breast was a monstrous child, really a beast, a leering, winged demon. He was drinking blood. "Choose," my mother said. "You must choose."' As the Abbot began to speak, the monk continued. 'All at once I saw my father. Perhaps he had been there all along. I don't know. In a rage, he began to beat me with his cane, as I cowered in the corner.'

'Poor Martin,' the Abbot said.

The monk continued without pause. 'The pain was intense, but I did not mind. I deserved it after all. So pleased was I that I became hard and almost ejaculated. I then turned to my father, bulging, monstrous, defiant. Shocked, he stopped beating me and retreated to the wall, his mouth gaping. He seemed to be looking at a stranger, not his son. My mother, now dressed, then said, almost sweetly, "Come here, Martin." As I approached her, she struck me with a whip, stuck my penis. Blood spurted everywhere. I prostrated myself at her feet, hoping she would continue to whip me. I wanted to drown in my own blood, drown in my sin. But nothing happened. I was alone. There was no sound but my sobbing. Then I screamed, "It isn't me. It isn't me." I awoke in my cell, drenched in sweat, shaking with fear, overwhelmed with shame.'

The Abbot took Martin by the shoulders and raised him to his feet. 'I do not know what to make of your dream, Martin. I will pray and I will think. I do know, however, that you must cease punishing yourself over nothing. You cannot, nor should you try, to close your ears to God…'

'To God? More like the Devil.'

'No, Martin, of that I am sure. You are open to God in a way neither you nor I understand. It's a rare, precious gift, no matter how terrifying. You must not destroy it, nor allow anyone else to either.'

'But what am I to do? How am I to live?'

'You must work. Work with God's gift to make it your gift to those who are not so close to God, but who long to be. You will be saved by your work and you will save others.'

The two men embraced, as the tears dried on Martin's face and flowed down the Abbot's.

> He [Luther's father] showed the greatest temper in his attempts to drive the temper out of his children. Here, I think, is the origin of Martin's doubt that the father, when he punishes you, is really guided by love and justice rather than by arbitrariness and malice this early doubt later was projected on the Father in heaven with such violence that Martin's monastic teachers could not help noticing…. It was clear that Martin, searching so desperately for his own justification, was also seeking a formula of Eternal justice which would justify God as judge. Erik Erikson[3]

> Staupitz…was the best father figure Luther ever encountered and acknowledged; he was a man who recognized the true *homo religiosus* in his subaltern and treated him with therapeutic wisdom. Erik Erikson[4]

THE FATHER OF THE MAN

What follows is not a psychological, much less a Freudian, explanation of Luther's thought. It modestly creates a human context for Luther's revolt against the theology of his times, against the Church, to which he was devoted and to which he had sworn multiple oaths of obedience. The first point is that categories, whether psychological, economic, sociological, or any other, have limited applicability to individuals. Whether or not they meet statistical niceties, they tend to filter idiosyncrasies, deriving their cogency from patterns.

An individual is the sum of his or her characteristics, the idiosyncratic often the most telling and revealing. In the great person categories are most suspect and least helpful. To say that Luther was a child of his age does *not* explain how *this* child responded to its pressures. Three important factors in his development prevailed in early sixteenth century Germany and, to a greater or lesser extent, in Christendom. (1) Fathers were almost always autocratic and frequently violent. (2) The world was believed to be populated by evil spirits. (3) God was a stern and wrathful Judge. According to Erikson: 'Faced with a father who made questionable use of his brute superiority; a father who had at his disposal the techniques of making others feel morally inferior without being quite able to justify his own moral superiority; a father to whom he could not get close and from whom he could not get away—faced with such a father, how was he going to submit without being emasculated, or rebel without emasculating the father?'[5] This problem, faced by countless boys and young men, has been met in a wide variety of ways, from submission to murder. Luther responded with classic symptoms: 'suspiciousness, obsessive scrupulosity, moral sadism, and a preoccupation with dirtying and infectious thought and substances....'[6] In testimony to his greatness, in the process, he created a theology, which 'justified' a violent indispensible father, whom he needed to love, and which brought forth the Reformation. Factors two and three will be treated as Luther's theology unfolds.

This analysis leaves to one side the apologists and dogmatists of the Roman Church, whose premise that the Church is the institutional manifestation, if not the incarnation of Christ, and is, therefore, perfect or, at the least, beyond human judgment. It also ignores Luther's apologists, whose premise is that he personified the Word or, at the very least, was its most profound interpreter and is, therefore, beyond the criticism of lesser mortals. Still the task remains daunting. Greatness—and there can be no caviling his greatness—by its nature resists normal categorization and standards of judgment. Luther's longevity, his fecundity, his combativeness, his impulsive, vitriolic, reckless, and scatological use of language compound the difficulties of comprehending a religious thinker who died five hundred years ago. Greatness of character, like originality of thought, must be understood as much as possible in its own terms. The normal should accommodate the great, if greatness is to be apprehended. This process requires sympathetic understanding and intuition more than scholarly exegesis.

Against Paul's seven letters are arrayed fifty volumes of Luther's work, making what may seem an arbitrary approach to Paul a virtual necessity for Luther. It would be tedious and fruitless to try to reconcile his works in the search of a treatise detailing what he really meant, an effort which would reduce his original, volcanic mind to the standards of academic exposition.[7] There are at least two ways to proceed. The first is to fashion Luther's words into a coherent whole of at least his major ideas, an effort more congenial to scholars than to original thinkers. Such a procedure inevitably shears off ideas which seem too awkward or too extreme to be consistent with the author's intent. This form of homogenization risks omitting the most original or profound of the author's thoughts. The further away the scholar is in time and sensibility from the author, the more acute the risk becomes. Homogenized according to unexamined prejudices of the critic, sour milk all too likely results. The second broad approach, employed here as in chapter one, focuses on the essence of the original mind, no matter how extreme or alien it might seem, either to the bulk of his writing or to the sensibilities of the scholar. Tolerating the contradictions and tensions of originality, instead of trying to resolve as much of the work as possible into a consistent framework, this approach tries to build coherence from the essential idea itself by filling in what the idea must assume and imply. Naturally, one person's notion of the essence of an original thinker will differ from another's. My purpose is fruitful inquiry not Truth, a way of discussing important ideas, not of consigning them either to the oblivion of falsehood or the indifference of a proven equation.

As Erikson argues, to impute normal reactions to the abnormal is a category mistake. Boehmer explains: 'Simply in a particularly delicate and sensitive conscience and unusually keen and lively sense of truth [did his abnormality lie]. In this tender conscience and in this severe, relentless truthfulness in the judgment of his own self, lay the real origin of his inward sufferings.'[8] What a normal healthy child can shrug off (seemingly at least), the hypersensitive one takes into his core. What to a normal child might seem a parental aberration questions the existence of a sensitive one. For the gifted child, pregnant with greatness or at least its vaguely apprised potential, there is no such thing as happenstance. Every sign or symbol portends, by its proximity to him, if for no other reason. It is not the beating for a nut (trivial precipitant) but the beating of *Martin* that was significant beyond its viciousness. The precipitant and the event are always trivial to such a child. What matters is that something happened to *him* and must be explained in relation to *him* and to *his* place in the great scheme of things. For the nascent religious thinker, the event must be related to God. For normal children, such a reaction would seem extreme, out of proportion, exaggerated. Far more than any normal child, perhaps too seriously for his own mental and physical well being, Luther cared, about himself, his life, his milieu, his salvation, his God. His enormous accomplishments, for good or ill, were the effects of taking himself so seriously, or 'meaning it,' as Erikson puts it. Many people have exceptional intellectual qualities. Many fewer have the character that chains these gifts to a perhaps obsessive quest for the answers to life's greatest questions. It is a measure of Luther's greatness that when he thundered his answers the mightiest institution since the Roman Empire shuddered.

We are bound to the past in the intellectual order as in every other, and if we were to forget that we are animals which are specifically political, we should be astounded to discover how historically we think, how traditional we are, even when we are claiming to make all things new. Jacques Maritain[9]

[Luther] was gifted with a nature at once realistic and lyrical, powerful, impulsive, brave and sad, sentimental and morbidly sensitive. Vehement as he was, there was in him kindness, generosity, and with it all, unbroken pride and peevish vanity. Reason was very weak in him. Jacques Maritain[10]

THE MEDIEVAL ECCLESIASTICAL ESTABLISHMENT

Rather than a detailed discussion of the Catholicism of Luther's time, I begin somewhat anachronistically by using the twentieth century Catholic philosopher/theologian Jacques Maritain to expound what Luther opposed, for several reasons. First, at the end of the fifteenth century Catholic dogma was not set. Within the Church there had always been debate about the central concerns of Christianity. Only with the Counter Reformation did Catholic dogma approximate the rigidity to which many of its popes had aspired and all of its critics condemned. Second, Maritain was a clear thinker with a polemicist's gift for simplifying his opponent's views. Third, a believer, who accepted Catholic dogma and the Church's exclusive right to discern and propound it, Maritain made no apologies for its absolutes. Fourth, he used reason to dismantle Luther's thought, mirroring his great antagonist, who also believed reason would destroy error, not Truth. For Maritain, Truth is the product of Revelation or Ecclesiastical Authority; for Luther, of Revelation or Scriptural Authority, the Word. Thus, Maritain's interpretation seems a way to cut to the bone of Luther's theology. Not doctrinal, neither Catholic nor Protestant notions of revealed Truth, however premised, disguised, or expressed, are my concerns. Nor is theology *per se*. Writing directly and indirectly about the social and political issues of his times, Luther's voluminous works have been central to German and thus European history. They prepared the way for the Third Reich.

Maritain's analysis dwells on Luther's 'vicious disposition,' his 'anger, calumny, hatred and lying, love of beer and wine, obsession with filth and obscenity—it all pours out in a flood.'[11] All of which stemmed from Luther's negative conception of God:

The unhappy man thinks he no longer trusts in himself, but in God alone. Yet by refusing to admit that man can share really and within himself, in the justice of Jesus Christ and in His Grace—which according to him is always external to us and cannot produce in us any vital act—he shuts himself up forever in his self, he withdraws from himself all support but his self, he builds up into a doctrine what had first been nothing but a personal disorder, he places the center of his religious life not in God but in man.[12]

Luther's unhappiness, the source of his vicious and reckless nature, derived from 'shutting himself up,' and by separating himself from 'Christ and His Grace.' Believing he put God at the center of his theology, Luther so placed himself, an egocentrism: [which is] 'something much subtler, much deeper, and much more serious than egoism; a metaphysical egoism. Luther's self becomes practically the center of gravity of everything, especially in the spiritual order.'[13] Maritain continues, 'What counts is his life, his history. Doctrine comes in as an extra. Lutheranism is not a system worked out by Luther; it is an overflow of Luther's individuality.'[14] So extreme was Luther's narcissism that 'let us make no bones about it; he put himself in the place of Jesus Christ.'[15]

Catastrophic individualism was the basis of Luther's theology: 'What is the Lutheran dogma of the certainty of salvation but the transference of that absolute assurance in the divine promises which was formerly the privilege of the Church and her mission to the human individual and his subjective state?'[16] The substitution of the subjective individual for the Church, Maritain concludes, has made for 'that immense disaster for humanity, the Protestant Reformation....'[17]

In the social order the modern city sacrifices the person to the individual; it gives universal suffrage, equal rights, liberty of opinion, to the individual and delivers the person with no social framework to support and protect it, to all the devouring powers which threaten the soul's live, to the pitiless actions and reactions of conflicting interests and appetites, to the infinite demands of manufacture and use. To all the greeds and all the wounds which every man has by nature, it adds incessant stimuli and the countless hordes of all kinds of errors, sparkling and sharpened, to which it gives the free circulation in the sky of intelligence. And it says to each of the poor children of men set in the midst of this turmoil: 'You are a free individual; defend yourself, save yourself, all by yourself.' It is a homicidal civilization.[18]

Luther's metaphysical egotism was fundamentally at war with authority, truth, morality, law and, therefore, with all civilization: 'Intellectual *magisterium*, human or divine, Church and revealed dogma, even more radically, authority of objective being and the moral law, are finally no longer conceivable except as external and mechanical restraints forced on a nature which suffers them under compulsion.'[19] His inability to accept authority left him desperate and bereft: 'From a Catholic point of view Luther's demand for certainty of salvation, achieved through direct experience, must inevitably appear as proof of a heretical disposition.'[20] Unable to secure the solace provided to millions of other Christians by the sacraments, ritual, dogma, and the community of the Church, Luther rebelled in equally gargantuan and metaphysical terms. He denied the authority of Christ's Church and thus Christ Himself, going so far as to assume His role.

Erikson differs from Maritain. Luther, when beaten brutally by his parents, especially his father, could neither reject nor accept the source of his pain and distress, which he considered just, regardless of his innocence or the disproportionate cruelty his misdemeanors provoked. Desperate for a psychological resolution Luther tried to become so good a son, young man, monk, and priest that a just God would have no reason to punish him. His heroic acts, his works, this process of mimicking Saul, the Pharisee of Pharisees did not work; neither did the consolations of the Church, whose forgiveness and absolution deepened his sense of unworthiness in the face of a wrathful and relentlessly just God. He, in his own mind, was irremediably, incorrigibly unworthy; sin itself, he hated his Creator.

Blasphemy it may have been, but hardly the egotism attributed to him by Maritain. Luther did not judge God anymore than he judged his father. Hating them, or being unable to accept the wrathful consequences of his sinfulness, was not a statement of his worth but of personal anguish. It reflected a feeling that itself may have furthered the sense of abjectness that lay at its source. Of what value could it have been to Luther that others found solace in the Church, when he did not? Who was more earnest than he in his efforts to derive from sacrament, dogma, ritual, and community what so many others sought and found? His failure added immeasurably to his sense of sin. Far from being better than others, he was worse. He asked: 'What could *he* do?' 'How could *he* achieve salvation?'

Luther's concern, for his critics, his obsession, was with his salvation. How could he, how could Martin, be saved, a question which remains as human as unavoidably personal? Luther's 'disorder' centered on the resolution of his distress, how he answered this question. Instead of developing a 'personality,' with the Grace of Christ, under the aegis of the Church, he became a 'monstrosity,' an individual impervious to all but inner compulsions. Instead of a healthy human being receptive to the teachings and consolations of Christ's Church, he became a metaphysical egotist, the progenitor of the disastrous Reformation. 'To someone such as Luther, who appears to have become increasingly uncertain about his own moral qualities…it must have seemed inevitable that God, in his righteousness, would condemn him.'[21] Having tried to be a monk among monks, a priest among priests, unable to accept or reject his father (or any other authority), incapable of receiving the blessing of the Church, unable to sustain his hatred of God, what could he to do? His great predecessor, Paul, facing the same question, inferred the Christ from Jesus' life, personality, and message, creating Christianity. Luther, with equal inadvertence, created the Reformation in the process of dealing with his torment; egotism perhaps, greatness, without doubt. When great men resolve their difficulties, the world trembles. Paul created Christianity, spawning innumerable profound consequences, social, political, spiritual, and metaphysical. Luther created the Reformation with scarcely less portentous effects. We shall examine the process again, when Hitler becomes the focus of inquiry. For now, however, let us retrace Luther's journey from troubled monk to great reformer. The following section discusses Luther's theology more in its own terms, that is, from a Protestant perspective.

> Is not the salvation of man, however, the work of God and His Christ? Beware: in the Lutheran theology Grace is always wholly extrinsic to ourselves, man is walled up in his nature and can never receive in himself the seeds of true participation in the divine life, nor (child of wrath as he is) can he produce a substantially supernatural act. Jacques Maritain[22]

TWO KINDS OF JUSTICE

Boehmer sums up the Church's view of salvation, which retains the core of Covenantal Judaism:

> Not that the Church is capable of directly effecting this application of Grace by its sacraments. That is God's own function. But He has so arranged that the bestowal of Grace takes place always at the same time as the ecclesiastical ceremony. So, although a man can of his own power carry out all God requires of him, he yet needs Grace and the Church, not that he may become a different being, but in order to obtain recognition from a despot God.... Not that he can force God to do any such thing. *But the Master of the World has bound Himself by a contract on this point, and, as He is truthful and immutable, He can be counted upon to fulfill the bargain conscientiously.*[23]

Luther simply could not accept this formulation, absolutely rejecting the idea that man can fulfill God's Will, while following his inevitable and ineradicable sinful nature. According to Cameron: 'These remorseless reinforcements of the moral law implied that it was not just supremely difficult for man in his natural state to fulfill the moral law, it was actually impossible.... So God, in laying down the moral law, must have commanded man to do something which his fallen nature made it impossible to do.'[24] The impossibility of success, according to his initial, quite traditional exegesis, could not be blamed on the intractability of the universe, for man had license to sin. 'Luther himself repeatedly designated as the chief cause of his inner distress the notion that man can do everything that he wills to do, and also that he is able to earn the reward of eternal blessedness by his own works.'[25] Luther writes: 'There are two things that are constantly assailing us, so that we fail to gather the fruits of the Mass. The first is that we are sinners and unworthy of such great things because of our utter worthlessness. The second is that, even if we were worthy, these things are so high that our faint-hearted nature does not dare to aspire to them or hope for them.'[26]

Premising the traditional Catholic view is the notion that: 'Christ and the Church are really made one, insofar as the same Church which administers the sacraments is also, is as the mystical body of Christ, one mystical person with Him. This is the fundamental insight of Medieval Catholicism....'[27] Luther spent his youth and young adulthood trying to live according to this dogma.

> If there was anything that was certain to him from childhood, it was the belief that God is just, that He holds inviolate the laws and regulations which He has created of His own free will, and that 'He guarantees His Grace unfailingly to everyone who does what he can.... But this idea became a source of the most dreadful inner torture only when he realized that he was at the mercy of the Being of Force, who could be moved to Grace or disfavor neither by human desire nor human acts, so that he himself had absolutely no power to change the fate to which he was destined from all Eternity....'[28]

According to Erikson, 'Luther pictured God Himself as a devourer, as if the willful sinner could expect to find in God's demeanor a mirror of his own avarice....'[29] This portrait of God was *not* softened by the concept of Christ: 'Even in the *Bible* he saw only the demanding, angry God, not the gracious, merciful Father; he saw in Christ only the Judge of the world "on the rainbow" who gives to each what he has earned while living in the body, not the Lamb of God who bears the sins of the world.'[30] What could union with the devouring God mean but annihilation? Luther found nothing in the Church's theology, dogma, rites or rituals, sense of community, sacrifice or anything else that could overcome the terror of confronting a righteous God and his equally righteous Son. Moreover, God seemed to enjoy the cruelty of His plan for man. Luther writes: 'As it were not enough that miserable sinners should be eternally damned through original sin, with all kinds of misfortunes laid upon them by the *Old Testament* law, and yet God adds sorrow upon sorrow through the *Gospel*, and even brings His wrath and righteousness to bear through it.'[31]

While all nearly all boys grow in the shadow of powerful and arbitrary fathers, often under the threat of severe beatings, few have viewed the world as morbidly as Luther. McKinnon, however, believes: 'Luther's fear of this righteous judge was, therefore, no mere product of a nervous imagination, though this element might enter into and aggravate it. It was the natural result of the ecclesiastical conception of a retributive God who will demand an account of actual sin committed after Baptism, and will weigh the merits and demerits of the sinner as well as the merits of Christ and the saints, to which he may appeal in his behalf.'[32] Luther's anguish was reinforced by the dominant unquestioned authority of *ecclesia*.

Terrified, Luther turned to the *Bible*, particularly to Paul's *Romans*. His reading proved disquieting, for Luther could not abandon the concept of the Righteous God. Dwelling in sin, man can be justly punished, *regardless of his behavior*. 'Paul holds Adam responsible for the entry of sin into the world and for the sinful state which his posterity inherited. But he does not say, as Augustine and Luther assumed, that all sinned in Adam, apart altogether from their own actually sin.'[33] Nor could Luther believe that God loved Creation, to say nothing of His continuing implication with all his creatures, including man. He could not see, as Paul saw, that we may abandon God, but that God could not abandon us.[34] God is Love, not Will. And this Love is identical with Creation. 'There is not the Pauline conviction of having passed by faith from death to life, here and now and forevermore.'[35] Calling Luther, Paul's 'the greatest of his disciples,' McKinnon concludes that 'Luther has not yet caught the absolutely confident tone of Paul in the triumphant conclusion to... *Rom.* 8: "There is, therefore, now no condemnation to those that are in Christ Jesus."'[36] Instead, Luther parsed Paul's concept of righteousness (*dikaiosyni*) or justice or justification or, as some scholars prefer, 'rightwising.' In this way Luther found a way to allow for salvation, a righteous God *and* irremedial sin.

Initially, Paul conceived righteousness in the context of the Wrathful God, the chastiser of the ungodly and the wicked. Combined with his conviction that man could not sufficiently live up to God's moral law, doom is guaranteed, foreordained. One has to wonder what 'salvation' could mean in these circumstances, except as a tantalizing fantasy. Was this a cosmic joke, with man as the principal fool in a divine comedy? Then Luther reconsidered. Assuming salvation to be a real possibility, despite man's irremedial sin, what could 'the Righteousness of God is revealed through faith for faith' mean, if it did not refer to retributive justice? Near the end of his life Luther recalled the experience, the importance of which the vividness of his prose demonstrates:

For I hated that phrase 'the Righteousness of God,' which according to the use and custom of all the doctors, I had been taught to understand philosophically, in the sense of the formal or active Righteousness, by which God is Righteous and punished unrighteous sinners. Although I lived an irreproachable life as a monk, I felt that I was a sinner with an uneasy conscience before God; nor was

I able to believe that I had pleased him to my satisfaction. I did not love—in fact, I hated—the Righteous God.... I began to understand that 'Righteousness of God' as that by which the Righteous lives by the gift of God, namely by faith, and this sentence, 'the Righteousness of God is revealed,' to refer to a passive righteousness, by which the merciful God justifies us by faith.... This immediately made me feel as though I had been born again, and as though I had entered through the open gates into paradise itself.[37]

In Boehmer's formulation: 'The Righteousness of God is revealed in the *Gospel*. "Thou shall live by faith." Therefore, he concludes, what is meant is not the punitive Righteousness of God, but rather the forgiving Righteousness of God by which in His mercy He makes us just....'[38] In other words, God rightwises or reconciles humans to Him by infusing them with faith. The secular meaning of justice no longer applies.

Fides Christi is now understood as the work of God in man and most emphatically not as a response which man is capable of making to God by means of his purely natural capacities. Whereas Luther had earlier regarded *fides Christi* as an indirect gift of God, in that God was understood to have established the theological framework within which man's faith could be reckoned worthy of justification, it is now regarded as a direct gift of God to the believer. Earlier *fides Christi* had been understood as a general gift of God, in that, the general framework having been established, it was up to the individual to make the necessary response to the divine initiative in the *pactum*; now it is understood as the specific gift of God to the individual.[39]

The importance of this rendition cannot be overestimated. For now God works *toward* man. God rightwises man. 'God offers his Grace to all men; He wishes all men to be saved. This necessarily implies that He shows the same degree of severity or leniency to all men....'[40] The cruel joke dissolves. Judgment remains, although here I prefer 'rightwising,' but it is no longer based on merit or demerit, which given the impossibility of being morally worthy of salvation could never be significant. McGrath sees this option as attractive but prefers his formulation, which adds the concept of the Covenant or the promise of God:

One solution...is that Luther understands *iustitia fidei* to be the divine gift of faith, irrespective of his merit or demerit, on the basis of which he can be accounted righteous before God. Attractive though this possibility may appear, there is every reason to suppose that Luther's intention here is totally different.... 'Even Grace and faith, through which we are justified today, would not justify us of themselves, without God's Covenant. It is precisely for this reason we are saved: God has made a testament and a Covenant with us, so that whoever believes and is Baptized will be saved. In this Covenant God is truthful and faithful and is bound by what he has promised.'[41]

The Covenantal idea retains some notion of reciprocity, but not equality, as McGrath, appreciated: 'The *pactum* thus defines a reliable framework within which the mutual rights and obligations of God and man have their context, so that what is just may be specified in each case.'[42] Luther's theology, as understood by McGrath, subverted the notion of human actions too fundamentally to have 'Covenant' mean more than 'promise.' 'Luther's emerging conviction that humans are prone to evil calls into question whether he is naturally able to make the necessary response to the divine initiative, expressed in the *pactum*. Luther no longer believes that humans are capable of the true humility required of them in order that he may receive the gift of Grace—he requires Grace in order to achieve this true humility in the first place.'[43] The barest reciprocity in this formulation is that man cannot avoid Grace. Luther's human is now the passive creature, impervious to Grace, that Maritain castigated. God becomes in this formulation pure Will, pure arbitrariness, devoid of Reason in principle, not only in man's limited capacity to reason. As God rightwises, God promises: no reciprocation, no mutuality. As Boehmer says: 'God is absolute, Eternal, omnipotent Will.... God could therefore at any time declare as good today what was evil yesterday, and punish as vice tomorrow what today he rewards as a virtue.'[44] Nothing is required of humans, not even being receptive to Grace: 'For the influence of the Holy Spirit has reached its goal only when man finds *that he is forced to submit unconditionally to the judgment of the Holy God* and no longer wills anything but what God wills. On this account it is the elect whom God allows to experience such things. And this is so because religion is concerned, not to satisfy the creature's desire for life and blessedness, but rather to do justice to the unabridged Will of God.'[45]

Christ did not figure in Luther's early struggles to formulate his theology. Perhaps Luther's reading of Paul subsumed Christ? Or, was Christ simply much more important to Paul's theology than to Luther's. This is not to say that Christ was not important for Luther, but He (or the concept) functioned in a peculiarly Lutheran fashion. Although Luther believed that Christ died for our sins, the Crucifixion must be read in the context of justification by faith. Hence, Luther's theology of the Cross, well analyzed by McGrath:

(1) The theology of the Cross is a theology of revelation, which stands in sharp contrast to speculation....

(2) This revelation must be regarded as direct and concealed.... Although it is indeed God who is revealed in the passion and the Cross of Christ, he is not immediately recognizable as God.... In that it is God who is made known in the passion and Cross of Christ, it is revelation; in that this revelation can only be discerned by the eye of faith, it is concealed....

(3) This revelation is to be recognized in the sufferings and the Cross of Christ, rather than in human moral activity or the created order....

(4) This knowledge of God who is hidden in his revelation is a matter of faith....

(5) God is particularly known through suffering.... God makes himself known through suffering. For Luther, God is active in this matter, rather than passive, suffering and temptation are seen as means by which man is brought to God....[46]

The hidden God (the God of Will) has Christ (God hidden in his human form) suffer a cruel and humiliating death. The generally accepted Christian tradition interprets the Crucifixion as a manifestation of God's love for us, that He gave His only Son for us and our salvation. Luther chose, however, to focus on Christ's suffering. 'For the Cross is to him both a symbol of God's gift, through which man becomes the child of God, and a symbol of the highest task laid upon him—*the imitation of Christ*—the holy sign in which the Christian, like Christ before him, may gain victory again and again over the powers antagonistic to God.'[47] God humiliated Jesus Christ (Himself in human form) to show that the only way humans can prepare for God's infusion of faith is to undergo a similar fate, and to do so willingly and joyfully, notwithstanding the prospect of damnation: 'To will what God wills even in this extreme case [damnation] is not to endure evil, and therefore the believer who attains to the highest form of love will even joyfully and freely desire to be eternally damned, if God so wills, in order that His Will may fully be done. But it is impossible for those who so absolutely conform to the divine Will to remain in Hell, because they would not be without God, and where God is there is no Hell.'[48] If God wills it, then even Hell is no Hell.

Luther knew this formulation would be difficult to understand and almost impossible to abide by. It is, however, precisely these difficulties based on natural inclinations or desires that must be overcome. Hence the necessity for humiliation:

> God humiliates man, in order that he may justify him; he makes man a sinner, in order to make him righteous—and both aspects of this matter are seen as works of God. How does God humiliate man? Through the experience of the wrath of God, the threat of Hell and eternal damnation, through *Anfechtung* [a state of hopelessness and helplessness] and suffering.... And thus he turns to God in his helplessness and hopelessness, and by so doing, is justified.[49]

This is the only reciprocity, the only shadow of a 'work,' Luther allows. 'The more' Luther writes, 'Christian a man is, the more evils, sufferings and deaths he must endure, as we see in Christ....'[50] Having suffered sufficiently, man 'turns to God.'

Justification by faith annihilates the concept of salvation by works and the value of the Mosaic Law, both of which implied that God was a deal maker, someone who could be obligated. More than abiding by moral and criminal law, acts of charity, or brotherly love, 'works,' in Church doctrine, included symbolic and devotional acts essential to religious observance: attending Mass, partaking of the sacraments, practicing rituals, and observing dogma. These observances were treacherous, because they suggested that a pious man could become holy, pleasing to God. Luther's devastating attack on the idea of the sacraments inhered in justification by faith. Sacraments, leaving aside for the moment Baptism and the Lord's Supper, were ritual acts which made an implicit demand on God similar to the Mosaic Law. 'If I do these things, in accordance with the rites and rituals ordained by you through your instrument, the Holy Church, I expect you to look upon me with favor,' a pious person might surmise. Of course, salvation could not be guaranteed by reputable clerics, but the suggestion is palpable. This is where the idea of indulgences achieved its importance beyond venality. Indulgences were sold with the guarantee that some benefit to the living or the dead would be procured, a contract pure and simple. Neither the gullibility of the people, who broadly supported indulgences, not their vast corrupt potential was at the core of Luther's objections to them. 'But as early as 1515 Luther was troubled more by the evil effects of indulgence preaching and the indulgence traffic upon the religious and moral life of the indulgence purchaser than by the base motives for granting indulgences.'[51]

In the light of indulgences, sacraments were merely older, more sophisticated forms of temptation, ways of misleading the people for the benefit of the Church, and therefore they were more profoundly pernicious. They established the basis of the two estates of Papal Christendom: clerics and laymen. Clerics, by virtue of their office as sacrament providers, were qualitatively superior to all laymen, including kings. By presiding over the sacraments, priests virtually commanded the presence of God, a power not given to the highest secular rulers. According to Holborn: 'He would have abolished them all. On this he had grounded two symbols, Baptism and the Lord's Supper, which received their meaning from the Word and man's faith.'[52] Only his commitment to the *Bible* forced him to retain Baptism and the Lord's Supper, although in modified forms.

Against the accepted Catholic doctrine of the Lord's Supper, Luther lodged three complaints or 'captivities.' The first is that 'The sacrament does not belong to the priests.'[53] *Bound* to administer the sacraments, priests have only minor authority. Failure to do so condemns *them*, not the people deprived. It is the idea of the Lord's Supper *as it has been appreciated by the faithful* that has the power, a power beyond words or priests. Secondly, Luther attacked the concept of transubstantiation. 'The Church kept the true faith for more than twelve hundred years, during which time the holy fathers never, at any time or place, mentioned this transubstantiation.'[54] He claimed that, although it cannot be understood philosophically, Christ was present in the bread and wine: 'Thus what is true in regard to Christ is also true in regard to the sacrament. In order for the divine nature to dwell in him bodily, it is not necessary for human nature to be transubstantiated.... Both natures are simply there in their entirety.... In a like manner it is not necessary in the sacrament that the bread and wine be transubstantiated....'[55] Catholic dogma maintained that the priest initiated transubstantiation. This capacity, however aided by Grace or any other concept, Luther denied. The third captivity is the claim that 'the Mass is a good work and a sacrifice.'[56] Luther's view of the Lord's Supper is strikingly simple and direct: 'What we call the Mass is a promise of the forgiveness of sins made to by God, and such a promise has been confirmed by the death of the Son of God. For the only difference between a promise and a testament is that the testament involves the death of the one who makes it.'[57]

Regarding Baptism, Luther had one major objection, it, too, striking at priestly power: 'It is far more forceful to say that Baptism signifies that we die in every way and rise to eternal life than to say that it signifies merely that we are washed clean of sins.'[58] And further: 'We must therefore beware those who have reduced the power of Baptism to such small and slender dimensions that, while they say that Grace is indeed impoured by it, they maintain that afterwards it is poured out again through sin, and that one must reach heaven in some other way, as if Baptism had become entirely useless.[59]

Luther's enmity focused on the Church's *power as administered by priests*; 'Priest craft is the essence of Medieval Christianity.'[60] Furthermore, the priestly office carried with it the power to bring God or Christ into the substance of the sacraments. Without priests, neither God nor Christ could be present in the Mass. Luther attacked these dogmas, believing that Baptism was self-sufficient, elevating the Baptized to the level of any priest, bishop, or pope. And, here too, any withholding of the rite does not condemn the person but the priest, for the power does not inhere in priests but in God and God alone. The vehemence of Luther's enmity to the claim of priestly power cannot be better put than by him: 'It would be better that all bishops would be murdered, all chapters and monasteries uprooted than that a single soul should perish, let alone all souls, on account of these useless fetishes.'[61] Although not his primary concern, the political and social implications of his captivities, especially the false claims of Church and priests, were clear.

The struggle between the Latins and the Germans had continued in the clashes of the Medieval popes and emperors and could be resolved only through a relentless war against all the secular powers of the Roman Church, particularly in Germany.... Hajo Holborn[62]

The German had always regarded religion as a personal and individual experience. The idea of the mystical body of Christ embodied only in the Roman Church and the hierarchy always seemed foreign to Teutonic thought. E.G. Schweibert [63]

God had instituted two orders of being, with two regimes of forms of government on earth. One, the 'realm of the spirit,' dealt only with the relationship between Christ and the believer's soul. This [spiritual] realm operated through the Word, not through any institution. The second, the real of the world, was the order of secular society, operating by visible structures, public rules and coercive force. Euan Cameron[64]

LUTHER'S TWO REALMS

Now, however, we must examine a major implication of Luther's theology: the Two Realms. Justification by faith, implying the diminution of the efficacy of works for salvation, along with the arbitrariness of God, His willful essence, the utter degradation of man, his need to suffer and to be humiliated, and the utter sinfulness of the world, all provided the basis of Luther's Two Realms.

Ever since humans became aware of their mortality, they became concerned with change. Cyclical change, the movement from season to season, from drought to flood, from birth to death to birth, had always been there, even when humans were dominated more by instincts and less by reason. Consciousness of linear change, the movement from *his* birth (or their child's) to death, called for answers to questions that cyclical change begged. As the process of deterioration, decay, and death became personal, so did the questions and answers they provoked. All early religions have been concerned with questions of life and death, its purposes, and meaning, as have all their successors. The boldest answers postulated Two Realms: the material or natural and the spiritual or supernatural. As philosophy emerged from these religious sensibilities, concepts became more sophisticated, that is, more closely tied to reason and logic. The Two Realms became: (1) the Eternal, the Perfect, the Unchanging and Real; and (2) the zone of Time and Space, the Imperfect, the Flux, and the Apparent. Christianity adopted these 'Platonic' conceptions, adding the Christ. Life now could be in Time and Space *and* be Eternal. If one had faith in Christ, one could exist in the world and partake of the Eternal. Dead to the power of flesh and alive in Christ, a Christians would be saved in this world, realizing his End (*Eschaton*) in existence. Luther, however, could not accept Paul's idea of the realized *Eschaton*. He could not believe that fundamentally depraved humans could partake of God in any way or that a righteous God would partake of them. How could God be in the world of sin, *via* his Church or any other way, and remain pure? Why would He have anything to do with depravity? Why would He acknowledge humans at all? If, for some unfathomable reason, God did have something to do with evil, what could He do but condemn it? Luther's answer was that the depraved world exists, so that humans would sin so greatly that notwithstanding their defiled state they would feel humiliated. Only in extreme humiliation would humans realize their abjectness, then, upon receiving a thoroughly unmerited infusion of faith-granting Grace, they would turn to God. Humiliation was, for Luther, the process of annihilating any sense of worthiness humans might retain, regardless of sin. Immersed in their unworthiness, only then might they submit to God's Will, be receptive to Grace, and be saved. The Fall, that is, the human sense of worth, instigated this entire process of sin, humiliation, faith, and submission. All questions that assume that man can understand the whys and wherefores of this process presume that reason can fathom God or that God partakes in reason. For Luther, God is Will and that is all the answer humans can have. As we have seen, the divorce of Will and Reason has lain at the heart of the dispute between Catholics and Luther. It also has lain at the core of *his* concept of Two Realms.

Instead of the Two Realms of existence postulated by the Church, the clergy and the laity, Luther asserted there were a Material Realm and a Spiritual Realm. No theological quibble, for by placing all existence in the Material Realm, including the Baptized, Luther located the Church and its priests in the world of sin. Any claim of the Church or priests to command God's presence in the world of sin by virtue of the sacraments or in any other way was blasphemy, an egregious expression of the Church's arrogance, proving it was in league with the Devil. Nor was Luther's doctrine of the Two Realms without political ramifications.

The Church's doctrine of the Two Swords was based on the superior position of the ordinary priest, to say nothing of bishops or popes, to any secular ruler. The economic implications of priestly power reinforced the Papacy's ability to rule temporally, by providing the economic resources to finance rational/legal authority, which Luther's theology undermined. The fewer the essential services priests provide, the less revenue they could supply Rome. 'The secularization of the Church in the fifteenth century led to the most dubious practices in financial matters, dubious because they exploited the religious devotion of the masses for the mere enrichment of the Papacy.'[65] The sale of Indulgences, the Holy Trade, as the Church called the practice, was but the most notorious of many dubious revenue measures the Church employed. Therefore, from the point of view of the Church, Luther's *The Babylonian Captivity* was a revolutionary manifesto going as much to the heart of their claims to secular rule as his treatise *To the Christian Nobility*.

Consider how Luther understood the political implications of his theology. He writes in *Christian Nobility*: 'I say therefore that since the temporal power is ordained of God to punish the wicked and to protect the good, *it should be left free to perform its office in the whole body of Christendom without restriction and without respect to persons, whether it affects pope, bishops, priests, monks, nuns, or anyone else.*'[66] The Church is in the world and it, therefore, must be subject to temporal authority. No one, no institution, nothing in the world is beyond the reach of God ordained temporal power. Far more than holding that Church and State have separate spheres of authority, by placing the Church in the world of sin, Luther demanded that it respond like a sinful person. The Church must submit to the degradation into which God has immersed Creation. The sinful Church should be restricted to the administration of Christian offices, without any extension into the authority of the temporal realm. 'In addition, the horrible extortion practiced by the judges in the bishops' courts must be forbidden...so that they no longer judge anything except matters of faith and morals, and leave matters of money and property, life and honor, to temporal judges.'[67] Luther, hereby, reversed the doctrine of the Two Swords with a vengeance.

Luther (intentionally, I believe) revisited the Investiture Contest. Gregory VII and his successors aborted the development of a German monarchy by subverting its spiritual authority. The German economy could not finance rational/legal authority to the extent necessary to rule without the support of spiritual authority. Now, by demolishing priestly power, Luther reduced the Church's ability to finance rational/legal authority. By the end of the fifteenth century, it was too late for the Church to rule in the name of spiritual authority alone, having become too worldly. Luther is in this sense the rooster who came home to scatter the priests in their temporal barnyards. The Papacy won its struggle with the German emperors. Luther's victory over the Papacy would culminate in the French Revolution and the apotheosis of the Nation-State. Luther's victory, as Maritain charged, would prove no less pyrrhic. The Two Realms of existence would soon be united in the Nation-State, which would successfully claim *both* spiritual and rational/legal authority, its most radical expression: the Third Reich.

Luther, moreover, reconsidered the Investiture Contest when he referred to the many 'German emperors [who] were in former times shamefully oppressed and trodden underfoot by the popes, although all the entire world feared the emperors.'[68] Not simply historically interesting: 'If the popes and Romanists have hitherto been able to set kings against each other by the Devil's help, they may well be able to do it again if we were to go ahead without the help of God on our own strength and by our own cunning.'[69] Moreover, the ability of the French to limit Papal powers, while the Germans could not, due to the power of the French monarchy and the weakness of the German, still rankled: 'How is it that we Germans must put up with such robbery and extortion of our goods, at the hands of the pope? If the kingdom of France has prevented it, why do we Germans let them make such fools and apes of us?'[70] While the nationalist implications of Luther's position were obvious, he was not so much defending temporal authority as just and proper, as condemning the idea that Church authority had either the right or the ability to correct its faults, powers which are God's alone. Notice that Luther is well aware that the Papacy has treated Germany far differently than France, a differential which will haunt German history into the twentieth century.

By placing freedom in the Spiritual Realm and by making the material world the Realm of the Devil (with God's approval), humans were compelled to be licentious. Rulers inferred from Luther's theology that they had virtually absolute authority in the world. Whether this inference was free or determined or whether their behavior was free or determined did not concern them any more than other philosophical or theological questions. Nevertheless, the support Luther gave to their actions did more than sanction tyranny; it made its coercive expression less necessary, and, thereby, made their rule more efficient. For resistance to secular rulers became resistance to the world ordained, if abandoned, by God. In Luther's mind this did not make coercion or violence legitimate. The depraved and degenerate world, devoid of ethical and moral concerns, had no use for concepts like legitimacy. One obeys because one must, physically must, for this is the only way to control humans under the Devil's sway. Physical coercion was thus, for Luther, a fact of life, necessitated by human nature, including its tendency to sin which would inevitably devolve into Chaos or Hell. Humans must obey under physical duress, because their sinful state made it impossible for them to obey without coercion. Luther expressed this in characteristically brutal language: 'Therefore must here we smite, choke and stab... whoever can be conscious that there is nothing more pernicious, obnoxious and devilish as a revolutionary man, as one must kill a mad dog.' Holborn concludes by saying: 'He could not have changed the defeat of the peasants if he had taken their side. But his stand had consequences that could be felt in German history for centuries.'[71]

Suffering under a tyranny becomes an opportunity to submit to God, *albeit* indirectly. 'The function of the State, according to Luther, is then to maintain a rough order in this sinful world of mortals so as to enable the chosen few to prepare for the kingdom of God.'[72] Holborn writes, 'And insofar as the modern *Machstaat*... required the subordination of the individual to the absolute power of the government, Lutheranism helped to pave the way for it.'[73] It is clear that the suffering subject of tyranny, the abject tool of the Devil, the essentially sinful human being cannot be free and should not be free in any sense. Their bondage, however convenient for tyrants, did free them in one important sense. Impervious to a sense of obligation, including citizenship, they were absolutely irresponsible for their actions, the one equality prevailing in Luther's world. Humans submit but only to force. Coercion and submission to coercion served the same purpose: they testified to the power of the Devil and sin, the threat of Chaos, and the unwillingness of God to allow the world its well deserved destruction.

Thus, in this respect, Luther anticipated Treitschke's power State. It follows that Luther's hatred of rebels was implied by his theology. Humans must obey rulers not as a moral or ethical duty or because rulers were ordained by God (they were). Rulers would be obeyed, because disobedience brought pain and death. Worse, rebellion was blasphemy: 'Without and imposed order, humans, corrupted by original sin, would lead the world into Chaos, which would terminate the very existence of the world.'[74] In their sinful condition, humans make primitive calculations: Does disobedience bring more pain than it is worth? Then, rulers should punish man without mercy, without the restraint that even the cruelest sometimes exhibit. In ordinary circumstances, man obeys his rulers in accordance with a primitive logic of survival. In extraordinary circumstances, that is, times when the logic of survival ceases to apply, rulers must respond with the logic of annihilation. Failure to kill rebels would place rulers in the rebellion. Worse, they would have allowed their subjects to descend into Chaos.

Luther had no regrets regarding the nature of this world and its suffering no matter how much the spectacle of suffering disturbed him. The consistency of this personality trait reached artistic levels in the Third Reich. His rationale was that, by making the world a living Hell, humans would be able to part the veil of their sin sufficiently—and realize that their real and only proper concern was salvation. By providing a world of infinite suffering, God in His mercy gave humans an opportunity to accept abjectly and absolutely his position as irremediably sinful and, therefore, justly punishable. In this sense rulers, the more oppressive and ruthless the better, were agents of God; so too was the Devil. For the few who understood this, submitting to it completely, by the Grace of God, Eternal salvation was in the offing.

NOTES

1. Quoted in Erikson, Erik: *Young Man Luther*, Norton, NY, 1958, p. 198.
2. *Ibid.,* p. 13.
3. *Ibid.,* p. 58.
4. *Ibid.,* p. 38.
5. *Ibid.,* p. 67.
6. *Ibid.,* p. 61.

7. Consider Plato. How many scholars have read Plato, as if he did not have the ability to write a treatise? How many have treated the dialogical character of his work as something literary, read irrelevant or unnecessarily ambiguous, rather than part of his central meaning? How many scholars have read the dialogues with a view to turning them into a treatise called, 'The Real Meaning of Plato'? Or, "What Plato Would Have Said, If He Had the Requisite Academic Training'?

8. Boehmer, Heinrich: *Luther and the Reformation,* translated by E.S.G. Potter, NY, 1930, p. 58.

9. Maritain, Jacques: *Three Reformers: Luther, Descartes, Rousseau,* London, 1970, p. 3.

10. *Ibid.,* p. 5.

11. *Ibid.,* p. 7.

12. *Ibid.,* p. 11.

13. *Ibid.,* p. 14.

14. *Ibid.,* p. 15.

15. Maritain, quoting Moeller, *ibid.*

16. *Ibid.,* p. 16.

17. *Ibid.,* p. 13.

18. *Ibid.,* p. 21.

19. *Ibid.,* p. 48.

20. Holborn, Hajo: *A Modern History of Germany: the Reformation,* NY, 1964, p. 128.

21. McGrath, Alister: *Luther's Theology of the Cross,* Blackwell, London, 1985, p. 111.

22. Maritain, *op. cit.,* p. 17.

23. Boehmer, Heinrich: *Martin Luther: Road to the Reformation,* translated by J. Doberstein & T. Tappert, Meridian, NY, 1957, *p. 56,* emphasis supplied.

24. Cameron, Euan: *The European Reformation,* Oxford, 1991, p. 116.

25. Boehmer, *Road, op. cit.,* p. 89.

26. Luther, Martin: *Three Treatises,* translated by many, Fortress, Philadelphia, 1970, p. 164.

27. Harnack quoted in Schweibert, E.G.: *Luther and His Times,* St. Louis, 1950, p. 160.

28. Boehmer, *Road, op. cit.,* p. 97.

29. Erikson, *op. cit.,* p. 121.

30. Boehmer, *Road, op. cit.,* p. 91.

31. Quoted in McGrath, *op. cit.,* p. 96.

32. MacKinnon, James: *Luther and the Reformation, Vol. I,* NY, 1962, p. 117.

33. *Ibid.,* p. 185.

34. For many years Luther studies Paul with increasing despair, and with good reason. 'For in the gospel righteousness is revealed, righteousness that is by faith from first to last' [*Rom.* 1.17]. This *New International Version* translation, continues, 'the wrath of God is being revealed from heaven against all the godlessness and wickedness of men who suppress the truth by their wickedness' [*Rom.* 1.18]. The *New Revised Standard Version* offers more hope. 'For in it [the power of God for

salvation to everyone who has faith] the righteousness of God is revealed through faith for faith...' [*Rom.* 1.18]. I do not believe either the English or the Greek admits of a univocal meaning. Neither did Luther, for he changed his mind.

35. *Ibid.,* p. 59.
36. *Ibid.,* p. 201.
37. Quoted in McGrath, *op. cit.,* pp. 96–7.
38. Boehmer, *Road, op. cit.,* p. 110.
39. McGrath, *op. cit.,* p. 132.
40. *Ibid.,* p. 110.
41. *Ibid.,* p. 116.
42. *Ibid.,* p. 105.
43. *Ibid.,* p. 129.
44. Boehmer, *Luther, op. cit.,* p. 55.
45. Boehmer, *Road, op. cit.,* pp. 144–5, emphasis supplied.
46. McGrath, *op. cit.,* pp. 149–51.
47. Boehmer, *Luther, op. cit.,* p. 78, emphasis supplied.
48. McKinnon, *op. cit.,* pp. 199–200.
49. McGrath, *op. cit.,* pp. 153&154.
50. Luther, *Three, op. cit.,* p. 290.
51. Boehmer, *Road, op. cit.,* p. 176.
52. Holborn, *Reformation, op. cit.,* p. 184.
53. Luther, *Three, op. cit.,* p. 142.
54. *Ibid.,* p. 192.
55. *Ibid.,* p. 151.
56. *Ibid.,* p. 152.
57. *Ibid.,* p. 155.
58. Ibid., p. 191.
59. *Ibid.,* p. 192.
60. McKinnon, *op. cit.,* p. 89.
61. Quoted in Holborn, *Reformation, op. cit.,* p. 168.
62. Holborn, *Reformation, op. cit.,* p. 140.
63. Schweibert, *op. cit.,* p. 157.
64. Cameron, *op. cit.,* p. 153.
65. Holborn, *Reformation, op. cit.,* p. 123.
66. Luther, *Three, op. cit.,* p. 15, emphasis supplied.
67. *Ibid,* p. 48.
68. *Ibid.,* p. 9.
69. *Ibid.,* p. 10.
70. *Ibid.,* p. 29.
71. Luther quoted in Holborn, *Reformation, op. cit.,* p. 176.
72. *Ibid.,* p. 191.
73. *Ibid.,* p. 193–4.
74. *Ibid.,* p. 88.

Chapter Four

The Clash of Virtues:
Jews in Christendom

PROLOGUE

'But, father, you must listen!'

Calm yourself, Isaac, calm. Are you badly injured?'

Exasperated, the boy did not realize the impression his appearance made upon his father and family. Flushed, streaked with dirt, his arms lacerated, clothes torn and singed, smelling of smoke and blood and fear, he seemed more a Christian apparition of Hell than the rabbi's son.

'Father, you're not listening.'

'Let your mother clean your wounds, while you tell me what happened.' The boy wanted to shout that they had to flee, now, that there was no time for words, for cleaning wounds, for anything but flight. With all the restraint he could muster, Isaac told his story, briefly, vividly, pretending that his father should not have anticipated it, should not have prepared for it. There had been many warnings, many incidents, ever since the great Crusade. Every abomination had occurred and with ever greater frequency, as the eleventh century dragged to a close. Forced conversions, street beatings, synagogue desecrations, murders, broken promises of protection and sanctuary and countless other humiliations—all had taken place within his father's circle of correspondence. Still his father remained serene in the belief that the bishop, his friend—as if a Christian could ever be a friend to a Jew—would protect 'his Jews.'

'We are, after all, his property, you know,' he would often say, smiling to his congregation. 'And you know how careful Gentiles are with their property.' Underneath the rabbi's irony lay a core truth. The bishop, who ruled the town and environs, a clerical prince, had invited Jews to settle in his town under his protection for his benefit. Negotiated, drawn up and signed, a Charter of Residence determined in exacting detail how many of them could reside in the town and where, street by street, what occupations they could pursue, what prices they could charge, with special reference to interest rates, relations with Christians in general, especially with regard to legal disputes, the right of the rabbi to rule his community, and much more. For protecting them from Christian animosity, the bishop would receive taxes and other fees from them. Keeping his word as faithfully as the Jews met their obligations, all had prospered, the Charter often renewed. Jews began to feel that they were permanent, not merely useful, residents of the bishop's domain. There was nothing to worry about. Who were the ignorant poor to the authority of the Church? Who indeed?

Reading his father's thoughts, recalling his oft repeated words, Isaac yearned to break through his complacent trust in the past, in the integrity of Christians, and in the Charter. He wanted to question his father's absolute faith that God would protect them, as long as they obeyed the rules. What was more, he wanted to question his father's conviction that God was God, no matter what, and especially was He God, when He asked His People to bear witness to Him, to honor His Holy Name. Jews delighted in the awesome presence of God and no more so and no more joyfully than when asked to sacrifice for Him. Chosen for favor, for a unique relationship with the One God, but also for obligation, for an unquestioning and absolute faith in the One God, this was the essence and beauty of Judaism. Revere the Law! Hear the prophets! Sing the Psalms! Live the *Torah*! What could be better than that? What was an eternity of life as a Gentile compared to a moment in the life of a Jew?

'Calm yourself, Isaac,' meaning, 'We are in God's hands. We have been faithful to His Law. We are the People of the *Torah*. There can be no greater protection than that, no better reason for serenity. We will survive as Jews because we have been chosen to survive, because we are His People. God manifests Himself through us. We must survive because we are testimony to the existence of the One God. Without us, no one would believe in Him. This is our mission, this is our life. We live to prove the existence of the One God. What is the life of an individual Jew or a community of Jews to that?' Isaac knew his father's words, knew them more clearly than he knew his own thoughts. He wanted to share his father's Abrahamic faith. He wanted to be Isaac, the first Isaac. He could not, neither as metaphor nor as a son, not after what he had seen.

'They came into the synagogue—a rabble, some wearing bits of uniform, some red crosses and such, but most in rags. They stank of alcohol, of pigs, of dung, of filth. Enraged, they broke windows and wrecked the sanctuary.'

'That's why the bishop....'

'Yes, I know, father, but can he, did he, protect the synagogue from the vandals?' Isaac continued, not waiting for an answer. 'Shouting, "Baptism or Death?" the drunken louts urinated on the altar, on the huddled elders, who just sat there, as if being defiled, humiliated and beaten were a holy ritual. "Baptism or death?" the Christians shouted. "Baptism or death?" As if they had been answered, they struck, swords descending on the elders, sending blood everywhere. It was ghastly. I escaped through a window and came here.'

'God be praised,' his father said.

'For what,' Isaac yearned to ask, 'his escape or the martyrdom of the elders?' knowing the answer. 'God be praised' *for whatever happened.* They were all the same to the rabbi. Only then did Isaac know his family was doomed, as much by his father's piety as by the Christian mob. What sort of God allows for the massacre of His People in His name by an ignorant rabble? What sort of God allows Himself to be praised by His People, as they are slaughtered? What sort of People worships a God, who allows their massacre, who hates His People for loving Him? Silently he asked these questions, knowing there would be, could be no answers from a father who had dedicated his life to serving the One God. His father had responses, not answers, responses which just were: responses appropriate to the great I AM. As Isaac contemplated the wonder of how so intelligent and otherwise reasonable man could be so irrational, he noticed the Christian artifacts which adorned the sacristy. The ultimate irony. His father was adhering to the One God, as Christ on the Cross gazed down on him, adhering to the One God in the hope of His protection in the presence of the Christian profanation of God, the so-called Messiah! His father, surrounded by apostasy, remained undeterred from his desires to serve Him and His Holy Name with the last full measure of devotion. Truly in the presence of his enemies, as he walked through 'the valley of the shadow of death,' his father prayed to the One God.

Just then the mob broke into the cathedral. As if by plan, his mother removed a knife from her skirts and cut his brother's and sister's throats. She then pleaded to her husband to dispatch her, tears flowing onto her bloody hands. With Abrahamic dignity, he plunged the knife into her breast, this time no divine hand stayed the stroke. Isaac shuddered in disbelief. 'Baptism or death?' The shouts became louder, as the mob searched the church for victims. The father stared imploringly at his son, who shrank away in horror. Then, as the mob burst into the sacristy, the rabbi fell to his knees and on to the sacrificial blade. Pausing to mourn their lost opportunity, the mob failed to see the boy leap through the window to safety.[1]

The relationship between Jews and Gentiles is at all times a reciprocal one.... A real insight into this relationship can therefore only be gained by concentrating our attention simultaneously on both sides of the barrier. Every attitude of the

Jew towards the non-Jew has its counterpart in a similar attitude of the Gentile towards the Jew.... Jacob Katz[2]

Only when historiography becomes...a debate without end rather than a continuation of war...only then does a humane historiography, which strives for both accuracy and fairness, become possible.... Israel Shahak[3]

INTRODUCTION: TROUBLED OBJECTIVITY

Few fields of inquiry are as vexed as the Jewish experience in Europe. As it has been difficult to avoid intentional misunderstanding, despite efforts to be objective, the field has been largely abandoned by non-Jewish interpreters. Equally unfortunately, if 'very understandably, since the history of post-Biblical Jews has been written primarily by Jews for a Jewish audience and against a background of anti-Semitism, ethnocentrism has marked the historiography on the Jews even more than majority historiography.'[4] Shahak and Mezvinsky have condemned a great deal of Jewish scholarship, as hopelessly ideological or religiously motivated: 'We believe that the great majority of the books on Judaism and Israel, published in English especially, falsify their subject matter. The falsification is sometimes a result of explicit lying but is mostly the result of omission of major facts that may create what the authors consider to be an adverse view of their subjects. Many of the books that fit into this category are comparable to much of the literature produced in totalitarian systems....'[5]

Langmuir has elaborated the confusions and the difficulties which have plagued these inquiries.

The implication that Jewish history can be properly understood only from a particular religious perspective brings us to the more basic factor that has made objectivity, as historians use the term, difficult in Jewish historiography. Since Judaism has always been the most essential distinguishing element in Jewish identity, there is an enduring tendency to confuse theological history, the history of a religion, Judaism, and the purely historical investigation of all the activities of those who have been associated with Judaism. The confusion of these three different kinds of inquiry has been aggravated by the extent to which Jewish history has been written by the rabbinate, but it has been aided by the religious commitment of many other Jewish historians.[6]

Confusion has enabled stereotyping: 'The counterpart to the majority stereotype of the Medieval Jew as unbelieving usurer is the minority stereotype of the Medieval Gentile as a violent Christian fanatic.'[7] Finally, the national identity component of Judaism has had powerful ideological impact:

Developed by a group to buttress its identity, it [tradition] serves to separate the group from other groups, almost inevitably drawing invidious comparisons in the process. And like prejudice, it tends to subordinate individuals to the group and its identity. That there may be good traditions, that traditions may have good effects, I would not wish to deny, but what I would like to stress here is that tradition not only has affinities with prejudice and the psychology of prejudice but also is an excellent perpetuator of prejudice—all the better because it makes the failings of out groups an essential counterpart of the virtues of the in-group. [8]

It is sometimes asserted *by scholars* that when a group has been oppressed, when it has been a victim over virtually its entire history, then it is *entitled* to resent its oppressors and to build its national self-esteem on this resentment. So stereotypical representations of its oppressors are understandable and justifiable building blocks of national identity. Groups inevitably build their identity or self-esteem out of anything they find ready to hand or anything they may imagine or manufacture. My issue is one of scholarship, not the inevitable ideological basis of political movements. *No notion of entitlement can justify ignoring the canons of scholarship.* No history, analysis, or interpretation can be soundly based on the idea that one standard of truth, honesty, candor, criticism applies to oppressors and another to victims. All too often, as Katz, Shahak, Langmuir, and others have pointed out, special pleading and double standards have marked this field of inquiry. Undoubtedly, the politically vulnerable status of Jews in Medieval Europe played a major role in determining the socio-economic position of the Jews and in turn impacted their relations with the Gentile majority, rulers and subjects alike. Without questioning the injustice of the their treatment by Gentiles or the legitimacy of an unvarnished critical analysis of the nature and sources of their oppression, a failure to apply equally keen scrutiny of Jewish misdeeds or to try to imagine how they were perceived by the majority, especially by those who saw themselves as victims of the Jews, is simply unacceptable scholarship.

Moreover, the unwillingness to account for the deficiencies of the victim group, whether or not properly understood as a response to majority provocation or domination, only worsens the minority in the eyes of the majority, as clever ideologues have long understood. Much of the antagonism of the Gentile community to Jews in Medieval Europe stemmed from their behavior: (1) They did not accept conventional standards; (2) They engaged in special pleading and sought privileges; (3) And, generally, they applied dubious ethics in their dealings with non-Jews. A leading Jewish scholar puts it this way: 'No moral teaching could change the realities of religious rivalry, social segregation, and the plurality of legal systems. All these must have encouraged a double standard of behavior. Those who were reluctant to be guided by the ideal of a higher morality had the letter of the law on their side.'[9] A non-Jewish scholar adds: 'They [Jews] began by working out a double standard for money dealings with Jews and Gentiles. Some elements of this remain even today....'[10] Katz goes further, attributing the ethical double-standard to Judaism, not simply the position of the Jews as a minority in need of money: 'The traditional Jewish texts presented a dualistic system of ethics and justice; that is, there was one law and ethic for the Jew and another for the Gentile.... The notion that a single system of justice could control relations between human beings without regard to ethnic and religious origins never occurred to anyone.'[11] Understandably, scholarship written before the European Judeocide tends to be less defensive and less prone to deny Jews misdeeds. Since the Hebrew prophets, the most searching critics of Jews have been Jews.

As the prologue suggests, the murder of Jews and the hatred of Judaism have a long history. Although there is no generally accepted theory which accounts for the prevalence of anti-Jewish and anti-Judaic outbursts by the masses, there are generally accepted reasons and factors. These include: the social and economic conditions of Jews in Europe, as well as, the conditions of the majority population; the state of relations between observant Jews and Christians; the political position of the Jews in a given jurisdiction. Let me say at the outset that no matter how hideous European Jewish behavior might have been, it could not have justified the murder of a single Jew, to say nothing of the murdered millions, or of the innumerable and relentless humiliations nearly every Jew has faced. Making this point more strongly, let us suppose that the negative Jewish stereotype has been in all respects true, fitting Jews perfectly. Let us suppose that no Jews had redeeming qualities in their relations with Gentiles. Let us suppose that the positive Christian self-image has been in all respects true and that they have been invariably honest, decent, and fair. If these fanciful suppositions were true, the enormous amount of antipathy, resentment, anger, and hatred of Jews might be understood. Notwithstanding these unlikely circumstances, the criminal violence of Gentile society could not be justified or made acceptable by the canons of civil society or the ideals of Christianity. The disproportionate treatment of Jews by Gentiles can neither be discounted nor understood on the basis of frictions attendant on the clash of these stereotypes. The hatred and oppression of Jews festered in the superstitions, ignorance, and fears of Medieval people, factors that are inexplicable without the anti-Judaism of the Church.

Let us further suppose that all Jews were deeply devout and literal adherents of the *Talmud*, including its many odious references to Jesus, Mary, and Christians generally. Let us suppose that every Christian lived in the imitation of Christ, incarnating God's Love. Let us assume that Christianity is true and Judaism is false. Let us add the powerful anti-Judaism, which would result from these 'truths,' to the anti-Semitism created by the bad behavior of Jews and the good behavior of Gentiles assumed above. Clearly much of the anger, resentment, and hatred of Jews might be understood, although, again, not without severely qualifying Christian ideals. Nonetheless, the persecution of Jews in these fanciful circumstances would remain disproportionate, a disproportion which lies at the heart of the Jewish question in Medieval Europe. To be sure, ignorance, superstition, and fear were at the root of Christian animosity toward Jews. But why did it take this form? This chapter only begins the discussion, for it is largely restricted to the period between the First Crusade and the Reformation, centuries which exhibited almost every form of anti-Semitism.

> The Jews were at once too close and too remote from their Christian neighbors. They attracted Christians by their sturdy piety and intense faith and repelled them by being at once too archaic and too advanced. Their tribalism made them appear so very primitive—as though they had not shaken off the dust of the desert and the burning ashes of Mount Sinai; and yet their enlightened doctors and educated elite were so very daring and progressive. Friedrich Heer[12]

> Jews did not belong to the place in which they lived but, expelled from their own country, had found a *temporary* abode among the nations. Jacob Katz[13]

A PRIVILEGED EXISTENCE:
RESIDENTS WITHOUT RIGHTS

Despite the bewildering variety of the terms of Jewish residence in Medieval Europe, generalization is possible. Almost never having a right of residence, either in law or custom, Jews had to be certified by political authority, residence normally limited by duration, number, location, and terms of behavior. The Jews were a 'Statist' people, because they could not exist without political sanction; they were *in principle* homeless. 'Everywhere in the North their term of residence was a limited one, and could only be renewed by a fresh act of their owner. It was this homelessness which made their rightlessness difficult to bear…. There was no Medieval machinery which could give him a home.'[14] This peculiar status, reinforced by physical and social estrangement, separated Jews from non-Jews. Although it was not unusual in Medieval Germany for various groups to be subject to different laws attendant on different status, Jews were always perceived as more than another guild or minority. Their presence and their undoubted importance could not be calculated as a simple economic equation, because their contributions had to be measured against the political, social, and religious 'costs' of their presence. The material benefits of granting Jews privileges had to be sufficient to pay for the political effects of their exploitation of the masses and their negative presence among Christians. Katz explains: 'The racial or national difference between Jews and Gentiles is here substantiated by the theological conceptions which underlay them. Neither Jewish residence, both settled and temporary, in Christian countries, nor even the very existence of the Jews, was taken for granted, nor had they to be justified in terms of some ideology that counterbalanced the theological conception.'[15] Often it was the ideology of money. The secular rulers had to 'earn' enough from the Jews to compensate both the masses and the Church. Since the masses were exploited largely for the benefit of the nobility, the compensation was, all too often, made in the coins of hatred, contempt, humiliation, and blood. Similarly, Jews made calculations. How much blood, how much hatred, contempt and humiliation could be assuaged by how much economic gain? When was it time to leave? When to renegotiate a deal? When to bribe a ruler to put down raging masses? Jews could not simply be there, residents like Gentiles. They had to pay their way, directly and indirectly. They existed to make money and in the process serve those who allowed them to reside in a given jurisdiction.

As Europe's economy began to revive, becoming more complex with the opening of the Mediterranean Sea, as trade between Europe, the Middle East and Asia developed, Jews became more valuable, especially to Europe's rulers. 'The very reasons which prevented Jewry from sharing the inner life of the peoples among whom it dwelt enabled the individual Jew to become an international carrier, to join hands with his fellow in remote lands and across remote seas to ship, in short, a bale of silk from Constantinople to Cologne.'[16] If Jews had been just another minority, their growing economic importance to emerging European states would have been an occasion for integration into the legal order without the contingencies implied by contractual privileges and permissions. Jews, however, were not just another minority. The occupational terms of Jewish residence reinforced estrangement. They were often allowed to reside in a town or city, because of their financial resources and expertise. This meant that Jews most often dealt with Gentiles who were desperate for money. As Parkes says: 'It was not the prosperous farmer who was taxed most heavily, but the farmer who could not make both ends meet....'[17] The normal resentment of those in need for those who are not and the contempt of lenders for borrowers could only rarely be assuaged by non-instrumental relations. Business relations were exacerbated by the varying need and power of their customers. Jews had to deal with their biggest customers, the nobility, delicately, for Jewish privileges were dependent upon good relations with the authorities. The nobility, therefore, received preferential terms regardless of credit worthiness or risk. This 'shortfall' was often made up by charging extortionate rates to those without political power.

Because usury has become identified with Medieval Jewry, the question of interest rates must be addressed. Cantor believes rates around 50% were normal and often justified by risk factors.[18] Some charters authorized rates as high as 173%.[19] It is fair to assume, whatever the rate charged, it was related to risk in a cash poor economy. Reasonably, to this calculation was added the risk of defaulting loans by politically important borrowers. In addition, it would be naïve to believe that Jewish businessmen, like businessmen in general, would have failed to charge whatever the circumstances would have borne. To the degree that the borrower believed he was dealing with a monopoly, one administered by a hated alien, his resentment would have risen more than his already parlous position entailed:

> When joined to the average lender's zeal for gain—a zeal surpassed only by the average borrower—the hazards of money-lending terminated in a vicious circle. The risks enlarged the rates and narrowed the terms, in this way increasing the burden upon the debtor and ultimately upon the entire German people. And the weight of the burden, expressed in hate, chicanery, and violence, heightened the risks. The cleft between Jew and Gentile became in the economic sphere as tragic as in the religious…. An immediate consequence was the progressive declassment of the Jew. In earlier centuries when Jew was synonymous with merchant, he was looked upon as an alien, yet not intolerable and certainly harmless. But now that he was synonymous with usurer…he became despicable and vile.[20]

Jewish privileges implied favors for their political superiors. The symbiotic relationship of Jews and nobility fueled the resentment of the masses, who paid for the privileges of the Jews *and* the special treatment of their masters with blood and sweat. Not only associated with money, Jews were a metaphor for usury, a process which cannot be understood without the anti-Judaism of Christendom. Parkes says: 'While hatred against them was often economic and based upon their usury, they were not the only chartered usurers. They were not even the only usurers who were persecuted or who suffered sudden expulsion. But when hatred directed against the Jews broke into violence, there was always his religious Otherness to lend it an air of respectability and even piety.'[21]

Despite exploiting the masses, the nobility were able in most instances to deflect peasant anger to Jews, much the easier target, despite being as much victims of exploitation as the masses. Gentile usurers or financiers were resented as well; this resentment, however, tended to be limited to the antagonisms of borrower and lender or to the Medieval antipathy to profit and interest. Jews were all too often perceived more ominously, becoming the metaphor for all that was evil, alien, and unnatural: archetypal exploiters. According to Roth: 'Since the tenth century, when the terms Jew and merchant were almost synonymous, much had occurred. The age of martyrdom for European Jewry had begun .... Little by little, the Jews had been excluded from all the ordinary walks of life.... Only one profession remained open to them—that of money lender.... By the close of the thirteenth century, the vast majority of the Jews subject to the Catholic Church...were overwhelmingly confined in spite of themselves to this degraded, and degrading, occupation.'[22]

Although Jews had lived in Europe since the Romans expelled them from Palestine, their alien status sharpened with the recognition of Christianity as the religion of the Empire. Nevertheless, they often thrived as traders through the Decline, the Dark Ages, and the revival of Europe, culminating in Charlemagne's Empire, but not without sowing seeds of resentment and hate: 'The particular spheres of Jewish commercial activity were thus three: a share in all the normal trade of Western Europe, a very important part of the land-borne trade with the East, and a predominant share of the trade with slaves.... References to this traffic in Christian slaves are not infrequent.... The evidence is enough to show that the Church possessed a genuine grievance against the section of the Jewish population involved in the slave trade.'[23] According to Lowenthal, the slave trade was the basis of Jewish capital: 'Slaves and furs much prized in Moslem lands were picked up for little more than nothing in the great Slavic reserves of men and beasts. So naturally, the profits were substantial. The foundations of Jewish wealth, later to be fatally enhanced by money-lending, can undoubtedly be laid to these favorable conditions....'[24]

Important as Jews were 'when his [Charlemagne's] Empire broke up, their position was left completely undefined.'[25] As Europe stabilized, in the wake of the breakup of Charlemagne's territory and the emergence of the Church as the main integrative force of the new Europe, the position of the Jews began to assume its Medieval character. Yet Jews continued to prosper in relative freedom, protected by whatever degree of law and order prevailed:

> The Jews of France and Germany from the ninth until the eleventh century were allowed to trade and to transact business almost without restriction.... Their religious liberty was guaranteed.... They were protected by the authority of the law from forced conversion by the Church or the laity.... A feature of the high political standing of the Jews...was the permission to bear arms, granted to Jews in France and Germany well into the thirteenth century.... The Jews ranked with the knights and the feudatories who belonged to the upper strata of Medieval society.[26]

Jewish privileges were, nonetheless, marks of precariousness. No amount of privilege, like no amount of wealth, could allow Jews either the fact or the feeling of security. 'The Jews therefore remained [under Germanic Custom] in the position of stranger.... A stranger was an object without a master.

Insofar as he was not protected, either by an individual, or by inter-tribal or international arrangement, he did not enjoy the most elementary rights.'[27] Despite Charters of Residence, Jews were without the rights of the peasantry.

While the idea of 'special protection' came into being when the relative security of Charlemagne's Empire dissolved, charters did not become widespread until after the First Crusade. 'The consequence of the First Crusade on the status of the Jews found a powerful expression in politics and law.... It was after the massacres that the idea of special protection for the Jews first entered the public consciousness and found legal expression....'[28] The need for special protection became a system of privileges most often granted by Charters of Residence. There is an ambiguity in the concept of privilege which helps to explain the existence of Jews in Medieval Europe. Privileges imply advantages, therefore, no one desires to be underprivileged. On the other hand, a privileged person may *need* privileges, grants of status from political authorities that others may not need to live and work in a given jurisdiction. No one wants permission to do what others do by right or custom. What is granted can be taken away, renegotiated, allowed to expire, or ignored by sovereigns. Privileges may have provided extraordinary scope for activity and profit, making Jews tantamount to nobility in many respects, yet: 'It was one of the basic causes of Jewish insecurity during the whole period that the most liberal grants, made with the most solemn assertions that they would remain unchanged either in perpetuity or at least for a number of specified years, might at a moment's notice be entirely revoked or at least sensibly modified. Both in the practice and in the theory of Medieval law, the Jew was fundamentally rightless.'[29] While few privileged Jews would have traded places with peasants or even with Gentile merchants, they remained alert to their tenuous status in Christendom.

Not all relations between Gentiles and Jews were negative or instrumental; however, they were limited, ultimately fatally, by religious differences which exacerbated commercial antagonism. Consider the conclusions of two scholars of European Jewry, one Christian, one Jewish:

> The Christian and Jewish communities were virtually two distinct societies. The fact that they nevertheless existed in the same economic and political framework was the source of their manifold problems and shortcomings.... It would, however, be a grave exaggeration to say that either Christian or Jewish society was entirely devoid of those humanitarian aspects in the light of which a tendency towards segregation would become morally delinquent. It is also true that, when they ignored the call of humanity, they did so in compliance with the demands of duties which were, in their estimation, of a higher value. These were the duties of religion in its Medieval form. It was in this field of religious devotion that both the Christians and the Jews of the Middle Ages excelled. We are, however,

entitled to know what the price of their devotion amounted to in terms of neglect of other values. When such a balance is drawn up in respect of other people's religion, this is done out of motives of self-defense. It is the test of the historian to be able to apply the same method to his own religious group. [30]

It is significant that Katz sees a 'price' to be paid for religious devotion, when it harkened to particularistic rather than humanitarian values. Consider Parkes:

> The Carolingian renaissance was followed by a dreadful period of chaos. The friendship which had reigned between Christians and Jews had nothing to do with the creation of that chaos. But the chaos was proof that the times were not yet ripe for the liberty of which that friendship was a symbol. In the actual and tragic course of history it was not because some Jews and some Christians abused their liberty that the friendship was to be drowned in blood, but because for good or ill it was the Church alone which possessed the power and the steadfastness to create a new spirit out of that chaos. And by the principles of the Church that friendship was a forbidden thing. [31]

Note that Parkes more directly places the responsibility for the tragic course of Jewish history at the feet of the Church, which, after all, had an opportunity to try to normalize relations between the two communities. Leaving aside the dubious assertion of paradox, Langmuir's point is apt: 'The paradox of the eleventh century is that, while the extreme decentralization of European society provoked local solutions to disorder, people began to think of Europe as Latin Christendom and to support development of a centralized Papal Church that would give it administrative and executive integration.' [32] The Church was the only institution that could have had a major positive effect on the relations between the two communities. Instead, 'the whole Jewry policy of the Church was purely negative. It lacked any constructive idea as to how the Jews were to be kept alive in the state of humiliation to which they were doomed until their ultimate conversion.' [33] Even when the Church was committed to protecting Jews, it could not do so without implying, homelessness, rightlessness, humiliation for all, and wretchedness for many. Katz believes that 'it may even be assumed that without the activity of these institutions [the Church and Rabbinate] the rules of segregation might have fallen into disuse.' [34] And with these rules came much of the tension and artificiality which has plagued Jewish-Gentile relations throughout the whole existence of European Jewry.

Later, the important theme of friendship will be discussed. In the meantime, it must be realized that whatever personal affection or respect may have obtained between a Christian and a Jew, under the circumstances of Medieval Europe, there was virtually no chance for affection and respect to exist between the communities. Without institutional support, personal relations remained idiosyncratic and fragile. To the degree they were not grounded in material self-interest, they were doomed by the mutual antagonism of communities, families, and socio-economic realities. 'To shun each other's religious rites was not merely prudent; avoidance of contact with the visible expression of the Christian faith became almost an instinct with the Jew, who felt himself endangered spiritually, and perhaps even physically, whenever he encountered a Christian gathering performing its religious rites.'[35] Two developments made matters worse: the intensification of belief and periods of economic privation, both of which made friendship or otherwise decent human relations more difficult and instrumental calculations more ominous. The greater the piety of the population or the more they were enflamed by anti-Judaic elements in the Church, like the friars, the higher were the costs of keeping the Jews in residence. For their sponsors had to spend political capital to protect Jews from religiously inspired or intensified reprisals. In periods of economic downturn, popular resentment of Jews, their privileges, the wealth, especially its basis in exploitation, raised the political costs of keeping them safe. When calculations of the rulers indicated that Jews cost more than they were worth, Jews were expelled or left to the ravages of the mob. Often the violence quenched itself; often circumstances improved and Jews were invited back. Mob violence scarred the Jewish folk memory, as homelessness became the essence of their existence, including Jews settled for generations. Christians and Jews tended to discount their advantages and exaggerate their disadvantages. The permanence of Gentiles, their unquestioned attachment to their land, both as real estate and as metaphor, seemed to Jews an awesome inheritance, beyond their means in principle. Jews believed Gentiles were more secure than they were. Gentile perceptions differed. The impermanence of Jews freed them from responsibilities and obligations which bound Gentiles, their voluntary presence conferring on them many privileges and economic advantages. They believed Jews were freer and more secure than they were. Fueled by misconceptions and exaggerations, envy and resentment all round resulted. Cantor concludes ominously:

> The new militancy of Latin Christianity and the growth of Papal piety [in the mid-eleventh century] contributed to a tremendous increase in Judeophobia.... Furthermore, changes in economic and political life resulted in the deterioration of the Jews' position. The proliferation of feudal institutions made it difficult for them to hold land because they could not enter into the necessary oaths involved in vassalage. The growth of the merchant guilds, which came to control international commerce, resulted in the exclusion of Jewish entrepreneurs from business by their Gentile competitors. By the early twelfth century their main recourse was to usury.... The Jewish usurers charged enormously high inter-

est rates—as much as fifty percent of the principal—not because they were a tribe of Shylocks, but because enormous risks were involved.... Incessant and violent anti-Semitism stems from the age of the Gregorian reform and the First Crusade.[36]

Homelessness and its psychic insecurity contributed to the Jews' attachment to movable wealth. More than a medium of exchange, money became a 'lease' to property the Jews could not own, as well as, a way to pay for the protection of their masters; a balm to homelessness, it became almost sacred: 'Ultimately the Jew could only live by means of money—not in the sense in which this is understood in our modern capitalist society, but in a much more significant sense: the right to life, which Christian society granted the merest yokel, had to be *bought* by the Jew at regular intervals.... Money became much more important to him than his daily bread—as necessary to him as the air he breathed. Under these circumstances, money finally acquired for the Jew a quasi-sacred significance.'[37] Thus understood, there is no need to discount or deny the empirical association of Jews with trade, usury, or money. Poliakov accounts for the link between money, social separation, survival and religion:

Given the instability of their kind of life, there frequent changes of residence and the necessity for concealment, it is not improbable, as Sombart suggests, that they played a part in the elaboration of that convenient instrument of 'mobilization and dissimulation of property', the letter of exchange.... All of which is of secondary importance compared with the final withdrawal of the Jews into themselves, leading to the formation of a hermetically closed society within which the complex of manners and customs [peculiar to the Jews] finds its definitive expression. *Of prime importance is the reverence for money, source of all life.... Without money, Jewry was inevitably doomed to extinction.* Thus, the rabbis henceforth view financial oppressions...as on a par with massacres and expulsions, seeing in them a divine curse, a merited punishment from on high.[38]

Katz makes the same point, emphasizing the link between Mammon and Judaism: 'There is no question that in this period Judaism approved wholeheartedly of the desire to amass capital.' And 'Hence, from the point of view of its social teachings, Judaism took a completely positive attitude toward economic activity.[39] Although often exaggerated, the association of Jews with money has been real and powerful, reinforcing the social isolation of Jews, advocated by Jews and Gentiles alike, making the consequent Jew hatred seem inevitable. Against this conceptual background, the trauma of the First Crusade can be understood.

From the time of the First Crusade the Holy War was substituted for the evangelization of the non-Christian world. Henri Pirenne[40]

By the beginning of the eleventh century the last flicker of the Carolingian freedom expired; and before its middle a new series of outrages heralded the massacres of the First Crusade. James Parkes[41]

'More bestial than naked beasts are all Jews, without a doubt... Many hate them, as do I, and God hates them, as well I wist, and everyone must hate them indeed.' Gautier de Coincy[42]

TRAUMA AND OPPORTUNITY:
THE FIRST CRUSADE AND THE JEWS

Few historical events better illustrate the gulf separating Jewish from non-Jewish scholars than the First Crusade.[43] Many detailed histories of the First Crusade barely mention its effects on Jews, while Jewish scholars mark the First Crusade as the beginning of Jewish misery in Europe. Parkes puts it this way: 'Though the Crusades were always nervous periods for the Jewish population, it is only in 1096 that the popular effervescence vitally affected their whole future development in Western Europe.'[44] Differing perspectives yield different priorities and points of emphasis; for example, the Egyptians failed to record the Exodus, one of the two or three most important events in Jewish history. Nonetheless, the First Crusade can not be understood without an appreciation of the anti-Jewish hysteria which murdered thousands of Jews. The central motivating factor may have been religious, a form of devotion to the Church Militant. Yet even this point cannot be granted without qualification: 'While the Crusaders in many cases forcibly Baptized large numbers of Jews, these Baptisms either followed the sack of the Jewish quarter or the acceptance of large Jewish bribes. In such circumstances it must be assumed that the desire for plunder and a religious blood lust were the real sources of their actions, not a sincere desire for the conversion of the Jews.'[45] The First Crusade may have been a sincere attempt to relieve the Eastern Church from Islamic pressure, religious and military, to liberate the Holy Land, or to reunify Europe after the disputes over the Investiture Struggle. It likely had more materialist motives, most probably a complex interplay of all these factors, Southern makes this assessment: 'The worsening position of the Eastern Empire, and the genuine desire of some to save it; the even more potent and secret desire of others to profit from its disintegration; the dim realization that Islam constituted a widespread and growing threat to Christendom; the sharper realization that the enemies of Christ were triumphing at the scenes of his early life. Some hoped to be saved by going; others didn't care if they were damned so long as they found new fields for profit and adventure.'[46] The First Crusade cannot be understood without appreciating the claim of the

Papal Monarchy to secular rule and the right to judge secular rulers. Part of this claim depended upon the Church's ability to motivate and discipline the masses.[47] In other words, the Church wished to demonstrate that secular rulers existed by the Church's leave.

While its motives may have been complex, ambivalent, and controversial, some of its effects were plain. Without diminishing the sincere religious motivation of many of the Crusaders, their experience with the Eastern Empire and with the Arab world accelerated Europe trade and economic development in general. In Poliakov's words: 'The great role the Crusades were to play in the development of Medieval civilization is well known: a general awakening of commercial and intellectual activities, followed by the rise of the urban bourgeoisie and, above all, that growing self-awareness of Christian Europe already reflected in the chronicles of the first Crusades.'[48] This long-term process made Jews more important than ever to Christendom, more anomalous to the Church, and more dependent upon sovereign authority, all of which increased the resentment of the masses. This portentous cycle became a litany and a lamentation for European Jews, which must be understood in the context of their roles as economic innovators and adherents of a faith which rejected Christ. The ground for massacre had been well-prepared. 'The popular reaction to the First Crusade was to be an early example of this problem [irrational religious fanaticism]. It is not surprising to find that the massacre of the Jews in 1096 as a popular response to the crusading appeal found its ultimate authority in the writings of Damiani.... The great increase of anti-Semitic literature in the late eleventh century began with [his] two pamphlets...whose passionate charity did not extend to those outside the Christian Church.'[49]

The tragic irony of European Jews has been that the more needed they were by Gentiles, the more anomalous and precarious their status became:

> The fact that the Jews' services could not be dispensed with did not reduce the ever growing intensity of popular sentiment against Jewish business activities.... There was very little or no understanding among the broad masses of contemporary economic changes and their requirements. The greatest obstacle to a universal recognition of the necessity of more modern economic methods was, however, the fact that theology and canon law conducted an almost permanent Crusade against usury and usurers. *Hence there is some truth in the remark that usury secured for the Jews official protection at the price of public detestation.*[50]

In place of the normal process of increasing interdependence, resulting in increasing acceptance and eventual assimilation on mutually acceptable terms, Jewish peculiarities were perceived as more pronounced and more important.

Kisch contrasts the experience of the Wends in Germany to that of the Jews: 'Both Wends and Jews had no definite territory of their owned, no closed region of settlement of any considerable extent, within Medieval Germany. *The most conspicuous difference of a basic nature was the religious one....* Although Wends were regarded as of foreign nationality, their social and legal assimilation was gradually accomplished. The Jews on the other hand... did not attain assimilation even locally....'[51] After all, the claim of authority of the Church as a spiritual institution could safely ignore Jews so long as their presence did not compromise the True Faith, although this approach was not without theological problems:

> In contradistinction to the absence of nationalism as a powerful factor in intranational relations, the *religious* factor, particularly in its theoretical aspect, holds a vastly predominant position in all spheres of Medieval thought and in all strata of Medieval life. This is a fact established beyond the slightest doubt. The dynamic influence of the theological factor on the other factors co-determinative for the social status of the Jews can hardly be overrated. The doctrine of the Jews as rejecters and killers of the Savior, the theological conception of the Jew as the deliberate unbeliever and deliberate usurer, will quickly come to mind.[52]

If theological problems could be fudged or suspended by the spiritual Church, the authority of the Church as a secular ruler could not. Jews either had to be accommodated as subjects or eliminated. Elimination of either Jews or Judaism was much the preferred solution. A cleaner solution perhaps, but in another one of the tragic ironies which beset European Jews, the Crusades opened vast economic opportunities for Europe, opportunities which made Jews less dispensable rather than more. Only fanatical friars pushed the consistency of the choice, 'Baptism or expulsion.' Only those who saw riches as inherently anti-Christian were willing to do without the economic benefits the presence of Jews almost always provided.

> The most predominant attitude of the friars toward the Jews was marked by an aggressive missionary spirit and often violent animosity. Since the friars represented the Christian middle classes both in their personal origins and in their religious program, their hostility toward the Jews may have derived in part from anti-Jewish sentiments typically harbored by European merchants. By the thirteenth century, the Jews of Europe were engaged almost exclusively in commercial activities, especially the lending of money; their success and influence in the marketplace set them among the chief competitors of the new Christian bourgeoisie.[53]

Like Jews, friars were located in the towns and cities: 'Drawn in large numbers from the rising middle classes, the orders came to represent a new brand of religious piety, one that did not demand withdrawal from the hubbub of worldly society. Rather the mendicants remained in society and sought to involve the laymen in their program of moral theology. The friars thereby accorded legitimacy to the commercial and profit economy of cities and towns; although they repudiated financial gain with their vows of poverty, they involved themselves in numerous aspects or urban life.'[54] The danger to Jews presented by the friars, largely the Dominicans and the Franciscans, was threefold. First, they incarnated an intensification of belief, which displayed itself in an aggressive missionary and anti-heretical spirit. Second, their commercial interests made them competitors of the Jews. Third, they studied Judaism from a hostile perspective:

> Only in the thirteenth century did the Church, with the friars in the forefront, undertake a systematic study of contemporary Judaism and Jewish literature and endeavor to demonstrate in public, officially conducted disputations with real Jews that the rabbinic tradition of Medieval European Jewry could not be tolerated in Christendom.... The Church now depicted 'living' Judaism of its own day as a heresy and a perversion, a pernicious oral tradition of religious law and doctrine, a gross deviation from the *Old Testament*.... Over the course of time, the Christian fear of heresy and misunderstanding of what was thought to be the Jews' life of perversity came more and more to dominate Europe's conception of its Jewry.[55]

In this way, a deadly anti-Jewish combination of social forces began to grow as part of the modernization process, which perceived Jews as victimizing pious Christians, respectable merchants, and town dwellers. Proving formidable enemies of the Jews, these forces would economically and politically transform Europe into the modern world. The undermining of the nobility and the Church, the chief defenders, however imperfect, of Jews, would leave them bereft of any form of institutional defense. 'They put their trust in cannon.... Synagogues were built with embrasures and had guns mounted on the roof.'[56] Of course, these events occurred in subsequent centuries. For now, the friars had an immediate target, the religious laxness of the institutional Church. 'Baptism or expulsion,' essentially the program of the friars, seemed to an increasingly worldly Church much too simple and too stupid a dichotomy. It soon was transmuted, as a practical matter, into 'Baptism or exploitation;' the doctrinal difficulties remaining largely unaddressed, leaving relations between the friars and the Church strained and often bloody.

In the aftermath of the First Crusade, the tenuousness of the Jews' position as resident aliens became all too apparent. The First Crusade ended this sense of mutual accommodation and mutual benefit, which characterized relations in the Carolingian period, with the awful finality of massacre: 'Recruitment

to the Crusade, in which Papal emissaries played their part, was made the occasion of religious-political propaganda aimed at the masses. Everything was
there, atrocity stories, over-simplification, lies, inflammatory propaganda; it
was small wonder that the masses often sought immediate relief from tension
in pogroms against the Jews and in riots against foreigners, classing them
all indiscriminately as enemies or heretics.'[57] The anger of the masses and
their amalgamation of violence and ignorance were too well known to admit
of surprises. More troubling to Jews was the inability or unwillingness of
the authorities to live up to their obligations to protect them. Again, it was
one thing to live precariously, when the entire society was bereft of law and
order, when sovereign authority was absent or in general decline, as in the
aftermath of Charlemagne's Empire. It was another matter altogether when
sovereign authority, whether secular or clerical, was established: '[Christian]
rulers regarded Jews as an exceptionally law-abiding and wealth-producing
element in the community. The stronger the authority was, the more likely
the Jews were to be safe. Trouble came…during waves of religious enthusiasm, when fundamentalist priests overawed the ruler or, worse still, turned
him into a zealous convert.'[58] For Jews the Crusades were traumatic. Without
understanding the ferocity of the massacres, 'it is not possible to understand
the subsequent history of the Middle Ages or the bitterness of the hatred of
the Jews for Christianity and for those Jews who accepted conversion to it.
For whether there was or was not some economic motive in their actions, the
Crusaders murdered in the Name of Christ, killing, "His enemies," mercilessly and with torture, as a deed pleasing in His sight.'[59]

Until the First Crusade, Jewish behavior, separateness, strangeness, sharp
practice, and peculiar vocations could have been understood by fair minded
Christians as a reasonable, if unpleasant, coping mechanism, a way to survive
in an alien environment. Destroying many modes of accommodation, the
Crusades opened a chasm between Jews and Gentiles. For Gentiles, it became
common to believe that Jews had to cease being Jewish or leave Europe: assimilation or expulsion. For Jews, their mode of living became: exploit or
vanish. It could not have been lost on many Jews that exploitation of Gentiles
might provide only short term security. Nevertheless, it had the promise of
creating a financial base that might extend Jewish security into the medium
term. Apart from the dangers of exploiting the majority, Jewish practices
faced the problem of diminishing returns. Christian merchants, traders, and
bankers began to exploit the opportunities of the New Europe, increasingly
perceiving Jews as economic rivals rather than enablers:

> The First Crusade was the decisive turning point in Medieval Jewish-Christian
> relations…. Any incident was enough to turn the general population, previously
> indifferent, into a mob seeking blood. This new insecurity had a profound effect

upon Jewish economic life. The Jew had been accustomed to the life of a traveling merchant.... Such trade was profitable, and was probably growing at the time when the Crusades occurred to interrupt Jewish participation in it. Within the next century much of it passes to the rising cities of Italy and Flanders.... An occupation containing fewer risks became desirable, and it was found in the ever-increasing demand for money in a society which was rapidly developing.... Yet other reasons than personal security contributed thereto. Money and precious objects could be hidden or carried away more easily than cumbrous merchandise—or crops, cattle and houses! Lastly money was the bulwark of security, in that it as the only form in which the Jews could buy protection, or bribe their enemies.[60]

Permit a digression on bribery. Having grown up in New York City, I can attest to its pervasiveness. Almost nothing can be done without 'greasing someone's palm,' a process which degrades everyone. For Jews in Medieval Europe, it became a way of life: 'The offering and reception of bribes was so universal a custom that at times the Jews actually received the written privilege that a present offered to an official for some service was not to be taken either as a precedent by that official or as entitling other officials to similar presents.'[61] Notice, bribery is not a payment for good service. It is a payment for the delivery of a service required by normal social or business relations, often buttressed by law. For Jews, a service which could be expected by a Gentile *gratis* had to be paid for, placing them outside of normal social relations, to say nothing of the community of care or obligation. The cycle of mutual contempt was reinforced with every bribe extended and every bribe accepted. This process had a more general and more pernicious effect: 'The variety and frequency with which the Jews owed their security to the giving of a bribe make it natural that the Medieval chronicler came to assume that, whenever any document was issued in favor of the Jews, bribery had been at the bottom of it.'[62] In other words, nothing favorable to Jews could ever be done, because it was the right thing to do or because it benefited the larger society. Every favorable action toward Jews was intrinsically based on a dirty transaction. Outside the law Jews had to pay to get within it, always conditional, always temporary. Alternatively, Jews used money to evade the law. Contempt for Jews, contempt for Gentiles, contempt for law—all these were inevitable outcomes. Thus, to the religious estrangement was added ethical and legal dubiety. The Jew was the contemptible outsider; the Gentile, the contemptible insider.

The period from early in the eleventh to the middle of the fourteenth century was one of sustained expansion, discernible in the size of the cultivated area, the number of peoples, and the productivity of the economy. Internal colonization and the expansion of Europe's frontiers considerably and quite visibly enlarged

the area of settlement.... The qualitative change, the appearance of a more var-
ied and complex economy certainly indicates a quantitative expansion in output.
This remarkable growth in turn sustained the brilliant flowering of Medieval
culture in the central span of its history. David Herlihy[63]

In [the next] two hundred years trade, industry and finance, under the influence
of nascent capitalism, superseded agriculture as the main economic basis of European society; town life grew in importance; the middle classes became more
influential, the lower classes more restive; freedom took the place of serfdom
among the rural masses; signs of the awakening of a national spirit became
visible; boundaries of States were more settled.... The most fundamental of
the changes that marked the passage from Medieval to modern times was the
increase of wealth, and the principal cause of the increase of wealth was the
extension of commerce. Edward Cheyney[64]

MAMMON AND THE DEVIL:
THE ROAD TO MODERN ANTI-SEMITISM

If no one could serve God and Mammon, the Jews, as it seemed to Christians,
had little trouble serving the Devil and Mammon. Moreover, they seemed
ordained for it. As the Middle Ages bled into the Reformation, the conflation of the world, the flesh, and the Devil seemed incarnated in Jews. The
irrationality of these views, their basis in fear, superstition and hate, did not
impede millions of Christians from believing them to one degree or another,
a belief which has plagued Christian-Jewish relations to the present. Nor was
the conflation of the natural and material, on the one hand, with the mystical,
superstitious and magical, on the other, limited to the ignorant, frightened
masses. In one way or another, using varying terminology, German elites
believed Jews embodied, sometimes literally, more often metaphorically, all
the contradictions, terrifying changes, and dislocations of modernity. When
Germans were damaged by the changes which destroyed the Medieval world
(or believed they were, even when they benefited materially), Jews thrived or
seemed to thrive as others suffered, thriving *because* others suffered. 'Why
do the wicked prosper?' became, 'Why do Jews prosper?' Or, 'Why do they
prosper at the expense of Christians?' Reality, as always, was too complex
to be reduced to the despair of the disadvantaged and exploited, who could
not see that Jews were as exploited, *albeit* in different ways, as they were.
Although Jews modified the forces of modernization, they could not create
or forestall them. That they optimized the opportunities provided by their allotted roles was to their credit as a resilient, intelligent people. It needs to be
understood, however, that, contrary to many commentators, Jews were not

'forced' into the occupations which enflamed the exploited masses, not in the sense of coercion. Only rarely were Jews 'imprisoned' and mandated to engage in usury or other odious practices. For the most part, within an ever-narrowing range of options, Jews chose to engage in usurious activities, just as they chose earlier to engage in the slave trade. There almost always was a choice, though the choice be unpleasant: exploit the masses or leave the region. For whatever reason—economics was probably the most important factor—Jews almost always chose to stay in Europe. Another part of Jewish willingness to engage in the exploitation of the masses was the satisfying contempt in which they held them.

At all events, many of them desired to remain settled *as Jews*. Whatever Christians believed, Jews must have become attached to their homes and towns. They, like Christians, longed for permanence and security, perhaps more, as it had proved so hard to come by, and especially during unprecedented times of change and uncertainty. To Christians, Jews may have seemed a strange people in a strange land, a people increasingly engaged in pernicious practices and exploitive vocations: 'Certainly the Jew exhibited many curious characteristics to the ordinary Medieval man. He often had a strange name; he spoke a strange tongue, and wrote with a strange writing; he ate different food; he had different legal customs; he belonged to a different religion.... All these were differences arising out of the will of the Jews themselves.'[65] To themselves, however, they were a community able to continue its religious and social practices, only insofar as they pleased the powers that be. In normal times, these parallel perspectives could rub together with a tolerable friction. Normal times, however, were becoming less frequent and more ephemeral, as the pace of economic and social change increased after the First Crusade.

By the middle of the thirteenth century, most modern structures were at least in embryonic form, and almost all feudal ones were dead or mortally wounded. Important innovators, Jews, according to Johnson, were major factors in the modernization process: 'Next to the development of credit itself, the invention and still more the popularization of paper securities were probably the biggest single contribution the Jews made to the wealth-creating principle.'[66] Far beyond their numbers, without political power, Jews were the midwives, if not the fathers, of the modern world: 'The Jews, through their talents and activities, have in every age and in every type of economy fulfilled an economic function. They were needed and used for certain pioneering activities (trade, money lending, pawn broking, etc.). This need existed as long as the majority of the population had either no interest in, or no ability for, such economic services. As soon as they learned to satisfy this need themselves, the mission of the Jew was finished.'[67] Kisch's point needs to be emphasized. As a rule Jews could not sustain their economic advantage, because they could not buttress it with political influence. At the same time, the absence of political power allowed Jews more freedom in the economic arena than they would have otherwise had. For their economic success could only benefit others politically. No matter how rich Jews became, they could never rule. What's more, their resources could always be appropriated by those who did. Jews were, hence, trebly valuable to their political masters: first, as sources of revenue; and, second, as major catalysts to economic growth; third, unable to become political rivals, 'The Jews' political powerlessness made them the ideal instrument for State protected capitalism in the eyes of those who held political power.'[68]

Pirenne describes in general terms how the capitalist spirit emerged. Appreciating their attachment to the land was much less pronounced, can one avoid reading 'Jews' into all of Pirenne's 'theys'?[69]

> Thus in this agricultural society, whose capital wealth was dormant, a group of outlaws, vagabonds, and poverty stricken wretches furnished the first artisans of the new wealth which was detached from the soil. Having gained a little, they wanted to gain more. The spirit of profit making did not exist in established society; those whom it inspired were outside the social system; *they* bought and sold, not in order to live, not because they had vital need of their purchases, but for the sake of gain. *They* did not produce anything; they were merely carriers. *They* were wanderers, guests...wherever they went. *They* were also tempters; offering jewelry for the women, ornaments for the altar, cloth of gold for the church. *They* were not specialists; they were one and all brokers, carriers, sharpers, chevaliers of industry. *They* were not yet professional merchants, but *they* were on the way to becoming merchants.[70]

There are several points to be made regarding this process. First, Christians predominated, except for brief periods of Jewish monopoly.[71] Second, this process, at least in its scope, was profoundly disturbing. Cohn describes some of the factors involves as follows: 'Materially the peasants often benefited greatly from the change [modernization]; but their attitude was determined rather by the snapping of a bond which, burdensome and oppressive though they had often found it, had yet possessed a certain paternal quality. As serfdom disappeared, material interest tended to become the sole criterion regulating the landowner's dealings with his peasants. And then there were many individuals to whom the collapse of the manorial economy brought sheer disaster.'[72] No matter how beneficial the material aspects of expanding commercial activities might become for all levels of society, the shattering of traditional norms and values was often traumatic, especially for the poor, the downtrodden, or the pious. Agrarian society, for all its misery, was the known quantity; commercial society, for all its temptations, seemed a brave new world. Third, while products changed hands and while financial services could be seen as renting money, for an agrarian people the separation of production from sale and profit seemed alien and necessarily pernicious. Fourth, and perhaps worst of all, the goal of the merchants was not to provide a product or a service, except incidentally: 'The bourgeois...was a stranger to both the noble and the peasant; both distrusted him and regarded him with hostility, and of this the traces have not entirely disappeared.... Compared with the noble and the peasant, the direct producers of the indispensable necessities of life, he was mobile and active element; the traffic of the country was in his hands, and he was an agent of transformation. He was not indispensable to human existence; it was possible to live without him.'[73] These proto-capitalists were in the business of making a small amount of money grow into a large amount of money, a process without limit and without rules, or so it seemed to the masses of the Middle Ages. More than a medium of exchange, money began to have a logic and life of its own. For all these reasons, it was easy for Jews to become associated with the negative aspects commerce, especially its impersonality and its destruction of communal relations. Although Jews certainly participated in these dubious activities, they were not alone. Gentile proto-capitalists, however, were able to assign the effects of their odious practices to Jews. It should be noted that what seemed exploitive to Medieval people might seem ordinary to those of us accustomed to business civilization. According to Bloch: 'Essentially, the burgess lived by commerce. He derived his subsistence from the difference between the price at which he bought and the price at which he sold; or between capital lent and the amount of repayment. And since the legality of such intermediate profit...was denied by the theologians and its nature ill-understood by knightly society his code of conduct was in flagrant conflict with prevailing moral notions.'[74]

More than the logic of money created antagonism to the changes implied by the emergence of a commercial society:

Many feelings no doubt contributed to [the hostility towards the new urban class]: the apprehensions of the powerful, directly threatened in their authority, their revenues, their prestige; the fears...aroused by the heads of the Church by the ambitions of groups with little respect for ecclesiastical liberties, which stood in their way; the contempt or ill-will of the knights for the trader; the virtuous indignation provoked in the heart of the clergy by the audacity of these 'usurers,' of these 'engrossers' whose gains seemed to spring from tainted sources. There was, however, another and deeper cause. In feudal society the oath of aid and friendship had figured...as one of the main elements of the system. But it was an engagement between inferior and superior, which made one the subject of the other. But the distinctive feature of the communal oath [among burgesses] was that it united *equals*.[75]

The entire fabric of human relations was shredding, largely as a result of the rise of the middle class and its notions of equality:

> The attainment of political recognition by the middle class was one of the principal characteristics of the period.... We have already noted the rise to prominence of many merchants and financiers, and we shall have to add to the list lawyers, scholars, soldiers, statesmen and travelers, who, though they sprang from the unprivileged classes, nevertheless achieved eminence and exercised great influence. But in addition to the success of individuals we have to consider the rise of the burghers as a class. The towns were the milestones in the progress of Europe from the dark ages to modern times.[76]

Although the concept of hierarchy might not seem a great loss, when it was inextricably interwoven with obligations of aid and friendship, which by definition transcended calculations of self-interest, we might appreciate the despair the domination of commercial considerations implied for agrarian societies. While commerce depends on contract, the keeping of promises and other forms of obligation, it can seldom be reduced to discrete exchanges.[77] Nevertheless, the idea that material self-interest should define virtually all relations seemed to people of the Middle Ages a world turned upside down. According to Southern, 'Trade encouraged usury; it promoted hypocrisy; it turned men from productive labor; it caused avarice to flourish and raised up men who profited from the misfortunes of their neighbors and so on.'[78] Against these perceptions, perhaps overdrawn, the idea of equality, especially when yoked to growing material inequality, seemed to many a poor substitute. When it seemed the result of the activities of an alien people, people who by definition were outside the community of concern, aid and friendship, the destruction of traditional society seemed more egregious. Even when Christians understood that Jews were as attached to tradition as they were and that they had much the same criticism of a world ruled by Mammon, they, no more than Jews, saw this as an occasion for inter-communal civility. Reinforced by religious leaders, all believed the traditions were too antithetical to allow for mutual curtailment of the harshness of their depersonalized exchanges: 'Medieval society was deficient, where the Jews were concerned, in that, although it included groups of Jews, the system of values on which it rested excluded them from participating in it. Conversely, the Jewish community, in spite of being part of another society, retained *in toto* it own system of values which presupposed the existence of a self-sufficing and separate Jewish society.'[79] Moreover, Christians perceived Jews as exclusivist, bestowing humanity only within their community, which seemed antithetical to their Christian ideals.

> The authors of the *Midrash* and philosophers like R. Judah ha-Levi had to distinguish between the natures of Jew and Gentile as the basis for the distinction

in faith and fate. They might see this distinction as stemming from a biological-racial factor. (Jews were descended from Abraham, Isaac and Jacob, while Gentiles descended from Esau, etc.) Alternatively, they might see it as deriving from some differing reaction to a historical-metaphysical event (Jews accepted the *Torah* and Gentiles refused it).... Differences in belief were now seen only as the product of a deeper division in the biological-metaphysical or historical metaphysical natures of the two camps.[80]

Mutual separation, even when it did not breed contempt—and Christian and Jewish religious leaders taught the evil of the other religion at every opportunity—had significant consequences. Commercial relations between Christians and Jews, including non-exploitive normal business transactions, only rarely could have ceased to have been instrumental. To the normal material self-interest of business relations was added the gall of mutual contempt, not the balm of community. Meeting each others' needs, the normal practice of a society, increasingly based on the division of labor and comparative advantage, was not a matter of economic convenience but a necessity reluctantly engaged in. Jews dealt with Gentiles when they had to: 'The Jewish household was dependent upon the Gentile for its meat, milk, grain, wine, and beer, and other food. Nor could the Jew have dispensed with the Gentile's services either inside or outside his household.'[81] Christians dealt with Jews, when they had too, usually for some sort of financial transaction. Separation, mutual contempt, economic necessity, exploitation, all these factors made double-standards inevitable and their application more harsh and invariant than was economically necessary. 'Although Weber pointed out that this was a universal social phenomenon—the members of any cohesive social unit observing different moral standards among themselves from those observed by it in relation to strangers—he was right in depicting the Medieval Jewish community as an extreme case in point, to demonstrate this sociological rule.'[82]

The very nature of economic rationality called its benefits into question; its association with Jews making it worse: 'It was the unconscious collective instinct of the Jews both to depersonalize finance and to rationalize the general economic process.'[83] Perhaps exaggerated, as are other statements of the sort which ascribe to the Jews genetic or religious advantages in commercial activities, Katz seems closer to the mark: 'The intensity of Jewish participation in the new economy was not the product of any internal tendency attuned to the spirit of capitalism; rather, it was first and foremost the result of the Jews' status in society [which] led the Jew to relate to his business dealings in a totally instrumental fashion. It was this attitude that led the Jew to evaluate every business deal solely on the basis of short-term profit.'[84] Their empirical association with commerce, for whatever reason, could not fail to be noted by the majority society. Nor did it fail to condemn Jews.

During periods of economic expansion, the day to day tensions between the two communities might diminish. Jews, however, seldom were credited for their contributions to economic development, and they were blamed for its dislocations and downturns. Although this asymmetry does not prove the inevitability of deteriorating Jewish-Christian relations as the modern age unfolded, it indicates a deep-seated problem. If the modern economy could have developed without the fluctuations that have occurred throughout its history, if there had been a straight line of improvement in the output of goods and services, and if the benefits of the material world had been distributed far more evenly and fairly than they were, Jews still would have been problematic in Christian society. The best way to make my point is to discuss *The Merchant of Venice.*

> Shylock, *albeit* I neither lend nor borrow
> By taking nor by giving of excess,
> Yet, to supply my friend,
> I'll break a custom. Antonio, I:3.57–60[85]
> Content, in faith: I'll seal to such a bond,
> And say there is much kindness in the Jew. Antonio I:3.148–9

LOVE, FRIENDSHIP AND EMERGING CAPITALISM

No work better captures the tragic confrontation between Jews and Gentiles in Europe than *The Merchant of Venice.* Shakespeare dealt with virtually every issue which has plagued the history of Jews in Europe: anti-Judaism, assimilation, anti-Christianity, greed, trade, usury, the law, friendship, marriage, deception, double-standards, brutality, willful misunderstanding, Baptism, stereotyping, the Other, capitalism (long-distance trade and finance), reconciliation, minority status, majority power, communal loyalty, among others. Few plays have created so many disagreements between Christians and Jews. Jewish scholars tend to focus on Shylock's predicament, his humanity, including his respect for Judaism, the admiration of his friends, and his love of his daughter. Christian scholars tend to focus on Portia, Antonio, and his Belmont friends. More than the manifold genius of Shakespeare lies behind Shylock's and Portia's immortal words. As a confrontation of virtues, the tragedy of Jewish-Christian relations required powerful expressions of each perspective. If Shakespeare were an unvarnished anti-Semite, he could not have given Shylock his great speech. It would have been unnecessary for Shylock to be more than a stock figure, the greedy usurer of countless anti-Semitic works, including early versions of him. As a man of virtue, his conversion was essential to the well-being of Venice, not a gratuitous insult. Gross captures the essential conflict: 'If Bassanio were pitted directly against

Shylock, the play would simply be a clash between two opposing worlds: Belmont... versus the Rialto. But what Shakespeare wrote was more complicated and more interesting. As the kinsman and friend of Antonio, Bassanio also has his inescapable links with the Venetian money-world, and it is Antonio who is Shylock's principal antagonist. There is a contrast in the play between Belmont and Venice, and a much sharper contrast within Venice itself, between two versions of capitalism.'[86] It is a measure of the power of the stereotypes which command the discussion of the Jewish experience in Europe that Shakespeare's great play has been systematically misunderstood. At the level of common knowledge, how many realize that the merchant of Venice is not Shylock? How many people, presumably acquainted with the play, believe that he was motivated by greed? So thoughtful and sensitive an observer as Parkes misleads, when he suggests that: 'It is the extortionate charges of the Jewish usurer, deeply imprinted upon the memory of Europe, enshrined in popular literature, canonized in Shakespeare's Shylock, which provides the foundation for economic anti-Semitism.'[87] The economic activities of Jews did create fertile ground for resentment by the larger community, an overwhelming empirical basis for the mutual antipathy of Jews and Christians. Religious differences, especially implying estrangement of the communities, added immeasurably to the always tense relation between Christian and Jew. But Shylock's difficulty with Venice was not *ressentiment*. Taking his Jewishness seriously, his first appearance establishes his contempt for Christians, rejecting an invitation to dinner:

> Yes, to smell pork; to eat of the habitation which
> Your prophet the Nazarite conjured the Devil into.
> I will buy with you, sell with you, talk with you,
> Walk with you, and so following; but I will not eat
> With you, drink with you, nor pray with you. I:3.30–34

To this gratuitous rudeness, Shylock adds an aside:

> I hate him for he is a Christian;
> But more for that in low simplicity
> He lends out money gratis, and brings down
> The rate of usance here with us in Venice. I:3.38–41

Yet neither Shylock's role as a creditor, nor his Jewishness, explains *The Merchant of Venice*. Understanding the significance of the transition to capitalism and the strains it entailed, Gross hits the mark:

> Such was the tradition that Shylock was born into. In many respects he is bound
> to strike us as a Medieval figure, still walking the same narrow groove marked
> out by his money-lending ancestors. Antonio, by contrast, seems a man of the

future—if we are to judge him by his business activities, that is. His reach extends to the Indies and the New World. From another point of view, however, the two men's roles are reversed. Antonio embodies the Medieval morality of friendship; Shylock represents the challenge of unrestrained bargaining and calculation. In this light, Antonio is the traditionalist and Shylock the innovator.[88]

Long accustomed to commerce and its values, by the fifteenth century, Venice was becoming a financial and commercial hub in the modern senses of the word, not just a strategically sited trading center: 'In the 1570s, the tide began to turn regarding the convenience of expelling usurers. With the spread of mercantilist thinking, of policies designed to foster trade, the economic skills and international connections of the Jews came to seem too valuable an asset to cast aside.'[89] Venice would have had many of the issues articulated in *The Merchant of Venice* had there been no Jews or any other minority involved in finance or any other important sector of its economy. Nonetheless, if we have learned anything from the history of Jews in Europe, it is that they have not been just another minority. As archetypal Others, they became scapegoats. It has been thematic in European history that almost every difficulty intrinsic to rapid societal change has been blamed on Jews. Much too subtle an observer to engage in so crass an accusation, Shakespeare portrayed Shylock and the Jews as obstacles to the necessary adjustments attendant to the dislocations of emergent capitalism. And he ascribed their continuing tense relations with Christians to their willful self-segregation and contempt for Christians, not to their commercial activities. Certainly Shakespeare made Shylock's Jewishness an issue:

> There are a number of other explicitly Jewish touches in the play. Shylock swears an oath 'by our holy Sabbath.' Recalling *Genesis* once again [the Jacob reference] (on this occasion the story of Ismael), he refers to Lancelot Gobbo as 'that fool of Hagar's offspring.' At a crucial turn in the plot, he tells his countryman Tubal to meet him 'at our synagogue'—a summons which sounds innocuous enough today, and can be made to sound deeply impressive, but one which would have carried inescapably sinister overtones for most members of the original audience.[90]

And Shakespeare tried to plumb the 'Jewish personality.' Gross quotes Harold Fisch:

> 'It is often said that in Shylock, Shakespeare penetrated into the psychology of the Jew. There *is* something Jewish about him certainly, or shall we say something of the Jew of the *Galut* [the Jewish term for the Diaspora], in his dark and gloomy resentments, his feverish care of his possessions, his sense of family (he prizes the jewel left him by his dead wife), his loyalty to his fellow Jews,

his love of his daughter, his gestures, his faith in the absolute validity of the written bond (the stress on this is a master-stroke), his appeal to law as against sentiment.' [Gross continues:] What is missing [is] the whole region of Jewish spirituality. There is no hint in Shylock of an inner faith, or of religion as a way of life, as opposed to a set of rules.[91]

While Shakespeare's powerful portrait of the Other created dramatic antagonism, it was unfair to the richness of Judaism and Jewish experience. Shakespeare's point, however, was not that Jews could not be integrated into the society, because they are not human or because they have strange practices. It is rather that they could not be integrated into Venetian society *as a separate community of virtue.* So Shakespeare favored the elimination of Jews *qua* Jews. His reason, however, is important. Shakespeare believed that for law to work properly it could not be literal. To approximate justice, law had to reside *within* a community of virtue. Danson is correct when he says that 'It is essential for Shakespeare's purposes in this play that Venetian law should seem to bear no signs of the concept of equity; it must be the unmitigated law of the *letter....*'[92] He is not correct, however, when he suggests that Shakespeare did not appreciate equity, when he knew better: 'So Shakespeare knew that even in 1596 or 1597 recourse from the unreasonable rigor of the common law was available in equity, despite the system's inadequacies and despite the fact—which has special bearing on the situation in *The Merchant of Venice*—that "the equity of redemption had not yet been elevated into a general rule, and mortgages were therefore liable to total forfeiture to unscrupulous speculators."'[93] The question was how to bring equity to bear when one of the parties to the dispute was *outside* the community of virtue. The link between willful stranger and voluntary criminal was too close to allow for the law to soften its literal application. Upon conviction, the criminal becomes an outsider, an outlaw, hence, literalness is appropriate. Jews, as members of another community, have always been outside this realm; legally speaking, they enter the everyday world on sufferance. To enter the legal world, where mercy obtains to others as a presumption of innocence does to criminality, Jews must first show they are capable of mercy, if the law were not to be applied literally. Thus, the legal asymmetry of Christians and Jews in Venice: 'In the Venetian court the literalist apparently finds his perfect arena. There is at least the show of reason why this court must be the "strict court" it is—and it is significant that, with the momentary exception of Bassanio's plea to have the law wrested by personal authority, everyone agrees with that reason.'[94] By forcing Shylock into the literal realm of aliens, especially of Jews, Christian Venice denied his claims to humanity, because one can be human, non-literal, only within a community. Note the tendency toward literalness of the law *per se*, Shakespeare's concern is literalness mandated by the presence of two conflicting communities of virtue within the same jurisdiction. In these circumstances literalness implies not only an absence of equity but an inability of the law do deal with the fluidities of a rapidly changing socio-economic order.

The point is not that Shylock's view of the law was too literal, too crude, to be up to its task of resolving property disputes, although it was. The law itself, as it has to be applied in a developing commercial and financial society, was too literal, *insofar as dealt with strangers*, a qualification Shakespeare appreciated. To be law, rules have to be applied impersonally and impartially, that is, as if personal characteristics and status were irrelevant. This application does not mean that law can ignore its human dimensions. Properly conceived, it is a human artifact which serves human needs, including equity and other non-literal values. The more the law is asked to do what lies outside its arena of ordinary concerns, the more it should be infused with a sense of justice. Justice, for Shakespeare, was a property of Belmont, a property which the Rialto needed to absorb. Absent love and friendship, law can at best approximate fairness, conceived as the literal application of Due Process. Shakespeare could not see how the values of the Rialto and Belmont could coexist, if business transactions were conducted by strangers.

> The relation of the individual to the community (in both its secular and religious aspects) is what is at stake in the condemnation of usury; and on that relationship the words of Archbishop Laud are particularly relevant: 'If any man be so addicted to the private, that he neglect the common, the State, he is void of the sense of piety and wisheth peace and happiness to himself in vain. For whoever he be, he must live in the body of the Commonwealth, and in the body of the church.' R.H. Tawney, who quotes Laud, says of this statement: 'To one holding such a creed economic individualism was hardly less abhorrent than religious nonconformity, and its repression was a not less obvious duty; for both seemed incompatible with the stability of a society in which Commonwealth and Church were one.'[95]

While Shakespeare did not value Christianity to this degree, he did believe that economic enterprise shorn of other values was necessarily odious. Further, he believed these other values had to be held in common, if the law were to approximate justice. Modernity had to be lubricated with traditional 'Christian' values, particularly love and friendship. This is the central message of *The Merchant of Venice*. The inability to locate Jews within the European community has been the root of their tragic experience in Europe. This point will become clearer when we consider the play in more detail.

Modernity implies depersonalization. As more and more facets of life free themselves from traditional constraints, economic possibilities multiply. Increasingly, time, talent, and energy are allocated to the production of wealth.

All material assets became subject to rational deployment. Change connotes opportunity. The nimble, armed with liquid assets, benefit disproportionately, and, from the perspective of their less flexible cohorts, unjustly. Time and time again, Jews have embodied and exploited these wealth-producing virtues. In Venice, much more so than in Central and Eastern Europe, Jews had powerful competitors in every area of commerce and finance. Nevertheless, their social and religious segregation marked them as necessary strangers, which leaked almost inevitably in the commercial hurly-burly into 'enemies.' Taunted by Shylock for coming to a despised Jew for help, Antonio responds:

> If thou wilt lend this money, lend it not
> As to thy friends, for when did friendship take
> A breed of barren metal of his friend?
> But lend it rather to thine enemy;
> Who if he break, thou may'st with better face
> Exact the penalty. I: 3.128–34

He established a dichotomy, which all but Portia accepted: if one is a friend, no business considerations apply; if not, the most exact, literal, or harsh penalty may be applied in good conscience. Like Portia, Shakespeare did not set the problem of Shylock so simply. A much greater writer than Dickens, Shakespeare did not focus on the humanization of a commercial man *simpliciter*. In *A Christmas Carol,* Scrooge becomes human by adopting the values of love, friendship and charity. All he had to learn was that, given the inevitability of death and the probability of Hell, it would be wise and beneficial to join the human race. In a much deeper predicament, Shylock had to deny the community of virtue he believed in to join a community of virtue he despised, if he were to retain his wealth and his standing. If he were simply a man of greed like Scrooge, his decision would have come down to this: is it more profitable for me to stay in Venice or go elsewhere? If he were simply a lonely, old man, it would have come down to this: will adopting the values of Bob Crachet make me happy? The facts were quite different. Not simply an unhappy or greedy man, Shylock was a man who valued his traditions and his religion.

The evidence seems conclusive. When he was offered three times the money due him, he declined in favor of a materially worthless pound of flesh. Making a point, not money, he testified to himself, to his community, and to the Gentiles that he was a Jew, and a Jew was nothing if not a man of principle. Viewing the Rialto as virtue and Belmont as trivial, Shylock mirrored the too simple dichotomy of the Belmont inconsequentials, who saw the Rialto as vulgar and Belmont as virtue. Shakespeare, in the figure of Antonio, appreciated the virtue of the Rialto *and* the virtue of Belmont. In the figure of

Portia, Shakespeare suggested how to infuse the one with the other. Portia's triumph makes *The Merchant of Venice* a comedy, goodness triumphing over evil. Antonio's ships coming home before the knife sliced his flesh creates comedy. Shylock's ultimate choice of conversion or death, whether the debt be paid or the ships come home or not, creates tragedy. It is, therefore, essential to see how conversion becomes the dramatic focus of the play, as well as, the condition for the reconciliation of Belmont and the Rialto.

The plot drew Shylock to the court of law. Having lent Antonio three thousand ducats with one pound of flesh as collateral, he presented himself for payment of the default. With Antonio's ships presumed lost at sea and with them all chance for payment in ducats, Shylock refuses to take a late payment, as urged by the Duke:

> I have possess'd your Grace of what I purpose;
> And by our holy Sabbath have I sworn
> To have the due and forfeit my bond:
> If you deny it, let the danger light
> Upon your charter and your city's freedom.
> You'll ask me why I rather choose to have
> A weight of carrion flesh than to receive
> Three thousand ducats: I'll not answer that:
> But say it is my humor; is it answer'd? IV.i.35–43

Confidently, Shylock rested his case on the prudence of Venice, a commercial city dependent upon the sanctity of contract and charter. The content of the contract was irrelevant, a point he underlines.

> If you deny me, fie upon your law!
> There is no force in the decrees of Venice.
> I stand for judgment: answer; shall I have it? IV.i.101–3

Simplicity itself, Shylock's case was: 'a deal is a deal and you, Venice, greedy Venice, cannot afford to renege.' Unstated was his deeper message: 'I can afford to do without the money and will gladly forfeit it, when my honor is at stake, something, you Christians will never understand or be able to do.' From Shakespeare's perspective, the *simplicity* of a literal application of the law was the problem. Within a community of virtue, the letter of the law must work within its spirit, a spirit of justice. Shylock concurred and would so acted within the Jewish community. In the Christian court, however, he was a stranger, so literalism seemed his best option, a less literal approach working against him as a Jew and a man of honor.

All his statements before the trial scene point to his desire for a literal interpretation of the contract, including his famous speech:

Hath not a Jew eyes? Hath not a Jew hands, organs, dimensions, senses, affections, passions? Fed with the same food, hurt with the same weapons, subject to the same diseases, healed by the same means, warmed and cooled by the same winter and summer, as a Christian is? If you prick us, do we not bleed? If you tickle us, do we not laugh? If you poison us, do we not die? And if you wrong us, shall we not revenge? If we are like you in the rest, we will resemble you in that. If a Jew wrongs a Christian, what is his humility? Revenge! If a Christian wrong a Jew, what should his sufferance be by Christian example? Why, revenge! The villainy you teach me I will execute, and it shall go hard but I will better the instruction. III.i.54–69

According to Gross, these words are anything but sophistical or rhetorical: 'They are wrenched from Shylock; they have the stamp of anger and spontaneity. And the fact they are in prose only heightens the impression. You feel that if Shakespeare had wanted Shylock to indulge in some specious rhetoric, it is far more likely he would have made him resort to verse.'[96] Prose is inherently more literal, less duplicitous, than poetry, and, therefore, more appropriate to legal interpretation. And Shylock wanted nothing so much as to demonstrate his honesty and candor. This magnificent outpouring, which so many have incorrectly read as a plea for universal rights, comes down to this: If a Jew be human, he is entitled to make contracts, notwithstanding the motives or character of the parties. His motive, revenge, must be allowed to flow from the contract, as if it were milk and honey, because the law between strangers must be literally applied. Justice, mercy, or compassion can have nothing to do with it, lest the law become unpredictable and inconstant. Shylock's indicated his understanding of the law:

I'll have my bond; speak not against my bond.
I have sworn an oath that I will have my bond. III.iii.4–5
I'll have my bond; I will not hear thee speak.
I'll have my bond, and therefore speak no more. III.iii.12–3

As if to underline the validity of Shylock's fear of Christian words, Portia, in disguise as a legal scholar, after establishing the validity of the contract, says, 'Then the Jew must be merciful.' [IV.i.182] 'Must' here is deeply ambiguous. It could mean 'should.' One must (should), if the application of the law implies extreme cruelty, avoid it. Or, it could mean, 'I am obliged to.' 'On what compulsion must I?' [IV.i.183] Portia initially chooses the first option in some of the most beautiful lines in literature:

The quality of mercy is not strain'd;
It droppeth as the gentle rain from heaven
Upon the place beneath: it is twice bless'd;

It blesseth him that gives and him that takes.
'Tis mightiest in the mightiest: it becomes
The throned monarch better than his crown;
His scepter shows the force of temporal power,
The attribute to awe and majesty,
Wherein doth sit the dread and fear of kings:
But mercy is above this sceptred sway,
It is enthroned in the hearts of kings,
It is an attribute of God himself,
And earthly power doth then show likest God's
When mercy seasons justice. IV.i.182–195

The sheer beauty of poetry placed tone-deaf Shylock in a different universe, outside of Belmont, in discourse and existence and, what was more important to him, outside of the Rialto. Emphasizing his fundamentally alien status, Portia concludes her speech:

Therefore Jew,
Though justice be thy plea, consider this,
That in the course of justice none of us
Should see salvation: we do pray for mercy,
And this same prayer doth teach us all to render
The deeds of mercy. I have spoke thus much
To mitigate the justice of thy plea,
Which if thou follow. This strict court of Venice
Must needs give sentence 'gainst the merchant
There. IV.i.195–203

For the non-religious Shakespeare, this evocation of Christian dogma is striking, particularly in the context of 'therefore Jew.' To Portia's request that he supply a surgeon to staunch Antonio's bleeding, Shylock confirms his estrangement from the Venetian community by responding, 'Is it nominated in the Bond?' She answers, 'It is not so expressed; but what of that?' [IV.i:260–1] Portia responds to his literalness by becoming as harsh and literal as he: 'Tarry a little,' and later, 'Soft, Jew.' Throughout the proceeding she calls him 'Jew,' which amounts to an accusation in the context of the play and the context of the times. More than mimicking his literalness, Portia links it to his inhumanity. If it is obvious why Shakespeare has Shylock default to literalism, it is startling to have Portia do so, and especially so after her plea for mercy. After Bassanio offered to pay twice the bond or ten times, Portia says:

It must not be. There is no power in Venice
Can alter a decree established:
Twill be recorded for a precedent,
And many an error by the same example
Will rush into the state. It cannot be. IV.i.216–20

This is no contradiction in Portia's character. First, disguised as legal scholar, Portia assumes a male professional role, although her purpose was the pursuit of love and friendship. Second, her literalness had several purposes: (1) It urged Shylock to reconsider her plea for mercy; (2) It underlined the harshness of law when applied in the absence of reason and compassion; and (3) It foreshadowed her willingness to apply the law against a Jew shedding Christian blood on pain of death. Danson sums up: 'Returning therefore to the law—from Shylock's point of view returning to it with a vengeance—Portia searches out every jot and tittle, not in order to wrest or overthrow the law but to fulfill it; and the paradoxical result of that rigor is to reveal the spirit of the law inherent in its letter, its mercy in its constraints.'[97] Finally, she relents and offers three times the bond:

Be merciful:/Take thrice thy money; bid me tear the bond. IV.i.231–2

Naturally, Shylock remained deaf to these appeals, not least because he expected Christians to demonstrate their prejudices. Moreover, now apprised of the statute forbidding the drawing of Christian blood, Shylock found himself in a dilemma. If his bond were granted, he could carve Antonio, doing so, however, would forfeit his life. At this point Shylock's principles melt, as he futilely tries to get a monetary payment instead of Antonio's fatal flesh. A way out is offered. 'Baptism or death.' Convert to Christianity. This loss of honor would be compensated by the retention of some of his property, his continued residence and business in Venice, and his life. Shylock accepts, saying, 'I am content.'

Content, but defeated, as father, Jew, and man. But what was cause of his downfall? Part of the answer is that he was vindictive, a man of his time: 'The Middle Ages, from beginning to end, and particularly the feudal era, lived under the sign of private vengeance. The onus, of course, lay above all on the wronged individual: vengeance imposed on him as the most sacred of duties—to be pursued even beyond the grave.'[98] Far from being a man defined by greed, he was a man of honor defined by his desire to avenge himself against those who would dishonor him. While his great speech asserted his humanity, much of it honored revenge. That Shylock and Jews have been reviled, insulted, and humiliated in Venice is beyond question. This outrageous treatment seems the worse to the extent that it originated in the feckless, witless, and profligate inhabitants of Belmont. The nature of the loan to Antonio, whom Shylock respected, indicates that he was more interested in achieving respect that making profits. There is no doubt that he would have accepted the timely payment of the debt in ducats. No Machiavellian creditor, who contracted a deal which could not be fulfilled in terms acceptable to the debtor, he was not above, however, having such terms enforced. Nor was he above being delighted in an enforcement mechanism which all too often has been a source of humiliation and prejudicial treatment of Jews: the Law. By its literal application, Shylock would avenge himself and his community for countless offenses perpetrated against them by Gentiles. This point of honor was worth more than three times the amount of the contracted indebtedness.

Here, again, is the contrast between Shylock and Antonio: 'Between them [they]…represent two extreme versions of Economic Man, one benevolent, the other malign. Jekyll-Antonio embodies the fantasy that you can enjoy the benefits of economic enterprise, and confer them on your society, without becoming competitive and self-assertive. Hyde-Shylock is the capitalist as total predator, conferring good on no one except himself. They are twin aspects of the same phenomenon; and a tremendous amount of the play's energy is spent keeping them apart.'[99] This is only part of the dichotomy, in a sense the easy part, the remedial part. Shylock in these terms could have been Scrooge and could have joined the human race. Danson captures a deeper difference between the merchants: 'His use of the world, and all the things of the world, appears to be all unblameworthy; everything he has or can get (for he must borrow in order to meet Bassanio's needs) is at the service of a friend…. Thus Shakespeare plays with his audience's expectations, giving them a merchant who is (apparently) so far from being guilty of a lack of charity that he comes perilously close to completing literally an *imatatio Christi*. But although a man of sorrow, Antonio is in fact no more a "Christ-figure" than is any man who acts with charity.'[100] No more, but no less, is Antonio a man of charity, a Christian. Antonio believes in other Christian virtues as well: 'The essential thing added to the law by Christ is forgiveness. Mercy, therefore, is made part of the law, rather than an opposing principle. Indeed mercy, or forgiveness, becomes the legal principle enabling all other legal principles….'[101] For Shakespeare, the trouble was that these values, charity, mercy, and forgiveness, however universal they might be in principle, could only be applied within a community. If Christian virtues cannot be applied outside the community, neither can Jewish ones. 'Needless to say, the notion that Judaism has an inadequate grasp on the concept of mercy is a travesty— as much of a travesty as it would be to suppose that Christianity has an inadequate grasp on the concept of justice. The word for mercy, *rachamim*, carries tremendous resonance in the Hebrew liturgy (it is related to *rechem*, the word for a womb), and endless exhortations to deal mercifully can be found in the writings of the Rabbis.'[102]

This issue was not a simple one of a clash of communities of virtue, of the differing perspectives of Christian and Jew. For Venice was not a tribal setting, where such conflicts have occurred from time immemorial. Shylock's effort to use modern means, the commercial law of Venice, forged to ensure the prosperity of the city, to pursue his code of honor, was unacceptable. Both Antonio and the Duke were prepared to accept it, as their understanding of the law and its principles mandated. Antonio was ready to die, and the Duke was prepared to have him killed to preserve Venetian legal integrity. Just as money lay at the origin of the flesh bond but did not define it, money lay at the origin of the law but did not define it. Shylock's conception of his integrity motivated his demand that the law be applied: 'I'll have my bond!' The Duke's conception of Venice's legal integrity motivated his acceptance of the death of Antonio at the hands of Shylock. Integrity versus integrity. Honor versus honor. Shylock, Antonio, and the Duke fully accepted the limitations of logic of commercial exchanges even (or especially) in this most commercial of cities. Commerce, without the underpinning of principles, could not have developed beyond discrete and necessarily petty exchanges of strangers. The merchants of Venice required enduring and reliable and law-bound structures, if they were to engage in the long-distance trade which marked the essence of emerging capitalism. If a literal, *albeit*, hateful, application of the law were required to demonstrate Venetian integrity, so be it. Notice this was not a simple dichotomy between traditional values, those entirely determined by honor and modern values, those entirely dominated by profit and loss. It was an understanding that only by honoring the law could the economy flourish. Law, despite its limitations, provides the essential infrastructure of modern transactions. At the very least, law must be applied impartially and impersonally. Shylock and Antonio must come to the bar shorn of their attributes, vices, and virtues. Capitalism requires Due Process.

This logic, however, was unacceptable to Belmont, where all was under the thrall of love and friendship. Just as Antonio worked in the Rialto with an appreciation of Belmont, Portia lived in Belmont with an understanding of the Rialto. Each symbolized the reconciliation of the two realms, differing in two important respects. Where Antonio accepted the limitations of the law, even at the cost of his life, Portia saw possibilities in the law, even at the cost of dishonesty and deception. Secondly, where Antonio accepted the necessity of Shylock, as a man of business and his strangeness as an unpleasant incidental to any commercial relationship, Portia saw the necessity for Shylock's participation, however limited, in the values of Belmont, which mandated that Shylock become a Christian, however nominally.

Portentous as *The Merchant of Venice* was for European Jews, it did not deal with two profoundly aggravating factors. Business was good at the Rialto; good fortune bathed Antonio, the actual merchant of Venice. Prosperity followed honor and goodness, which were the basis of the reconciliation of Belmont with the Rialto, the world of love and friendship with commerce and finance. If Venice were going through an economic downturn, the need for reconciliation would have been greater, its likelihood less. Secondly, Shylock's adversaries, despite their anti-Judaism and dislike of him as a man and a Jew, were not ignorant, irrational, or violent. Shylock did not have to account for masses. Other Jews would not be so fortunate, as Parkes explains: 'The Jews might secure for themselves charters which seemed to give them every security. Individuals might seek a still more sheltered position, enjoying the general toleration accorded to Jewish settlements and avoiding the burdens which they bore, but, in the end, the last word lay with public opinion and the mob.'[103]

> The fantasy of the demonic Jew existed before the reality of the Jewish money-lender, whom indeed it helped to produce. Norman Cohn[104]

> In the fourteenth and fifteenth centuries…European society suddenly stopped expanding. Economic depression was accompanied by political chaos and social disorder, in which competing forces struggled to the death. Norman Cantor[105]

A PLAGUE UPON BOTH YOUR HOUSES

The fourteenth century brought two catastrophes; the ending of a long economic expansion and the Black Death, which killed approximately thirty percent of Europe's population. Huizinga describes the situation in memorable prose:

> Is it surprising that the people could see their fate and that of the world only as an endless succession of evils? Bad government, exactions, cupidity and violence of the great, wars and brigandage, scarcity, misery and pestilence—to this is contemporary history nearly reduced in the eyes of the people. The feeling of general insecurity which was caused by the chronic form wars were apt to take, by the constant menace of the dangerous classes, by the mistrust of justice, was further aggravated by the obsession of the coming end of the world and by the fear of Hell, of sorcerers and of Devils. The background of the world seems black. Everywhere the flames of hatred arise and injustice reigns. Satan covers a gloomy earth with his somber wings.[106]

These shocks had varying impact on Jews and Gentiles and even more varying effects on their mutual perceptions. Just as the economic expansion benefited the Jews more than the Christians, the downturn did not hurt them as much. An urban, merchant class simply has more economic resilience and more options than peasants and landless poor: 'The great Jewish strength lay in the ability to take quick advantage of new opportunities; to recognize and unprecedented situation when it arose and to devise methods of handling it. Christians had long learned how to deal with conventional financial problems, but they were conservative and slow to react to novelty.'[107] When Jewish creditors were squeezed, they pressured the indebted masses. According to Johnson, 'many Jews were not in a position to exercise benevolence, being sub- and sub-sub-lessees, forced to grind the peasants in order to pay their own rents.'[108] This pernicious process worsened when elites failed to meet their obligations to their Jewish creditors. In the poisoned atmospherics of Jews and Gentiles, these differing results were often exaggerated, raising levels of resentment past the point of violence and the ability of the rulers to protect Jews.

The Black Death exacerbated an already parlous situation, causing the deep substratum of superstition of the Medieval world to surface. Desperate times revived old demons in an effort to account for the unprecedented misery and death the plague produced. More than another period of intensifying irrational beliefs, fantastic explanations of the catastrophe of the Black Death created violent movements: 'In the great massacre of European Jewry which accompanied the Black Death...the flagellants played an important part.... Whenever the authorities had so far protected the Jews, these hordes now demanded their massacre. When in July 1349, flagellants entered Frankfort they rushed straight for the Jewish quarter, where the townsfolk joined them in exterminating the entire community.'[109] The Devil seemed triumphant. 'The Black Death seemed to come as God's visitation on a sinful world, but more particularly on a sinful church, and most particularly of all on a sinful papacy. Especially in Germany, where political confusion added to the agitation of spirits, popular religious movements sprang up...movements to expiate the sins of the day, but which soon turned against the hierarchy, and particularly against ecclesiastical property and the wealth of the church, which seemed—and was—the main cause of evil.'[110] Thus, the groundwork for the penultimate piece of anti-Semitism was laid, awaiting nineteenth century racism to lay the final stones.

Langmuir's effort to define the various kinds of anti-Semitism is now apt:

Realistic assertions about outgroups are propositions that utilize the information available about an outgroup and are based on the same assumptions about the nature of groups and the effect of membership on individuals as those used to understand the ingroup and its reference groups and their members.

Xenophobic assertions are propositions that grammatically attribute a socially menacing conduct to an outgroup and all its members but are empirically based only on the conduct of a historical minority of the members; they neglect other, unthreatening, characteristics of the outgroup; and they do not acknowledge that they are great differences between individuals who compose the outgroup as there are between individuals who compose the ingroup.

Chimerical assertions are propositions that grammatically attribute with certitude to an outgroup and all its members characteristics that have never been empirically observed.[111]

In the malaise of the fourteenth century, in the wake of the Black Death, 'chimerical assertions' became the most important factor in the murder of Jews. These assertions, although different in kind from 'realistic and xenophobic assertions,' nonetheless presumed their virulence. Langmuir's last form of anti-Semitism is logically final, if we begin with the material, the factual, and the evidentiary. In periods of rapid change, political catastrophe, or natural disaster strikes, when God seems to have abandoned the world, irrational explanations pour forth: 'Toward the end of the Middle Ages, the simultaneous appearance of numerous movements—flagellants, dancers, millenarians, mystics, and others—indicates that powerful currents of social unrest existed in a period of plague, famine, war, and rapid social change.'[112]

The Middle Ages were awash in superstition, magic, and other forms of irrationality. Both Church and Synagogue had to distinguish their supernatural premises, acts attributed to divinities in defiance of science, philosophy or any other explanation that finds sufficiency in the material world, from events which seem to be the result of the Evil One or the Devil from magic and superstition. No more than a distinction between white magic and black, it cannot satisfy the rational mind. If one supernatural event is possible, then logically all are. As a consequence, Judaism and Christianity have had a great deal of difficulty purging their adherents of superstitious beliefs and practices. Calling some of these beliefs 'mystical' cannot remove their irrational structure. In these circumstances, it can hardly be surprising that the cataclysms of the last half of the fourteenth century stimulated a great deal of irrational behavior based on absurd renditions of events. As archetypes of the Other, aliens who benefited from and created disastrous changes, Jews became targets of mass fear and rage. Poliakov captures the interrelationship of many of these factors: 'In an age when the distinction between the sacred and profane was never very clear, when every social activity was simultaneously a charitable deed and one pleasing to God, the two images were superimposed: the Devil's hand was seen behind all evil, which is why it is impossible to distinguish between the Jew-Devil (who haunted all Europe) and the Jewish usurer (present in this period in only certain regions).'[113] Sacrificing Jews, seen increasingly as the agents of the Devil, if not the incarnation of the Evil One, became the preferred way to propitiate the Wrathful God. The increase in piety represented by the friars added to the reality of Satan. 'Only from this period [the thirteenth century] were Jews portrayed as real, active agents of Satan....'[114] In the calamitous fourteenth century, 'the friars' attacks on the Jews were no longer fortuitous; they represented a deliberate effort on the part of groups of mendicants to rid Europe of contemporary Judaism.'[115]

Almost of all of the anti-Christian acts attributed to Jews were explained in religious terms and the response of the masses, however violent and however much official Church policy might have abhorred and condemned it, were justified by the pious. According to Parkes: 'There was...the menace of religious superstition, for the accusations of ritual murder, poisoning of wells, and profanation of the Host were all believed by the more superstitious of the clergy.'[116] Notice the dogmatic blending: 'profanation' with criminal acts, 'ritual murder' and the 'poisoning of wells.' All were of a piece, all part of the Jewish plan to defeat Christianity and to harm Christians. Jews were killing Christ again and again. And doing so in the service of the Devil: 'The two inexorable enemies of Jesus, then, in Christian legend were the Devil and the Jew, and it was inevitable that the legend should establish a causal connection between them.'[117] As inhuman deniers of Christ, '[They] joined...in a war against the Church and its civilization.... Christendom was summoned to a holy war of extermination, of which the Jews were only incidentally its objects. It was Satan whom Christian Europe sought to crush.'[118] The religious basis of the violence against Jews cannot be overestimated: 'Social tensions in the Middle Ages, expressed it terms of transcendental Christian myth, produced crazes of fear that were directed against outcasts from Christian society. Jews were accused of praying to the Devil, doing him homage, practicing sexual orgies, cannibalism, and murder, and using in their rites loathsome materials like blood and semen.'[119] As the most potent source of Jew-hatred, at least until the racial anti-Semitism of the Nazis, anti-Judaism must be considered the principal motivator of violence against Jews, its Christian basis endowing it proponents with a clear conscience. 'Small wonder, then, that in view of this attitude the conscience of Christendom was little burdened by the unexampled persecution to which the Jews were subjected. They had it coming to them, the average Christian contended; for Christian treatment of the Jew was mild compared to what *they* would suffer were the world in Jewish hands.'[120]

With the Church's Jewish relations increasingly influenced by the friars, the economy slowing, and having absorbed the ravages of the Black Death, few Jews mourned the passing of the fourteenth century.[121] Nevertheless, ever resilient, alert to opportunities, searching the rubble of every disaster for ways to thrive not merely survive, Jews recovered in the fifteenth century, disproportionately benefitting from the effects of the plague. The huge loss of life increased *per capita* capital, the fundamental tool of commerce. Once the Black Death burned itself out, although it would recur in less virulent forms over the next hundred years, Jews, like other Europeans, recovered their footing and believed again in the future. This absolute condition for investment could now be credited. Jews played key roles in the recovery, the exploration of the world, the discovery of the New World, and the increase in long-distance trade—developments which placed Jewish internationalism, finance, and commerce at the forefront of the exploitation of new resources, including new capital, new products, and new markets.

Ominous trends, however, continued, trends which prosperity could not eliminate and in some respects reinforced. The declining Papal Monarchy, while hardly friendly to Jews, weakened one of the major doctrinal and institutional supports of Jewish presence in Europe. The piety of the friars made the worldly Church seem Christian in name and ritual only. The Papacy's efforts to secure secular authority undermined its claim to a monopoly of spiritual authority. Within the Church hierarchy, voices were raised calling for change which would restore the Church to its proper role in the lives of Christians. Possessed of information and brains, the Church hierarchy understood its need for reform. Like the KGB on the eve of the dissolution of the Soviet Union, the Church bureaucracy could not bring its knowledge and competence to bear. Intrinsically conservative and self-protective, bureaucracies have been congenitally unable to reconstitute themselves. Throughout the fifteenth century, reform was in the air, its particles as visible and undeniable as those of eighteenth century France and nineteenth century Russia. It took the genius and the volcanic energy of Martin Luther to transform these particles into cannon shot.

Luther's Reformation was not progressive in the sense of improving the world. To the contrary, Luther wanted to reduce the significance of the world, except to hope its misery and horrors would bring Christians to their knees, their will destroyed, ready to receive the Will of God into their souls, or better, to beg that God notice their misery and their willingness to absorb more, if it be God's Will. Luther's fundamental criticism of the Church was that, by glorifying itself, it glorified the world and thereby aborted the process of bringing Christians to the Cross. Worse, the Church led people to believe that their acts, moral and sacramental, could earn favor with God. Thus, the intensification of piety that Luther incarnated was far more extreme than that of the friars, notwithstanding their self-flagellation and other mutilations of body and soul. The friars believed that the Church could become more pious and more sound spiritually, just as they believed Christians could become better by performing acts of piety. Luther believed that the Church was the problem and that friars made the problem worse. The Church glorified itself and the world. The friars glorified penance, privation, evangelical zeal, and those who fulfilled these requirements. The worldly Church, for all intents and purposes, behaved like Jews. Friars, by promulgating their own 'Law,' were similarly participating in this grievous Jewish fallacy of expecting God's favor in return for pious actions. The world, as conceived by the Church and the friars, was Luther's enemy. Little wonder that he would find the most worldly of people anathema: 'Luther spoke to a responsive and understanding audience when he lashed out, with rabble-rousing accusations and vituperation, against Jewish usury, and concluded with savage irony: "Should the Devil not laugh and dance, when he enjoys among us Christians such a fine Paradise, when he, through the Jews, his saints, devours our substance, and in return fills our mouths and nostrils with his effrontery, and mocks and curses God and man, in the bargain.'"[122] The world, the Jews, and the Devil, overlapping and conjoined, in fact and in metaphor, would be subject to unrelenting vituperation and humiliation over the next five hundred years: 'As soon as the Jews were present [at the end of the fifteenth century in Germany], the traditional hatred erupted; moreover, it was given new impetus as the Germans discovered that the deicidal (i.e., homicidal) and usurious race was at the same time a foreign people. Many texts by clerical and lay authors, theologians and humanists, show how during this period the three motifs—religious, economic, and national—had become amalgamated.'[123]

Bespeaking a rejected lover, Luther's extreme and often scatological language reflected more than normal Christian anti-Judaism and anti-Semitism. Initially, he believed the Jews would welcome the Reformation's downgrading of the sacraments, its emphasis on the *Bible* as the Divine Word and its respect for the long neglected *Hebrew Bible*. While likely many Jews did welcome these changes which seemed to indicate new respect for Judaism. Luther, however, expected Christian respect for the *Bible* to result in massive Jewish conversion, which it did not: '[He] grew embittered to discover that the Jews were as deaf to Martin of Eisleben as they had been to Paul of Tarsus. He became alarmed to find among them the sects which sprouted like mushrooms in the fertile soil of Protestant revolt a dangerous tendency to revert to Jewish type; to deny the Trinity, to look upon Jesus as a prophet rather than a deity, to observe the seventh day as the Sabbath, and to take the *Old Testament* with a literalness embarrassing to the New—in short to go Jewish as the Humanists had gone ancient.'[124] Thus another element of the rejectionist thesis was borne. To Jewish rejecters of *Jesus as the Christ* were added German Jews as spurners of the generous hand of the Luther's Reformed Church. This thesis would have another variation after the French Revolution, as we shall see in the next chapter. Harbison explains: 'It is of the essence of understanding the Age of Reformation to remember that it was still too early for the mass of Europeans to accept a worldly skepticism and a faith in the omnicompetence of the State as the logical way out of their intellectual and institutional difficulties. Among other things, the fact that the sixteenth century witnessed the climax of the witchcraft mania should remind us that there were profound unresolved tensions in European society untouched by rational control.'[125]

It would await the French Revolution to complete the development the omnicompetent State, which, by increasing skepticism and rationalism, would undermine witchcraft and other supernatural absurdities. Insofar as the State implied rationality and law, Jews expected to benefit. The difficulty was that the Revolution yoked the Nation to the State. 'The Reformation gave large groups of people across Europe their first lessons in political commitment to a universal ideology. In the sixteenth century, religion became mass politics. Other ideologies, more secular in tone, would take its place.'[126] The Nation-State, far from abjuring the irrational, would employ the fears, anxieties, ignorance, and superstitions of the masses in behalf of its own interests. Nation-States would supplant the Church for millions of its citizens as the principal source of transcendent meaning and authority. This highly irrational process would produce a high degree of loyalty that Nation-States would use to extract unprecedented devotion and sacrifice from the masses. To the rational/legal authority of the omnicompetent State was added the spiritual authority, once the property sacerdotal entities. Nation-States, no less than Medieval political organizations, would find in Jews the Other, who would, by negative example, help create national identities in almost every European State. Moreover, the disruptions implied by the destruction of Medieval European social, political, and economic structures, as modernity accelerated, would find in Jews a perfect receptacle for the anger and resentment of the masses. After all, Jews could never be loyal to the Christian Nation-States of Europe for two interrelated and reinforcing reasons. They had rejected Christ, and as self-proclaimed members of the Jewish Nation, they could never be fully German or French. As being German or French became more important, Jewishness became dangerously tenuous.

NOTES

1. This prologue is a fictional version of several historical events which occurred during the First Crusade.

2. Katz, Jacob: *Exclusiveness and Tolerance,* Oxford, 1961, p. 3.

3. Shahak, Israel: *Jewish History, Jewish Religion,* London, 1994, p. 22.

4. Langmuir, Gavin: *Toward a Definition of Anti-Semitism,* Berkeley, 1990, p. 47.

5. Shahak, I. and Mezvinsky, N.: *Jewish Fundamentalism in Israel,* London, 1999, p. 150.

6. *Ibid.,* p. 51.

7. *Ibid.,* p. 53.

8. *Ibid.,* p. 42.

9. Katz, *Exclusiveness, op. cit.,* p. 61.

10. Johnson, Paul: *A History of the Jews,* Harper Row, NY, 1987, p. 247.

11. Katz, Jacob: *the Teaching of Contempt,* McGraw Hill, NY, 1965 *Tradition and Crisis: Jewish Society at the End of the Middle Ages,* Schocken, NY, 1993, p. 32.

12. Heer, Friedrich: *The Medieval World: Europe 1110–1350*, translated by Janet Sondheimer, NY, 1998, p. 260.

13. Katz, Jacob: *Out of the Ghetto: The Social Background of Jewish Emancipation, 1770–1870*, Schocken, NY, 1978, p. 5.

14. Parkes, James: *The Jew in the Medieval Community*, 2d, Hermon, NY, 1976, p. 206.

15. Katz, *Exclusiveness, op. cit.,* p. 4.

16. Lowenthal, Marvin: *The Jews of Germany: a Story of Sixteen Centuries*, Philadelphia, 1936, p. 17.

17. Parkes, *op. cit.,* p. 360.

18. Cantor, *op. cit.*, p. 365.

19. Parkes, *Community, op. cit.,* p. 180.

20. Lowenthal, *op. cit.,* p. 65.

21. Parkes, *Community, op. cit.,* p. 206.

22. Roth, Cecil: *History of the Jews in Venice*, Schocken, NY, 1930, 1975, pp. 12–3.

23. Parkes, *Community, op. cit.,* pp. 45–6.

24. Lowenthal, *op. cit.,* p. 18.

25. Parkes, *Community,* op. cit., p. 23.

26. Katz, *Exclusiveness, op. cit.,* pp. 5–6.

27. Parkes, *Community, op. cit.,* pp. 102–3.

28. Kisch, Guido: *The Jews of Medieval Germany*, Chicago, 1949, p. 338.

29. Parkes, *Community, op. cit.,* p. 111.

30. Katz, *Exclusiveness,* pp. 11–12.

31. Parkes, *Community, op. cit.,* p. 52.

32. Langmuir, *op. cit.,* p. 87. It is not a paradox when a group of humans deals with their problems by following two tracks, especially when they complement rather than contradict each other.

33. Kisch, *op. cit.,* p. 352.

34. Katz, *Exclusiveness, op. cit.,* p. 10.

35. *Ibid.,* p. 43.

36. Cantor, *op. cit.,* p. 365.

37. Poliakov, Leon: *The History of Anti-Semitism: From the Time of Christ to the Court Jews*, translated by Richard Howard, Vanguard, NY, 1976, p. 76.

38. *Ibid.,* p. 156, emphasis supplied.

39. Katz, *Crisis, op. cit.,* pp. 5 8 & 59.

40. Pirenne, *op. cit.,* p. 180.

41. Parkes, *Community, op. cit.,* p. 58.

42. Quoted by Poliakov, *op. cit.,* pp. 53–54.

43. I tend to rely on scholars who essentially agree on the facts and differ only marginally on interpretation. In this way I hope to minimize the differences in perspective and values which have tended to produce unusually diverse sets of facts and interpretations.

44. Parkes, *Community, op. cit.,* p. 59.

45. *Ibid.,* p. 67.

46. Southern, *Making, op. cit.*, p. 54. Cantor explains: [Urban's reasons for the First Crusade]: First, it would help to reunite Christendom after the bitter and divisive disputes over Gregorian reform, and second, it would increase Papal prestige at a time when there were supporters of the German emperor even in the city of Rome. Third, it would work toward ending the schism between the Western and Eastern Churches…. The fourth value that Urban saw in a Crusade was a consequence of his own French background. [The Crusade would meet] the needs of many French lords and knights and at the same time employ their energies in the service of the church. Cantor, *op. cit.*, pp. 291–2.

47. I am aware that the most of the massacres of Jews did not take place with the approval of the Papacy. Yet in a period when the masses were being enflamed by the piety of the friars and by many high ranking and influential clerics, I cannot absolve the Papacy of guilt in this matter. If the Papacy did not know what it had unleashed, it should have.

48. Poliakov, *op .cit.*, p. 41.

49. Cantor, *op. cit.*, p. 253.

50. Kisch, *op. cit.*, p. 329, emphasis supplied.

51. *Ibid.*, p. 313, emphasis supplied.

52. *Ibid.*, p. 337.

53. Cohen, Jeremy: *The Friars and the Jews*, Cornell, Ithaca, 1982, p. 43.

54. *Ibid.*, p. 41.

55. *Ibid.*, p. 76.

56. Johnson, *op. cit.*, p. 259.

57. Heer, *Medieval, op. cit*, p. 107.

58. Johnson, *History, op. cit.*, p. 199.

59. Parkes, *Community, op. cit.*, p. 78.

60. *Ibid.*, pp. 81–3.

61. *Ibid.*, p. 150.

62. *Ibid.*, p. 154.

63. Herlihy, David, 'Ecological Conditions and Demographic Change' from DeMolen, Richard L.: *One Thousand Years: Western Europe in the Middle Ages,* Houghton Mifflin, Boston, 1974, p. 21.

64. Cheyney, Edward: *The Dawn of a New Era: 1250–1453*, Harper, NY, 1936, p. 2.

65. Parkes, *Community, op. cit.*, p. 239.

66. Johnson, *op. cit.*, p. 283.

67. Kisch, *op. cit.*, p. 322.

68. Katz , *Crisis, op. cit.*, p. 46.

69. 'The Jews' economic potential stemmed from more than their possession of liquid assets. Their chief economic virtue lay in the fact that they actively employed these funds, and therefore served as an economic catalyst at times without parallel in Christian society…. In fact, the Jews tended not to invest in land because they had no real desire to do so.' Katz, *Crisis, op. cit.*, p. 41

70. Pirenne, Henri: *A History of Europe: From the End of the Roman World in the West to the Beginnings of the Western States,* Vol. I, translated by Bernard Miall, Doubleday, NY, 1956, p. 194, emphasis supplied.

71. For an extensive discussion, see Parkes, *Community, op. cit.*

72. Cohn, N.: *The Pursuit of the Millennium*, Oxford, N.Y., revised edition, 1970, p. 99.

73. Pirenne, *op. cit.*, p. 204.

74. Bloch, Marc: *Feudal Society: The Growth of Ties of Dependence, Vol. 1*, translated by L.A. Manyon, Chicago, 1961, p. 353.

75. *Ibid.*, p. 355.

76. Cheyney, *op. cit.*, p. 64.

77. Marginal economics depends on the concept of discrete exchange. Each transaction is isolated and self-justifying. Normal economic transactions take place in a social context. Transactions are based in part on experience and on expectations, that is, relations. Relational exchange tries to take this context into account. The more distinct communities are, the more like discrete exchanges their activities are. Or, worse, their necessary relations are read in a negative light.

78. Southern, R.W.: *Western Society and the Church in the Middle Ages*, Michigan, 1970, p. 47.

79. Katz, *Exclusiveness, op. cit.*, pp. 56–7.

80. Katz, *Crisis, op. cit.*, p. 24.

81. Katz, *Exclusiveness, op. cit.*, p. 38.

82. *Ibid.*, p. 56.

83. Johnson, *op. cit.*, p. 283.

84. Katz, *Crisis, op. cit.*, p. 50.

85. All quotations are from Shakespeare: *The Merchant of Venice*, edited by Roma Gill, Oxford, 1979.

86. Gross, John: *Shylock: A Legend and Its Legacy*, Simon and Schuster, N.Y., 1992, p. 53.

87. Parkes, *Community, op. cit.*, p. 385.

88. Gross, *op. cit.*, p. 56.

89. *Ibid.*, pp. 31–2.

90. *Ibid.*, p. 45.

91. *Ibid.*

92. Danson, Lawrence: *The Harmonies of The Merchant of Venice*, New Haven, 1978, p. 83, emphasis supplied.

93. *Ibid.*, p. 85.

94. *Ibid.*, p. 93.

95. *Ibid.*, p. 144.

96. Gross, *op. cit.*, p. 67.

97. Danson, *op. cit.*, p. 20.

98. Bloch, *op. cit.*, p. 125.

99. Gross, *op. cit.*, p. 54.

100. Danson, *op. cit.*, p. 31.

101. Danson, *op. cit.*, p. 65.

102. Gross, *op. cit.*, p. 96.

103. Parkes, *Community, op. cit.*, p. 237.

104. Cohn, *op. cit.*, p. 79.

105. Cantor, *op. cit.,* p. 481.

106. Huizinga, J.: *The Waning of the Middle Ages*, Doubleday, NY, 1954, p. 30.

107. Johnson, *op. cit.,* p. 253.

108. *Ibid.,* p. 259.

109. Cohn, *op. cit.,* pp. 138–9.

110. Barraclough, Geoffrey: *The Medieval Papacy,* Norton, NY, 1979, p. 154.

111. Langmuir, *op. cit.,* p. 328, original emphasis.

112. Russell, Jeffrey Burton: *Witchcraft in the Middle Ages*, Cornell, Ithaca, 1972, p. 2.

113. Poliakov, *op. cit.,* p. 149.

114. Cohen, *op. cit.,* p. 244.

115. *Ibid.,* p. 246.

116. Parkes, *Community, op. cit.,* p. 124.

117. Trachtenberg, Joshua: *The Devil and the Jews*, Jewish Publication Society, Philadelphia, 1983, p. 20.

118. *Ibid.,* p. 22.

119. Russell, *op. cit.,* p. 269.

120. Trachtenberg, *op. cit.,* p. 42.

121. 'Probably never in the entire Western experience has Europe endured such ferocious blows and suffered such tremendous human losses as in the fourteenth century. War, plague, famine, and death...savagely attacked and reduced the population.' Herlihy, David: 'Ecological Conditions and Demographic Change' in DeMolen, *op. cit.,* p. 33.

122. Trachtenberg, *op. cit.,* p. 194.

123. Poliakov, *op. cit.,* p. 211.

124. Lowenthal, *op. cit.,* p. 159.

125. Harbison, E. Harris: *The Age of Reformation*, Ithaca, NY, 1955, p. 132.

126. Cameron, Euan: *The European Reformation*, Oxford, 1991, p. 422.

Chapter Five

National Socialism and the Triumph of Time and Space

The strength of the old State rested on three pillars: the monarchistic form, the civil service, and the army. The Revolution of 1918 eliminated the State form, disintegrated the army, and delivered the civil service to party corruption. Hitler[1]

It is important to keep in mind that the Nazis found their greatest support among respectable, educated people.... What differentiated the Germany of this period from other Nations was a profound mood, a peculiar view of man and society which seems alien and even demonic to the Western intellect. George Mosse[2]

THE GOSPEL OF RESPECT

As the most promising of Charlemagne's heirs, Germans have been feared by their rivals: France and the Roman Church. West Europeans strove to keep Germans from reaching their political and military potential. The Investiture Contest contributed to this result by inhibiting the development of a hereditary monarchy, notwithstanding a succession of competent German Emperors. This sabotaging of German unity by the Papal Monarchy, with the connivance of France, kept Germany from becoming a significant rival to France until late in the nineteenth century. Moreover, when enmeshed in the Romantic Movement, German unification promised to fulfill German Destiny. Realizing their true natures, materially, politically, and spiritually, Germans would assume their rightful role as the saviors of European civilization. Re-established as Charlemagne's heir, the Reich would rescue Europe from the decadent materialism of France and Rome. Luther's Reformation, apart from its theological purposes, fostered German autonomy and identity. In addition to attacking the worldliness of the Papacy, Luther denied the legitimacy of the Church's interference with the material and political, as well as, the spiritual lives of Germans. Reducing the Church's claims to the loyalty and the purses of Germans resonated with their secular princes. There were other nationalist elements to the Reformation: Luther created the modern German language, and he subordinated the Lutheran Church to secular authorities. In time, these factors might have yielded a unified German State under a hereditary monarchy. In the areas where Lutheranism triumphed, however, the princes retained and increased their capacity to enforce their sovereignty, now having first claim on the material resources of their territories, reinforcing Particularism. In the Catholic regions, the princes or bishops had more reason to resist centralization, for they would have been subordinated to Protestant monarchs. Furthermore, Protestants disintegrated into countless, often hostile, sects. Finally, a period of religious and political violence spread over German lands. The Hundred Years War impoverished Germany, making it impossible for the economy to produce a sufficient surplus to finance a modern State. It would take two hundred years and German unification under Prussian domination to strengthen Germany sufficiently to defeat the long dominant French. Complete unification by the Third Reich almost enabled Germany to unify Europe. But we anticipate. Let us review German history from the perspective of preparing the ground for the victory of National Socialism.

Whether isolated or ostracized, whether a consequence of the Reformation or its violent aftermath, Germany seemed more distinct than ever from the West: 'The hardening of the Lutheran revolution is not the only or even the main reason why around 1600 the [German] Empire no longer occupied the same place in the world as a hundred years earlier. Germany, which so far had shared all Europe's great experiences—the Roman occupation and Christianity, feudalism and the Crusades, the monastic movement and the universities, cities and middle classes, Renaissance and Reformation—now failed to share the greatest of them all: the incipient Europeanization of the world.'[3] Unable to participate in the great European expansion across the globe and its concomitant prosperity, Germans struggled for subsistence, as the French dominated Europe for three hundred years, first under the monarchy and then under the aegis of the Revolution. Meanwhile, Britain established a worldwide empire. For Germans, the Post-Revolutionary imperialist expression of French energies was the most ominous. The first to realize the military potential of the union of Nation and State in modern terms, France attempted to dominate Europe, including Russia. Driven by Napoleon's military genius, it almost succeeded. Napoleon's aggression did not so much undermine the Revolution as manifest its imperialist nature. For many Germans, French aggression, more than the Terror, revealed the hypocrisy of republican ideals. Hardly universal, Enlightenment values were intrinsically anti-German. These developments, including the Terror, were considered normal by the French; the progressive and enlightened, consequences of their profound Revolution. Having incurred the difficulties of radical social change, the French were eager to secure its military and political benefits. Europe, under French influence, would throw off its archaic social, political, and economic forms and move into an era of prosperity and peace. The Revolution and the burgeoning power of their Nation-State were signs of progress and hope.

Viewing these developments differently, German States, fearful of French power and terrified by revolution, helped defeat Napoleon. The peace contrived at the Congress of Vienna was the reactionaries' best effort to forestall other nationalist revolutions, which in the American and French versions, destroyed aristocratic and clerical privileges. The French Revolution gave the age-old fear of Germans a new urgency. Metternich's reactionaries reasoned: If the French could come close to dominating Europe under a revolutionary structure, whatever its form of government, imagine what the Germans could do. Perhaps more than in any other area of Europe, the Congress succeeded in the Germanic states. In the wake of the Congress, instead of nationalistic revolutionary fervor, German elites created the Romantic Movement. In place of the Enlightenment, the intellectual basis of the Revolution, the Germans pursued *Kultur*. Coupled with German personality, culture would redeem the world without violence, without war, without imperialism, without revolutionary chaos. These ideas were in some sense confirmed by Prussia's partial unification of German States, a process which lacked both the fervor and the widespread participation of the people which characterized revolutionary States. Nor was there political change beyond the extension of the jurisdiction of Prussia. No foreigners were evicted, no aristocrats were guillotined, no powerful legislatures emerged representing, at least in theory, the Nation. Germany seemed uniquely able to undergo both structural economic change and political amalgamation, while keeping irrational politics and violence to minimums.

Less idealistic, the French viewed these developments, especially the German fear of revolution, as defects, signs of retardation, a failure of nerve. Ignoring the German lack of one of the principal provocations of the Revolution, a grievously corrupt Divine Right monarchy, French virtues *and* excesses signified the inferiority of the Germans; incapable of participating in progressive developmental processes, they were pre-political barbarians. These differing worldviews came to a head in the Great War. German outrage, including its basis in the perceived antipathy of the Roman-French world to everything German, was expressed by Thomas Mann, among others.

We will build Germania's cathedral without the Jews and without Rome. Hitler[4]

The whole tendency of the Germans ran counter to the Enlightenment and to the revolution of society, which, by a crude misunderstanding, was considered its consequence: piety toward everything still in existence sought to transform itself into piety toward everything that has ever existed, only to make heart and spirit full once again and to leave no room for future goals and innovation. The cult of feeling was erected in place of the cult of reason. Nietzsche[5]

THOMAS MANN AND THE GERMAN ALTERNATIVE TO THE ENLIGHTENMENT

During the last grim years of World War One, Thomas Mann wrote *Reflections of a Non-Political Man*.[6] This complex, profound, and troubling work is perhaps the best analysis of enduring German values. Moreover, understanding *Reflections* is the single best way to comprehend why National Socialism had so deep and broad an appeal among the educated classes in Germany, a point all the more salient because *Reflections* is not in the tradition of Lagarde, Moeller, and Langbehn that Fritz Stern dissects in *The Politics of Cultural Despair*.[7] Yet Mann admires Lagarde, a notorious anti-Semite who said, referring to Jews: 'You don't talk about what to do with parasites and bacilli…. They are as quickly and fully as possible destroyed.'[8] While Mann makes no such statements, he never disavows Lagarde, whom he quotes frequently. Furthermore, *Reflections* contains many ideas antithetical to the Enlightenment.

Perhaps the most vexing question of the twentieth century has been, 'How could the most cultured and best educated European Nation pursue aggressive war and genocide?' Much of the answer to the German Question is embedded in the pages of *Reflections*. Before beginning my analysis of Mann's ideas, I should indicate some of my initial and often surprising impressions. The first is Mann's sustained attack on Rome, as power State and Empire and Rome as Papal Monarchy, the differences between them largely unimportant for Mann. Post-Revolutionary France is targeted, as the legatee of Rome, secular and sacerdotal. The occasion for writing *Reflections* was the Great War; the reasons for writing it were Rome's abuse of Germany since the Caesars, its humiliation by Popes since Gregory VII, and its ostracism by the West since the French Revolution. So deep is Mann's animosity for the Latin World that he cannot view the Great War as a European *civil war*. So far from being a fratricidal, it is the war of the anti-European, imperialist power, 'Civilization,' against the sole 'European' power, Germany, a conception which by itself jars West European sensibilities. Nor should the war be conceived as a clash of civilizations, for Germany is not a civilization; it is a culture. Mann's implication is that, if Europe is to survive, it must retain its humanitarian values, best exemplified by Germans, most subverted by the West.

The second impression is Mann's admiration of the Russians, personified by Dostoevsky. Ignoring the age-old European dread of the Asiatic East, Mann quotes Dostoevsky repeatedly. The great Russian appreciates Germany's role: 'Since the first moment of its appearance in the historical world, that it [Germany] has never, neither in its destiny nor in its principles, wanted to be united with the far Western World, that is, with all the heirs of the ancient Roman destiny.'[9] He shares Mann's view of the unity of the Latin world: 'The concept of the Roman universal monarchy was replaced by that of the unification of Christ; whereupon there followed that split of the new ideal into an *eastern* part, which Dostoevsky says is characterized by the ideal of the wholly spiritual unification of mankind, and a *western* European part, which was Roman Catholic, papal. In its western form...it preserved the old Roman political-imperial tradition.'[10] Because this unity has always been anti-German, Germany's task has been Protestantism: 'not merely that form of Protestantism that developed at the time of Luther, but her *Eternal* Protestantism, her *Eternal* protest as it began with Arminius against the Roman world, against everything that was Rome and Rome's mission, and later against everything that was transmitted from the old Rome to the new, and to all Nations that received the Roman idea, formula, and element, protest against the heirs of Rome and against everything that constitutes this heritage.'[11] He accounts for Germany's antipathy to Rome: 'During the era of Roman Christianity, more than any other Nation, she fought with Rome for supremacy. Finally, she protested in the most powerful way by taking the new formula of protest from the most spiritual, most elementary foundations of the Germanic world. The voice of God resounded in her, proclaiming the freedom of the spirit.'[12] The conservative protest, exemplified by Luther, against the Latin World's domination of Europe, is thus confirmed by Dostoevsky. Mann admires both Orthodox and Protestant resistance to their common enemy: Rome in all its incarnations. Rome has undermined the political, economic, cultural and spiritual security of Russia and Germany and, therefore, of Europe as a whole. This powerful adversary has had the support of a fifth column, Russians and Germans, who have taken sides with the West in the name of progress and freedom.

My third impression concerns the fraternal animosity that pervades *Reflections*. Mann pillories his brother, Heinrich, as the worst sort of German, a Francophile, and a Literary Man: 'A sublime and brilliant but basically Latinized literary man, who long ago renounced every feeling for the particular ethos of his people, yes, who even ridicules the recognition of such a special national ethos as bestial nationalism, and who opposes it with his humanitarian-democratic civilization and social internationalism.'[13] Mann targets, not only writers who are sympathetic with the Enlightened West, but literature itself, because: 'In the innate and eternal conviction of Roman civilization, not only humanism [but] humanitarianism in general, human dignity, respect for human beings, and human self-respect are inextricably bound to literature.'[14] The irony of this charge does not elude the novelist. Without irony Nietzsche earlier made Mann's point with typical acuity: 'Compared with music all communication by words is shameless; words dilute and brutalize; words depersonalize; words make the uncommon common.'[15]

My last impression is that Mann poured his heart, soul and mind into *Reflections*. Not only are its brilliance, passion, and intensity worthy of Mann's Noble Prize winning novels, it deserves to rank with the best books of his generation. By contrast, Mann's lectures of the 1930s and 1940s, presented to American audiences, are set pieces, dry, predictable, simplistic, and banal. In these lectures, which advocate much of what he condemns in *Reflections*, Mann does his duty, with all the enthusiasm of taking out the trash. In *Reflections* the impassioned, fully engaged Mann illuminates a complex and profound alternative to the Enlightenment.

Not a period of history the Enlightenment was, for Mann, a collection of ideas, which were born with the Roman Empire and which reached its apotheosis in the French Revolution, the unnatural coupling of the power State and Latin Nationalism, its scion, the French Revolution. What this coupling continues to spawn is chaos and, worse for an artist, mediocrity. When democracy, equality, and the politicization of society become different aspects of the same concept, power for power's sake, demagogues, in the name of the people, undermine and need to undermine all values which have proved their worth and their capacity to endure. For these values necessarily limit the exercise of power. 'And what are the highest goods of mankind? God, Fatherland, emperor, freedom, love and loyalty, beauty, science and art.'[16] To a Westerner, a child of the Enlightenment, these highest goods, to the degree they are not self-contradictory, indicate what has been wrong with Germany. Where are justice, equality, Natural Rights, rule of law, democracy, and the people? What do love, beauty, science, and art have to do with politics? How can freedom—of all terms, freedom—be squared with Fatherland and emperor? And Fatherland, why not Nation? Perhaps because 'Nation' suggests the people, while 'Fatherland' suggests paternalism bred in Blood and Soil. Consider loyalty. The Enlightenment values loyalty to principles, but not loyalty to tradition, monarchy, or other human beings. Consider the Enlightenment's God; acceptable as the Designer, a distant, cool Clockmaker, but certainly not the Judge of the Universe, and certainly with no capacity or inclination to limit the power of the people, who are omniscient and omnipotent. After all, as Robespierre said, 'the people are just, wise and good. Everything they do is virtuous and true, nothing exaggerated, mistaken or criminal,'[17] implying an infallible Nation.[18]

It seems reasonable to conclude that, whether or not based on a shallow materialism, the Enlightenment lent itself to one-sided and simple-minded views of human perfectibility, to anti-human and anti-humane individualism, whose earmarks are getting and spending, and to mispremised and anti-historical optimism, indentured to an unsupported belief that politics could cure the ills and conflicts of mankind, creating a pre-Fall garden of delights. This critique seems less reactionary to those who would live through the horrors of the twentieth century, which Mann prophesies would reprise the eighteenth: 'The twentieth century declares the character, the tendencies, the basic mood of the nineteenth century to be discredited, it defames its form of truthfulness, its weakness of will and submissiveness, its melancholy lack of belief. It *believes*—or at least it teaches that one must believe. It tries to forget what one knows of the nature of the human being—in order to adapt him to his utopia. It adores the human being completely in *dix-huitieme* fashion; it is not pessimistic, not skeptical, not cynical and—most of all—not ironical.'[19]

To this more or less standard list of the shortcomings of the Enlightenment, Mann adds complex and less predictable elements, many of which seem absurd to non-Germans, indicating that Germans are not like West Europeans. First, the Enlightenment denied what we know of human nature and the natural world.[20] While Mann does not posit Social Darwinism, he denies that nature is the Garden of Eden or Rousseau's State of Nature. Surfeit with human violence, depravity, conflict, war, pestilence, famine, and many other horrors, all of which would make existence unendurable, without the human capacity to draw strength and nobility from suffering and travail. Here Mann seconds Nietzsche's belief that good *Eris*, strife, can be embedded in violence: 'Just as the individual Greek fought as though he alone were right and an infinitely sure measure of judicial opinion were determining the trend of victory at any moment, so the qualities wrestle with one another, in accordance with inviolable laws and standards that are imminent in the struggle.'[21] Not only wrong, the Enlightenment's portrait of nature diminished human existence by denying human nobility.

Second, the Enlightenment denied the metaphysical nature of human beings. By defining humans as social animals, who distinguish themselves by
individual achievement, the Enlightenment consigned human beings to the
trough of society. 'I am what I consume.' 'I am my social position.' 'I am
my political office.' 'I am my fame.' Profoundly flawed this conception of
individualism was self-contradictory. Mann quotes Hammacher: 'Nietzsche's
greatest service is the *separation of metaphysical from social life*.... He redis-
covered the insight that individualism is a mistake and that superindividuality
is still realized through personality itself and only through it; for him, social
individuality, society, is relatively unimportant and inferior to metaphysical
superindividuality.'[22] Only by transcending social existence, by being true
to nature, can humans become true to themselves, as personalities, as super
individuals. In Nietzsche's and Mann's writings, a personality emerges by
embracing nature and all its life-giving potential, by perfecting itself in the
face of all the suffering living to the full entails. The distinction between the
personality (good, profound, spiritual) and the individual (bad, shallow, materialist) will be emphasized by Hitler.

The resonance with Dostoevsky is striking, as Mann's appreciation of
Dmitri Karamazov makes clear: '[His] infamy is not egotistical; in every
other sense than the civic one, it is anything but vulgar. It is a sacrifice, a
casting away, a self-debasement, a relentless, fanatic, and humiliating devotion that not only is not without generosity, but is rather itself a dirty and
bloody form of generosity. To the pure person—but I should rather say: to
the clean one—the sight of infamy may awaken disgust, but not without at
the same time inspiring him with certain awe and teaching him presentiments
of a mystical morality.'[23] Without paradox, Mann argues that life presents
opportunities for transcendence, for spiritual expression, for profound self-
expression, and moral action in nearly every moment, for nearly everyone,
including the infamous and the depraved. Is this not why a scoundrel is easier
to admire than a politician, who makes his or her way by always going with
the wind, always securing approval, always calculating benefits and costs,
and who believes in nothing? Mann condemns politics, not for its inevitable
corruption, but for its emptiness.

Third, the Enlightenment was anti-intellectual. Here, Mann seemingly
contradicts himself. First, he cites Nietzsche: '[He]...signified: the self-denial
of intellect in favor of life, of strong and especially beautiful life. This is
undoubtedly a most extreme and final escape from the domination of ideals,
a submission to power that was by now no longer fatalistic but enthusiastic,
erotically intoxicated....'[24] Then, he writes: 'The difference between intellect and politics includes that of culture and civilization, of soul and society,
of freedom and voting rights, of art and literature; and German tradition is

culture, soul, freedom, art and *not* civilization.'[25] In the first quotation, intellect is negative, because it denies life. In the second it is positive, because it is antithetical to politics. Mann is *not* saying that, when compared to life, intellect is unimportant, but, when compared to politics, it is. He uses 'intellect' to refer to two entirely different processes. The first indicates the use of intellectual capabilities like a machine, that is, *divorced* from culture, society, freedom, and art. The second process, on the other hand, indicates a mental activity that is interpenetrated with these values. The Enlightenment sees intellect as subordinate to society, civilization and politics. Intellect is part of the policy process; and, therefore, a tool for Everyman to shape society at will, impervious to doubt: 'Every Frenchman considers himself capable of overcoming all difficulties with a little spirit. Never did so many people imagine they were all lawmakers, and their task was to correct all the mistakes of the past, to remove all delusions of the human mind, to insure the happiness of coming generations. There was no room in their minds for doubt....'[26] Much of the shallowness of the Enlightenment derives from this misuse of intellect as the process of creating an illusion of certainty in matters of the utmost complexity and profundity which defy rational or scientific analysis. For Mann, intellect is moral, spiritual, metaphysical, personal, and physical: 'This solidarity [of intellectuals] is organic, it is constitutional. It rests on the homogeneity of the form of existence, on a higher, tenderer, form of existence that is more capable of suffering, more willing to suffer, more foreign to comfort than the ordinary one. It is comradeship in nobility, brotherliness in pain. *Here* is the source of all tolerance, conscientiousness, all courtesy of the heart and gallantry, in short, of all *morality* of the intellect.'[27]

Fourth, the Enlightenment collapsed the concepts of civilization, politics, democracy, and equality, making it impossible to consider one without meaning them all: 'Civilization is politics through and through, politics itself, and its hatred too, can only be, and must immediately be, political. The political spirit as democratic enlightenment and humanitarian civilization is not only psychologically anti-German; it is also by necessity politically anti-German....'[28] The effect of this collapse of concepts is not limited to an inability to understand Germans; it's purpose is to destroy them: 'Our good natured, non-political humanity has always led us to think that understanding, friendship, peace, and good relations were possible, and we would never have allowed ourselves to dream, we had to learn for the first time in the war with shock and horror, how much *they* hated *us* (and not we them!) all this time....'[29] Note the asymmetry of the relationship. The German *cannot* hate, while the civilized Westerner *must* hate, because, unlike the German, the Westerner expresses his or her individuality in the power State, first as a bourgeois, then as an imperialist: 'But he [the German] will never become a State philistine, a Reich philistine. He will never come to believe that the State is the purpose and meaning of human existence, that the destiny of the human being is found in the State and that *politics makes people more human....*'[30] The asymmetry derives from the fact that the German is a personality: 'The human being is not only a social but also a metaphysical being; in other words, he is not only an individual but also a personality.... The Nation, too, is not only a social but a metaphysical being; the Nation, not the human race as the sum of the individuals, is the bearer of the general, of the human quality; and the value of the intellectual-artistic-religious product that one calls national culture, that cannot be grasped by scientific methods, that develops out of the organic depth of national life....'[31]

For these reasons, Germans have been assaulted for their self-perceived virtues: profundity and their true understanding of what it means to be a free, cultured, metaphysical and spiritual personality. Their role has been constrained by the antipathy of the Roman world:

> Dostoyevsky's formulation of the German character, of German primeval individuality, of what is eternally German, contains the whole basis and explanation of the lonely German position between East and West, of Germany's offensiveness to the world, of the antipathy, the hatred she must endure and defend herself against—in bewilderment and pain at this universal hatred that she does not understand because she knows little about herself and has not developed very far at all in all matters of psychological understanding—the basis and explanation also of her enormous *courage* that she has unflinchingly displayed to the surrounding world....[32]

Therefore, Mann writes, [Germany's] 'Eternal and innate mission' [has been to engage in a] 'terrible, perilous, and in the most magnificent sense, irrational struggle against the world *entente* of civilization.'[33]

To appreciate how Mann arrives at this portrait of the Enlightenment and Germany's sacred duty to defy it, the cardinal distinctions he makes between concepts often used as synonyms must be clarified. His usage is much too complex and nuanced to assign clear definitions to the concepts his analysis employs. Far from apologizing for this inability to be precise, Mann insists that precision cannot be achieved without engaging in the very reductionism that has made Enlightenment thought trivial. A discussion of some of his cardinal distinctions fulfills this claim in some measure. (1) Civilization and culture: Civilization, including its association with humanitarianism, is the enemy of culture, because it signifies the superiority of the social to the metaphysical and of the political to the spiritual, and of and the individual to the personality and the true community. 'Culture binds together; civilization dissolves. This is obvious.'[34] (2) Bourgeois and burgher: personality *and* the true community are what he means by 'burgher.' A burgher is a personality, because '[he] never elevates social problems above moral ones, above inner experience.'[35] Mann suggests that only Germans could be burghers: 'The German burgher is really the German human being; and everything that strove for freedom and intellectuality, both from above and below, strove toward his center.'[36] (3) Individual and personality: Having already discussed this contrast, here I stress that the individual is immersed in the material and the political. 'Politics is the sphere of the democratic individual, not of the aristocratic personality.'[37] The personality, by contrast, 'knows that politics, namely enlightenment, social contract, republic, progress toward the greatest good for the greatest number, is no way to reconcile social life; that this reconciliation can be achieved only in the sphere of personality, never in that of the individual, only on a spiritual path, that is never on a political one, and that it is insane to want to raise social life even the slightest bit toward religious consecration.'[38]

Mann dichotomizes other pairs of concepts which, while not synonyms, often seem to have family resemblances, for example, literature and music. While it is normal to treat music and literature as two art forms, two expressions of culture, he believes this practice is misleading, because literature is part of civilization *etc*, while music is part of culture. Mann approvingly quotes Luther, 'I have always loved music; it is a beautiful, affectionate gift of God and close to theology.'[39] He says, moreover, that 'Wagner is so powerfully German that to me it has always seemed one absolutely had to passionately experience his work, if one were to understand, or at least to divine, something of the deep magnificence and painful ambivalence of the German character.' And further, 'In itself alone, Wagner's art would be this portrait of the German character.'[40] Mann is fully aware that his novels, no matter how German they are in character, no matter how critical of the Literary Man, contribute to civilization and, thereby, undermine culture. Music is aesthetic, literature is not. Music is art; literature is not, at least not in the absolute sense. This is not a taxonomic exercise, for art is the proper expression of life, just as literature is the proper expression of politics.

In the nineteenth century, Germany flowered as never before. A.J.P. Taylor writes: 'On almost every test of civilization—philosophy, music, science, local government—the Germans come out at the top of the list; only the art of political behavior is beyond them.'[41] Many scholars would add technology, higher education, and literature. According to Hans Kohn, 'The Germans, in the nineteenth century, began to feel themselves fundamentally different from and culturally and morally superior to France and the West.'[42] For Mann and the Romantics, these achievements more than sufficed to demonstrate Germany's pride of place in Europe. They and many ordinary Germans would have been content to live their lives in this cultural garden. They could not, because they saw themselves, against their nature, wrenched into a Europe comprised of power States: 'The Germans certainly could not remain as innocent and peace-loving as cosmopolitan, as they had been in Kant's day. Napoleon had taught them too roughly what power was and what was the reward for weakness. The misery of State and Nation made them discover State and Nation, though they still approached the new problems with high idealism.'[43]

The Defeat in the Great War brought the continuation of this cultural superiority into question; its moral base seemed to be deteriorating: 'The abrupt and challenging breach with previous standards of morality touched people at their most sensitive point.... There was a strong streak of self-mockery, typified by the final scene of...*Mahogany*, where the actors step up to the footlights and raise placards reading, "Up with the chaotic State of our cities," "Up with love for hire," "Up with honor for assassins," or "Up with the immortality of vulgarity."'[44] To this standard complaint of the *avant garde*, Mann adds a more sophisticated concern, one which typically goes against his aesthetic grain:

> Must we not, even against our will, recognize in this phenomenon an aspect of the artist's character? We are ashamed to admit it, but the whole pattern is there: the recalcitrance, sluggishness and miserable indefiniteness of his youth; the dimness of purpose, the what-do-you-really-want-to-be, the vegetating like a semi-idiot in the lowest social and psychological bohemianism, the arrogant rejection of any sensible and honorable occupation because of the basic feeling that he is too good for that sort of thing. On what is this feeling based? On a vague sense of being reserved for something entirely indefinable. To name it, if it could be named, would make people burst out laughing. Along with that, the uneasy conscience, the sense of guilt, the rage at the world, the revolutionary instinct, the subconscious storing up of explosive cravings for compensation, the churning determination to justify oneself, to prove oneself....[45]

For Mann, this capacity to see phenomenon in the round, to be self-critical to the point of self-destruction, is what has given the German artist and burgher his distinctive character. This candor stems from an ironic appreciation of the world and man's place in it.

Nietzsche, along with Luther, Schopenhauer, and Goethe, influenced Mann's *Weltanschauung*. It should not surprise that he shares some of their misconceptions. For example, like Nietzsche, Mann wishes Germany were more like Greece, ancient and orthodox, and less Latin and French. Yet his notion of Greekness, like Nietzsche's, is limited to heroic aesthetics. 'There are ages in which the rational man and the intuitive man stand side by side, the one in fear of intuition, the other with scorn for abstraction. The latter is just as irrational as the former is inartistic. They both desire to rule over life; the former, by knowing how to meet his principal needs by means of foresight, prudence, and regularity; the latter, by disregarding these needs and, as an overjoyed hero, counting as real only that life which has been disguised as illusion and beauty.'[46] While capturing the significance of art, including the art of the hero, it ignores its basis in the *polis*. The *polis*, even in its most democratic phases, never forgot its heroic and artistic ideals. Its creative outburst in the fifth century was the result of the tension between heroic individualism, warrior and artist, and the needs of the *polis*, political and military. Mann's one-sided appreciation of the Greeks ignores Aristotle's conception of the citizen and *polis* as mutually dependent. One could not exist without the other. This conception fundamentally differs from the bond that Mann celebrates by his dyad of personality and community, because he ignores the Greek passion for participation in the social-political arena. In so doing, he suggests that freedom can be achieved through inner virtue, that its pursuit is a solitary and lonely endeavor. This may be true, but this is not how the Greeks viewed it. A free man must participate in the political. He must rule and be ruled in turn. It is possible that Mann, like Nietzsche, is trying to import as much of Greek culture as he could given the realities of the modern State. There is no indication, however, that he is making the best of a bad bargain. On the contrary, he believes that Germany had achieved high culture, an amalgamation of art, freedom and discipline. He fears that their nineteenth century achievement was about to be squandered by the victory of the Enlightenment over German culture, hence his enthusiasm for the Great War. His support of war, moreover, is generalized, as an ennobling, mystical experience. For all his praise of doubt, Mann seems altogether too certain of the value of war.

My final concern deals with the notion of rights and the modern State. Mann is openly contemptuous of human rights, which, since he links the idea with the French Revolution, must include Natural Rights. While he decries the Roman power State, as it has manifested itself in Western Europe, he ignores how the concept of Natural Rights might limit the State. He does not say the concept of rights is fragile and often fails to be applied, but that it is empty: 'The German concept of freedom will always be of a spiritual nature: an individualism that, in order to reveal itself politically, must always create institutions other than those barren-abstract ones of the political West and of human rights.'[47] Pre-societal rights, rights as an endowment by birth as a human being, simply make no sense to him. Moreover, freedom, for Mann, does not mean a zone of liberty into which coercive State power may not trespass. Freedom is spiritual, echoing the Lutheran conception that however oppressed an individual might be, a Christian is free. For those who believe the material world is insignificant, then slaves might be as free as a king. Freedom is spiritual not material.

Mann's idea of what might limit the power State in the Here and Now is even more troubling. He believes the State has a metaphysical character which prevents rulers from becoming tyrants and the people from becoming an individualistic mass. 'Never has the difference between the people as a mystical character and the individualistic mass appeared more visibly; and no sense of awe for the former, no heartfelt participation in its heroic, protects one from seeing the basically miserable nature of the latter, its cowardice, impudence, wickedness, lack of character, and meanness.'[48] He suggests that the metaphysical State endows it with a mystical character. Not only does this conception deny intrinsic value to human beings, it suggests that only a metaphysical State can limit their depravity, echoing Luther. Mann praises the German personality, really the nexus between this personality and the metaphysical State, because: 'He [the German] knows that politics, namely enlightenment, social contract, republic, progress toward the greatest good for the greatest number, is no way to reconcile social life; that this reconciliation can be achieved only in the sphere of personality, never in that of the individual, only on a spiritual path, that is never on a political one, and that it is insane to want to raise social life even the slightest bit toward religious consecration.'[49] Furthermore, social life and the political arena are futile, because they are antithetical to 'religious consecration.' Mann suggests further that the way toward consecration is through an immersion of the individual in the Nation. He affirms Lagarde: 'The Nation speaks only when Nationhood...is expressed in individuals....'[50] Moreover, he suggests that individuals become personalities only through the Nation. 'The one and only possibility for Germany is for *national affirmation to imply negation of politics and democracy*—and vice versa.'[51] Only by these negations can individuals avoid devolving into the mass; by them they can dwell in *the* Nation and thus become personalities. How UnGreek all this is: no justice, no life of virtuous activity, no political participation, no liberty, no rebellion against tyranny. Instead, Mann offers a pathway to religious consecration by aesthetic endeavors. For those without creative ability, he offers life as a burgher. 'I do not want politics. I want objectivity, order, and decency. If this is philistine, then I want to be a philistine.'[52] As Mann comes to understand to his regret in his exile, one should be careful what one wishes for. In 1933, he recanted his support for the National Socialists with typical perspicacity:

> The primitiveness, the disappearance of culture, the increase in stupidity and the reduction to a petit bourgeois mentality are not recognized as fright by the intellectuals but are welcomed with a perverted approval. Propagators of the irrational, as they prevailed in great masses in Germany during the period of growing

National Socialism, educated the people to a moral san-culottism and to an apathy to all cruelty.... Cryptic sciences, pseudo sciences and frauds, formation of sects and quackery were the vogue and had mass appeal. Intellectuals did not consider all this as a low, modern fad or as cultural degradation. Instead they welcomed it as the rebirth of mystic powers of life and the soul of the people. The soil was ready for the most absurd and lowest mass superstition. That was the faith in Adolf Hitler.[53]

By then Hitler was in power, and his early successes seemed to make intellectuals that supported him, like Heidegger, seem more prophetic than Mann.

To be sure, we need history; but our need for it is different from the pampered idler in the garden of knowledge—regardless of the noble condescension with which he might look upon our crude and inelegant needs and afflictions. That is, we need it for life and for action, not for an easy withdrawal from life and action, let alone for whitewashing a selfish life and cowardly, base actions. Nietzsche[54]

GERMANY: THE NINETEENTH CENTURY BACKGROUND

Unwittingly confirming Mann's critique, West Europeans, however much they might have admired Germany's cultural achievements, emphasized the primacy of politics. From their perspective, 'the most significant event in modern German history is the revolution that did not take place. Often this incapacity for revolution has been seen as a characteristic of a particularly submissive character.'[55] In Kohn's view, before 1806 'Germany knew hardly any nationalism or political activity. The people lived peacefully, unmoved by French revolutionary appeals, without any understanding of Western aspirations.... Even the liberals did not demand participation in government but only freedom of mind and the insulation of society from the State.'[56] This 'failure' suggests that Germans were hostile or at least indifferent to freedom, to say nothing of Natural Rights. It is fair to say that the Germans did not need a French style revolution, because they were not ruled by a decrepit monarchy, a corrupt bureaucracy, a rapacious aristocracy, and a venal and self-serving clergy; nor were they seduced by the concept of the Divine Right of Kings. Of course, there were many German States which suffered from one or more of these afflictions, but never did all German States do so. In this respect Particularism, often provided sanctuaries for Germans who ran afoul of one sovereign or another.

It is clear in Locke and Rousseau that the notion of Natural Rights, taken as myth or fact, was needed to defeat the Divine Right concept and its corrupt effects: decadence and misrule. It seems equally clear that their emphasis on individualism derived from a desire to defeat the privileges and immunities that arose from rigid caste and class systems. Although the German situation was much more variable and stable, it was difficult for Germans to find satisfaction in this relative passivity: 'Things happened to Germany, but they were done to it by others…. It [adapted], voluntarily or compulsorily, to great happenings elsewhere. The storm [French Revolution] blew elsewhere, Germany felt only the effects. As a result the Germans had in years to come no wish to look back and be proud of the great political and social transformation that occurred at the beginning of the nineteenth century; they saw it as a time of shame, however lasting or positive its achievements.'[57] The importance of Golo Mann's judgment, apart from reflecting the feelings of many Germans, is its conviction that adapting to great events is shameful. The corollary of this notion is that no matter how great its achievements might be, Germany could not play an admirable role, until it ceases to be passive. This is not quite the idea that Germany has a mission to save Europe, but it approaches it; the underlying temperament is the same. German initiatives must comport with their abhorrence of violence and mob action: 'Civil war does not suit the German character either. The Germans have never had one. Even the Thirty Years War was a war between the princes, not a civil war…. From the beginning until 1939 the dictatorship cost only a few thousand lives, in executions, murders and suicides; no one was killed in open battle. If there was something to be said for this compared with a genuine civil war, there was something particularly repulsive about this self-indulgent, mercilessly exploited but bloodless victory of one part of the Nation over the other.'[58] Consider how Golo Mann renders the incendiary events of 1848:

> Conditions in Germany in 1848 differed fundamentally from those of France in the late eighteenth century. There was no bankrupt administration on the verge of collapse; the Austrians were not badly governed and the Prussians were well governed. No helpless monarch convened the old estates because he was in financial difficulties. On the contrary, the Germans rebelled against the effective, often all too effective bureaucratic State. Their demand was for greater freedom of action, legal safeguards, political participation…and above all for National unity, the participation of the whole Nation in important questions.[59]

In response to the first agitation for more freedom, many German sovereignties gave in without a fight. 'The words "everything is granted" heard so often with joy in Germany at the time [March 1848], show that the people wanted freedom to be granted by traditional authority.'[60] When the reaction took place, the people likewise acquiesced. What is too easily given is often as easily taken. Enduring freedom is not granted but won. Both quotations indicate the endemic dilemma of German political character: facing agitation, authorities comply; facing reaction, the people acquiesce. When resistance

occurred in the name of freedom, it seemed divorced from reality and destined to ineffectuality. Moreover, Germans have defined freedom and other
cardinal Enlightenment terms differently from their West European rivals.
According to Krieger, 'they named their own values and actions in Western
terms and saw in their divergence only their positive cultural creation within
the common Western pattern.'[61] Golo Mann goes further: 'The clear-cut concepts of French politics—reactionary, conservative, progressive, revolutionary, left, right—were useless for the understanding of German problems.'[62]
At the same time, many Germans envied the French for their sense of national
unity which the Revolution stimulated. As the first truly modern Nation-
State, bringing all segments of society into the Nation, under a doctrine of
Natural Rights, France, driven by Napoleon's genius, came remarkably close
to recreating Charlemagne's Empire on a larger scale, alarming and intrigu-
ing Germans. According to Golo Mann: 'The shape of Germany's political
and legal and administrative life, which was preserved through the nineteenth
century and in many cases until well into the twentieth, was molded under
his spell. Napoleon also gave the Germans new notions of politics, the State,
power, war, success and greatness; they accepted these.'[63] The alarm grew
out of the feeling that Germany again was being drawn into a French way of
thinking. German thinkers began to wonder if there could there be a German
equivalent of the power State which would retain the spiritual, aesthetic, and
nonpolitical nature of their people.

Before the Germans could confront this question as a practical matter,
European events intervened. Appreciating the anti-aristocratic implications of
the Nation-State, as well as its tendency toward aggression, the Congress of
Vienna, under Metternich's leadership, impeded further national development
in Europe, delaying the inevitable. Reaction, however, was perceived by many
Germans as specifically anti-German, notwithstanding their ambivalent attitudes toward a French style Nation-State. Golo Mann believes that 'it would
have been excellent if at Napoleon's fall Germany had become a State, a national republic, a democracy.... But to speak of missed opportunities is meaningful only where genuine opportunities existed, which was not the case....'[64]
Very few Germans thought this kind of Nation-State would be ideal, as Mann
admits: 'His [Bismarck's] great achievement was not that he created German
unity.... What makes his achievement so very clever, daring and unnatural is
the fact that he brought about German unity without the elements associated
with it for fifty years: parliamentary rule, democracy and demagogy.... In
the end the German Reich was proclaimed among princes and generals, at an
army camp, where a middle-class deputation looked drab and timid.'[65] And,
moreover, the class which led the democratic revolution elsewhere has had a
different role in Germany: 'The liberals preached freedom but the result of

their efforts was to make the State omnipotent. They glorified the Nation, the good, the infallible people, though in reality they distrusted the masses and represented the interests of the well-to-do who were only a small minority.'[66] Taylor acerbically criticizes them:

> They had a sincere liberal faith, but assumed from the start that their faith must be ineffective; in fact they soon made the further assumption that power was, by its very nature, illiberal and unprogressive. To achieve power for themselves never entered into their calculations; and in view of the economic backwardness of the German bourgeoisie this omission was no doubt inevitable. But they wished to see their ideas succeed and so arrived at the comforting conclusion that, in time, liberal ideas would triumph not by acquiring power, but merely by their innate virtue. The belief in the victory of ideas, without the foundation of an effective political organization or of a coherent class backing, was to be the ultimate ruin of German liberalism; and, though it has many sources, its most important origin lay in the days of Napoleonic rule, when the men of liberal ideas saw their ideas established in Germany without any effort of their own.[67]

For Germans liberalism was a way to free the economy feudal or mercantile constraints, not a political doctrine which strove to free the individual from the power State. Moreover, the distinction between political and economic liberalism was legitimated by success. The partnership of commerce and government transformed Germany into Europe's leading industrial State, meeting the security needs of the middle classes, who, unlike the West, did not appreciate the State's threat to liberty:

> In economics liberalism also defended the interests of the bourgeoisie by demanding the creation of conditions favorable to the growth of industrial capitalism. It urged the expansion of the *Zollverein* to embrace all of Germany, the removal of restrictions on the growth of the factory system, freedom of movement, freedom of occupation, and freedom of enterprise. Railways, rivers, telegraphs, and roads were to become part of a united system of transportation and communication serving a national market. Such residues of the past as artisan guilds, corporate monopolies, trade privileges, and mercantilist regulations should be swept away to make way for a system of liberty under which skill and ambition could find a fit reward. For among the most precious rights of the citizen was the freedom to exercise his talent in the pursuit of financial gain, and only through it could the aptitude and ingenuity of a progressive people contribute to the welfare of the State.[68]

So long as these sorts of changes occurred, liberals were content to have a modest voice in government. The symbiotic relationship between Bismarck and the bourgeoisie tended to ignore the needs of working class Germans.

Despite the remarkable changes in the economic and social structure of Germany in the late fifties, there was little mass support for the liberal cause in the constitutional conflict of 1862–1866 as there had been in the later stages of the revolution in 1848. The weakness arose from an inadequate penetration of liberal ideas into the lower working strata of German society, but also from the deliberate unwillingness of the liberals to look after the material needs of the working class. The alliance of the aristocratic and middle classes consummated by Bismarck in 1866 left the working class no other recourse than to find in proletarian socialism its spiritual home.[69]

Furthermore, in Bismarck's Germany, the liberation of the German economy from 'feudalism' became a force for conservatism: 'The word *"libertat"* made its debut in the German language as an expression of the corporate rights of the princes against the emperor rather than of the Natural Rights of man.... In this way the German idea of freedom became associated with the absolute State. Despite the many social and political upheavals which subsequently occurred, this association was never really dissolved.'[70] Dahrendorf amplifies this semantic point: 'There are certain words that come up time and again in connection with economic and social policy of Imperial Germany: Nation, State, tight control, the interest of the whole, adaptation and subordination. Not even industrialization managed...to upset a traditional outlook in which the whole is placed above its parts, the State above the citizen, or a rigidly controlled order above the lively diversity of the market, the State over society.... Instead of developing it, industrialization in Germany swallowed the liberal principle.'[71] Germany's digestion was aided by the competence and reach of its bureaucratic tradition. One of the properties of belated German industrialism was that it was coordinated and sometimes directed by governmental bureaucracy. Taylor frames this virtue negatively, drawing an extreme and over dichotomized conclusion: 'The German capitalists became dependents of Prussian militarism and advocates of arbitrary power as naturally and as inevitably as English or American capitalists became liberals and advocates of constitutional authority. Where Anglo-Saxon capitalists demanded *laissez-faire*, German capitalists sought for State leadership; where Anglo-Saxon capitalists accepted democracy, however, grudgingly, German capitalists accepted dictatorship.'[72] Furthermore, bureaucratic rationalism led to an emphasis on size, to efficiencies of scale. The flexibility or disorder of *laissez-faire* entrepreneurialism did not take root either as an ideology or as an approach to the relations of the private and public sector. With the government responsible for raising the capital necessary for economic development, 'Large economic units and a powerful but small group of industrial leaders emerged so early...as to leave no place for the traditional liberal infrastructure of the medium sized enterprises and bourgeois entrepreneurs.'[73]

The relatively complete absorption of bourgeois economic values and the incomplete absorption of liberal political values allowed Germany to undergo a profound economic structural transformation without the political upheaval that accompanied equivalent changes in the West. Moreover, half-hearted political liberalism had a concomitant effect on German nationalism. The yoking of the Nation to the State did not follow French precedent. The People or the Nation were not absorbed into Bismarck's Germany even as an ideal. Just as political liberalism was restricted to the bourgeoisie, nationalism was restricted to patriotism. The idea that the People defined the Nation never took hold for the same reasons that the People conceived as a legitimate political force never took hold: fear of bringing irrational elements into the body politic or the government. Only with the Third Reich would the Nation come into its own, not however, as the main support of democracy, but as the most irrational devotees of the Hitler Movement. The ironic consequences of the German's fear of the irrational in politics were catastrophic. Germany's success in cabining the forces of irrationality in the nineteenth century would be matched by Hitler's success in unleashing them in the twentieth. But we anticipate.

We have seen Thomas Mann's ambivalence towards the concept, captured more sharply by Hans Delbruck [1899]: 'It was the high ideal of our fathers that the German national State should come into existence without the Germans deteriorating into the hatefulness and exclusiveness which in the case of other countries we brand as chauvinism, jingoism, moscowism. The firm authority of the State was to go hand in hand with the free unfolding of individuality which for no people is more indispensable, because no people are more richly endowed with it than our own.'[74] Many educated Germans concurred. There was a general concern not only that the lower classes would have a say in a liberal State, but that it would be fundamentally uninformed and irrational, unable to rise to the level of self-interest, to say nothing of the common interest.

Bismarck, who was notoriously suspicious of emotionally driven policy, agreed. German unification agreed without the normal nationalist fervor. One of the ironies of this approach is that Prussia ceased to exist as a national entity, despite its leading role in unification. Acquiescing in this subordination of Prussia to Germany, Bismarck believed that German nationalism was unlikely to occur, due to an inability to overcome a great many disintegrative factors, including Particularism. Besides, he believed that a competent power State would keep the nationalist furies at bay, by providing the material benefits of a thorough-going realism in foreign policy. The Franco-Prussian War perfectly manifested Bismarck's attitude, especially as it contrasted with the grandiose program of Napoleon. To fulfill Napoleonic dreams required developments that Bismarck abhorred: a Nation-State armed with an

intense feeling of nationalism with its associated senses of political entitlement and ethnic superiority. Secondly, it required a greater sense of political
participation by the middle classes, who were to pay for military adventures.
Bismarck incompletely unified Germany, partially released bourgeois energies, partially allowed nationalism to emerge, partially released militarism,
but only in support of realistic, limited goals. Bismarck financed his control
of German developments by creating economic security: 'There is one thing
the authoritarian welfare State does not and cannot permit: the development
of the subject into the citizen with all the rights of this social character....
What is remarkable about Imperial Germany is that throughout the industrial
revolution it managed to miss the road to modernity and instead consolidated
itself with an industrial feudal society with an authoritarian welfare State.'[75]
The uneasy and unstable alliance which resulted from this grafting of State
capitalism on to premodern social structures persisted due to the remarkable
international success of the German State, as 'a kind of State socialism corresponded to the prevailing system of State capitalism.'[76]

Dahrendorf similarly over dichotomizes German and Western economic
development, assuming that only a liberal political regime can be modern, effective, or legitimate. All modern States are power States, regardless of their
form of government. With no opportunity to wield power, the people, including
the middle classes, judge their government by their prosperity. The political for
them is subsumed by their need to have a successful economy. Dahrendorf, like
Taylor, believes the people can exercise real power in a liberal State, despite
their inability to participate politically, save periodic meaningless elections.
The real 'people' in power States are those who can turn their economic preferences into political programs. These 'people' invariably control vast economic
power and use their political influence to gain more wealth. The middle classes
acquiesce in this process so long as they feel economically secure. Political action is the last resort, the sign of a failed economy, not of an unfilled desire to
participate in the political process. Bismarck's Germany succeeded because it
met the needs of the political/economic elite and the middle classes. The elite,
in partnership with the government, grew wealthy and therefore more politically powerful; the middle classes grew more secure by virtue of social welfare
programs and therefore more acquiescent. This is the same formula that was
implemented by Roosevelt's New Deal and various British governments in the
twentieth century. The test of the power State is its ability to survive in a hostile
international arena. The survival of power States depends on the increasingly
important nexus of wealth and military power. Political participation becomes
a factor only when significant sections of the population believe that the State
is failing to provide them security. The kind of regime, liberal or conservative,
is irrelevant, so long as it meets this basic need.

Having resolved one of the tensions of modernization, Germany, by the last quarter of the nineteenth century, became the dominant power in Europe: 'Bismarck's triumph in Germany and Europe was complete. He had split his opponents at home and formed a new majority for his rule. He had defied or duped all Europe; he had created a new order without fully destroying the old.... Beaten, too, was the dream of a liberal, humane Germany, and born was a mighty, militaristic country that would idolize power even when that power was unrestrained by intellect or moral realism.'[77] The preeminence of the Fatherland seemed to be a wedding gift of the newly unified German State. Bismarck's synthesis seemed to avoid the Scylla and Charybdis of modernity: 'To quote Nietzsche... "The whole tendency of the Germans went against the Enlightenment, against rationalism." The belief in a special path for Germany—neither Western civilization nor Eastern barbarism, neither capitalism nor Marxism—was incredibly strong and persistent.'[78]

Containing some of the effects of political dislocation allowed for economic and demographic expansion: 'Total German industrial production overtook that of France in the seventies, caught up with the British around 1900 and surpassed it substantially by 1910.... Around 1830 four-fifths of the German population lived on the land and earned their living in agriculture; in 1860 the number had fallen to three-fifths, in 1882 to two-fifths and in 1895 it was barely one-fifth.... This is the essence of German history in that period.'[79] Another good indicator of industrial development is coal. According to Keynes, 'The output of German coal grew from about 30,000,000 tons in 1871...to 190,000,000 tons in 1913.'[80] This was the nineteenth century German transformation *par excellence*. Where Napoleon unleashed the military potential of the unified Nation-State, Germany's partial unification unleashed its economic potential. Germany became the largest economy in Europe and its population increased by more than twenty millions, while France's stagnated.[81]

More troubling to the West was that Germany's domestic production miracles, not only enabled them to become the dominant economic force east of the Rhine, it made Eastern and Central Europe as well as Turkey increasingly dependent on Germany:

There was no European country except those west of Germany which did not do more than a quarter of her trade with her; and in the case of Russia, Austria-Hungary, and Holland the proportion was greater. Germany not only furnished these countries with trade, but, in the case of some of them, supplied a greater part of the capital needed for their own development.... And by the system of peaceful penetration she gave these countries not only capital, but, what they needed hardly less, organization. The whole of Europe east of the Rhine thus fell into the German industrial orbit, and its economic life was adjusted accordingly.[82]

With rapid development came the need to make societal adjustments:

> For Central Europe the early years of industrial production were thus a period of difficult adaptation to new conditions. A sleepy land of noblemen and peasants was miraculously turning into a bustling Nation of entrepreneurs and work-ingmen, experiencing the strains of far-reaching economic and social change. Within the lifetime of one generation of Germany was forced to accept new forms of production, new methods of transportation, new social classes, new civic ideals, new demographic pressures. It proved too much for a bewildered people. The masses in their agitation began to mutter, complain and threaten, and finally they rose in open revolt against the effects of technological progress.[83]

Notwithstanding internal difficulties, including a crippling depression, Germany's economy continued to expand. This success and the anxiety it created fueled the kind of nationalism that worried Bismarck and which seemed so UnGerman to Thomas Mann. At all events, the age-old French nightmare of German power became real. What had been forestalled for almost 900 years had come to pass, with much more economic and political development on the horizon, France's domination of the Continent was over. To prevent further relative decline, France prepared for a new war hard on their humiliating defeat in 1871. Aware that the French would never accept the outcome of the Franco-Prussian War, Germany knew that they would have to defeat the French decisively to achieve what they had long expressed culturally, their political hegemony on the Continent. The day would come, *der tag*, sooner or later, and every Frenchman and German knew it. A German victory would undo centuries of humiliation and restore the Holy Roman Empire in all but name. The Roman-French Latin world, which had seduced Europe, including many Germans, would be seen for what it was: effete, weak, shallow, materialistic, imperialistic, intolerant, decadent, slavish—fundamentally anti-German. Victorious Germany would provide Western Europe with spirituality and Eastern Europe with freedom.

In the wake of the Third Reich, it is difficult to credit this lofty mission, yet Mann and countless other German authors conceived it in precisely this way. According to Fest, '[after 1866] German became a word with a virtually moralistic cast, carrying strong missionary overtones. It developed into a concept imperiously and pretentiously opposed to everything foreign.'[84] Mann's romantic vision with a negative tone. After World War Two, his notion of the German burgher seems more like a bad joke than a description of an ideal-type. Who can see a black uniform without conjuring the SS? After Auschwitz, the very notion of German ideals seems suspect. In the West, the idea of an inherently barbaric Germany has been reinforced by generations of anti-German education. Yet, unless non-Germans see the Germans as they saw themselves, they will never understand their reaction to the Great War. Mann's *Reflections* mirrored the views of the majority of educated Germans. With the Defeat, much more than a war was lost; the greater and more profound loss was Europe's last chance, under German leadership, to defeat Eastern tyranny and Western decadence. Only Germany, it was thought, appreciated the importance of a spiritual alternative to the Roman-Latin-French world view, to say nothing of its brutal alternative Soviet Russia. According to the liberal Max Weber: 'We warded off something...much worse—the Russian knout.'[85] The new Europe would host the contest between Bolshevism and Capitalism. No matter which kind of world resulted, it would be far worse that what could have been achieved with German leadership:

> Among the men who pledged themselves to the 'ideas of 1914' were Thomas Mann, Ernst Troeltsch, Frederick Meinecke, Walther Rathenau, Max Scheler, Werner Sombart, and Frederick Naumann. Despite many differences, these men generally agreed that Anglo-American liberalism was without real moral spine and wittingly or unwittingly reinforced various forces of social decay with its easy gospel of moral relativity, affluence, and universal happiness. In place of bourgeois liberalism and its materialistic values they stressed a more conservative way of life in which a sense of tradition, honor, love of country, and consciousness of the past would be highly prized. In social terms this meant an organic community without class divisions, a society in which each individual or group worked for the common good.[86]

This Defeat made the 'organic community' seem more utopian than ever.

Of course, the German view was as partial as the French. A more politically realistic, perhaps more Machiavellian, way to account for Germany's development between the Congress of Vienna and Versailles was suggested by Weber: 'Only complete political dishonesty and naïve optimism can fail to recognize that, after a period of peaceful competition, the inevitable urge of all Nations with bourgeois societies to expand their trade must now once more lead to a situation in which power alone will have a decisive influence on the extent to which individual Nations will share in the economic control of the world....'[87] The emotional fuel of the Nation in arms exacerbated international tensions, as Friedrich Paulsen warned in 1902: 'A supersensitive nationalism has become a very serious danger for all the peoples of Europe; because of it they are in danger of losing all feeling for human values. *Nationalism, pushed to an extreme, just like sectarianism, destroys moral and even logical consciousness. Just and unjust, good and bad, true and false, lose their meaning; what men condemn as disgraceful and inhuman when done by others, they recommend in the same breath to their own people as something to be done to a foreign country.*'[88]

Yet neither materialist nor Machiavellian explanations, taken by themselves, can account for the profound sense of German despair. Nor could Weimar's successes convince Germans that in defeat they gained something valuable: parliamentary government. To the contrary, the importation or, what seemed to many, the imposition, of the Weimar Republic, foretold that Germany would no longer be German. Life as *ersatz* Frenchmen appealed to few Germans:

> We know the spirit of the Weimar Constitution. It was unitary and democratic.... Insofar as the idea of a united Nation which gives itself a constitution was first realized by the French Revolution it must be said that the official philosophy of the German Republic came close to the French tradition. But only a few people believed in it.... It represented the comfortable spirit of progress without force and without excessive costs to the propertied classes: humanization of justice, constitutional reform...international understanding, particularly between Germany and France, and indifference to religious questions. These were radical bourgeois ideals from the last century. They were advocated in more extreme and more critical form...by a few writers who... now became the semi-official spokesman of the Republic, like Heinrich Mann.[89]

From the perspective of the Enlightenment, it is almost impossible to appreciate this sense of despair, this sense that the War, Weimar, and Versailles destroyed the idea of a spiritual German people. Perhaps this sense of spirituality, minimally, a sense of the limitations of materialism, romantically, a sense of transcendence, did make Germans different from other Europeans. The West did not, and perhaps could not, take German spirituality seriously. And for this reason, among many others, the West could not take the German answer to despair seriously either. Not merely defeat, but humiliation, created a sounding board for Hitler's views. Not merely material loss, as great as this was, but the loss of German identity as the savior of Europe, created an atmosphere in which extreme nationalism could flourish. The Western inability to respect or even understand how the Germans saw themselves in Europe contributed to Hitler's success. The vindictiveness and stupidity of the Versailles Treaty confirmed this proposition.

> In Paris, where those connected with the Supreme Economic Council received almost hourly reports of the misery, disorder, and decaying organization of all Central and Eastern Europe, allied and enemy alike, and learnt from the lips of the financial representatives of Germany unanswerable evidence of the terrible exhaustion of their countries, an occasional visit to the hot, dry room in the President's house, where the Four fulfilled their destinies in empty and arid intrigue, only added to the sense of nightmare. J. M. Keynes[90]

VERSAILLES: HATRED CONFIRMED

The Versailles Treaty proved to Thomas Mann and many others that Western Europe and especially France, held Germany in contempt: 'In the first place he [Georges Clemenceau, its architect] was a foremost believer in the view of German psychology that the German understands nothing but intimidation, that he is without generosity or remorse in negotiation, that there is no advantage he will not take of you, and no extent to which he will not demean himself for profit, that he is without honor, pride, or mercy.'[91] As the reverse image of Mann's view of the French, this portrait indicates the level of estrangement between the legatees of Charlemagne's Empire. Bullet-headed gorillas in dinner jackets, Germans were part of the Roman Empire as the rot from within, its insidious barbarizers and ultimate destroyers, unable to participate or contribute to Roman culture. Germany has never been part of the European story, which was written west of the Rhine. This portrait interprets the Reformation as repudiation, not only of the universal Church, but of Renaissance and Mediterranean values in general; moreover, the absence of the Spirit of 1789 amounts to a profound rejection of the Enlightenment, that is, of true European values. Things German were peculiarly and ineradicably Teutonic, that is, mystical or tribal; hence, its accomplishments in the irrational arts, music and romantic poetry. Its rational achievements were considered derivative and superficial, monkeys singing Bach or, worse, Bach as a monkey mouthing Gregorian chants. The absence of a German Nation-State testifies to its barbarity; its nationalism, primitive, particularistic, tribal, and, above all, an inability to be French. German economic development and capitalism were perceived as deeply flawed and incompletely absorbed, aborting the birth of an independent and politically active middle class. Worse than failing to conceive of the Rights of Man, Germans rejected them when presented by Napoleon as a gift. Their conceptions of freedom were contradictions in terms, a barbaric inability to understand that freedom depends on constitutionally guaranteed Natural Rights, enforced by citizens.

Their barbarism was pervasive. Instead of Paris, Germans had Berlin: 'The great pulsating city had no links with the German past; it resembled Chicago more than the small, elegant provincial capital it once had been. It was here that by far the strongest concentration of the changing German character was found. The Germany that was at odds with itself, that hatred of its own present, did not get on with Berlin; it like to think of its capital as a morass of corruption, a Babel of every sin.... Berlin lived entirely in the present, it was Germany's America....'[92] For Germans, this was far more than an aesthetic or moral judgment of a particular city in a particular time. It was a condemnation of urban life in principle, a way of living that necessarily corroded the basic agrarian, small town decency of Germans. Its sudden appearance, as the urban symbol of how Germany was becoming modern, made visible all that was wrong with the present: its pleasure-seeking, lack of discipline, 'flattering minorities by experiments of all kinds...[valuing] the snobbish and the lurid, pretending to be new and progressive.'[93] For Germans, Berlin, like Chicago, denied the German equivalent of Jeffersonian values; for the French, Berlin proved the vulgarity and unsophistication of Germans.

In conclusion, the Western imagination perceived Germany as a threat to Europe as much as it was and for the same reasons that it destroyed the Roman Empire and Christendom. Not only a product of war time propaganda or its bitter residue, it reflected the enduring antipathy of Foreign Minister Clemenceau, among many others, for Germany: 'The Old Tiger had been reared on *revanche*, and his overriding aim was to redeem French sacrifices by permanently crippling Germany.'[94] Since it was impossible to redress the balance of populations, he targeted Germany's economy, especially its industrial base. Keynes puts it this way: 'The German economic system, as it existed before the War, depended upon three main factors: I. Overseas commerce as represented by her mercantile marine, her colonies, her foreign investments, her exports, and the overseas connections of her merchants; II. The exploitation of her coal and iron and the industries dependent built upon them; III. Her transport and tariff system.... The Treaty aims at the systematic destruction of all three, but principally of the first two.'[95] Golo Mann concludes: 'With the best will in the world the Germans could not have made such an effort; their whole country was hardly worth more than the ridiculous sums demanded from it, which it was to pay in the course of a century....'[96]

As harsh as its economic provisions were, the humiliating guilt clauses rankled Germans most:

> In general the psychological affronts rather than the material exactions were what produced the extraordinarily traumatic effects of the Treaty of Versailles, so that from Right to Left, running across all factions and parties, it produced a sense of unforgettable humiliation.... The contradictions and the hypocrisies in the 440 articles of the treaty were all too evident. The victors assumed the pose of judges and insisted on the Germans' confessing their sins, where in fact their interests were purely material. The pointless and vengeful moralism was what awoke so much hatred and ridicule.[97]

The Treaty asserted that Germany was the *sole* cause of the War, the *only* guilty party, and that, as such, it had a moral obligation to compensate the Allies for its damages. Considered a betrayal of the preconditions for the Armistice, the Treaty confirmed Western duplicity and arrogance. Keynes agrees: 'The nature of the Contract between Germany and the Allies [which produced the Armistice]... is plain and unequivocal. The terms of the peace are to be in accordance with the Addresses of the President, and the purpose of the Peace Conference is "to discuss the details of their application."'[98] I am not suggesting that Germany did not lose the War. Nevertheless, it seems clear that there would have been no Armistice, if the Allies' true intentions had been stated.

Moreover, this duplicitous Allied behavior was stupid and futile, not simply dishonest and vindictive: 'The reason lies largely in the tactlessness of the victorious Allies who, boldly anticipating the findings of scholars, prejudged their own case by including in the peace treaty a reference to Germany's sole guilt for the war. On this paragraph they based their demand for reparations; therefore in order to destroy the whole moral and legal foundation of the Versailles Treaty German historians only had to refute the theory that Germany alone was responsible for the war.'[99] The Treaty was both too harsh and too lenient, making almost every error possible in a peace settlement. It was too harsh to induce Germans to see themselves as respected members of the European community and too lenient to prevent Germany from menacing France, even for a generation. Clemenceau could not turn Germany into the world's biggest dairy and still have Germany pay reparations for decades, his contradictory goals forcing compromise.

Beyond the Treaty's provisions, its manner of negotiation and its historical context made it nearly impossible for it to succeed. The Germans were instructed to sign it—take it or leave it. '[Many Germans] called the Treaty a dictation which indeed it was, because genuine negotiations had taken place only between the victors, not between victors and vanquished.'[100] Fatefully, the precarious Weimar Republic acquiesced to this gratuitous ultimatum, a shame it never expiated: 'These deceptions [of Versailles] hung like a millstone round the neck of the new German republic and oppressed the future of Europe as the great war itself, had it been terminated with a modicum of sense, could not have done.'[101] To reject the Treaty courted invasion. To accept it, in the face of nearly unanimous condemnation by the German public, now encouraged to speak out, reduced Weimar's chances of success. By accepting a treaty, which most Germans saw as a dishonorable and preposterous denial of German humanity, Weimar gave its many enemies weapons it could not combat. According to Fest, 'To a growing number of Germans the very term "republic" seemed synonymous with disgrace, dishonor, and powerlessness. The feeling persisted that it was something imposed on the Germans by deception and coercion, that it was something altogether alien to their nature.'[102] Furthermore: 'To [Germans] all this [the Weimar Republic and Versailles] was a fall from grace, an act of metaphysical treason and profound unfaithfulness to true selfhood. Only treachery could have delivered

Germany, romantic, pensive, apolitical Germany, into servitude to that idea of Western civilization which threatened her very essence.'[103]

It should now be obvious that the Versailles Treaty did not *conclude* the Great War. A pause in hostilities, Versailles was as ephemeral as the Weimar Republic and for many of the same reasons.[104] It did punish Germany, only temporarily disabling German militarism. It did not intend to unite the Germans under a charismatic dictator, but, by so doing, nearly destroyed Europe. Versailles failed and deserved to fail, because it was conceived in anger, vengeance, ignorance, perversity, and fear. Worse, it did so in the name of the Enlightenment, as it denied reason, fundamental rights, universal values, and common humanity. In the name of civilization, it extolled force. In the name of prudence, it applied force foolishly, incompletely, and ineffectively. In the name of civilization, it contributed to the rise of the Third Reich, whose victory would have plunged Europe into a new dark age, the more horrific for being under the aegis of a modern State with a racial Social Darwinist ideology. Keynes concludes: 'The policy of reducing Germany to servitude for a generation, of degrading the lives of millions of human beings, and of depriving a whole Nation of happiness should be abhorrent and even detestable, even if it were possible, even if it enriched ourselves, even if it did not sow the decay of the whole civilized life of Europe.'[105] It requires no deep understanding of human nature or European history to predict in 1919 that Germany would even its score with France and Britain or die trying.

> Unprepared politically and psychologically, the Nation...which believed in the superiority of its arms as in a gospel was plunged into an abyss. Joachim Fest[106]

PARTICULARISM *RECIDIVUS*

The following analysis, by no means uncontroversial, lends credence to Hitler's account for the German collapse. The ensuing discussion of *Mein Kampf* focuses on Hitler's remedies, which, while far more controversial than his diagnosis, derive from it. German victory in the Great War depended on several factors, most important of which was that hostilities would last only a few months at most. Outnumbered and out produced by the Franco-Russian alliance, only a short war would give German military superiority in leadership, planning, training, tactics, and strategy a chance to prevail. Secondly, German victory depended on the aloofness of the Sea Powers, Great Britain and the United States. Britain, however, continued its Balance of Power policy, whose prime imperative was the prevention of a master State in Europe. Ignoring age-old Franco-British animosity, Britain supported France with significant ground forces and a naval blockade, which, when reinforced by the United States, caused severe shortages of food and fuel in Germany. Finally, American intervention in 1917–1918 administered the *coup de gras*. In these circumstances, after four years of unprecedented carnage, despite the early capitulation of Bolshevik Russia, Germany knew it could not win. Collapsing under the weight of a million fresh American troops, famine at home, and unacceptable casualties in the field, Germany recast its plans in line with President Wilson's Fourteen Points, summed up as a 'peace without victors,' hopes which the Versailles Treaty destroyed. Its monarchy overthrown, a parliamentary government installed at Weimar, headed by the Marxist Social Democrat Party, betrayed Germany signed the Treaty, reluctantly and despairingly.

Age-old fault lines fissured, the most important of which was Particularism. After the Defeat, it took a form suited to modern representative governments. Instead of scores of sovereign German States, the aftermath of the War produced a score of parties, most of which were identified with a single interest, religion, or region. Nation-States with traditions of parliamentary rule and experience with interest group politics find it difficult to advance common goals. Each pressure group, if it cannot achieve its principal purpose, strives to block actions in the public interest. In Weimar Germany, the lack of parliamentary experience by ordinary Germans and by party activists aggravated the problem. The sordid jockeying for petty preferment, the overweening expediency, which marks all party systems, seemed worse to Germans. Rather than accept selfishness, ambition, corruption, or short-sightedness as endemic to human nature, Germans saw it as fundamentally anti-German, inherent in the West, but alien to Germany. The dream of the German united in a Nation-State seemed, in its expression in the Weimar Republic, an unfunny joke. In addition to the many severe problems consequent to the Defeat, a near universal despair set in, taking two forms. One was the cynicism reflected in 'Mahogany' and the degeneration of traditional German values incarnated by post-war Berlin. The other was a resurgence of the traditional *Volkisch* values and attitudes.

These developments revived the romantic concept of the German Nation, often wrapped in Christian garments:

> Fichte believed in man and humanity and probably also in God with a seriousness that only a few no-longer Christians have shown. He believed in the spirit as the creator of all things which are nothing without it and in the right of the individual to develop himself properly in freedom .... From the right of the individual he came to the State as the omnipotent agent which alone could guarantee that right, and from there he quickly arrived at what today is called the totalitarian State, the State as unrestricted ruler of education and economic life. From the all-powerful State he came finally to the Nation and the Nation-State.[107]

Note the significance of philosophers and poets in German political thought. Even the heavily theoretical American Founding was more legal than philosophical. Unique in another respect, German poets, especially in the nineteenth century, tended toward nostalgia: 'Novalis, Brentano, Arnim, and Tieck wrote beautiful poems. They created a magic garden for the Germans in which new gardeners continued to labor until the middle of the century. But this was another world from that of society and politics, and for our purposes we should not be discussing it. Except that even here there were links with politics. It was the German Middle Ages that attracted the poets....'[108] The partial unification under Bismarck resolved some of the difficulties of Particularism, as the Franco-Prussian War demonstrated. A power to be reckoned with, Germany was not, however, the sort of State for which many Germans had longed. Providing effective government, the German State, nonetheless, kept its people at arm's length. By not integrating Germans into the State, even as an ideal, the major conflict of the Bismarck era 'was between the German people and the Prussian State, between majority and authority, ruled and rulers.'[109] Few Germans came to love the power State: 'The frightening thing about the German victory [in the Franco-Prussian War] was that new-Germany only showed force, blank, effective force, without any happy message. Its triumph was nothing but a material one and such triumphs bring no blessing.'[110] Nor could the power State create more than a shallow and ephemeral unity: 'This feeling of unity [at the beginning of the Great War] was an illusion. The old contradictions survived behind the image of a Nation reconciled. A welter of motives underlay the surge of rejoicing: personal and patriotic wishful thinking, revolutionary impulses, antisocial rebellions, dreams of hegemony, and, always, the yearning of adventurous spirits to break out of the routine of the bourgeois order.'[111] Many Germans believed bourgeois prosperity submerged its warrior spirit, a dominant theme in *Mein Kampf*.

Hitler's views found fertile soil, prepared by no less a thinker than Nietzsche. Scholarly opinion runs the gamut from adulation to outrage, nowhere more so than regarding Nietzsche's views on war. He invited reductionism, making him all-too-easy for Hitler and other National Socialists to co-opt. His aphoristic style, his brevity, his ellipses—all tend to isolate his thoughts, making them seem complete, more final than Nietzsche intended. Presented the way a jeweler presents diamonds, singly on a velvet cloth, dancing under a bright light, cold and hard, his ideas perform. Consider the following quotations. They resonated again and again in the words of National Socialists:

'Only fighting yields/ Happiness on earth, / And on battlefields/ Friendship has its birth. / One in three are friends: / Brothers in distress, / Equals, facing foes, / free—when facing death.'[112]

'Hatred, the mischievous delight in the misfortune of others, the lust to rob and dominate, and whatever else is called evil belongs to the most amazing economy of the preservation of the species.'[113]

'The strongest and most evil spirits have so far done the most to advance humanity....'[114]

'Soldiers and leaders still have far better relationships with each other than workers and employers. So far at least, culture that rests on a military basis still towers above all so-called industrial culture: the latter in its present shape is altogether the most vulgar form of existence....'[115]

'One cannot fail to see at the bottom of all these noble races the beast of prey, the splendid blond beast prowling about avidly in search of spoil and victory; this hidden core needs to erupt from time to time, the animal has to get out again and go back to the wilderness: the Roman, Arabian, Germanic, Japanese nobility, the Homeric heroes, the Scandinavian Vikings—they all shared this need.'[116]

'The deep and icy mistrust the German still arouses today whenever he gets into a position of power is an echo of that inextinguishable horror with which Europe observed for centuries that raging of the blond Germanic beast (although between the old Germanic tribes and us Germans there hardly exists a conceptual relationship, let alone one of blood).'[117]

'The *sick* are man's greatest danger; *not* the evil, *not* the beasts of prey. Those who are failures from the start, downtrodden, crushed—it is they, the *weakest*, who undermine life among men, who call into question and poison most dangerously our trust in life, in man, and in ourselves.'[118]

'*Unfortunately*, man is no longer evil enough; Rousseau's opponents who say "man is a beast of prey" are unfortunately wrong.'[119]

'I am glad about the military development of Europe; also of the internal States of anarchy.... Personal *manly virtu, virtu* of the body is regaining value; estimation becomes more physical, nutrition meatier. Beautiful men are again becoming possible.... The barbarian in each of us is affirmed; also the wild beast.'[120]

'Life is will to power.'[121]

'*In summa*: so that man may respect himself he must be capable of doing evil.'[122]

'Now, no philosopher will be in any doubt as to the type of perfection in politics; that is Machiavellianism. But Machiavellianism *pur, sans mélange, cru, vert, dans toute sa force, dans toute son âpreté*, is superhuman divine, transcendental, it will never be achieved by man, at most approximated.'[123]

'The victory of a moral ideal is achieved by the same immoral means as every victory: force, lies, slander, injustice.'[124]

'My insight: all the forces and drives by virtue of which life and growth exist lie under the ban of morality: morality as the instinct to deny life. One must destroy morality if one is to liberate life.'[125]

'Everyone desires that no doctrine or valuation of things should come into favor but that through which he himself prospers. The basic tendency of the weak and mediocre of all ages is, consequently, to weaken and pull down the stronger: chief means, the moral judgment. The attitude of the stronger toward the weaker is branded; the higher States of the stronger acquire an evil name.'[126]

'And if you do not want to have a destiny, do not want to be pitiless, how can you come with me—and conquer? And if your hardness will not flash and cut to pieces, how can you come with me—and create? For the creators are hard. It must be bliss to press your hands on the will of millennia as on wax—bliss to engrave the will of millennia in steel—harder than steel, more precious than steel. The most precious can only be very hard.'[127]

The content and the tone of these remarks make the transition to *Mein Kampf* all too easy.

We have a different faith—we consider the democratic movement not only a degenerate for of political organization but a degenerate and diminished form of man, the cause of his mediocrity and devaluation. Nietzsche[128]

It certainly is no pleasure to examine Hitler as a political thinker to the point that critical analysis demands. Nevertheless it seems necessary to do so for two opposite reasons. First, because until it has been done a greater portion of Hitler's theoretical ideas than one might think will survive, and not only among Germans or among the avowed followers of Hitler. Secondly, because until the misconceptions in these ideas are clearly separated from what was more or less correct in them, the correct elements are in danger of being made taboo simply because Hitler thought so. Sebastian Haffner[129]

MEIN KAMPF: THE SOURCES OF DEFEAT

It cannot be surprising that *Mein Kampf* has been controversial. In virtually every respect, its reviewers and interpreters, even leaving aside the ideologically committed, have disagreed regarding its value, honesty, and purpose. Though a best seller, some scholars claim it was not influential. Moreover, *Mein Kampf* has been widely ridiculed, as a turgid, incoherent outpouring of clichés, half-truths and racist nonsense, the notions of a self-educated (read ignorant) crank. Subjected to facile destructive criticism, *Mein Kampf* has been dismissed as the delusions of a maniacal racist. Since *Mein Kampf* must be read in the shadow of Auschwitz, to treat it seriously inevitably condones racism and genocide. Consider, for example, Hitler's emphases on youth, health, and beauty. While no one praises old age, infirmity, or ugliness, readers are invited to associate youth, health, and beauty with National Socialism's racism.[130] Acknowledging that preferring youth, health, and beauty might have racist implications, can it be proper to condemn the concepts in principle? Accepting *arguendo* that it is politically incorrect to evaluate people entirely by these criteria, can we properly ignore the positive role they have played in nearly all societies? More to the point, is it possible to understand Hitler or his appeal without considering how these values grounded his political approach?

Less justifiable is the virtual silence of Hitler's commentators regarding his views on unemployment, the plight of the working poor, the difficulty of holding family life together in periods of economic uncertainty, the necessity for responsible behavior by employees and employers, and a host of other similar concerns. To cripple the ability to understand an author for fear of making a manifestly evil person into a complicated human being does more than distort reality; it allows evil a free ride. To turn such a person into a Hollywood caricature, as Chaplin did in *the Great Dictator,* disarms his enemies. Clowns inspire ridicule not fear: 'The fellow who had obviously had to overcome his insignificance and borrow character for himself from a mustache, a forelock, and a uniform...was for some time the favorite butt of European humor.'[131] At best, *Mein Kampf* has been praised for its analysis of propaganda and to a lesser extent for its organizational insights. Although some scholars have credited Hitler's acumen regarding international politics, only a handful of the innumerable serious works on the Third Reich have treated *Mein Kampf* as coherent political analysis. One of the exceptions is Ian Kershaw. 'However base and repellent they [the ideas in *Mein Kampf*] were, they amounted to a set of clearly established and rigidly upheld political principles:'[132] Nor does Kershaw grudge its importance: 'The very inflexibility and quasi-messianic commitment to an idea, a set of beliefs that were unalterable, simple, internally consistent and comprehensive, gave Hitler the strength of will and a sense of choosing his own destiny that left its mark on all who came into contact with him.'[133]

To be sure, *Mein Kampf* has many flaws. What seven hundred page book doesn't? Yes, it does not meet scholarly standards, and it is suffused with many dubious ideas. For all that, it must be remembered that it was the work of a practicing politician. Before dismissing *Mein Kampf,* one should ask how many world class political leaders have been capable of writing a work of equivalent scope and coherence. Perhaps only Churchill. Certainly not Stalin or de Gaulle. Roosevelt did not even try. None of Churchill's works has had the importance of *Mein Kampf.* No other leader in history has explained what he wanted to do and why he wanted to do it better than Hitler. No other leader has come closer to fulfilling his program than Hitler. *Mein Kampf* needs to be understood, if only as a warning. For, according to Fest, 'Hitler did not come as a thief in the night. With his histrionic verbosity he revealed, more perhaps than any other politician, what he had been aiming for through all the byways and tactical maneuvers: dictatorship, anti-Semitism, conquest of living space.'[134] One of Hitler's greatest advantages was that he was underestimated by his adversaries, left and right, in and out of Germany. Kershaw asks in his introduction: 'How do we explain how someone with so few intellectual gifts and social attributes, someone no more than an empty vessel outside his political life, unapproachable and impenetrable even for those in his close company, incapable it seems of genuine friendship, without the background that bred high office, without even any experience of government before becoming Reich Chancellor, could nevertheless have such an immense historical impact, could make the entire world hold its breath?'[135] The force of Kershaw's statement is intensified by his inability to answer it without contradiction. His account of Hitler's accomplishments makes it impossible to conceive of Hitler without remarkable traits, which Kershaw fails to acknowledge. Fest puts it this way, although not without a discussion which separates goodness from greatness: 'The eruption he unleashed was stamped throughout almost every one of its stages, down to the weeks of final collapse, by his guiding will.... To a virtually unprecedented degree, he created everything out of himself and was himself everything at once; his own teacher, organizer of a party and author of its ideology, tactician and demagogic savior, leader, statesman, and for a decade the axis of the world.'[136] He adds, 'In this ability to uncover the deeper spirit and tendencies of the age and to represent those tendencies, there certainly is an element of greatness.'[137] I have tried hard not to underestimate Hitler. Here, I deal only with *Mein Kampf's* political theory; its political theology and its racial anti-Semitism are reserved for latter chapters.

Mann wrote *Reflections* before the Defeat, before the Weimar Republic, before Versailles, before the Communist take-over of Munich, the hyperbolic inflation, and before the massive suffering of the German people in the years after the War—in short, before all his worst fears were realized. Hitler dictated the first volume of *Mein Kampf,* while serving his prison sentence in 1924. His appreciation of the continuing catastrophe is much more intense than Mann's premonitions. So, too, are his convictions regarding the root of the German Defeat and, as he termed it, 'collapse.' Weimar, with its Marxist Social Democrats in the lead and with the Communists at their heels, could not but make matters worse. It is important to realize 'worse' does not mean materially worse, important as economic hardship was to the extreme parties, right and left. According to *Mein Kampf*, the cause of the German collapse was a persistent decline in spiritual values and a concomitant rise in the belief in the sufficiency of the material world, its goods and its services. The strength of Marxist parties, democratic and revolutionary, signified this deterioration. The economic

fortunes of Weimar Germany were irrelevant to his concerns, except as economic downturns decreased confidence in republican Germany. Like Mann, and
countless other Germans, Hitler believed that the price of prosperity, coming at
the expense of Germany's national culture and mission, would be too high. To
Mann's critique he infuses a powerful strain of *Volkisch* thought, radicalized by
a race-based anti-Semitism. To Mann's general respect for war and warrior virtues, *Mein Kampf* adds that war is not only natural and necessary but desirable,
a creative and purifying force. Not only would war annihilate their enemies,
it would cleanse Germans of decadent ideas. *Mein Kampf* does not deny that
the War was lost on the battlefield, but characteristically lays the blame on the
deterioration of German society: 'No, this military collapse was itself only the
consequence of a larger number of symptoms of disease and their causes, which
even in peacetime were with the German Nation. This was the first consequence,
catastrophic and visible to all, of an ethical and moral poisoning, of a diminution of the instinct for self-preservation and its preconditions, which for many
years had begun to undermine the foundations of the people and the Reich.'[138]
While civilian cowardice and duplicity did contribute to an erosion of the home
front's support of the military, the reason for the Defeat lay much deeper in
German society: 'Unfortunately, the military defeat of the German people is not
an undeserved catastrophe, but the deserved chastisement of Eternal retribution.
We more than deserved this defeat. It is only the greatest outward symptom of
decay amid a whole series of inner symptoms....'[139] The extraordinary successes
of the German economy in the nineteenth century immersed Germans in a web
of materialist values. 'We no longer had the slightest idea concerning the essence of the force which can lead men to their death of their own free will and
decision.'[140] Practical concerns have their place: [But] 'the material interests of
man can always thrive best as long as they remain in the shadow of heroic virtues; but as soon as they attempt to enter the primary sphere of existence, they
destroy the basis for their own existence.'[141] Germany lost because its spiritual
foundations of heroism and victory were undermined by materialism, defined
as the belief in the sufficiency of material life, expressed individually and insti-
tutionally in the stock exchange. 'In proportion as economic life grew to be the
dominant mistress of the State, money became the god whom all had to serve
and to whom each man had to bow down.'[142] And further, 'The stock exchange
began to triumph and prepared slowly but surely to take the life of the Nation
into its guardianship and control.'[143] Hitler's reasons for the Defeat do not deny
its material factors. Nor do they differ significantly from Mann's *Reflections*.
Mein Kampf calls for a rebirth of the German spirit, heroically defined, ignoring
Mann's belief that the burgher can be part or the revitalization of the German
Spirit. Nor does *Mein Kampf* agree with the historians who blame Germany's
inability to absorb a modern economy.

Before we elaborate, appreciating how much Hitler's remedies diverge from German mainstream thought, it is necessary to note his sympathy with the plight of ordinary Germans: 'The entire economy suffers bitterly from the individual's insecurity in earning his daily bread.'[144] *Mein Kampf* depicts the difficulties of unemployment in terms which an American social worker could subscribe to:

> The consequence [of unemployment] is that once the man obtains work he irresponsibly forgets all ideas of order and discipline, and begins to live luxuriously for the pleasures of the moment. This upsets even the small weekly budget, as even here any intelligent apportionment is lacking; in the beginning it suffices for five days instead of seven, later for only three, finally scarcely for one day, and in the end it is drunk up the very first night. Often he has a wife and children at home. Sometimes they, too, are infected by this life, especially when the man is good to them on the whole and actually loves them in his own way.... It ends badly if the man goes his own way from the very beginning and the woman, for the children's sake, opposes him.... When at length he comes home on Sunday or even Monday night, drunk and brutal, but always parted from his last cent, such scenes often occur that God have mercy.[145]

Nor is unemployment the sole difficulty of the German worker. His employers have made his situation a misery: '*Since on innumerable occasions the bourgeoisie has in the clumsiest and most immoral way opposed demands which were justified from the universal human point of view, often without obtaining or even justifiably expecting any profit from such an attitude, even the most self-respecting worker was driven out of the trade-union organization into political activity.*'[146] Bourgeois attitudes add insult to injury: 'As long as there are employers with little social understanding or a deficient sense of justice and propriety, it is not only the right but the duty of their employees, who certainly constitute a part of our Nationality, to protect the interests of the general public against the greed and unreason of the individual; for the preservation of loyalty and faith in a social group is just as much to the interest of the Nation as the preservation of a people's health.'[147] *Mein Kampf* concludes that workers need to organize to counter their employers' tyrannical behavior. '*And this makes it obvious that the power of the employer concentrated in a single person can only be countered by the mass of employees banded into a single person, if the possibility of victory is not to be renounced in advance.*'[148] *Mein Kampf* is unusually sensitive to the humiliation of charity, however well meaning. 'I do not know which is more terrible: inattention to the social misery such as we see every day among the majority of those who have been favored by fortune or who have risen by their own efforts, or else the snobbish, or at times tactless and obtrusive, condescension of certain women of fashion...who feed the people.'[149] Concluding: '*Social activity must never and on no account be directed toward philanthropic flim-flam, but rather toward the elimination of the basic deficiencies in the organization of our economic and cultural life that must—or at all events can—lead to the regeneration of the individual.*'[150]

Of course, Hitler did not want Western style labor unions. Yet, until National Socialism took over German society, he believed organized labor was the only way that German workers could relieve their conditions. '*The National Socialist trade union is no organ of the class struggle, but an organ for representing occupational interests.*'[151] Labor organization implies responsibility for both workers and employers: '*The National Socialist worker must know that the prosperity of the National economy means his own material happiness. The National Socialist employer must know that the happiness and contentment of his workers is the premise for the existence and development of its own economic greatness.*'[152] On the basis of these ideas, Hitler attracted non-Marxist German workers to National Socialism.

Had the Weimar Republic and its left of center parties been able to deal with the political aspects of the German economy, they might have blunted Hitler's appeal to workers, building on its material successes. Golo Mann explains:

> Although immediately after the War the income of the Nation had fallen to about half of its pre-war level, ten years later it was back to where it had been, or even higher. All the worn-out, antiquated equipment, all the things handed over after the War were replaced. Germany had the most modern merchant fleet, the fastest railways and an adequate system of roads. In matters of high politics the State behaved as though it were stumbling from one crisis to another.... But the administration was good, the workers worked well, the inventors, engineers and technicians were good. Industrial planning was magnificent and effective.[153]

Unable to exploit its accomplishments; much less take credit, as all successful governments do, for the good things that happen during their rule, Weimar's difficulty was more political than economic. When unemployment moderated or wages rose, employers took the credit. 'One cannot accuse the German industrialists of not taking their job seriously. In a certain sense they regarded themselves as responsible for the Nation and for their workers, as implied by the German word *Arbeitgeber*—one who gives work—for employer, which has no equivalent in English or French.'[154] When the government operated effectively and honestly, the State, not Weimar, received the credit. Fest sums up the real accomplishments of Weimar and their negative effects on Hitler's reach for power: 'The government meanwhile had successfully continued the stabilization efforts of 1923–4. A new reparations agreement, the Treaty of Locarno, the acceptance of Germany into the League of Nations, the Kellogg

Pact, and finally some reconciliation between Germany and France...all these factors indicated that the trend of the times was toward the relaxation of tensions, a trend to which the strained radicalism of Nazism was opposed.'[155]

Weimar contributed to its failure. The Marxist ideology of its iconic party, the Social Democrats, prevented it from praising the still essentially bourgeois economy. Despite behaving like bourgeois parties, with whom they increasingly cooperated, Social Democrats bathed in Marxist clichés. Political incompetence made it impossible for Weimar to attract loyal supporters beyond the grounds of 'What have you done for me lately?' The Social Democrats not only confused their constituents, they confused themselves: 'Their [Social Democrats] theoretical position, however, remained obscure. Although in fact they had left the Communist Manifesto a long way behind, they had never openly rejected it.... [They] continued to use Marxian jargon and ideas in their speeches. But for Marx the bourgeois republic has at best been only a springboard to other things. What then was the Weimar Republic? Was it a State of the people, of the workers? If not, was the real thing, the socialist revolution, yet to come?'[156]

Typical of parliamentary regimes, the Weimar Republic compromised, falling between two stools, giving workers more than employers could absorb, without providing workers a sense of self-esteem or employers a sense that they were not class enemies. The Republic fed the workers' bodies, for a while, without feeding their souls, while driving employers further to the Right. Consider Franz Neumann's account of Weimar's dilemma: 'The Revolution of 1918 had not been the work of the liberals, but of the Socialist parties and trade unions, even though against the will and inclination of the leadership. True, it had not been a socialist revolution: property was not expropriated, the large estates were not subdivided, and the State machine was not destroyed, the bureaucracy was still in power. Nevertheless, working class demands for a greater share in determining the destiny of the State had to be satisfied.'[157] The failure of left-wing parliamentary democracy to develop loyalty allowed the masses, which *per force* meant the workers, to see in Hitler a possible solution to their plight. It needs to be remembered that many of Hitler's early followers, like Goebbels and the Strassers, were avowed socialists. Fischer describes the form of socialism that was able to lure traditional socialists into the National Socialist movement:

Socialism in Hitler's mind was not to be taken in its degenerate Marxist sense of class struggle and proletarian equality but in Oswald Spengler's meaning of Prussian socialism based on class harmony, hard work, obedience, and service to the State.... Socialism was thus ultimately linked with nationalism because a homogeneous and prosperous whole requires the love and commitment of its members; but that commitment is also reciprocal: the whole must care for the individual parts. Germans must be taught that they work not just for their own selfish ends but for the good of the Nation; and by working for the collective, Germans should be secure in the knowledge that the State, in turn works on their behalf by guaranteeing them a good livelihood, conducive working conditions, unemployment benefits, old-age pensions, free education, and other social benefits.[158]

Despite some significant improvements in the economy during the twenties, the German economy remained brittle and volatile, confirming Keynes's predictions. The Versailles Treaty made Germany the disproportionate victim of every economic downturn. Waiting for disaster, the Republic seemed to welcome the barbarians, if only to relieve the drabness of German life. According to Golo Mann:

> The Weimar Republic somehow survived the melancholy facts of its origin, the Treaty of Versailles, the limited, but ugly, civil wars of the first four years, the occupation of the Ruhr, the inflation, the blind fury of the Communists, the arrogant indifference of the Army, the sullen refractoriness of the upper classes, bureaucracy, judiciary and universities—and to its own surprise it even experienced a period of reasonable health. But the arrival of the second economic crisis and the unleashing of all the furies of demagogy—that was the last straw.[159]

The Republic's weakness did not surprise Hitler, any more than it surprised Max Weber, one of its founders, who said, 'A new order which is the product of this terrible defeat and violation is unlikely to take roots.'[160] While Hitler appreciated how devastating Versailles was to the economy, his critique of Weimar struck deep in the heart of parliamentary politics. The 'November criminals,' who fashioned it, were as much a consequence of long term economic and political deficiencies as they were of the Defeat. By eroding the German character, materialism left it vulnerable to opportunists. To believe that the political expression of bourgeois society, parliamentary politics, could cure the defects of materialism was absurd. The Great Depression made Hitler seem as prophetic as Keynes and for more profound reasons, calling into question German adjustments to the changes of the nineteenth century. According to Fest, 'The most prominent characteristic of the Depression in Germany was its totality.... The turn of events in Germany simply cannot be adequately considered in terms of the objective economic conditions. For it was more than an economic slump; it was a psychological shock.'[161] When the Western economy proved to be as shallow, fragile, and unable to right itself, as Weimar, the reestablishment of true German values seemed the only way out. Of course, even among those who agreed with the diagnosis of German problems, there was wide disagreement regarding their remedies. Nonetheless, Hitler's were about to be given a chance.

Mein Kampf offers three remedies to German difficulties. The first: revivify the concept of the *Volksgemeinschaft* as the basis of German Nationalism. The second: make Germany economically self-sufficient by the acquisition of *lebensraum*. The third: the development of and adherence to the *Fuehrer* Principle. Implicit in these three objectives is the destruction of anything or anyone who would impede their development: the Versailles Treaty, the Weimar Republic, and Western values. Their imputation to Jews by anti-Semites is reserved for a later chapter. Here I consider the appeal these remedies had for the great majority of Germans.

The centerpiece of the revivified German society, the *Volk* should not be translated because: "*Volk*" is a much more comprehensive term than "people," for German thinkers ever since the birth of German Romanticism in the late eighteenth century "*Volk*" signified the union of a group of people with a transcendental "essence." This essence might be called "nature" or "cosmos" or "mythos," but in each instance it was fused with man's innermost nature, and represented the source of his creativity, his depth of feeling, his individuality, and his unity with other members of the *Volk*.'[162] To this cardinal principle *Mein Kampf* adds a racial emphasis, distinguishing the concept from its materialist conditions: 'It is not a collection of economic contracting parties in a definite delimited living space for the fulfillment of economic tasks, but the organization of a community of physically and psychologically similar living beings for the better facilitation of the maintenance of the species and the achievement of the aim which has been allotted to this species by Providence.'[163] Always under attack, racial purity must be defended: '*What we must fight for is to safeguard the existence and the reproduction of our race and our people, the sustenance of our children and the purity of our blood, the freedom and independence of the Fatherland, so that our people may mature for the fulfillment of the mission allotted to it by the Creator of the universe.*'[164]

Hitler's religious terminology reflects *Volkisch* ideas, especially when linked with *Geist,* meaning in this context, 'Spirit:' 'The community of the *Volk* constituted the unity for which the soul yearned. Its existence and vitality were a prerequisite for that intuitive grasp of the cosmos which signified the function of the true *Geist*…. The true community consisted of those who lived in the *Geist*; its members were bound together by a shared experience of the absolute which gave them strength and heightened their sense of life.'[165] Consistent with his assessment that Germans have been corrupted by materialism, Hitler writes that building the *Volksgemeinschaft* would require a major educational effort, an undertaking which would radically transform contemporary educational models which emphasized academic excellence: 'First place [in education] must be taken by the development of character, especially the promotion of will power and determination, combined with the training of joy in responsibility, and only in last place come scientific schooling.'[166] Moreover: '*His whole education and training must be so ordered as to give him the conviction that he is absolutely superior to others....*'[167] It is important to realize that contemporary Germans were not yet Aryans; their superiority consisting in their Aryan potential. 'The process of transformation and equalization will not be completed in ten or twenty years; experience shows that it comprises of many generations.'[168] Note that by 'equal' Hitler does not mean 'equality,' as the West tends to conceive it, but that 'it must be a greater honor to be a street-cleaner and citizen of this Reich than a king in a foreign State.'[169] The significance of this sort of equality, based on belonging to the *Volk*, enables its members to feel superior to everyone not included, leaving open the possibility of a meritocratic society, while avoiding the resentment generated in societies that oscillate between notions of equality of opportunity and of outcomes. Spiritual equality allows for material inequality to prevail without the resentment normally entailed. 'The best State constitution and State form is that which, with the most unquestioned certainty, raises the best minds in the National community to leading position and leading influence.'[170] Less gifted people would not be ignored. 'Rooted in the *Volk*, the worker would recapture his individual and creative self, and would thus be able to function as a Medieval artisan rather than as an alienated modern proletarian.'[171] In conclusion, notwithstanding the exclusiveness of the *Volksgemeinschaft*, the concept appealed to many Germans, who would not have considered themselves racists or anti-Semites. Pride in the *Volk* did not, for them, imply contempt of others. *Volk* could mean what 'burgher' meant for Thomas Mann, a spiritually infused concept, one peculiarly German, neighborly, not racist or aggressive. Kershaw disagrees, conceiving *Volkisch* thought as follows:

> The central strands of *Volkisch* ideology were extreme nationalism, racial anti-Semitism, and mystical notions of a uniquely German social order, with roots in the Teutonic past, resting on order, harmony, and hierarchy. Most significant was the linkage of a romanticized view of Germanic culture (seen as superior but heavily threatened by inferior but powerful forces, particularly Slavs and Jews), with a Social Darwinian emphasis upon the struggle for survival, imperialist notions of the need for expansion to the Slavic east in order to safeguard national survival, and the necessity of bringing about racial purity and a new elite by eradicating the perceived arch-enemy of Germandom, the spirit of Jewry.[172]

There is no question that Kershaw has correctly stated *Volkisch* thought, *as radicalized by Hitler*. Nor is there any doubt that Hitler implemented the homicidal version of *Volkisch* ideology. It is important, however, to distinguish mainstream *Volkisch* ideas from their extreme versions. Although *Volkisch* ideas are undoubtedly racist, their most radical expression did not occur until years after Hitler achieved power.

The second pillar of Hitler's program, *lebensraum*, living space, is more difficult to see benignly, even when shorn of its racist underpinnings, for it represents business as usual for Big Power politics.[173]

> They were all alike, the great powers, new and old, the would-be great powers and the little ones, Germany and Russia, Italy and Serbia and Montenegro. They all wanted to inflict diplomatic defeats on their neighbors, to extend their territories under some pretext or other, to protect their protégés, to redeem their unredeemed brothers, to play their national anthems where hitherto they had not been allowed, to raise their flags and to introduce their police in new places. They all wanted to enlarge their armies, to improve their guns and to make every conceivable preparation for war which was bound to come one day.[174]

The nineteenth century, culminating in the Great War, reinforced the powerful nexus between wealth and military capability and its consequent militarism. Hence forward, the struggle for the preservation of the Nation-State implies that all the resources of a given society were at the disposal of the military. To be militarily effective implies economic self-sufficiency, at least with regard to strategic resources, food, fuel, metals, technology, population, and the like: if possessed, protected, if not, taken. Not so situated before the War, Germany paid a heavy price. Typically, Hitler struck at the core of German weakness: the lack of strategic resources, principally, food and energy.

Taking Eastern lands, weakening the Bolshevik State, achieving economic independence would guarantee Germany's survival. France would either accept the German hegemony or be conquered. Britain would tend to its Empire, so long as it had little to fear from the Continent. '*England's desire is and remains the prevention and rise of a continental power of world-historical importance; that is, the maintenance of a certain balance of power between the European States; for this seems the presupposition of British world hegemony.*'[175] Fest argues that Hitler had reason to believe that the British would accept a more powerful Germany. 'British Statesmen who believed in [Balance of Power] policy had long been watching with uneasiness France's overpowering influence on the Continent.'[176] Fest concludes, 'The core of his [Hitler's] thesis was that Germany, in her militarily, politically, and geographically threatened middle position, could survive "only by ruthlessly placing power politics in the foreground."'[177] Although Hitler generally understood British foreign policy objectives, he overestimated their traditional enmity with France. Furthermore, he did not seem to realize that their overseas Empire seemed more precarious to the British than it did to him. Britain was well aware of the ability of nineteenth century Germany to threaten British control of the Middle East and the trade routes to Asia. Still pursuing Balance of Power policies, Britain's prime objective remained the prevention of a European master State.

Perhaps the point can be made clearer by considering U.S./Japanese relations. In the Pacific, Japan tried to make itself impervious to economic sanctions by the West. With virtually no strategic resources, Japan had to dominate its region, then in European imperialist control, or be subordinate to the U.S. When in 1941, the U.S. tightened it embargo of strategic goods, Japan responded with the attack on Pearl Harbor. Branding Japan an aggressive, immoral State, the Sea Powers, the U.S. and Great Britain, cast themselves as defenders of peace and prosperity. If one discounts their many provocative acts, the Sea Powers acted defensively. The question remains, 'Were they not simply preventing Germany and Japan from following in their footsteps to economic autarky and military supremacy in their regions?' Regional hegemons always find it impertinent for others to achieve a similar status. Unless one applies a double standard, the reach for regional hegemony has to be either condemned or accepted in all instances. Japan and Germany avoided hypocrisy, which, as Thomas Mann and countless other observers have pointed out, has become an art form in the West. Hitler's drive for *lebensraum* and its presumptions of power politics, including the use of preemptive war, must be understood in the context of political Realism, which Hitler phrased in racial Social Darwinist terms.

Mein Kampf's first premise is Social Darwinist: 'Nature knows no political boundaries. First, she puts living creatures on the globe and watches the free play of forces. She then confers the master's right on her favorite child, the strongest in courage and industry.'[178] Not only is this the way it is, it is good; not 'morally good,' but good in terms of functional development. 'Mankind has grown great in eternal struggle, and only in eternal peace does it perish.'[179] Worse, from his point of view, has been the tendency of the best European Nations to undermine their own development and survival by following absurd doctrines. 'The talk about the peaceful economic conquest of the world was possibly the greatest nonsense which has ever been exalted to be a guiding principle of State policy.'[180] The consequence of this folly has been to renounce natural superiority in favor of the inferior, who have no qualms about violent territorially acquisitions. 'Since in general, unfortunately, the best Nations, or, even more correctly, the only truly cultured races, the standard-bearers of all human progress, all too frequently resolve in their pacifistic blindness to renounce new acquisitions of soil and content themselves with internal colonization, while the inferior races now how to secure immense living areas in this world for themselves....'[181] Therefore, *'the foreign policy of the Volkisch State must safeguard the existence on this planet of the race embodied in the State, by creating a healthy, viable natural relation between the Nation's population and growth on the one hand and the quantity and quality of its soil on the other hand.'*[182] *Mein Kampf* concedes that *lebensraum* implies war, acknowledging that Germans, still reeling from the Defeat and its consequences, preferred peace. Hence, it urges Germans to see *lebensraum* as an entitlement, something deserved, an endowment. 'We [must] *secure for the German people the land and soil to which they are entitled on this earth.'*[183] The conquest of the East would be a natural development, an outcome of decent German values, not an Alexandrian or Napoleonic search for glory: '*Our task, the mission of the National Socialist movement, is to bring our people to such political insight that they will not see their goal for the future in the breath-taking sensation of a new Alexander's conquest, but in the industrious work of the German plow, to which the sword need only give soil.'*[184] Well aware that in *Volkisch* thought that 'industrious work of the German plow' had romantic overtones, Hitler makes the Sword and the Plow partners, not in the search for aristocratic glory, but for bourgeois land and security.

The duty of the Leader is to prepare his people to meet its destiny. For those who yearn for Athenian democracy or its Lockean or Madisonian variants, however irrational, however flawed, few concepts are as troubling as the *Fuehrer*, the concern deepening when the Leader is perceived to have extraordinary attributes or charisma. *Mein Kampf* denies the viability of democratic values and practices. In the wake of a left-wing revolution, a regime change which replaced a failed monarchy, Hitler espoused a virtual dictatorship, calling it a return to the Leader principle. First, *Mein Kampf* attacks the Weimar Republic at its root. Fundamentally irresponsible, parliamentary democracy could not defend the most basic rights of its people; it could not properly represent them. Real democracy, German democracy, entails leadership. Weimar denied what is essential German: 'Juxtaposed to this is the truly Germanic democracy characterized by the free election of a Leader and his obligation fully to assume all responsibility for his actions and omissions.'[185] The Republic failed not because Weimar politicians were not up to the job, or that they were corrupt or incompetent, although he believed they were. Weimar failed, because representative democracy is fundamentally and fatally flawed. 'Mustn't our principle of parliamentary majorities lead to the demotion of any idea of leadership? Does anyone believe that the progress of the world springs from the mind of majorities and not from the brains of individuals?'[186] Moreover, 'The parliamentary principle of majority rule sins against the basic aristocratic principle of Nature....'[187] And finally, 'For no one can believe that these men elected by the Nation are elect of spirit or even intelligence!'[188] By denying Nature's hierarchical dispensations of abilities and character, parliament cannot accomplish its principle *raison d'être*, representation: 'What gave me food for thought was the obvious absence of any responsibility in a single person. The parliament arrives at some decision whose consequences may be ever so ruinous—nobody bears any responsibility for this, no one can be taken into account.... Can a fluctuating majority of people even be made responsible in any case?'[189] Furthermore, 'What luck to be able to hide behind the skirts of a so-called majority in all decisions of any real importance!'[190] This criticism seems harsh, more due to its tone than to its content, for it has been reaffirmed by many scholars, including Golo Mann:

> The great party of the masses, the Social Democrats, had decided that Germany must be a democracy. The people must govern themselves, the majority must decide, regardless of what the majority decided, regardless of whether a viable majority could be found. This attitude was courageous and from a democratic point of view consistent. It was optimistic, assuming, as it did, that a sensible, constructive majority would be found. It was also an easy way out because it transferred responsibility from the leaders to the people. The people were a chaos of conflicting hopes and fears. Chaos does not resolve itself on its own; what is needed are ideas and determination and not just a well-prepared constitution.[191]

When Germans make this point, it is taken to reveal an authoritarian bias; it, nevertheless, is a standard critique of modern legislatures, becoming more salient with the rise of mass media. Countless American political scientists have decried the irresponsibility of Congress, its unwillingness to look past the next election, its desires to appear powerful, while avoiding painful decisions for decades. Congress, like the public, waits for a President to do the necessary work, to spend executive political capital, allowing Congress to take the credit, notwithstanding, their efforts to obstruct executive policies. Hitler believed these weaknesses could not be overcome by better politicians. All politicians are, by definition, irresponsible, self-serving, or corrupt. To deal with severe problems, fundamental structural change is necessary. Attempts to overcome parliamentary deadlock or irresponsibility are doomed. The parliamentary device of setting up independent agencies or commissions to deal with urgent, enduring problems does not suffice, for it compounds fraud with evasion:

> And so the commissions come together to revise the old program...in which everybody gets his share. The peasant gets protection for his agriculture, the industrialist protection for his product, the consumer protection for his purchase, the teachers' salaries are raised, the civil service pensions are improved, widows and orphans are to be taken care of most liberally by the State, trade is

promoted, tariffs are to be reduced, and taxes are pretty much, if not altogether, done away with.... [After 4–5 years of inability to pass any significant part of the program] the commission comes back to life, and the swindle begins again from the beginning. In view of the granite stupidity of our humanity, we have no need to be surprised at the outcome.[192]

A Leader, sufficiently heroic and Messianic to meet the challenges of the times, is called for. Although in *Mein Kampf* Hitler does not cast himself for the role, others did, once he asserted total control of the National Socialist Movement. Consider Hanns Ludin:

I never succeeded in taking his measure. Perhaps I never shall, perhaps history never will either. Sometimes I thought he was a genius, at others I wondered whether it was a madman who was leading us.... When I try to find the proper word for him, it is 'remote,' a man who could not stand the light, a man of the shadows, emerging from the shadow, speaking from the shadow, and forcing back into the shadows everything that strove towards the light....and all the same I could not get away from him. If I felt one thing with certainty, it was this: that he was a man with a fate, a man of fate, and that fate I could never grasp since for me it was always a great shadow. But apart from him I have never met a man who had such a fate, who was so fateful; and since his fate was also that of the German people, to whom I wished to devote my life, I had to identify him with my Nation.... If I was guilty, if we were all guilty, then our guilt was based on love.[193]

Virtually impossible for non-Germans or for Germans, who did not experience Hitler in the flesh or even on the radio, to credit this sort of statement, Ludin's reaction is neither unique nor exaggerated. Capable of a nuanced portrait, Ludin, wondering if Hitler were a madman, noting his shadowy image, and his fatefulness, which in this context is as ominous as it is promising, attributes Hitler's appeal to 'love.' *Mein Kampf* is more prosaic in its description of the Leader: 'Any man who wants to be a Leader bears, along with the highest unlimited authority, also the ultimate and heaviest responsibility. Anyone who is not equal to this or is too cowardly to bear the consequences of his acts is not fit to be a leader; only the hero is cut out for this.'[194] More than heroic character is necessary: 'Leadership itself requires not only will but also ability, and a greater importance must be attached to will and energy than to intelligence as such, and most valuable of all is a combination of ability, determination and perseverance.'[195] To this, *Mein Kampf* adds a spiritually enriched set of concepts:

Conceptions and ideas, as well as movements with a definite spiritual foundation, regardless whether the latter is false or true, can, after a certain point in their development, only be broken with technical instruments of power if these physical weapons are at the same time the support of a new kindling thought, idea, or philosophy. The application of force alone, without the impetus of a basic spiritual idea as a starting point, can never lead to the destruction of an idea and its dissemination, except in the form of a complete extermination of even the very last exponent of the idea and the destruction of the last tradition.[196]

Mein Kampf argues that leadership consists of an extraordinary amalgam of traits, which cannot be understood, but must be apprehended. 'Anyone who wants to win the broad masses must know the key that opens the door to their heart. Its name is not objectivity (read weakness) but will and power.'[197] In addition, 'The important thing is not what the genius who has created the idea has in mind, but what, in what form, and with what success the prophets of this idea transmit it to the broad masses.'[198] Yet genius remains important: 'The progress and culture of humanity is not a product of the majority, but rest exclusively on the genius and energy of the personality. To cultivate personality and establish its rights is one of the prerequisites for recovering the greatness and power of our nationality.'[199] Finally, the truly exceptional Leader combines theoretical truths with practical political acumen:

> The basic correctness of an idea is decisive and not the difficulty in execution. As soon as the theoretician attempts to take into account of so-called utility and reality instead of the absolute truth, his work will cease to be a polar star of seeking humanity and instead will become a prescription for everyday life. The theoretician must lay down its goal, the politician strive for its fulfillment. The thinking of the one, therefore, will be determined by Eternal Truth, the action of the other by the more practical reality of the moment. The greatness of the one lies in the absolute abstract soundness of his idea, that of the other in his correct attitude toward the given facts and their advantageous application; and in this the theoretician's aim must serve as his guiding star.[200]

Hitler also writes, 'for if the art of the politician is really the art of the possible, the theoretician is one of those of whom it can be said they are pleasing to the gods only if they demand and want the impossible....'[201] Leadership is the ability to convince the masses that the Leader's policies are pleasing to the gods. 'All selfish interests and all social antagonisms are abolished within him; a total unity of the German people corresponded to the total enemy on the outside. The *Fuehrer* had the power to bind and loose; he knew the way, the mission, the law of history.'[202] 'Bind and loose,' it will be recalled, is a religious term allowing the possessor of this power to make some act mandatory or optional. Hitler had real and easily recognizable leadership skills, a Fest explains: 'His insight into the true nature of situations, his knack for penetrating the various strata of interests, for spotting weaknesses and setting up temporary coalitions, in short, his tactical instinct, certainly contributed as much to his rise as his oratorical powers, the backing of the army, industry, and the judiciary and the terrorism of the Brown Shirts.'[203] Hitler's Leader is a gift of nature, a romantically conceived solitary genius, who embodies his race, an artist who sacrifices his art for the benefit of Eternity. The *Fuehrer* Principle is much closer to Nietzsche than to Plato.

More analytical explanations of leadership have been offered. Speaking of charismatic personalities, 'Weber saw such a Leader as the counterforce to the inhuman bureaucratic structures of the future.'[204] Fest, in addition, sees in Hitler a fulfillment of Burckhardt's historical confluences: 'To a great extent his special charisma, a mixture of obessiveness, passionate banality, and vulgarity stemmed from this sharing [the plight of the bourgeoisie]. He proved the truth of Jacob Burckhardt's saying that history sometimes loves to concentrate itself in a single human being, whom the world thereupon obeys; time and the man enter into a great, mysterious covenant.'[205] A less mystical and more theatrical appreciation comes from Golo Mann: 'In the audacity of his attacks, in the boldness of his self-praise, in the captivating, ingratiating cunning of his arguments, in hatred and ridicule, even in the physical intensity of his screams and tears he had no equal anywhere. People compared what he said with the long chain of their own bitter experiences—war, defeat, inflation, economic crisis—and found it worth listening to.'[206] And worth voting for:

> As the economic and political situation, deteriorated the rationality of voting for a small and weak interest party rather than a massive and strong *national* party—upholding interests but transcending them—was less and less compelling. A vote for the Nazis could easily seem like common sense.... The process was only in its early stages in summer 1930. But it would make rapid advances following the Nazi triumph of 14 September 1930. What happened that day was a political earthquake. In the most remarkable result in German parliamentary history, the NSDAP advanced at one stroke from twelve seats and a mere 2.6 per cent of the vote gained in...1928 to 107 seats and 18.3 per cent, making it the second largest party in the Reichstag.[207]

As the Depression deepened and Weimar's ineffectuality became ever more manifest, the appeal of the extreme parties increased. The enormous German fear of the Bolsheviks, coupled with their experience in the brief Communist reign in Munich, made the National Socialists seem a reasonable alternative to the unendurable status quo. Through a combination of miscalculations by his opponents, his political acumen, the failures of Weimar, and the advent of the Great Depression, Hitler became Chancellor of Germany. Fest sums up the factors which paved the way to power:

> Hitler must be shown against a dense pattern of objective factors that conditioned, promoted, impelled, and sometimes braked him. The romantic German

notion of politics and the peculiarly morose grayness of the Weimar republic belong equally in this background. So also do the declassing of the Nation by the Treaty of Versailles and the secondary social declassing of large sections of the population by the inflation and the world-wide Depression; the weakness of the democratic tradition in Germany; fears of the miscalculation of conservatives who had lost their grip; finally, the widespread fears aroused by the transition from a familiar system to one new and still uncertain.[208]

National Socialism was the expression of totalitarianism which drew on the pathology of a modern mass society in which the individual had lost his ties and values and all sense of direction. National Socialism…became the sinister embodiment of a dynamic nihilism devoid of ideological commitment. Martin Broszat[209]

The real miracle would have been a decision to resist Nazism. Joachim Fest[210]

THE INTOXICATION OF SUCCESS (1933–1939)

Having relied on Golo Mann for his powerful descriptions and trenchant analyses, here, perhaps ungratefully, I criticize his interpretation of National Socialism. Mann represents a strain of German thought which sees National Socialism as an alien intrusion on German society, a foreign element: 'The Nazis behaved like foreign conquerors, exploiting the country, putting the people in their place with massive vulgar monuments, with rallies and parades designed to make the individual feel small, with columns of enormous limousines occupied by black uniformed men and in the last resort with prison watch towers and machine guns.'[211] It had no past, and can have no future in Germany, hardly having a presence, despite of twelve years of rule. As a power grab, National Socialism was no more German than Mann's Literary Man. National Socialism just happened to Germany, just as Heinrich Mann happened to have German parents. Golo Mann contrasts National Socialism with Communism, finding it empty, ephemeral, and unable to leave an ideational or ideological residue. 'It was a historically unique phenomenon, dependent on an individual and on a moment, a phenomenon which can never reappear in the same form. It was a form of intoxication produced by a gang of intoxicated experts, kept up for years. It was a machine for the manufacture of power, for the safeguarding of power and for the extension of power.'[212] Understandable as a way of distancing Germans from National Socialists, this view is dangerously flawed. It assumes that there was not and cannot have been an underlying set of values, concerns, fears, or convictions, which under the proper circumstances, would have lent credence to National

Socialist proposals. It further assumes that National Socialism, taken as a means, rather than a set of objectives, was equally UnGerman. It was, in the final analysis, a criminal conspiracy from the beginning led by a demagogic serial killer whose insanity would in the end manifest itself, a fever German society contracted when in a weakened condition. Once it ran its course, the fever would subside and never recur. Would that this were true!

There was far more to the Third Reich than a criminal conspiracy, for it reflected long-standing German objectives, values, and anxieties, notwithstanding *Mein Kampf's* radical rendition of them, and notwithstanding its horrific expression in Auschwitz. At least two of these, *Volksgemeinschaft* and the *Fuehrer* Principle, were, if not exclusively German, were German in their emphasis. *Lebensraum* was not, notwithstanding its racist justifications; the pursuit of material advantage has been a near universal objective of the power State, forming the basis of almost all international political activity. Moreover, the successes the National Socialists achieved were extraordinary; no other political movement accomplished so much, so quickly. National Socialism became by far the most effective and popular regime in Europe. Its real price in terms of civil liberties, political participation, Natural Rights and human decency were not perceived or were ignored. Once Germany was restored, many Germans believed, there would be time enough to reestablish their values. Only when the costs of war became their concern did doubts and questions arise, awaiting Stalingrad to become significant. Accepting success without asking questions is not a peculiarly German trait. Few societies, coming out of the multiple crises and humiliations that Germans endured, would have questioned the means which provided relief or leadership which solved or seemed to solve enduring problems. If their support for the Third Reich seemed too enthusiastic, it was as much a measure of their despair as of an inherently authoritarian character, to say nothing of homicidal racism.

In any event, many conservatives believed Hitler would be a temporary solution to a severe crisis, a bulwark against the revolutionary impulses of the masses, dispensable when the flood waters subsided. They would pay dearly for this miscalculation. In a deal, which otherwise favored the conservative establishment, they formed a Hitler government. Despite the lack of a clear cut mandate, a parliamentary majority, and only three National Socialist members of the cabinet, the new government, as harbinger of great expectations, was greeted euphorically. 'From now on the political order of the past was no longer a concept in whose name some hope, let alone opposition, might have gathered. The feeling of great change, which had affected people vaguely, as a kind of euphoric expectation, when Hitler entered government, now overcame wider and wider sectors of the population.'[213] Less enthusiastically, some Germans believed that Hitler's Chancellorship would be another Weimar government with a new addition, the Leader of the largest party. He would have his moment in the sun and then be overwhelmed by circumstances that had defeated men greatly his superior. When the public got the National Socialists out of their system, the serious business of governing Germany would again be in the hands of rational adults. This conservative consensus was joined by Communists, for opposite reasons. When Hitler failed, they prophesied, the Marxist program would seem Germany's last best hope. Few realized, despite the rapturous mass response, how much events had outstripped these inside the *Reichstag* strategies of the traditional parties, to say nothing of Communist fantasies. The enthusiastic acceptance of Hitler brought the back room onto stage front and center with 66 million Germans in the audience. 'The dramatic ceremonial with which Hitler took over the Chancellorship, the accompaniment of torchlight parades and mass demonstrations, bore no relationship to the constitutional importance of the event. January 1933 brought nothing more than a change of administrations. Nevertheless, the public sensed that the appointment of Hitler as Chancellor could not be compared with the cabinet reshufflings of former years.'[214] The masses were better prophets than the elites.

As if to confirm mass hysteria, Hitler swiftly emasculated his conservative enablers. Ready for the Leader and his 'legal revolution,' his decisiveness reinforced the public's acceptance of the new regime, confirming Hitler's conviction that Germany wanted something completely new from him. Moving on parallel tracks of boldness and caution, building acceptance for more radical changes, Hitler introduced Germans to the technique he would employ for the duration of the Third Reich. In March, 1933, he participated modestly in a ceremony, which was led by President Hindenburg: 'Hitler's speech was pitched on the same note [as Hindenburg's] of moderate, deeply felt solemnity. He looked back upon the greatness and downfall of the Nation and then declared his faith in the "eternal foundations" of its life, the traditions of history and culture.'[215] Fest concludes: 'These scenes had an extraordinary effect upon all the participants, upon the deputies, the soldiers, the diplomats, the foreign observers, and the public. That day in Potsdam truly proved to be a turning point in history.'[216] This effect was not limited to ceremonials. 'For years he astonished them [world leaders and diplomats] by a schooled statesmanlike manner which he could easily put on and for which they were totally unprepared. Eden [the British Foreign Minister] was amazed at Hitler's smart, almost elegant appearance, and wondered at finding him controlled and friendly.'[217]

At virtually the same time, Hitler demanded that the *Reichstag* pass the Enabling Act: 'By virtue of the Act, the entire apparatus of the government bureaucracy was at Hitler's disposal. This included the judiciary, which was indispensable to his far-reaching plans. The Act offered a basis that satisfied both the consciences and the craving for security of the bureaucrats. Most governmental officials were pleased to note the legal nature of this revolution, which in spite of the many isolated outrages contrasted so favorably with the chaos of 1918.'[218] Achieving dictatorial power, Hitler never lost sight of the need to appear legal. Little more than *post hoc* coverings of naked acts of power, these legalities placated the longing for law and order. Whatever Hitler really thought about these old fashioned men, he required them, for their expertise and for their respectability, at least temporarily. With remarkable ease and swiftness, he secured both: 'Actually, Hitler needed less than three months to outmaneuver is partners and checkmate almost all the opposing forces. To realize the swiftness of the process we must keep in mind that Mussolini in Italy took seven years to accumulate approximately as much power. Hitler's purposefulness and his feeling for the statesmanlike style had made their impression on Hindenburg from the start and soon prompted the President to drop his former reservations.'[219] With the *Reichstag* sidelined, Hitler pursued his objectives, ignoring the residue of political parties, including the Communists, who were hounded, dispersed and silenced. He then eliminated the only institution, other than the Army, which could limit his freedom of action: Rohm's Storm Troopers, the SA. Meanwhile, he confronted the economy's weakness, especially its high unemployment levels. Then, he dismantled the Versailles Treaty. Finally, he completed the unification of the German Nation-State, including Austria and other large German populations in neighboring countries. Let us deal with these briefly in turn.

The Bolshevik Menace

Scholarship is divided on how serious the Bolshevik movement was in Germany. Nearly a century after the fact, it requires a good deal of historical imagination to understand the enormous impact of the Bolshevik Revolution on Germany. Germany's perennial Eastern threat, the Asiatic horde, was now under the control of a government which preached world revolution. Lurid accounts of the horrors of the East abounded: '"Dreadful times in which Christian-hating Asiatics everywhere are raising their bloodstained hands to strangle us in droves...." Yet the horrifying reports of atrocities in the East were not unfounded and were confirmed by credible witnesses.'[220] Moreover, Marxism had a powerful intellectual European following, including Germans. Dominated by the Social Democrat Party, flanked by Communists, who like the National Socialists, took their message and thugs to the streets, Weimar Germany was awash in violent confrontations. The majority of Germans were appalled by chaos in the streets and terrified of its revolution potential.

'The tendency of the Enlightenment throughout Europe was to challenge existing authorities. But the spokesmen of the Enlightenment in Germany refrained from criticizing the government of princes; some even lauded it— so ingrained were the terrors of the past. The German mind accords unusual respect to the categories of order, discipline and self-restraint.'[221] And finally, there was the experience of a Communist government in Munich, which, however short-lived, scarred the German psyche: 'The leaderless State was left to the muddled gospel of the poets, who soon found themselves supplanted by a group of hardboiled professional revolutionaries. Chaos and terrorizing of the citizenry followed. It was an experience that could not be forgotten. The arbitrary confiscations, the practice of seizing hostages, the curbs on the bourgeoisie, revolutionary whim, and increasing hunger accorded all too well with recent horror stories of the October Revolution....'[222] From this perspective, revolution promised only chaos. Moreover,

> Marxism itself was only the metaphor for something dreaded that escaped definition. Anxiety was the permanent emotion of the time. It sprang from the intuition that the end of the war meant not only the end of familiar prewar Europe with its grandeur and its urge to world domination, its monarchies, its gilt-edged securities, but also the end of an era. Along with the old forms of government, the accustomed framework of life was being destroyed. The unrest, the radicalism of the politicized masses, the disorders of revolution were interpreted as the after pains of the war and simultaneously as harbingers of a new, strange, and chaotic age.[223]

With his acute understanding of German anxieties, Hitler made anti-Bolshevism the centerpiece of his program, viewing it as a 'negative, destroying spirit [which] spared nothing of all that is highest and most valuable. Beginning with the family, it has undermined the very foundations of morality and faith and scoffs at culture and business, Nation and Fatherland, justice and honor. Fourteen years of Marxism have ruined Germany; one year of Bolshevism would destroy her.'[224] Wanting to eliminate the Communists, but avoiding direct official action, the Nazis awaited a provocation, which came as the Reichstag fire. Blamed on Communists, it precipitated the Enabling Act. Contrary to expectations, the still legal Communists withered away: 'Now a Communist following numbering in the millions, forming a powerful and effective threat, terrifying the bourgeoisie, had evaporated without even token resistance....'[225] Of course, the Bolshevik threat remained, incarnated in the Soviet Union and the perfidious Jew. The German Communist Party, however, ceased to exist, apparently having few mourners. The fear of violence and revolution, however, persisted in a much more dangerous way.

The SA and the Second Revolution

If the demise of the Communists and the debasing of the Reichstag were all too predictable, the reduction of the SA to a social service organization was not, if only because Hitler had so frequently expressed his undying support for his 'old fighters.' Offering an alternative to Hitler's leadership and a more socialist version of National Socialism, the SA endangered Hitler's Vision for the new Germany. The demolition of the party system foretold the reduction of the SA, for without the need for elections, the SA, which had essentially been a get out the vote organization for Nazi sympathizers and a suppression of the vote for their opponents, lost its only acceptable function. Of course, Rohm, its shrewd and ambitious leader, had different ideas all along. The SA would become *the* Army of the Third Reich. This fundamental misunderstanding of Hitler's plan for Germany would have led to Rohm's fall, even if he had learned to keep his mouth shut. Dependent on the Army, including its highly competent High Command and its representation of German glory and sacrifice, Hitler would temporarily tolerate their potential disloyalty, so long as he could rely on their expertise and exploit the respect the people had for them. Politically checkmated, the Army would not pose a threat, until defeat in World War II became all but certain. The SA played a role in this process, though certainly not the one Rohm had envisioned. The reduction of the SA, moreover, proved to the High Command that Hitler was not the thug they feared. Seldom has cold blooded murder had the effect of raising the murderers' respectability, yet this is precisely how the High Command responded to 'the Night of the Long Knives.' Asking Hitler to accept a personal oath of loyalty from the officers and men of the army, to which he immediately acquiesced, the High Command believed they were binding Hitler to them. For the tradition conscious officers, oaths were sacred, absolute, and *mutually* obligatory. For the anti-traditional Hitler, they were mere tools. He, after all, had the power 'to bind and loose,' a power which included abrogation of any agreement, contract or oath.

Besides, Rohm could not keep his mouth shut, calling for 'the Second Revolution,' making many off-hand comments about Hitler's inadequacies, including his tendency to sell-out to the establishment, especially the Army High Command. 'Adolf is rotten. He's betraying all of us. He only goes around with reactionaries. His old comrades aren't good enough for him. So he brings in these East Prussian generals.'[226] Trading on his prior service, relying on the four hundred thousand strong SA to protect him, Rohm never understood that these defenses were intolerable to Hitler. 'The smashing of the SA removed the one organization that was seriously destabilizing the regime and directly threatening Hitler's own position.'[227] Another reason for Rohm's elimination was his friendship with Hitler. Far from protecting

Rohm, assuming that Hitler had genuine feelings for him or at least his early indispensable role in his ascent to power, his friendship with Hitler made his elimination more necessary. A test for Hitler and an object lesson to those who pledged absolute loyalty to the *Fuehrer*, Rohm's murder proved that friendship, love, loyalty, no more than any other value, would obstruct the fulfillment of the *Fuehrer's* Vision for the new Germany and the creation of the Aryan people. Fest describes the problems that the destruction of the SA and Rohm helped solve: 'To sum up, the challenge facing Hitler before June 30 required the simultaneous solution of no fewer than five problems. He had to quash Rohm.... He had to satisfy the demands of the Army. He had to dispel public dissatisfaction with the rule of the streets and visible terrorism. He had to head off the conservatives' counter plans. All this he had to do, without becoming a prisoner of one side or the other.'[228]

The Dismantling of Versailles Treaty

Once Hitler attained dictatorial power, he turned his attention to another of his oft repeated avowals: the destruction of the hated Versailles Treaty. Reparations had been halted in 1932, as a result of the Great Depression and the threat of Hitler's ascension. Facing hostile and superior military forces, Hitler moved prudently. 'Until 1938, Hitler's moves in foreign policy had been bold, but not reckless. He had shown shrewd awareness of the weakness of his opponents, a sure instinct for exploiting divisions and uncertainty. His sense of timing had been excellent, his combination of bluff and blackmail effective, his manipulation of propaganda to back his coups masterly. He had gone further and faster than anyone could have expected in revising the terms of Versailles and upturning the post-war diplomatic settlement.'[229] Protesting the essential unfairness, harshness, and gratuitous humiliation of the Treaty, Hitler often found receptive ears, especially among the British and Americans. He moved on multiple fronts: He secretly rearmed. The Saar was reincorporated into the Reich, as a result of a plebiscite in 1935. Military conscription was reintroduced in March of 1935 and the Anglo-German Naval Agreement was concluded in June. In 1936, he successfully entered the demilitarized Rhineland, over French protests, and he signed agreements with Italy and Japan for mutual support. In 1938, he annexed Austria and the Sudetenland, unifying virtually all Germans living in Europe. Unmourned, the Versailles Treaty died.

The Power of Success: the Positive Program

Not content with destroying his enemies, Hitler worked to improve the lot of Germans, praising his accomplishments:

I overcame chaos in Germany, restored order, enormously raised production in all fields of our National economy.... I succeeded in completely resettling in useful production those seven million unemployed who so touched all our hearts.... I have not only politically united the German Nation but also rearmed it militarily, and I have further tried to liquidate that Treaty sheet by sheet whose 448 Articles contain the vilest rape that Nations and human beings have ever been expected to submit to. I have restored to the Reich the provinces grabbed from us in 1919; I have led millions of deeply unhappy Germans, who have been snatched away from us, back into the Fatherland; I have restored the thousand-year old historical unity of German living space; and I have...attempted to accomplish all that without shedding blood and without inflicting the sufferings of war on my people or any other. I have accomplished all this...as one who 21 years ago was still an unknown worker and soldier of my people, by my own efforts ....[230]

Haffner comments 'Sickening self-adulation.... But damn it, it was all true, or nearly all.'[231] As appreciation of Hitler's successes became widespread, his popularity soared. So great and so unexpected was his success that it caused many Germans, otherwise skeptical of National Socialism, to question their assumptions and convictions, adding to Hitler's support and placing it on a more firm foundation than popular acclaim: '[In the face of] Hitler's undeniable achievements and his never-ending miracles [Germans asked]: Can it be that my own yardsticks are wrong? Can it be that everything I was taught or that I believed in is right? Am I not being proved wrong by what is happening here before my own eyes? Does [his success] not compel me to revise all my concepts, including aesthetic and moral concepts?'[232] It is difficult for me to criticize the process of reconsidering assumptions, convictions, methods of analysis, and the like. This is what an educated person is supposed to do. Yet, when it is occasioned by the successes of a charismatic leader, it should cause concern. When political theory and practice degenerates into a religious movement under the aegis of a charismatic Leader, supernatural authority replaces rational/legal authority, imperiling rationality itself. To this process we now turn.

NOTES

1. Hitler, A.: *Mein Kampf,* translated by Ralph Mannheim, Houghton, Boston, 1925, 1971, p. 518.

2. Mosse, George: *The Crisis of German Ideology,* Grosset & Dunlap, N.Y., 1964, p. 1.

3. Mann, G.: T*he History of Germany Since 1789,* translated by Marian Jackson, NY, 1968, p. 11.

4. Quoted by Fest, Joachim: *Hitler*, translated by Richard & Clara Winston, NY, 1974, p. 41.

5. Quoted by *ibid.*, p. 97.

6. Mann, Thomas: *Reflections of a Non-Political Man*, translated by Walter Morris, NY, 1918, 1983.

7. Stern, Fritz: *The Politics of Cultural Despair*, Doubleday, NY, 1965.

8. Kershaw, Ian: *Hitler: 1889–1936: Hubris*, Norton, NY, 1998, p. 151.

9. Mann, *op. cit.*, p. 26.

10. *Ibid*, p. 25, original emphasis.

11. *Ibid.*, original emphasis.

12. Quoted in *ibid.*, p. 26.

13. *Ibid.*, p. 20.

14. *Ibid.*, p. 32.

15. Nietzsche, Friedrich: *The Will to Power*, translated by W. Kaufmann & R.J. Hollingdale, NY, 1967, p. 428.

16. Mann, *Reflections, op. cit.*, p. 113.

17. *Ibid.*, p. 269.

18. *Ibid.*, p. 219.

19. *Ibid.*, p. 14, original emphasis.

20. See Pinker, *op. cit.*

21. 'On Truth and Lies in a Nonmoral Sense' (1873), quoted in *Nietzsche Reader, op. cit.,* p. 108.

22. Mann, *op. cit.*, p. 151, original emphasis.

23. *Ibid.*, p. 141.

24. *Ibid.*, p. 13.

25. *Ibid.*, p. 17, original emphasis.

26. *Ibid.*, p. 219.

27. *Ibid.*, p. 234, original emphasis.

28. *Ibid.*, p. 18.

29. *Ibid.*, p. 21, original emphasis.

30. *Ibid.*, p. 97, original emphasis.

31. *Ibid.*, p. 179.

32. *Ibid.*, p. 31, original emphasis.

33. *Ibid.*, p. 34, original emphasis.

34. *Ibid.*, p. 123.

35. *Ibid.*, p. 20.

36. *Ibid.*, p. 97.

37. *Ibid.*, p. 184.

38. *Ibid.*, p. 185.

39. *Ibid.*, p. 232.

40. *Ibid.*, both quotes, p. 53.

41. Taylor, A.J.P.: *The Course of German History*, Capricorn, NY, 1946, 1962, p. 7.

42. Kohn, Hans: *The Mind of Germany*, Scribner's, NY, 1960, p. 24.

43. Mann, Golo, *op. cit.*, p. 38.

44. Fest, *op. cit.*, p. 94.

45. Quoted in, *ibid.*, p. 49.

46. 'Nietzsche, 'On Truth and Lies in a Nonmoral Sense,' quoted in *The Nietzsche Reader, op. cit.*, p. 122.

47. Mann, *op. cit.*, p. 201.

48. *Ibid.*, p. 182.

49. *Ibid.*, p. 185.

50. *Ibid.*, p. 198.

51. *Ibid.*, p. 191.

52. *Ibid.*, p. 189.

53. Broszat, Martin: *German National Socialism*, Clio, Santa Barbara, 1966, p. 41.

54. Nietzsche, F: 'On the Utility and Liability of History for Life,' (1874), *The Nietzsche Reader, op. cit.*, p. 124.

55. Fest, *op. cit.*, p. 378.

56. Kohn, *op.cit.*, p. 69.

57. Mann, G., *op. cit.*, p. 21.

58. *Ibid.*, p. 434.

59. *Ibid.*, p. 115.

60. *Ibid.*, p. 95.

61. Krieger, *op. cit.*, p. 4.

62. Mann, G., *op. cit.*, p. 58.

63. *Ibid.*, p. 25.

64. *Ibid.*, p. 41.

65. *Ibid.*, p. 172.

66. *Ibid.*, p. 150.

67. Taylor, *op. cit.*, p. 37.

68. Hamerow, Theodore: *Restoration, Revolution, Reaction*, Princeton, 1958, p. 63.

69. Pflanze, Otto: *Bismarck and the Development of Germany*, Princeton, 1963, p. 12.

70. *Ibid.*, p. 23.

71. Dahrendorf, Ralf: *Society and Democracy in Germany*, Doubleday, NY, 1969, p. 39.

72. Taylor, *op. cit.*, p. 88. By over dichotomizing German and Western economic development, Taylor reveals his anti-German bias or an ignorance of American history. *Laissez-faire* became important as a political doctrine only after a populist backlash to reckless and rapacious capitalism, in league with Republican politicians, had run its course from the end of the Civil War to the 1890s. In these circumstances, the monopolies or trusts were not afraid of government interference *per se*, for they had long used or abused their political connections to great effect. For nearly a hundred years the government, despite Jeffersonian rhetoric to the contrary, actively assisted national economic development, mostly by creating or financing economic infrastructure. *Laissez-faire*, especially as interpreted by the Supreme Court, became important because under populist pressure the honeymoon between corporate interests and the government was over.

73. Dahrendorf, *op. cit.*, p. 35.

74. Quoted by Meinecke, Friedrich: *The German Catastrophe*, translated by Sidney Fay, Boston, 1950, p. 21.

75. Dahrendorf, *op. cit.*, p. 60.

76. *Ibid.*, p. 37.

77. Stern, Fritz: *Dreams and Delusions*, Knopf, NY, 1987, p. 94.

78. *Ibid.*, p. 155.

79. Mann, G., *op. cit.*, p. 201.

80. *Ibid.*, p. 14.

81. Keynes, John Maynard: *The Economic Consequences of the Peace,* Dover, NY, 1920, 2004, pp. 10–1. 'In 1870, Germany had a population of about 40,000,000. By 1892 this figure had risen to 50,000,000, and by June 30, 1914, to about 68,000,000.... This great increase was only rendered possible by a far-reaching transformation of the economic structure of the country. From being an agricultural and mainly self-supporting, Germany transformed herself into a vast and complicated industrial machine, dependent for its working on the equipoise of many factors outside Germany as well as within.'

82. *Ibid.*, p. 15.

83. Hamerow, *op. cit.*, p. 20.

84. Fest, *op. cit.*, p. 26.

85. Mann, G., *op. cit.*, p. 340.

86. Fischer, Klaus: *Nazi Germany: a New History:* Continuum, NY, 2003, p. 25.

87. Quoted by Mann, G., *op. cit.*, p. 262.

88. Quoted by Meinecke, *op. cit.*, pp. 23–4, emphasis supplied.

89. Mann, G., *op. cit.*, p. 369.

90. Keynes, *op. cit.*, p. 5.

91. *Ibid.*, p. 29.

92. Mann, G., *op. cit.*, p. 368.

93. *Ibid.*

94. Fischer, *op. cit.*, p. 61.

95. Keynes, *op. cit.*, p. 60.

96. Mann, G., *op. cit.*, p. 356. It should be remembered that Germany imposed a harsh peace on the new Soviet government: the Treaty of Brest-Litovsk. Revenge, especially by a third party, is, however, a poor rationale and a worse justification.

97. Fest, *op. cit.*, p. 82.

98. Keynes., *op. cit.*, p. 55.

99. Mann, G., *op. cit.*, p. 299.

100. *Ibid.*, p. 346.

101. *Ibid.*, p. 344.

102. Fest, *op.* cit., p. 83.

103. *Ibid.*, p. 99.

104. For elaboration, see Mayer, *op. cit.*

105. Keynes, *op. cit.*, p. 209.

106. Fest, *op. cit.*, p. 77.

107. *Ibid.*, p. 38.

108. *Ibid.*, p. 37.

109. *Ibid.*, p. 182.

110. *Ibid.*, p. 233.

111. Fest, *op. cit.*, p. 65.

112. Nietzsche, Friedrich: *The Gay Science*, translated by Walter Kaufmann, Vintage, NY, 1974, p. 59.

113. *Ibid.*, p. 73.

114. *Ibid.*, p. 79.

115. *Ibid.*, p. 107.

116. Nietzsche, Friedrich: *Genealogy of Morals*, translated by Kaufmann & Hollingdale, NY, 1967, [11] 40–1.

117. *Ibid.*, [11] p. 42.

118. *Ibid.*, [14] p. 122.

119. Nietzsche, *Will, op. cit.*, p. 61.

120. *Ibid.*, p. 78.

121. *Ibid.*, p. 148.

122. *Ibid.*, p. 163.

123. *Ibid.*, p. 170.

124. *Ibid.*, p. 171.

125. *Ibid.*, p. 189.

126. *Ibid.*, p. 189.

127. Nietzsche, Friedrich, *Nietzsche and the Death of God: Selected Writings*, Peter Fritzsche, editor & translator, Boston, 2007, p. 121.

128. Nietzsche, *Death, op. cit.*, p. 133.

129. Haffner, *op. cit.*, p. 77.

130. For an intelligent treatment see, Mosse, George: *The Image of Man*, Oxford, NY, 1996.

131. Fest, *op. cit.*, p. 442.

132. Kershaw, *Hitler, op. cit.*, p. 244.

133. *Ibid.*, p. 243.

134. Fest, *op. cit.*, p. 374.

135. Kershaw, *Hitler, op. cit.*, p.xxiv.

136. Fest, *op. cit.*, p. 3.

137. *Ibid.*, p. 4.

138. Hitler, *op. cit.*, p. 231.

139. *Ibid.*, p. 230.

140. *Ibid.*, p. 153.

141. *Ibid.*, p. 152.

142. *Ibid.*, p. 234.

143. *Ibid.*, p. 235.

144. *Ibid.*, p. 26.

145. *Ibid.*, p. 28.

146. *Ibid.*, p. 45, original emphasis.

147. *Ibid.*, p. 47.

148. *Ibid.*, p. 47, original emphasis.

149. *Ibid.*, p. 24.

150. *Ibid.*, p. 30, original emphasis.

151. *Ibid.*, p. 600, original emphasis.

152. *Ibid.*, p. 601, original emphasis.

153. Mann, G., *op. cit.*, p. 365.

154. *Ibid.*, p. 366.

155. Fest, *op. cit.*, p. 250.

156. Mann, G., *op. cit.*, p. 372.

157. Neumann, F., *Behemoth: The Structure and Practice of National Socialism*, N.Y., 1942, 1966, p. 9.

158. Fischer, *op. cit.*, p. 125–6.

159. Quoted in Mann, G., *op. cit.*, p. 365.

160. *Ibid.*, p. 340–1.

161. Fest, *op. cit.*, p. 268.

162. Mosse, George: *The Crisis of German Ideology*, Grosset & Dunlap, NY, 1964, p. 4.

163. Hitler, *op. cit.*, p. 150.

164. *Ibid.*, p. 214, original emphasis.

165. Mosse, *op. cit.*, p. 56–7.

166. Hitler, *op. cit.*, p. 408.

167. *Ibid.*, p. 411, original emphasis.

168. *Ibid*, p. 339.

169. *Ibid.*, p. 441.

170. Hitler, *op. cit.*, p. 449.

171. Mosse, *Crisis, op. cit.*, p. 21.

172. Kershaw, *op.cit.*, p. 136.

173. See Mearsheimer, John: *The Tragedy of Great Power Politics*, Norton, NY, 2003, for a cogent analysis of international politics, in which pre-emptive war is perceived as a normal approach to improving one Nation-State's security *vis a vis* all others. It should be stressed this is an emphatically non-ideological approach, having far more similarities to Bismarck than to Hitler or other emotionally or racially driven nationalists.

174. Mann, G., *op. cit.*, p. 269.

175. Hitler, *op. cit.*, p. 618, original emphasis.

176. Fest, *op. cit.*, p. 486.

177. *Ibid.*, p. 215.

178. Hitler, *op. cit.*, p. 134.

179. *Ibid.*, p. 135.

180. *Ibid.*, p. 143.

181. *Ibid.*, pp. 134–5.

182. *Ibid.*, p. 643, original emphasis.

183. *Ibid.*, p. 652, original emphasis.

184. *Ibid.*, p. 655, original emphasis.

185. *Ibid.*, p. 91.

186. *Ibid.*, p. 80.

187. *Ibid.*, p. 81.

188. *Ibid.*, p. 88.

189. *Ibid.*, p. 79.

190. *Ibid.*, p. 82.

191. Mann, G., *op. cit.*, p. 379.

192. Hitler, *op. cit.*, pp. 374–5.

193. Quoted in Salomon, Ernst von: *The Answers*, translated by C. Fitzgibbon, London, 1954, p. 540.

194. Hitler, *op. cit.*, pp. 345.

195. *Ibid.*, p. 349.

196. *Ibid.*, p. 170.

197. *Ibid*, p. 338.

198. *Ibid.*, p. 342.

199. *Ibid.*, p. 345.

200. *Ibid.*, pp. 210–11.

201. Quoted in Fest, *op. cit.*, p. 202.

202. *Ibid.*, p. 445.

203. *Ibid.*, p. 262.

204. *Ibid.*, p. 102.

205. *Ibid.*, p. 149.

206. Mann, G., *op. cit.*, p. 391.

207. Kershaw, *Hitler, op. cit.*, p. 333.

208. Fest, *op. cit.*, pp. 6–7.

209. Broszat, *German, op. cit.,* p. 89.

210. Fest, *op. cit.*, p. 367.

211. Mann, G., *op. cit.*, p. 448.

212. *Ibid.*, p. 446.

213. Fest, *op. cit.*, p. 415.

214. *Ibid.*, p. 373.

215. *Ibid.*, p. 405.

216. *Ibid.*, p. 404.

217. *Ibid.*, p. 443.

218. *Ibid.*, p. 412.

219. *Ibid.*, p. 411.

220. *Ibid.*, p. 91.

221. *Ibid.*, p. 378.

222. *Ibid.*, p. 111.

223. *Ibid.*, p. 93.

224. Hitler quoted by Fest, *op. cit.*, p. 388.

225. *Ibid.*, p. 395.

226. *Ibid.*, p. 452.

227. Kershaw, *Hitler, op.* cit., p. 521

228. Fest, *op. cit.*, p. 474

229. Kershaw, Ian: *Hitler: 1936–45: Nemesis*, Norton, NY, 2000, p. 91

230. Haffner, *op. cit.*, pp. 32–3

231. *Ibid.*, p. 32

232. *Ibid.*, p. 34

Chapter Six

The Hitler Movement

To Partake of the Eternal

> The fascination with Heidegger's thinking is based primarily on this religious undertone of an epochal and eschatological consciousness.... How distant is this eschatological-historical thinking, for which everything counts merely as seed-sowing and preparation for an arriving future, from the original wisdom of the Greeks, for whom the history of time was philosophically insignificant because they directed their view toward eternal beings.... Karl Lowith[1]

PROLOGUE: HEIDEGGERIAN MUSINGS

Language and Becoming

Can I say that I am becoming through the language of my poem? No, but not perhaps for the reason which may leap to mind—something like, 'I am I' or 'I make the poem' or 'I, by the use of my language, make the poem' or 'I make the poem, and, therefore, become a poet, becoming myself.' All these statements are false, because they misunderstand the nature of language. Language makes the poem. The poet is but its instrument, ready to hand, more or less. When I listen to the appeal of language, when I dwell in the language, language is ready to use me to make its poem. Better, but not quite sufficient. For something happens to the instrument which denies its instrumentality. The poem is not the poem; the instrument is not the instrument. My poem is not mine. Language is not *my* instrument. But neither am I *its* instrument, notwithstanding that language uses me to *reveal* the poem, not to make it. The poem dwells in the language. If I dwell in it, as well, I may be a poet. When I dwell in the same space as the particular poem, language uses me to reveal it. Then, am I but the workman who stumbles upon a coin? Can *reveal* only mean cleaning dirt off a coin? Is there no less contingent relationship between me and the poem I reveal or is revealed through me? Has it become my poem, at least slightly, since I discovered it? My treasure? Not in the sense of my possession, for poems cannot be possessed. Yet, is it not significant that I found the poem? Surely, this must signify some non-contingent relationship between me and what I found. Do I not differ from those who did not find it? Yes, perhaps, but how much does this matter? For, all it may say is that the one who did not or could not find it did not listen to the appeal of language with respect to the particular poem that dwelt within language at that particular moment. Yes, but I did listen. I heard the appeal; I dwelt in the language at that moment. There must be a connection more important than stumbling on a coin. If so, perhaps in reverse. The treasure stumbled on me. The language heard *my* appeal. It listened to me in the one precise moment and found me a useful instrument. As I did not make the poem by listening to the appeal of language, language did not make the poet by listening to my appeal. Yet, if the poem became revealed by me, then can I not say that I was revealed by the poem? Can I not say that I dwelt in the language with the poem? Can I not say that the language dwelt in me with the poem?[2]

Ajax Hero Artist[3]

It may seem absurd to conceive of Ajax as an artist. What does he create? What is his medium? The short answer is that he creates himself, by conceiving himself a hero. He is his own work of art. Consider this notion in the light of the relationship of language and poetry, the poet and the poem. The poet creates (or reveals) the poem and equally the poem creates (or reveals) the poet, because they dwell in the same moment in a particular language. To put this in heroic language, both Heideggerian and Nietzschean, the poem is as willed as the poet and as willing. Art is located in both of them, not each of them, for poet and poem exist only as part of a willed/willing dyad. Art, it may be more precise to say, dwells in this willed/willing relationship. Note the ambivalence of 'willing.' The willer, the person or thing that wills, and the person who accommodates will, who is willing to be willed. So long as this ambivalence is honored, so long as one is not merely willed, the object of another's willing, so long as one is willing, able to accept being willed and able to reject being willed, all is well.

And Ajax? As a hero Ajax lives (or is spawned by) his heroic acts. Ajax's willed acts will Ajax into existence. The heroic act of Ajax's willing, in both senses, creates Ajax, enabling Ajax to unconceal of himself and become unconcealed to us. His shameful acts in response to the unjust allocation of Achilleus's armor, therefore, amount to a willful self-denial of Ajax the Hero, of Ajax who is his heroic deeds. The injustice of Agamemnon's decision diminishes Ajax, for it asserts that a lesser hero is the greater, Ajax must set things right, for he cannot be Ajax and accept his diminution. To accept the allocation makes him an unwilling person, leaving him as a willed subject, acted upon merely and solely. Athena reinforces his abject status, by making it clear to all that Ajax has been willed, acted upon, by her superior willingness or will to power. Worse, by intoxicating him, she causes (wills) him to act in a shameful manner, a process which undermines further Ajax's self-conception and self-creation. Is Athena *Parthenos* making another point as well? First, Ajax is the object of her will; second, he is willed to act anti-heroically, becoming anti-Ajax in two senses. It matters not in the least that the god, Athena, has superior will. Her divine power is heroically irrelevant *to Ajax*. Heroes overcome their adversaries, human or divine, or they lose their status, their self-conception, themselves. It they cannot overcome being willed upon, they cannot be self-conceived, self-willed, self-willing. Life as a willed creature cannot be countenanced, much less tolerated, by a hero. If a hero cannot conceive (create) himself, by his willing actions, he cannot conceive (imagine) of his existence. Ajax kills himself, his willing act, an effort to expunge Ajax the willed upon. Suicide is his ultimate assertion or reassertion of his self-conception. Ajax *Parthenos*.

Leader Volk Spiritual Mission

What is pregiven to the Leader and how it is given so that it can be regiven to the spiritual Nation as its mission are critical to the process of revealing the mission and empowering the Leader, by revealing how he is embodied in the *Volk*. As the poem dwells in the language, the Leader dwells in his people, the *Fuehrer* in his *Volk*, for the *Volk* entails its mission, its destiny. Similarly, to the degree of his authenticity, the *Volk* is revealed in him, becoming unimaginable without him. Once unconcealed, once shorn of its encrustations of thoughtlessness, habits, customs, by ceaseless struggle, *Eris*, the *Volk* Leader then presents, reveals, incarnates the new *Volk*, now spiritualized in the form of its mission. Yet, to the degree that this formulation suggests Time, by employing the terms 'becomes,' 'now,' 'once,' and 'ceaseless,' it misses the simultaneity, the immanence, the enfoldedness of these ideas in an ever-present, but concealed, moment. The spiritual mission has always dwelt in the *Volk*. The Beginning and the End are an identity, the true nature of which is revealed by the Leader who dwells in the *Volk*. The more truth there is, or rather, the more, by our confrontation with What Is in its totality, is unconcealed: *Volk* Leader Spirit Mission. The more immanent truth there is in this manifold, the less Time is seen as part of its nature.

The assumption of the rectorate is the commitment to the *spiritual* leadership of this institution of higher learning. Martin Heidegger[4]

THE RECTORAL ADDRESS MARCH 1933

The ideas written in a Heideggerian manner in the Prologue were not intended to represent Heidegger's ideas, though, I hope, their provenance is clear. They were presented to illustrate how a philosophical turn can be given to many ideas current in German thought in the century leading up to the Third Reich. Consider the many ideas, convictions, values, and predispositions Heidegger shares with Thomas Mann: (1) that there is a substantive difference between the German and other European nations, which includes elites and ordinary people; (2) that there is a substantive difference between the German language and other European languages, especially marked in the Romance languages; (3) that there is an antagonism to the Roman and Latin world and a love of Greece; (4) that there is a frank appreciation of the value of conflict, including war, rather than an attachment to violence for its own sake; (5) that there is a contempt for the material, the shallow, the trivial, the decadent, and the West in general; (6) that there is a special spiritual mission of the German Nation. This far from complete list is sufficient to indicate more than the many affinities between the great novelist and the great philosopher. It is to show that many ideas, values, convictions, and predispositions antedated the rise of Hitler, ideas that found adherents who were not National Socialists.

But Heidegger for a time was an enthusiastic supporter the Hitler Movement. Unlike Thomas Mann and many others, equally critical of Western thinking, he did not leave Germany in protest. The weight of the evidence supports the conclusion that Heidegger, until perhaps the late 1930s, believed that the Hitler Movement offered best chance to transform Germany along *his* lines. Neither a careerist nor an opportunist, he supported the Third Reich, because he believed Hitler offered Germany its one best hope to fulfill its spiritual mission. So it becomes essential to examine Case Heidegger.[5] Let me make some disavowals. I am not interested in indicting Heidegger or in debunking his philosophy *via* his political activities. Not only is this project highly dubious, it is irrelevant to my purpose: to explain the affinities that so many elites, including some of the world's most brilliant people, had for National Socialism, Hitler, and his Movement. Let me also say, it is incomprehensible that anyone having the most cursory acquaintance with Heidegger's writing can believe that his philosophy *derived* from the Hitler Movement's ideology or that he learned anything at all from it. He did, however, believe that the Movement provided an opportunity to have his vision for the German university actualized. An opportunity he had to chance, because, like Plato at Syracuse, the call to life, the call to live one's philosophy, was too tempting to ignore. Unlike Plato, who thought he could transform a dictator, and thereby his *polis*, Heidegger thought he could transform his university and, by so doing, spiritualize the German Nation. Though this project failed, Heidegger went to his grave believing in its value. That Heidegger was naïve is hardly surprising. That he was naïve to the extent that he believed he could infuse the Hitler Movement with his philosophy is astounding, but perhaps not to those familiar with the delusions of professors.

In the midst of Hitler mania, Heidegger became Rector of Freiburg University, his Rectoral Address becoming a document of the Hitler Movement. The Address remains deeply controversial. My purpose is not resolve the controversy but to analyze why Heidegger believed in the Hitler Movement. Profoundly German in its essence, not merely in its nationalist assertions of the superior character of the German language and culture—many nationalisms make similar claims—only a German rector would make so many demands on his audience. As Thomas Mann and countless other Germans have said, 'to think philosophically is to think in German.' Heidegger's address suggests that to be an educated German is to be a philosopher. Moreover, the Address serves as a prolegomena to the Hitler Movement's political theology.

In Heidegger's view: To perform its great mission, the German university must be 'self-administered,' but this cannot happen without understanding German students and teachers. He asks, 'Can we know all this without the most constant and unsparing *self-examination*.'[6] This self-critical, unrelenting process reveals not only the essence of students and teachers but the 'primordial common will [of the German university] to its essence.... The will to the essence of the German university is the will to science as will to the historical spiritual mission of the German people as a people that knows itself in its State.'[7] This remarkable idea needs some discussion, for it counters one of the most hallowed notions of education. The unexamined life has not been considered worth living since Socrates, if not before. The purpose of this life is, however, not to serve the State, nor to serve a historical mission of a people, but to lead a good, virtuous, and just life. While this could not be accomplished outside the *polis,* the *polis* should not be conceived as a State with a historical mission or as a modern State at all. The *polis* did not have a will, primordial or otherwise, to its essence. My point is not to contrast Greek notions of the educated life with the German, but to indicate how far a great student of Greek thought like Heidegger could miss the mark, despite believing he was getting back to 'the *beginning* of our spiritual-historical existence.... This beginning is the departure, the setting out, of Greek philosophy. Here, for the first time, Western man rises up, from a base in popular culture [*Volkstum*] and by means of his language, against the *totality of What Is* and questions and comprehends it as the being that it is.'[8]

Heidegger's concept of the 'beginning' lies at the heart of his philosophy. While the beginning stands *before in Time*, it also stands *before us in Space*, that is, in front of us, confronting us. In this respect, the beginning still is and always must be before us. Greek thought is the beginning for Heidegger, not only because it is the 'first' thought to use the totality of *What Is* and the method of relentless Questioning to keep *the What Is*, in both senses, before us. The Greeks discovered thought *in* their language. They became Greeks because of Greek, and Greek became Greek because of the Greeks. By this process of self-discovery or self-unconcealing, they revealed the What Is *and* what always has been. In this sense, the Greeks did not develop from a non-Greek line of thinkers; they were the first people to think at all. They were the beginning of thought, because they were the first to confront the totality of the *What Is* with relentless Questioning. It must be kept in mind that *the Questioning and the What I*s are part of the same idea, separable only heuristically. Without Questioning there can be no What Is; without the What Is, there can be no Questioning. Therefore, not only were the Greeks the first people to think, they were the first or primordial people. Other human beings have been trapped or suspended in Time, moving from event to event mindlessly, under the power of necessity without being aware of their thralldom. Such people have been colloidal, not primordial. They could not confront the What Is, because their languages did not embed the Questioning. Therefore, the What Is remained concealed. Necessity may be stronger than knowledge. But knowing or Questioning reveals it, names it, and limits it, by placing it within the language and the language within it.

Supposing the plausibility of this reading of Heidegger, it remains difficult to accept that Heidegger faced the Greeks in all their totality of what they were. Like Nietzsche, Heidegger ignored the centrality of the *polis* to Greek philosophy, a process only partially justified by their appeal to the Pre-Socratics. Unlike Nietzsche, Heidegger substituted the State for the *polis*. Then, he compounded the distortion by imbuing the State with a spiritual-historical mission. He further elaborated this idea: 'For the Greeks, science is not a cultural asset but the innermost determining center of all popular and national existence. The Greeks thought science not merely a means of bringing the unconscious to consciousness, but the power that hones and encompasses all existence.'[9] Moreover: 'Then this will to essence will create for our people its world of the innermost and most extreme danger, i.e., its truly *spiritual* world.... And the *spiritual world* of a people is not the superstructure of a culture any more than it is an armory filled with useful information and values; it is the power that most deeply preserves the people's earth-and blood-bound strengths as the power that most deeply arouses and most profoundly shakes the people's existence. Only a spiritual world guarantees the people greatness.'[10]

Can one imagine Pericles uttering such sentences? Can one imagine Aeschylus, whom Heidegger quotes in his Address, making these points?

'Knowing, however, is far weaker than necessity (*Prometheus*, Aeschylus, ln.514).' Heidegger amplifies, 'That means that all knowing about things has always already been surrendered to the predominance of destiny and falls before it.'[11] Without denying the power of necessity, it is difficult to see how Aeschylus suggested, especially through Prometheus, that humans must '*surrender* to the predominance of destiny' or necessity. Prometheus is chained to his rock, not because he surrendered but because he defied the gods to serve man, becoming himself. Can anyone believe that Aeschylus suggested that Prometheus should have done otherwise? Or that he should have recanted? There is a great deal of difference between surrendering and going down fighting. Is not fulfilling one's destiny, defiantly and without apology or regret, what *Eris* is all about, as Heidegger and Nietzsche repeatedly made clear? Necessity, for Prometheus, and countless other Greek heroes, historical or mythological, meant that one must be who one is, the consequences be damned. All other necessities must be confronted. Surely, Nietzsche concurs with the tragedians in this. Necessity should be defied not kowtowed to.

There is another issue. Heidegger believed that the Germans, following the Greeks, could will themselves to their essence as a spiritual people and that it was no coincidence that only these two peoples—the only Nations able to confront and question the What Is because of the power of their languages to reveal to the people their spiritual-historical mission—have appreciated the power of necessity. While Germans may have been a people whose spirituality enabled them to subordinate knowledge to necessity, it is a far different matter to so conceive the Greeks. The most that can be said, if Greeks are to be the primordial precursors of Germans, is that knowing *of* necessity (in the sense of being aware) may allow a people to dwell *in* necessity, as they dwell in the language which unconceals necessity. Knowing, reason, and logic, all bundled in *Logos,* define Greek manhood, not just Greek thought. A Greek may be defeated by necessity, or fate, or the will of a god, but he will never submit himself to it.[12]

At all events, when a great thinker, like Heidegger or Nietzsche, distorts, wittingly or not, the views, values, or ideas of another person or culture, one must ask why? Nietzsche ignored the *polis*, in his call to recapitulate as much of Greek society as possible in mid to late nineteenth century Germany.[13] Having no possibility of recreating the *polis*, the best that could be done was to transform (or allow the self-transformation) citizens into artists. Heidegger reconceived the *polis*, without mentioning it, into the spiritual-historical State. Where Nietzsche tried to create the conditions under which individuals could express themselves in their full natures, Apollonian and Dionysian, despite the constraints of modern society, Heidegger tried to create conditions under which Germans could fulfill their destiny within the confines of the spiritualized State. One of the most important elements of this process entailed the spiritualization of the German university.

Implying a major recasting of the university, Heidegger did not shrink from the difficulties of his project: 'Instead of giving oneself over to the universal enterprise of education, as if one had been given the mission of saving the culture, one must [engage in] a radical dismantling and rebuilding or a destruction...without concerning oneself with idle talk of those sensible and enterprising people who reckon time with clocks.'[14] Learning is no longer for learning's sake; its purpose is to preserve 'the people's earth- and blood-bound strengths as the power that most deeply arouses and shakes the people's existence.'[15] Academic specialties will have to be reordered to achieve this objective. Under the relentless force of 'questioning' that 'unfolds its most authentic strength to unlock the essential in all things... the encapsulation of the sciences in separated specialties [is shattered and thus] brings back from their boundless and aimless dispersal in individual fields and corners, and directly exposes science once again to the productivity and blessing of all world-shaping powers of human-historical existence, such as nature, history, language; people, custom, state; poetry, thought, faith; disease, madness, death; law, economy, technology.'[16] It is easy to sympathize with Heidegger's impatience with specialization. More than one critic has complained that academics know more and more about less and less. His emphasis on questioning as a means and form of knowing is also consonant with many well thought out notions of liberal education. Yet, for all the attractiveness of his ideas, their nationalistic context, inevitably condoning, if not idealizing violence, makes Western scholars shudder.[17] Moreover, nationalism and academic freedom are incompatible, as Heidegger candidly granted: 'The much lauded academic freedom will be expelled from the German university; for this freedom was not genuine because it was only negative. It primarily meant a lack of concern, arbitrariness of intentions and inclinations, lack of restraint in what was done and left undone.'[18] We have already encountered, in our examination of Thomas Mann, the German critique of the West's concept of freedom as liberty and, therefore, essentially negative. It is, of course, negative in the sense that liberty does not empower the scholar *to do*; it does not include the *freedom to*.[19] Yet in the context of the modern power State, the *freedom from* should not be so casually disparaged. Academic freedom, for all its possible abuses, including irresponsibility to the larger society, must be honored, because it conditions the freedom to do research, to learn, and to teach without the interference of the power State. The responsibility of the university cannot be to the State, however it is disguised as the destiny of the spiritual people. It must be to learning itself, to the relentless questioning and the confrontation with the What Is that Heidegger so values.

How little the 'self-administered' or 'self-asserted' university could with-
stand, how little it could imagine resisting the influence of the Third Reich
is indicated by Heidegger's list of what the new university would demand of
students. There would be three bonds of the German student: 'The first bond
binds them to the *Volksgemeinschaft*...[Labor Service]. The second bond
binds to the honor and destiny of the nation...[Military Service]. The third
bond...binds them to the spiritual mission of the German people...[Knowl-
edge Service].'[20] I am aware how perilous and unfair it is to take Heidegger's
words literally or out of context. Nevertheless, it is difficult to escape the
feeling that he did not value either the student or the pursuit of truth, however
defined, as intrinsically valuable or that Heidegger's vision of the new university was to be geared to or coordinated (*Gleichshaltung*) with the Third Reich
and that the value of students and leaning were dialectically tied to the fulfillment of Germany's destiny. More than an effort to understand Heidegger's
elective affinities with the Hitler Movement, his ideas will help to clarify my
interpretation of the Hitler Movement as political theology. The great literary
scholar, J.P. Stern, will assist us on our journey.

> Now we are meet here, we are all filled with the wonder of this gathering. Not
> every one of you can see me and I do not see each one of you. But I feel you,
> and you feel me! It is faith in our Nation that has made us little people great, that
> us made us poor people rich, that has made us wavering, fearful, timid people
> brave and confident; that has made us erring wanderers clear-sighted and has
> brought us together. So you have come this day from your little villages, your
> market towns, your cities, from mines and factories, or leaving the plough, to
> this city. You come out of the little world of your daily struggle for life, and
> of your struggle for Germany and for our Nation, to experience this feeling for
> once: Now we are together, we are with him and he is with us, and now we are
> Germany. Hitler[21]

HITLER'S POLITICAL THEOLOGY

Hitler's remarkable words divide interpretations of the Hitler Movement.
One view, largely that of historians, social scientists, and others whose reality tends to be exhausted by the empirically verifiable, either discount or ignore Hitler's speeches as propaganda or insane (or infantile) self-promotion.
Devoid of meaning, his writings and speeches were theatre, to be judged by
how much his audience was moved, however momentarily. They believe
that only those already committed to Hitler could have ignored the falsity,
absurdity, and blasphemy of Hitler's effusions. What appealed to the ignorant, the superstitious, no less than to the desperate and the panicked, could

not but offend the educated and the sophisticated. In the long run, the very
irrationality of Hitler's words should have undermined his support among the
educated. The material world and the limitations it entails inevitably would
have prevailed. Hitler, like other false Messiahs, should have dissolved like
mist in the morning sun. That Hitler succeeded continues to baffle many
interpreters of the Third Reich. Consider Ernst Nolte, an exceptionally able
interpreter of Hitler and his Movement. At the end of his magisterial analysis
of fascism, he writes:

> Theoretical transcendence...means the reaching out of the mind beyond what
> exists and what can exist toward an absolute whole;...all that goes beyond, that
> releases man from the confines of the everyday world and which...makes it
> possible for him to experience the world as a whole. Practical transcendence...
> means the social process...which continually widens human relationships,
> thereby rendering them more subtle and abstract—the process disengages the
> individual from traditional ties and increases the power of the group until it
> finally assails even the primordial forces of nature and history.[22]

Nolte flatly denies that fascism, including the Hitler version, could have
made any valid claim to this sense of transcendence.[23] Fearing a misreading
of his analysis of the Third Reich, I was gratified to learn that Stern contradicted Nolte: 'Hitler's onslaught on "the world as one whole"—on the idea
of our common humanity—is the successful thing it is precisely because it
is conducted under the image and in the language of transcendence, as the
answer to a religious longing and demand.... Why should the gigantic dream
of destruction...not be seen as a project to transcend the human condition in
the direction of a (racially pure) whole, and to free men from the constraint
of everyday?'[24]

Let us consider his analysis of Hitler's speech which was epigraph of this
section:

> After an initial illusion to 'the voice crying in the wilderness (*John* iii. 4),
> Christ's epiphany (*John* xx. 19–31) is presented, with its exhortation to tran-
> scending faith, 'blessed are they that have not seen, yet have believed.' The next
> passage ('Not every one of you...') continues the messianic parallel by alluding
> to *John* xvi. 16–7), 'A little while, and; ye shall not see me: and again a little
> while, and ye shall see me;' and so does the subsequent enumeration ('us little
> people...us poor people...') with its allusion to *Luke* vii. 22, 'how that the blind
> seem the lame walk...to the poor the gospel is preached.' The last paragraph
> opens with Hitler's favorite antithesis on the theme of 'your little lives...my
> great mission:' the topos of 'little villages' has no direct parallel in the *English
> Bible* but relates to Luther's rendering of *Micah* v. I (and *Matthew* ii. 6), 'And
> thou, Bethlehem, which art little among the towns of Judah....' The final clarion

call, 'We are with him and he is with us!' takes up the earlier 'I feel you and you feel me,' again in Luther's version of *John* xiv. 3, 'I will come again and take you unto me, so that ye shall be where I am.' And the Johannine allusion is joined by a reference to some of the most famous and familiar of German medieval mystical love poetry, '*du bist min, ich bin din/ des solt du gewis sin:*' Tristan wooing Isolde, Christ the Bridegroom wooing the Church, Hitler wooing the communicant members of the Nation....[25]

While it can hardly be disputed that Hitler self-consciously made religious appeals, claiming that his Movement was transcendent, it remains necessary to try to explain why it worked, not only among desperate masses but among educated elites. Before I consider Stern's analysis in more detail, allow a social scientific parenthesis, which provides a basis for analyzing the Hitler Movement from a different academic perspective. It will complement the philosophical prologue of this chapter and ground Stern's and my interpretation in non-literary terms. Intending no disparagement of literary analysis, my point is that no single method suffices to understand the Hitler Movement.

Despite Weber's warning regarding defining 'religion,' consider Peter Berger's argument.[26] 'Religion is the human enterprise by which a sacred cosmos is established.'[27] Further, 'The cosmos posited by religion thus both transcends and includes man. The sacred cosmos is confronted by man as an immensely powerful reality other than himself. Yet this reality addresses itself to him and locates his life in an ultimately meaningful order.'[28] Simultaneously, human beings place themselves in the enormity of a cosmos which 'should' find them insignificant, powerless in the face of awesome reality, yet, by providing them with an arena of meaning, by noticing them, grants them significance. By establishing the sacred cosmos, humans establish the anti-Chaos, a meaningful reality, so long as they remain right with the universe. 'To be in a right relationship with the sacred cosmos is to be protected against the nightmare threats of Chaos,' man's most profound enemy.[29] Hence the importance of Order: 'The anthropological presupposition of this is a human craving for meaning that appears to have the force of instinct. Men are congenitally compelled to impose a meaningful order upon reality.'[30] At the same time, the power of this imposition or this constructed reality depends largely on its implicit character.

> Let the institutional order be so interpreted as to hide, as much as possible, its *constructed* character. Let that which has been stamped out of the ground *ex nihilo* appear as a manifestation of something that has been existent from the beginning of time, or at least from the beginning of this group.... Let them believe that, in acting out the institutional programs that have been imposed on them, they are but realizing the deepest aspirations of their own being and putting themselves in harmony with the fundamental order of the universe.[31]

Humans may be aware that they are in a theatre, watching a drama of their own devising, yet they prefer not to notice its artifice. They wish to be drawn into the dramatic, orderly, meaningful space, without noticing the props, the makeup, the garbled lines, the concentration of time and the collapsing of space or any of the other essentials of dramatic presentation. Religion can be understood as the most effective drama, because 'All legitimation maintains socially defined reality. Religion legitimates so effectively because it relates the precarious reality constructions of empirical societies with ultimate reality.'[32] Religion works, because it transcends Time and Space, the artificiality of human constructs, including the concept of reality, because by so doing it creates an orderly reality, all the more powerful for seeming natural. Moreover, 'Religion implies the farthest reach of man's self externalization, of his infusion of reality with his own meanings. Religion implies that human order is projected into the totality of being.'[33] Being is Eternal. Being defeats Chaos, by restricting it to Time and Space. 'Religious legitimation purports to relate the humanly defined reality to ultimate, universal and sacred reality. The inherently precarious and transitory construction of human activity is thus given the semblance of ultimate security and permanence.'[34] At least so long as the drama absorbs its audience.

By defeating Chaos, Being also defeats Death. Although it cannot be denied, its significance is dissolved in two senses. First, humans now see themselves as part of Eternity. Secondly, human life is not a 'tale told by an idiot signifying nothing.' Life has meaning, insofar as it is sheltered under the sacred canopy, which takes the sting out of death by giving life a point, however mortal. 'Every human society is, in the last resort, men banded together in the face of death. The power of religion depends... upon the credibility of the banners it puts in the hands of men as they stand before death, or more accurately, as they walk inevitably toward it.[35] Religion makes the path, not the end, significant. This understanding of religion and its functions enables us to appreciate that Stern's interpretation of the Hitler Movement is more than a literary exercise, more than a gifted critic's reading of a text. Along with the philosophical prologue, Berger's sociological framework provides Stern's interpretation with multidisciplinary underpinning.

He is the maker of his kingdom: the powerful embattled personality we find in Balzac, Dickens or Melville (and German novelists like Gustav Freytag, Otto Ludwig, and C.F. Meyer) imposes its demands upon the world and attempts to fashion the world in its own image. Romantic, Faustian man forms, and in all but literal sense creates, his own conditions and thus the world.
J.P. Stern[36]

THE CALL OF TRANSCENDENCE

It was possible for many Germans approve of Hitler based solely on his successes before World War II and perhaps until the Fall of France. Success collects adherents. Here I suggest why many would have followed Hitler *irrespective* of his successes or failures. For this group, Hitler's successes confirmed their faith in him as a transcendent personality, the *Fuehrer*, and for some, the Messiah, including attributes of divinity. So powerful was this faith that any failure which attended the Third Reich would have been attributed to the deficiencies of the world, which knew not what to do, further confirmation that Hitler was the Messiah: 'But above all the Will becomes a pseudo-religious concept: in speaking of himself as one sent by History, or again as the agent of cosmic forces or natural laws, Hitler comes close to Christ's affirmation, "I am of mine own self do nothing: as I hear, I judge; and my judgment is just: because I seek not mine own will, but the Will of the Father which hath sent me" (*John* v.30)....'[37] I realize applying terms like 'theology,' 'sacred,' and 'Messiah' to Hitler offends. In mitigation, many scholars have felt obliged to resort to scare quotes or qualifiers like 'pseudo' or 'false.' Understandable as these protective procedures are, they make more difficult the already formidable task of appreciating Hitler's appeal. Moreover, calling one set of spiritual (non-material) values 'pseudo' suggests that there is a true set of such values, a true religion opposed to the false. Unlike theologians, secular scholars normally avoid truth claims regarding religion.[38] Labeling something 'pseudo,' without substantiating or at least disclosing what is 'authentic,' panders to prejudice. Worse, applying these labels to phenomena as complex as the Hitler Movement makes comprehension almost impossible. Failure to understand how Hitler could captivate an entire people, not only dishonors its victims, it courts a reprise. It is one of the many strengths of Stern's interpretation is that he does not make this mistake, notwithstanding his occasional use of 'pseudo.'

Stern does not stint Hitler's gifts as a politician: 'The more we come to know about these groups and organizations [which constituted the Third Reich], the more clearly we perceive the astonishing fact that this huge array of jealous and mutually hostile factions, beset with internecine conflicts, plots and counterplots, was held together, until April 1945, by the promises, cajolings, the threats and tantrums, the appeals to loyalty and invitations to expedient betrayal, the contempt and praise, the self-assurance, the realism and fantasies, the cynical and professed commitment, of one man.'[39] Only a charismatic leader could have brought the Third Reich to power, and only one person could have kept it together until the final catastrophe. 'The Hitler phenomenon—the reality and the myth—remains the most important phenomenon of its age.'[40] 'Charismatic,' when applied to Hitler, cannot be reduced to a gifted politician who connects with the masses. It signifies something much closer to its religious connotations, a gift of God, not in the sense of an attribute among many, like charm, but in the sense of a being touched by the divine. In a political setting, this kind of Leader speaks *for* God and, for some of his followers, speaks *as* God. His words flow from his *inneres Erlebnis*, his authentic experience, which was inextricably tied to his personality. To use Heideggerian language, Hitler's experience dwelt in his personality and *vice versa*. If the personality be charismatic, the experience-personality dyad approaches the divine, either as divine instruction or divine presence. Stern approximates this idea: 'His acts are judged according to the criterion of immanent, inward coherence: that is, according to the degree to which a man's utterances and action express his total personality and indicate his capacity for experience. Utterances are seen as actions and actions as poetry, and poetry as the consummation of *Erlebnis*, of living experience.'[41] 'Poetry,' in this context is not simply verse or ornamental speech; it is rather the sign that the personality dwells in the language and has been chosen by the language as its embodiment. As poets make or unconceal poems, Leaders make or reveal worlds, as the epigraph indicates: 'Romantic, Faustian man forms, and in all but literal sense creates, his own conditions and thus the world.' This Creator is not Nature or God in Spinoza's sense. This Creator is a personal God, not necessarily in the sense of a loving or caring divinity, but in the sense of a powerful, awesome existential personality:

> Existentialism is the final and most radical form of this heroic Romanticism— most radical because at the farthest remove from the moral and social sanctions of earlier, more stable conceptions of man. In its popular, least technical aspect existentialism is a philosophy for heroic living. Its values are authenticity, commitment, and for want of a better word we may call personal truth. As such, existentialism from Kierkegaard through Nietzsche to Heidegger and Sartre rejects all values which are not expressive of an individual self and which are not created by the self.... The commitment of the self is authenticated not by the value and worth of its objective—the value of what a man is committed *to*—but by strength, energy and originality of the willing self.[42]

In the German context and with respect to Hitler all the more, it is important not to see the existential self in the Western sense of individualism. This self is embedded in the *Volk*. With uncharacteristic modesty, Hitler said: 'I have come from the people. In the course of fifteen years I have slowly worked my way up from the people, together with this Movement.... It is my ambition not to know a single statesman in the world who has a better right than I do to say that he is a representative of his people.'[43] He would later conceive of this process as much more immanent than the concept of 'working up' suggests, seeing himself much more in the Faustian mode, not simply a hardworking politician. Stern concurs in Hitler's self-image as an indispensable Leader: 'His originality consists in a deliberate reversal of the functions normally attributed to personal-existential values on the one hand and social-political values on the other.... Hitler's discovery...is to introduce a conception of personal authenticity into the public sphere and proclaim it as the chief value and sanction of politics. What he does is to translate the notions of genuineness and sincerity and living experience...from the private and poetic sphere into the sphere of public affairs....'[44] Much more is suggested here than notions like 'the art of politics.' By this transposition from the normally private to the normally public, Hitler redefined public affairs as poetry, as an expression of his *inneres Erlebnis*. He was the Leader who dwelt in the *Volk*, as a poet dwells in language. More than representing the *Volk*, he was the *Volk*. His Will was their Will, because his Being was their Being: 'The "Will" was for Hitler what, in German popular mythology, it was for Schopenhauer and Nietzsche: the agent of the law of nature and of history, an all-encompassing metaphysical principle; in short, creator of the world and all that is in it.'[45] Stern draws the theological implications of this world-creating Will: 'At the point where the self is so imperiously asserted a curious reversal, from complete subjectivity and arbitrariness to what looks like its opposite is said to take place. In declaring the Will absolute, the ideologist makes a show of replacing the subjective self by an objective principle; the Will is now to be seen as cosmic law and as an element of a religious faith.... But above all the Will becomes a pseudo-religious concept.'[46] Lest there be any doubt that Hitler was aware of the power of religious faith, consider his words:

> In helping to raise man from the level of mere animal survival, faith really contributes to the securing and safeguarding of man's existence. Take away from present mankind its religious-dogmatic principles which are upheld by its education and whose practical significance is that of ethical-moral principles, by abolishing religious education and without replacing it with something equivalent, and the result facing you will be a grave shock to the foundations of mankind's existence. One may therefore state that not only does man live to serve higher ideals but that, conversely, these higher ideals also provide the presupposition of his existence as man. So the circle closes.[47]

Hitler intended to do more than lay a foundation from which Germans could face life's vicissitudes. Stern argues that Hitler believed in his role as a spiritual Leader, not as a simple manipulator of the masses, quoting Nietzsche: 'In all great deceivers a remarkable process is at work, to which they owe their power. In the very act of deception with all its preparation, the dreadful voice, expression and gestures, amid their effective scenario they are overcome *by their belief in themselves;* it is this belief which then speaks so persuasively, so miracle-like, to the audience....'[48]

In this self-deception, if that is what it was, Hitler had powerful allies, his audience. Over the years, crowned with self-validating and self-creating success, Hitler believed he was the savior of the German people for all times, not merely a politician who met their transitory needs. Stern qualifies his suggestion, when he writes: 'What lifts Hitler out of the sphere of the banal and commonplace...is his wholly political perception of a religious need in contemporary German society, and his a growing confidence of being able to exploit that need for his own ends.'[49] Yet this qualification assumes that Hitler's ends differed from the *Volk's.* Hitler and his followers believed their ends were identical, an identity entailed in the notion of the mutual indwelling of his personality and the *Volk.* Stern comes close to appreciating the power of this mutually created identity: 'The self-assertion of the leader's undivided personality is matched by the devotion of his followers' undivided belief.'[50] He, however, is not willing to grant the Heideggerian notion that the personality and the belief it engenders are profoundly interpenetrated. Undivided belief creates an undivided personality, or, rather, the belief dwells in the personality and the personality in the belief, the dividedness inherent in Time and Space dissolving, while revealing and creating the Will to German destiny. Heidegger's concept of mutual indwelling helps us understand the nature of Hitler's appeal.

It is one thing to convince the masses to believe in saviors, their embodiment in the people, and the identity of ends. It is quite another to convince elites. Yet, as Stern realizes, many of them were, including the leading lights of German thought. I am not suggesting that the likes of Mann, Heidegger, Benn, Schmitt, Jung, or Jaspers agreed with each other regarding the nature of the Hitler Movement, or that Hitler would have agreed with them or even understood their views. Nor am I suggesting that the Hitler Movement contained an explicit doctrine, notwithstanding my effort to make it coherent. It was more than a reflection of the ideas and feelings, the values and the predispositions, the anxiety and the despair, the hope and the visions that were in the air. By no means simple-minded, several leading German intellectuals believed that the Hitler Movement had elective affinities with their values and modes of thought.

Stern dissects some of them. Consider his treatment of Carl Jung: 'The religious dimension of National Socialism is for Jung not a matter of propaganda but the psychic given of contemporary Germany. [Jung] "There are representative of the German Faith movement who, both intellectually and in human terms, are fully in a position not merely to believe but also to know that the god of the Germans is Wotan and not the universal God of the Christians."'[51] Stern concludes that Jung, like the 'fascists,' is enamored of energy: 'What is at work here is that dynamic fallacy, according to which all psychic energy is *ipso facto* positive, all movement is a sign of vigor, all vigor is divine, and all divinity dynamic. So numerous are the affinities of this fallacy with the view that authenticity is the supreme value and with the religious element in what I have called the ideology of Will, that we may speak of three aspects of one and the same thing. And the thing itself is the chief metaphysical aspect of fascism.'[52] This assessment hardly does justice to the notorious Jung essay. In 'Wotan,' Jung, far more than indicating his attraction to movement and energy as a sign of physical and mental vigor, he comes close to identifying Hitler with Wotan and indirectly with Christ.[53]

> But what is more than curious...is that an ancient god of storm and frenzy, the long quiescent Wotan, should awake, like an extinct volcano to new activity in a civilized country that had long been supposed to have outgrown the Middle Ages. We have seen him come to life in the German Youth Movement, and right at the beginning the blood of several sheep was shed in honor of his resurrection. Armed with rucksack and lute, blond youths...were to be seen as restless wanderers on every road from the North Cape to Sicily, faithful votaries of the roving god. Later, towards the end of the Weimar Republic, the wandering role was taken over by the thousands of unemployed.... By1933 they wandered no longer, but marched in their hundreds of thousands. The Hitler Movement literally brought the whole of Germany to its feet.... He could be seen, looking rather shamefaced, in the meeting-house of a sect of simple folk in North Germany, disguised as Christ sitting on a white horse.[54]

Jung, like Stern, concludes that Hitler has changed the course of German history: 'The impressive thing about the German phenomenon is that one man, who is obviously possessed, has infected a whole Nation to such an extent that everything is set in motion and started rolling on its course towards perdition.'[55] And this, despite Jung's assertion of the uncontrollability of the life of Nations:

> The life of the individual as a member of society and particularly as part of the State may be regulated like a canal, but the life of Nations is a great rushing river which has always been stronger than men.... Thus the life of Nations rolls on unchecked, without guidance, unconscious of where it is going, like a rock crashing down the side of a hill, until it is stopped by an obstacle stronger than itself. Political events move from one impasse the next, like a torrent caught in gullies, creeks and marshes. All human control comes to an end when the individual is caught in a mass movement. Then the archetypes begin to function.... [56]

Can one reconcile these ideas? How can there be an entire Nation be infected by a possessed individual, directing its course, breaking its perennial political impasses and at the same time be a Nation that in principle denies human control? Whence the sources of infection and possession? Even if Nature or God, do they not have human existence and expression. Jung's 'Wotan' does not have the courage to make explicit the most obvious resolution: that Hitler *was* Wotan or so possessed by him that any distinction between the possessed man and the god is insignificant, a distinction without a difference. 'Wotan is an *Ergreifer* [one who seizes] of men, and, unless one wishes to deify Hitler—which indeed has actually happened—he really is the only explanation.'[57] I realize the 'he' probably refers to Wotan. Jung believed that Hitler was the *Ergreifer* of the German people, whether he was under Wotan's thrall or embodied in the god of storm and frenzy. It might be objected that in 'Wotan' Jung believes that the course of events is moving toward perdition. Whatever the end of the Hitler Movement, Jung's linkage, if not identity, of Wotan and Hitler, goes a long way of explaining the power of the Hitler Movement. Benign or not, gods must be all-powerful. Notoriously wrathful, arbitrary, cruel, blood-thirsty, and insatiable, demanding (or are imputed to demand) worship, adoration, obeisance, submission, and reveling in human degradation, above all, they demand sacrifice. The survival of the tribe depends on the propitiation of this awesome, unquestioned power, its strength deriving from proximity to this divine force. Such was the nature of Abraham's Yahweh and countless other tribal deities. Such was the nature of the followers of Hitler, whether conceived as divine embodiment or agent.

Why would anyone accept such a god?[58] Why would anyone worship a god who demands sacrifice, the death of children, and threaten general annihilation? One reason is fear, a cowering before the Awful. Cassirer writes: 'Myth and religion in general have often been declared to be the mere product of fear. But what is most essential in man's religious life is not the fact of fear, but the *metamorphosis* of fear.... Myth is filled with the most violent emotions and the most frightful visions. But in myth man begins to learn a new and strange art: the art of expressing, and that means of organizing, his most deeply rooted instincts, his hopes and fears.'[59] Another is respect for the Awesome, hoping that proximity will provide security or salvation.[60] More positively, such gods defy Chaos, and by so doing create a zone of meaning under the sacred canopy. Death cannot be so denied, but its implication for nihilism can be undermined. One believes that 'I will live or I will be significant beyond the grave because I have become part of Absolute Power. Alternatively, my tribe will live or become significant because it has tied itself to Absolute Power.' Not from mere existence, meaning derives from proximity to the Absolute or an ability to glimpse the Absolute through the personality of the charismatic Leader, who dwells in the Absolute and it in him.

How closely the Hitler Movement approximated these ideas can be seen through Stern's treatment of the idea of sacrifice. He begins with Hitler's words: 'So if somebody tells us, "The future will demand sacrifices," then we say, "Yes, indeed, it will!" National Socialism is not a doctrine of inertia but a doctrine of conflict. Not a doctrine of happiness or good luck, but a doctrine or work and a doctrine of struggle, and thus a doctrine of sacrifice.'[61] If this notion can be read in the sense of working for a better future, then it is more appropriate to the previous chapter than this one. Yet in the context of charismatic leader saving his Nation, sacrifice takes on more profound and troubling connotations. Stern amplifies: 'Again and again, this generation had to hear how privileged it was to have Hitler in its midst and to be placed by him (or the Lord God, or providence or history) in the vanguard of the revolution. The blood-sacrifices demanded of it were the signs of its worthiness, and its reward: but were they enough?'[62] Note Stern's important linkage of worthiness and reward. The blood-sacrifice is its own reward, because it signifies the worthiness of the *Volk*. Therefore, Stern's question answers itself. There can never be enough of the worthiness/reward dyad. Here the idea of sacrifice retains the idea of a self-abnegating decision on behalf of a greater good. The member of the community sacrifices his material well-being for others or for a higher conception of him or herself. Hence the term self-sacrificing. But what if these actions make victims of others? What if others are sacrificed by the self-sacrificing actions of believers? Again Stern is apt: 'No doubt the simple idea of "sacrifices" for the sake of future material gain is part of the message. But again a fatal ambiguity, exploited by the word "*Opfer*"—it is as though the German language itself, in its inability to distinguish between "victim" and "sacrifice," were an accessory to the ideology....'[63] More than an accessory to an ideology, ambiguity correctly sees the victim and the actor engaging in a sacrificial dance. The most obvious sense is that a suitable victim is offered in propitiation to an awesome deity. Less obvious but equally important, victimhood includes the person making the sacrifice. Abraham must overcome his abhorrence of killing his son, must sacrifice his sense of humanity, to obey Yahweh by meeting this extreme test of faith. Willing to sacrifice Isaac to prove his worthiness to Yahweh and to himself, Abraham received his reward. Sacrificer and sacrificed are inextricably entwined in religious ritual. Removing the ambiguity of '*Opfer*' would create too much space between Abraham and Isaac for the act to be understood. One is tempted to make a triad of the dyad, by adding Yahweh to the sacrificial act. All that would be needed would be for Abraham to lose his love for Yahweh. Then Yahweh could be understood as having sacrificed the love of a good man for his submission. In addition, the concept of the loving father God dissolves in the blood of the beloved son at the hand of his father.[64] *Opfer* with a vengeance.

Stern makes a further point. The logical conclusion to the concept of ritual sacrifice is annihilation, as Hitler understood. 'All in all it is surely best for someone who has no heir for his house to be burned in it with all its contents, as though on a magnificent funeral pyre!'[65] Before this holocaust could come, Hitler had to demonstrate that he was prepared to fulfill the requirements of sacrifice in all its connotations. Sacrifice was profoundly tied to the *Fuehrer* Principle. 'The supremacy of *his* ideas—his absolute rule—begins…with the destruction of the SA in the summer of 1934.'[66] Hitler sacrificed his earliest supporters, because he believed with good reason that Rohm and the SA constituted, if not rivals for power, obstacles to his absolute authority. The SA was sacrificed to his faith in himself as Absolute Leader. Hitler had little animosity toward the SA or Rohm: 'Once dead, Rohm and his SA bravos enter the hagiography of "party comrades who went wrong," and serve the renewal of its "revolutionary spirit" in the same way as the blood-sacrifices of November 1923.'[67] And many of the SA went to their deaths saying 'Heil Hitler!' Grotesque this certainly was from the perspective of Time and Space, but not from the perspective of the Hitler Movement: 'The revolution must go on! It will take many years, many generations will pass, before the victorious emblems of the Reich will be engraved on all hearts—and only then will the National Socialist revolution have succeeded, only then will Germany be saved!'[68] To achieve this glorious revolution of the heart, all means are acceptable. Faith in the Absolute in pursuit of the Eternal is a hard mistress. 'The path of his revolution lay through the blood-sacrifice of *any* group of society, German or foreign, Jewish or Aryan, ultimately of Germany itself.'[69] Furthermore, the SA represented Chaos to most Germans. By sacrificing them, Hitler reinforced one of the most important functions of the sacred canopy: to defeat Chaos. While I believe that Stern appreciates the religious appeal of the Hitler Movement far better than any other scholar, I must disagree with him in one important respect. Consider his definition of the sacrifice syndrome: 'Among conservative writers of the older generation, who spoke powerfully of the noble tradition of *Geist* and of literature's national responsibility, the same strangely self-destructive temper—we may here call it "the sacrifice syndrome"—prevailed. Not even Thomas Mann, far and away the most perceptive of them, seems to have grasped the full significance of this mode of thought when it was presented, not merely as a literary theme, but as a pattern of national values.'[70] Stern here has an impoverished, and certainly not a German or a Greek, sense of self. Recall our discussion of Ajax. By his suicide, did Ajax destroy himself? If one credits his wife or the Chorus, the answer is, 'Yes.' What could be more self-destructive than suicide? Would Ajax have concurred? A hero with a hero's self-conception, Ajax was far more than a hominid creature creeping in Time and Space in search of his next meal or breath. By polluting himself by a shameful act, not in any way his fault, Ajax made *living as Ajax* impossible. Mere existence was insufficient. Ajax sacrificed himself to himself, his physical existence to his image, or better, his self-imagining. Nothing was more important to him, not his wife, his child, nor any others who might need his presence. That Thomas Mann has more understanding of Ajax than Stern is evident in Stern's criticism of Mann. 'In sum [for Mann], a scheme emerges in which *value is commensurate with the catastrophic nature of man's existential project.*'[71] Ajax's *telos* was to be Ajax whatever the cost or however others might assess it. The value of the self is commensurate with what one will sacrifice to be that self. The catastrophe for Ajax would have been to live as someone other than a self-defined hero.

Like Stern I am troubled by turning this 'literary theme' into 'a pattern of national values,' if by 'national' is meant an 'organic nation,' a '*Volk*.' If 'national,' however, refers only the values of a self-designated people, it might have benign effects. The heroic *Volk* can have both meanings. As organic, it measures its value by what its willingness to sacrifice, itself in a funeral pyre, its victims, or both. As the locus of common values, there is no such implication. There is, however, a problematic tendency in German thought to move from the personal to the public, a process which includes infusing concepts like the public or the Nation with an organic property: 'Whereas in other Western countries politics based on the analogy with private experience comes to be distrusted as arbitrary and tyrannical, and is superseded by politics based on and regulated by constitutional and parliamentary devices, German thinking is apt to distrust these devices as mere form and sham.'[72] In the Hitler Movement, however, politics itself was suspect to the degree that it deviated from the Will of the *Fuehrer*. From the perspective of Time and Space, there is nothing worse than death or the annihilation of the world. From a religious perspective, as apocalyptic movements have repeatedly asserted, the destruction of the world can be necessary to achieve the reconciliation of man and God, perhaps the only way to witness their mutual indwelling. At the heroic level, Ajax confirms his self-conception by killing the *shamed* Ajax, the anti-Ajax. At the level of the Apocalypse, the destruction of the world or the End of Days confirms the Leader's Messianic status, his worthiness and his people's worthiness to transcend the limitations of Time and Space.

Finally, Stern is ambivalent about the notion of sacrifice in a religious context: 'As examples of moral heroism and of that "reasonable service" of which St. Paul speaks...the actions of the White Rose [a non-violent resistance group] are unsurpassed in European history and worthy of our highest admiration. Considered as a political act in defiance of a political system, however, the conspiracy was conceived on the level of a moral utopia, executed with a heedless enthusiasm, and attended by no tangible results....'[73]

Was this not a sacrificial act of self-destruction? Is it to be judged by the terms of Time and Space or *sub specie aeternitatis*? What would the parents of the members of the White Rose have felt? It is certainly unpleasant to contemplate that many followers of the Hitler Movement believed they were similarly motivated and directed by spiritual longings. Yet, notwithstanding the content of the causes, the principle seems all but identical. Failure to appreciate either the idealism or the spirituality of the devotees of the Hitler Movement expresses a perverse unwillingness to understand the phenomenon in question. Revulsion is a luxury scholars must learn to do without or deal with less troubling issues.

The last rejectionist of the Enlightenment is Karl Jaspers. Stern writes incisively:

> Writing about 'the spiritual situation of the age,' Karl Jaspers describes its danger as that of a mass-society ruled by 'anonymous powers.' ...Bolshevism and the 'mechanical dialectics of Marxism,' atheism, bureaucracy, even homosexuality and psychoanalysis are listed as the factors leading to the alienation of modern man and to the collapse of human values. 'Man in his present situation' is incapable of responsible political decisions.... Democracy means mob rule, egalitarianism, and hatred of excellence.... What is needed is spiritual aristocracy and 'genuine leaders' who are capable of 'being themselves.' They are contrasted with 'those who, though knowing no cause other than their own, feel and inner emptiness and are thus attempting to escape from themselves.'[74]

For Enlightenment thought, following the Greeks in this respect, political participation confirms authenticity and freedom, not quietism.

> With Jaspers's repeated emphasis on the self-being of man we are back to the theory of authenticity. The form Jaspers gives...is of course wholly unaggressive and non-violent: the remedies he offers are to be found not in personal or collective heroism but in the purely private sphere of spiritual recollection.... Yet by stamping political and prudential thinking as inauthentic and by denying to the institutionalizing of a group conflicts the dignity of serious thought, Jaspers—like Heidegger and countless others before him—implicitly advocates an attitude of political quietism and conformism. And freedom? 'Man's history is a vain attempt to be free,' and his freedom lies in his acceptance of this failure (*Scheitern*).[75]

Nowhere do Stern's Enlightenment values reveal themselves more powerfully than in his treatment of Jaspers, which was a specification of his condemnation of the German concept of freedom generally: 'At the height of his power he [Hitler] proclaims that the readiness to forego freedom is the sign of a truly cultured nation; adding that "the more primitive men are, the more strongly do they feel every restriction of their personal freedom as an act of undue coercion.'"[76] So complete was the absence of any strong feelings for personal freedom that even today, few historians of the Third Reich refer to it.

Much of course depends upon what one means by 'personal freedom.' Is it entailed in notions of Natural Rights, or is it based on a more European notion of contract, where civil rights are negotiated between the ruler and the people or estates? In a sense, Hitler seems in this passage more cognizant of *natural* rights than Stern, for he suggests that primitive, pre-political peoples have a greater regard for liberty than a 'truly cultured Nation.' An undercurrent of German thought, largely concurs with Hitler, when it posits that liberty is indeed primitive and corrosive of 'real' freedom, the freedom appropriate to cultured Nations. From this perspective, far from being freedom in its negative phase, liberty is no form of freedom at all. The idea is that to be free one must be able and willing to engage fully in the life of the community or *Volk*. This participation is made virtually impossible by a concept of liberty that assumes that an individual can be fully human *outside* of civil society. Under this assumption, the free individual could not avoid feeling restricted by any rules imposed by the community at all. By denying the legitimacy of the concept of liberty, many German thinkers have argued that they have released the individual from a primitive misconception, enabling him to be free *within* the social order. Freedom in this sense is exhausted by the concept of freedom *to*, the freedom to participate in civil society, the freedom to become fully human as a result of this participation and the freedom to make a personal contribution to the life of the community. Compared to these life-fulfilling acts, liberty is a primitive thing, little more than acquiescence to *anomie* and loneliness. Moreover, liberty from the perspective of the life-sustaining community is tantamount to treason, for it implies that the individual is less than fully committed to the community which defines him and provides him with transcendent significance.

Although it is possible to disagree with this denigration of 'personal freedom,' disagreement does not warrant dismissing alternate ways of conceiving freedom. Or, to conclude with Stern that 'Jaspers's book has a wrong—and in the circumstances disastrous—sort of timelessness about it....'[77] I suppose this means that Jaspers should have been more cognizant of his historical circumstances and less philosophical in his approach. And if he had been wise enough to do so, he, and others like him, would have avoided 'political quietism and conformism' and perhaps taken up the leaflets of the White Rose. Here Stern reveals his Western understanding of the political as public strife and the competition among interest groups, precisely the kind politics that the German critics of the Enlightenment abhorred. This rejection may have been, in the circumstances of the 1920s and 30s, misconceived or naïve or too detached from the hurly-burly of the times. This finding is, however, far different from concluding that this entire school of thought was wrong because it was 'timeless.' Moreover, in the circumstances following the Great War, to find a way to transcend the series of disasters that descended upon the Weimar Republic and the German people was understandable. To condemn this as 'timeless,' as in effect irresponsible, is to impose one set of values on another. Following the catastrophe of the Hitler Movement, it is appropriate to hesitate before imposing a set of values on any one, much less a proud and accomplished people. After all, are not such coercive impositions what the Hitler Movement attempted to justify with terrifying results?

> What is achieved here—by a complete outsider—is the German Romantics' dream of an organic national community…but at the price of compete unfreedom. J.P. Stern[78]

> The history of this age is no longer a witty game conducted in polite social forms and concerned with a nicely calculated less or more, a game from which one may withdraw at any time. To stand fast or go under—there is no third way. Oswald Spengler[79]

THE HITLER MOVEMENT: *WELTANSCHAUUNG*

It is not possible to describe the Hitler Movement without an analysis of anti-Semitism and the Judeocide it engendered. Anti-Semitism was as central to the Hitler Movement as it was peripheral to chapter five's analysis of National Socialism. In accord with the preliminary nature of this chapter's analysis, I reserve anti-Semitism, including its murderous assumptions and consequences, for the next chapter. In this way, the ideas of the Hitler Movement can be presented coherently, realizing that such coherence has rarely been made explicit. By distilling anti-Semitism from the Hitler Movement, its *Weltanschauung* might appear positive, even praiseworthy. To include anti-Semitism here, however, would interfere with appreciating the Hitler Movement's appeal to German intellectuals, who were not racial anti-Semites. That these intellectuals should have been aware of the homicidal implications of their support of the Hitler Movement is another issue. It is significant that many of them continued to support it even after the Judeocide. History failed the Movement, events preventing the actualization of its Vision. Heidegger, the most brilliant advocate of this thesis, was not alone.

A common objection to the proposition that the Hitler Movement had a coherent doctrine stems from the idea that Hitler *was* the Hitler Movement. The Movement was too idiosyncratic and too personalistic to admit of a doctrine.

That whatever Hitler did, whenever he did it, whether or not it contradicted any previous action or compromised any stated value or objective, comprised the Hitler Movement. This view is incorrect, for it implies that the Movement had no core values and no principles. Hitler was the Movement in the sense that there was a mutual indwelling of his and the Movement's values. I believe that vagueness of 'was' is why Heidegger preferred to use the verb 'to dwell.' Dwelling has the additional advantage of emphasizing Space, making Time a derivative, ultimately dispensable element, of the primordial concept. At all events, the absence of an explicit and coherent *Weltanschauung*, that is, one more systematic than *Mein Kampf*, need not trouble us. Many authors have been incapable of stating the meaning of their works, a proposition especially valid regarding political theologians delivering the Word to the masses. Furthermore, what *Hitler* meant was beside the point. How his message was received or conceived by German elites was decisive. The Hitler Movement allowed German intellectuals, in various ways and in varying degrees, no more consistent with each other than they were with Hitler, to find in the Movement a way of overcome their normal reluctance to adhere to an irrational set of ideas or to follow its charismatic Leader.

Notwithstanding, the German rejection of the Enlightenment—its veneration of Reason, the individual, the material, its optimism, its sense of man's perfectibility, its anti-spiritualism, and other ideas that Germans for centuries thought were trivial and anti-German—these intellectuals, with few exceptions, were not willing to succumb to barbarism. To the contrary, they believed that only Germans could arm European society against the barbarism (and imperialism) that the Enlightenment implied. They saw themselves as the cultural and intellectual saviors of Europe, the reincarnation of the primordial people: the Greeks. Listen to Cassirer: 'Germany stood alone as the last remaining hope for the preservation and continuance of Europe.... The poet [Stefan George] thus sees the surest guarantee that Germany will not become extinct in that it alone can complete the...task of reanimating the Hellenic dream.'[80] Conceiving the Hitler Movement as the political expression of this Messianic project, many intellectuals agreed with its Life philosophy: the primacy of Nature, the authenticity of the human personality, the importance of the community and the Nation, and the necessity for struggle, including violence and war; all of which would free Germans from the morass of materialism and capitalist exploitation. In the process they would unconceal who they always were. For some, like Nietzsche, this freedom had a profound individualistic and anarchistic cast—an artist's absolute claim to ignore all conventions which might make his life more comfortable, less dangerous, and less creative. The ultimate freedom is the ability to transcend mediocrity, the mediocrity that modern society all but makes mandatory. This is the Life philosophy expressed one Overman at a time. For others, like Heidegger, Jung and Jaspers, freedom was membership in the *Volksgemeinschaft,* thereby participating in the Nation's destiny. Cassirer amplifies: 'It is a deep and ardent desire of the individuals to identify themselves with the life of the community and with the life of nature. This desire is satisfied by the religious rites.'[81] Hitler writes, suggesting the link between personality and the *Volk*: 'The progress and culture of humanity are not a product of the majority, but rest exclusively on the genius and energy of the personality. To cultivate personality and establish its rights is one of the prerequisites for recovering the greatness and power of our nationality.'[82] For those who sensed something like this, the Hitler Movement exerted a profound attraction.

It all began with Paul, especially as he was interpreted (wrongly in my view) by Luther. Insofar as he subordinated Mosaic Law and ritual to faith, Paul denied that the world was a testing place. Instead Paul asserted that Creation was an expression in Time and Space of God's Love. If one has faith, the goodness of the world and man's place in it would be obvious. Unable to give up the concept of the Wrathful God, Luther subverted Paul's notion of faith by his doctrine of the Two Realms, denying the Goodness of Creation in the process. The first Realm, the World, is a cess pool, intentionally foul, intentionally an arena of sin, the worse the better. God made the world odious, so that human beings would *not* be tempted by its Satanic attributes. Only when humans give up on the world, overcoming all their worldly or Satanic instincts, would they be prepared to submit to God. Then and only then might God not *impute* to them their ineradicable sin. The only purpose of the Worldly Realm is to demonstrate to humans that salvation requires abject submission to arbitrary divine authority. Then, God in his mercy, despite his Righteousness conceived as the necessity to punish sin, *might* allow sinful humanity a pass into the Divine Realm and Life Eternal. Drawing the political implications of the necessary depravity of humanity in a world run by Satan, Luther believed that human beings must submit to their princes no matter how corrupt or evil; for resistance suggests the significance of the world and the efficacy of human efforts to improve the unimprovable. While Luther did plead, somewhat inconsistently, that Christian rulers act like Christians, he abhorred rebellion.

One of the most important objectives of the Hitler Movement was to make the separation of the Two Realms less radical, if not to reconcile them completely. The world became a testing place again, but not in the sense of a superhuman effort to obey punctilious rules. Hitler was more antagonistic to the idea of the Law than St. Paul. At most, Hitler agreed with the *Theologia germanica*: 'Thus order, laws, precepts, and the like are merely admonitions to men who understand nothing better and know and perceive nothing else;

therefore are all law and order ordained. And perfect men accept the law along with such ignorant men as understand and know nothing other or better, and practice it with them, to the intent that thereby they may be kept from evil ways, or if it be possible, brought to something higher.'[83] The world is an arena where the *Volk* demonstrates its worthiness to partake Eternal harmony, achieving this ultimate goal by conforming to the *Fuehrer's* Will. Not be confused with the absolute authority of autocrats, Hitler's authority embodied God's Will, redeeming the world in the process by giving it a positive role in salvation. The world, in effect, must be purified to be the pathway to the Divine Realm. Not the effect of actions done in accordance with ritual or legalistic practice, purification results from actions which conformed to the *Fuehrer's* Will. Nor should these actions be confused with Christian forbearance and passivity, to say nothing of forgiving one's enemies, so ridiculed by Nietzsche and others. Purifying actions signified that the *Volk* knew that the world was an arena for the life and death struggle against relentless enemies, whose prime purpose was to defile Germans, preventing them from fulfilling their role as the saviors of Europe. Physical and metaphysical, internal and external, these enemies had to be eliminated, defeated, annihilated. More than removing adulterating elements from the *Volk*; purification would demonstrate the worthiness of the Germans to be purified. Self-justifying, not merely prudential, purifying actions would demonstrate the German potential to become, in the fullness of time, Aryans. Moreover, this demonstration of worthiness must not be thwarted by anti-Aryan values. The normal human reluctance to inflict pain, to hear the screams of its victims, to wallow in the blood and filth of the tortured and the murdered had to be overcome. In this sense, the concentration camps were holy places, the ultimate temples, where Germans prove that they were willing to sacrifice their humanity to fulfill their Aryan promise. Although it is difficult to imagine anything more alien to the death camps than the cult of the Virgin, consider Spengler's insight, which, at the very least, suggests a justification of annihilation: 'But this world of purity, light and utter beauty of soul would have been unimaginable without the counter-idea, inseparable from it, an idea that constitutes one of the *maxima* of Gothic, one of its unfathomable creations—one that the present day forgets, and *deliberately* forgets. While she sits there enthroned, smiling in her beauty and tenderness, there lies in the background another world that throughout nature and throughout mankind weaves and breeds ill, pierces, destroys, seduces—namely, the Realm of the Devil.'[84] The Hitler Movement reminded Germans what pious Christians had forgotten, to wit, that it is impossible to revere Mary, the symbol of compassion and virginity, without hating the Devil. Moreover, no mere condition of existence that has to be tolerated like death, the Devil could be defeated, annihilated by a purified and purifying people, a people whose greatness would be manifested in struggle. As Hitler often said, 'Mankind has grown great in Eternal struggle, and only in Eternal peace does it perish.'[85]

Not all, perhaps not a majority, of the intellectual adherents of the Hitler Movement met this standard or accepted it. Certainly, neither Heidegger, nor Jung, nor Jaspers advocated genocide or any other form of extreme violence, or countenanced its purifying effects, or this extreme form of holy sacrifice. Yet, they did agree that the spiritual nature of the *Volk* had to be rescued from the materialism of the West. They believed that Primordial Germanness was the only way to achieve this victory against the material proclivities of human beings and nearly two thousand years of history. The spirit of the German Nation would redeem the *Volk*, preparing them to meet their destiny as Europe's saviors. For some, this destiny could be measured by Germany's political ascendance. For others, it could be fulfilled by partaking in the Eternal. At all events, the role of the leading personality, the *Fuehrer*, was essential. Unlike Plato's gifted cave dwellers, who only glimpsed the Eternal, due to the mutual indwelling of Hitler and the *Volk*, Germans would become Aryans and partake in the Eternal. The affinity with Christology is striking.

The *Fuehrer* revealed that to become Aryans more than ceaseless vigilance and strife and more than the destruction of anti-German forces was required. Being manifests itself in the great personality and a great people by sacrifice. Consider Thomas Mann's assessment of Frederick the Great, one of Hitler's few role models: 'He was a sacrifice. He felt, indeed, that he had sacrificed himself: his youth to his father, his manhood to the state. But he erred if he believed that a choice was open to him. He was a sacrifice. He had to do wrong, he had to lead a life contrary to his thoughts, he had to be not a philosopher but a king, in order that the destiny of a great people might be fulfilled.'[86] Spengler pushed the idea further back in German history: 'In the myth of the Holy Grail and its Knights one can feel the inward necessity of the German-Northern Catholicism. In opposition to Classical sacrifices offered to individual gods in separate temples, there is here the *one never-ending* sacrifice repeated everywhere and every day.'[87]

The superiority of the Aryan depended on his capacity to sacrifice for the *Volk*: 'The Aryan is not the greatest in his mental qualities as such, but in the extent of his willingness to put all his abilities in the service of the community. In him the instinct of self-preservation has reached its noblest form, since he willingly subordinates his own ego to the life of the community and, if the hour demands, even sacrifices it.'[88] More than the acid test of worthiness, sacrificial acts signify that the divine is absolute but not arbitrary. It is not sufficient that the Eternal dwells in Time and Space. Human existence must recognize its relation to the Eternal, a relationship that is unconcealed

and fulfilled by sacrificial acts. Time and Space is significant to the degree
that it unconceals its property and goal of transcendence, its capacity and
destiny to partake in the Eternal. Now transformed Luther's God is more than
the Creator. He is the God of Sacrifice. God and Sacrifice dwell in each other,
simultaneously unconcealing and fulfilling their natures in Time and Space;
the Hitler Movement's version of the realized *Eschaton*. Pauline only to this
extent, for the Movement's End of Days will not come at the end of Time and
Space, when God absorbs Creation into His Being. Hitler's Final *Eschaton*
will occur when all Germans become indwellers in the *Volk*: Aryans

Berger indicates how harrowing this process could be: 'Man's own works,
insofar as they are part of a social world, become part of a reality other than
himself. They escape him. But man also escapes himself, insofar as part of
himself becomes shaped by socialization. The otherness of the social world
and the concrete human beings who are the others of social life are internal-
ized into consciousness.... As a result it becomes a possibility not only that
the social world seems strange to the individual, but that he becomes strange
to himself in certain aspects of his socialized self.'[89] Hitler's most devoted
followers did not need to escape, believing that they were infused and always
had been such, in the *Volk*, the Nation, and the Eternal, facts which Hitler
made manifest. They were their socialized, purified Aryan selves.

For intellectuals, the process was less straight forward. Unable to credit the
Blood and Soil basis of their membership in the *Volk*, unable to overcome
their social and personal alienation, intellectuals were suspended between
longing for an organic community and realizing its artificiality. Confronting
the enemies of Eternal Order would not result in victory; it would, nonetheless, demonstrate the worthiness of intellectuals to participate in the *Volksgemeinschaft*, to partake in its struggle to purify itself and perhaps partake of
the Order itself. Ritual words, sacrificial acts, and adherence to the Will of the
Fuehrer proved that the *Volk* dwelt in the Eternal as a matter of Being *and* as
a matter of Destiny. Again, the apparent tension between Being as timeless
and Destiny as temporal was not countenanced. The temporality of Destiny
was part of existence in Time and Space, contingent, ephemeral, not real,
except as Destiny dwells in the Eternal and thus overcomes its temporality.
Faith in the Hitler Movement implied that Being would triumph over existence, Time, and Chaos. More than a sense of security against their enemies
in the world, faith in the Hitler Movement gave its adherents spiritual significance that could not be destroyed by anything that happened in the world,
so long as they remained vigilant to the demands of the faith as articulated
by the *Fuehrer*. His exact relationship to Being, to the Eternal and to the Divine did not have to be specified. Whichever relationship or combination of
relationships was felt by the faithful transcended the limits of reason. Faith

dwelt in the words of the *Fuehrer* under the sacred canopy: 'Now we are meet here, we are filled with the wonder of this gathering.' It was this feeling that, from the earliest times,' Cassirer affirms, 'supplied the impulse to religious thought and language. The immediate *perception of the Infinite* has from the very beginning formed an ingredient and necessary complement to all finite knowledge.'[90] This connection helped assuage the doubt endemic to intellectuals, because it re-privileged knowledge, their *raison d'être*, while binding them to Hitler's most devoted followers. What would prove more deadly was the need of intellectuals to validate their worthiness. Incapable of simple acceptance, only by perpetual sacrifice could the *Volksgemeinschaft* include them; only then could it and they achieve metaphysical transcendence. They needed unlimited victims, upon whose corpses they would hurl their reservations and doubts. Intellect could dwell in the *Volk*, after all; and, therefore, the *Volk* could dwell in the metaphysical. Reason Knowledge Faith, mutually indwelling, became the long sought for antidote to the loneliness and *anomie* of German thinkers and artists. Cassirer's universal claim is thus reserved for Germans; its wonder, this *ecclesia*, the possession of Germans, not defined legally as citizens, but racially. Its bonding power, therefore, depended on excluding those who were not Blood and Soil Germans. All those who seemed or could be made to seem the antithesis of Hitler and his Movement had to be eliminated. Principal among the excluded, these Others, were the Jews.

NOTES

1. Lowith, Karl: *Martin Heidegger and European Nihilism*, Richard Wolin editor, translated by Gary Steiner, Columbia, NY, 1984, 1995, p. 39.

2. See Heidegger, M.: *Poetry, Language, Thought*, translated by Albert Hofstadter, NY, 1971.

3. Ajax, it will be remembered, while attempting to revenge himself, was intoxicated by Athena and shamefully slaughtered cattle instead of Agamemnon and Menelaus. Unable to live with this act, he killed himself. For a fuller treatment, see Vasillopulos, 'To Defy the Gods: Ajax and the Problem of the Self,' *Skepsis*, 2008, pp. 133–44.

4. Heidegger, M., "The Self-Assertion of the German university," [the 1933 Rectoral Address] reproduced in Neske, G. & Kettering, E.: *Martin Heidegger and National Socialism*, Paragon, NY, 1990, pp. 5–13, p. 5, original emphasis.

5. The controversy of Heidegger's support of National Socialism was rekindled by the publication of Farias, Victor: *Heidegger and Nazism*, edited by Joseph Margolis and Tom Rockmore, translated by Gabriel Ricci, Philadelphia, 1989. See also, Wolin, Richard, editor: *The Heidegger Controversy*, MIT, Cambridge, 1993.

6. *Heidegger, op. cit.*, pp. 5–6, original emphasis.

7. *Ibid.*, p. 6, original emphasis.

8. *Ibid.*, pp. 6–7, original emphasis.

9. *Ibid.*, p. 7.

10. *Ibid., op. cit.*, p. 9, original emphasis.

11. *Ibid., op. cit.*, p. 7.

12. I realize Heidegger believed he dealt with this and similar objections by preferring the pre-Socratics to Plato and Aristotle. My view is that he pushes the distinction too far. Moreover, when he referred to 'The Greeks,' if he meant only the pre-Socratics, he should have said so.

13. For elaboration, see Vasillopulos, "The Passionate Embrace: Romanticism and Nietzsche," *Existentia, an International Journal of Philosophy,* Vol., XVI, 2006, Fasc.3–4, pp. 255–62 and Vasillopulos, "How Greek Was My Nietzsche," *Dialogue and Universalism,* vol. XV, No.5–6, 2005, pp. 35–42.

14. Lowith, *Heidegger, op. cit.*, p. 18.

15. Heidegger, 'Self-Assertion," *op. cit.* p. 9. It would be difficult to imagine a more anti-Aristotelian idea, for he valued contemplation higher than all other activities.

16. *Ibid.*

17. Lowith echoes this combination and attraction and repulsion: 'Nobody will be able to dispute that Heidegger is more perceptive than practically any other contemporary interpreter, that he is an expert in the art of reading and interpreting when it comes to carefully taking apart an intellectual or poetic system of language and assembling it anew. But neither will anyone be able to overlook the violence of his interpreting.' Lowith, *Heidegger, op. cit.*, p. 106.

18. Heidegger, 'Self-Assertion,' *op. cit.*, p. 10.

19. For a classic treatment of this distinction, see Berlin, Isaiah: *Four Essays on Liberty,* Oxford, 1969.

20. Heidegger, 'Self-Assertion,' *op. cit.*, p. 10.

21. Quoted in Stern, J.P.: *The Fuehrer and the People*, Berkeley, 1975, p. 90.

22. Nolte, Ernst: *Three Faces of Fascism*, translated by Leila Vennewitz, NY, 1963, p. 542.

23. *Ibid.*, p. 566.

24. Stern, *op. cit.*, p. 97.

25. *Ibid.*, p. 91.

26. Weber, Max: *The Sociology of Religion,* translated by Ephraim Fischoff, Boston, 1922, 1964, p. 1.

27. Berger, Peter, L.: *The Sacred Canopy, Elements of a Sociological Theory of Religion*, NY, 1969, p. 25.

28. *Ibid.*, p. 26.

29. *Ibid.*, p. 26.

30. *Ibid.*, p. 22.

31. *Ibid.*, p. 33.

32. *Ibid.*, p. 32.

33. *Ibid.*, pp. 27–8.

34. *Ibid.*, p. 36.

35. *Ibid.*, p. 51.

36. Stern, *Fuehrer, op.* cit., p. 43.

37. *Ibid.*, p. 77.

38. See Dunham, Barrows: *Heroes and Heretics*, Knopf, NY, 1963 for an exposition of the separation of theological from secular (scientific) arguments and proofs, especially chapter 13.

39. Stern, *Fuehrer, op. cit.*, p. 14.

40. *Ibid.*

41. *Ibid.*, p. 44.

42. *Ibid.*, pp. 44–5.

43. *Ibid.*, p. 18.

44. *Ibid.*, pp. 23–4.

45. *Ibid.*, p. 70.

46. *Ibid.*, pp. 76–77.

47. Quoted in *ibid.*, p. 94.

48. *Ibid.*, p. 35, original emphasis.

49. *Ibid.*, p. 93.

50. *Ibid.*, p. 112.

51. *Ibid.*, p. 109.

52. *Ibid.*, p. 110.

53. Jung, C.G.: *Civilization in Transition*, 2d edition, translated by R.F.C. Hull, Princeton, 1975 'Wotan,' first published *Neue Schweizer Rundschau*, (Zurich), n.s., III, (March 1936).

54. *Ibid.*, p. 180.

55. *Ibid.*, p. 185.

56. *Ibid.*, p. 189.

57. *Ibid.*, p. 185.

58. For a scathing rationalist critique of Yahweh and all other wrathful gods, see Dawkins, Richard: *The God Delusion,* Mariner, NY, 2008, p. 51 and *passim*.

59. Cassirer, E.: *Myth of the State,* Yale, New Haven, 1946, p. 48.

60. See Otto, Walter: *Dionysus: Myth and Cult*, translated by Robert Palmer, Bloomington, 1965.

61. Stern, *op. cit.*, p. 33.

62. *Ibid.*, p. 165.

63. *Ibid.*, p. 33.

64. Of course Judaism does not see it this way. Abraham's willingness to sacrifice Isaac proves his devotion to Yahweh. His submission to the Will of God, far from dissolving Yahweh in the blood of Isaac, exalts Yahweh by manifesting his absolute faith.

65. *Ibid.*, p. 34.

66. *Ibid.*, p. 156.

67. *Ibid.*, p. 166.

68. *Ibid.*, p. 164.

69. *Ibid.*, p. 158.

70. *Ibid.*, p. 29.

71. *Ibid.*, p. 32.

72. *Ibid.*, p. 24.

73. *Ibid.*, p. 137. Stern has high praise also for Georg Elser who attempted to assassinate Hitler, pp. 147f.

74. *Ibid.*, p. 104.

75. *Ibid.*, p. 105.

76. *Ibid.*, p. 99.

77. *Ibid.*, p. 105.

78. *Ibid.*, p. 41.

79. Quoted by Stern, *ibid.*, p. 41.

80. Norton, Robert: *Secret Germany: Stefan George and his Circle,* Cornell, Ithaca, 2002, p. 548.

81. Cassirer, *The Myth, op. cit.*, p. 38.

82. Hitler, *Mein, op. cit.*, p. 345.

83. Berger, *Sacred, op. cit.*, p. 98.

84. Spengler, Oswald: *The Decline of the West*, Oxford, NY, , 1918, 1991, p. 331, emphasis original.

85. Hitler, *Mein, op. cit.*, p. 135.

86. Mann, Thomas: *Three Essays,* translated by H.T. Lowe-Porter, Knopf, NY, 1929, p. 215.

87. Spengler, *op.cit.*, p. 99.

88. Hitler, *Mein, op. cit.*, p. 297.

89. Berger, *op. cit.*, p. 85.

90. Cassirer, *Myth, op. cit.*, p. 20.

Chapter Seven

Danse Macabre

The Sacrifice of the Jews

It is 3 o'clock. So 4000 are ready to go. The orders are that there must be 9000 by 4 o'clock. *Judenrate* Chairman Czerniakow's diary[1]

PROLOGUE

Bent over a poorly lit table an old man prepared a list, yet another list. For transportation, the heading said. 'A sad business,' he mumbles, 'but necessary, all things considered, life saving.' Yawning as he stands, trying to stretch the aches from his joints, sipping a little lukewarm tea. Either I make the selections with all my wisdom or they do. My family would be first to go, that is clear, then anyone at hand. Is it not my duty to protect one's own and then try to be fair? To save the most valuable? What else can I do? Who else could do better? Is it not important to retain some semblance of authority? Do not our people need to believe in something? For this duty, I get some soup for my children. Should I be begrudged these blessings? Who would refuse them? I couldn't, if I wanted to. The Germans believe I am corrupt, selling my people for some food. It confirms their view of us. Besides, look at what the ghetto police do, the beatings, the humiliation, for what, clean clothes? Jew on Jew, an outrage! My lists save people, give us some hope, some dignity. The few, the sick, are sacrificed. To save many, at least for a while, for the remnant will survive this Hell. Resuming his seat, he folds the list. In the morning, it would be picked up. By the afternoon it would be over, until the next time. Time, time, time to survive, no matter how, no matter how few.

More lists were demanded, then his son asked him, 'But, father, I thought we were safe. Why are we going?'

'The time has come. We are among the last.'

231

'But you said…'

'That I was doing all I could to keep us together. But the Germans are in charge.'

'I thought you were.'

'Only up to a point.'

'What?'

'They let me help them. Now there is nothing more for me to do.'

'But why?'

'Perhaps to teach a lesson? I don't really know.'

'I am afraid, father.'

'And I, my son, but we must trust in God. His Will must be served.'

'Is it God's Will that Germans kill us?'

'No one knows the ways of God?'

'Why does He let the Nazis rule?'

'No one knows. We must simply obey His Will.'

As one of the corollaries, however, that very faith [in the *Fuehrer*] brought with it widespread acceptance, passive or not, of the measures against the Jews: Sympathy for the Jews would have meant some distrust of the rightness of Hitler's way, and many Germans had definitely established their individual and collective priorities in this regard. The same is true in relation to the other central myth of the regime, that of the *Volksgemeinschaft*. The national community explicitly excluded the Jews. Saul Friedlander[2]

ELECTIVE AFFINITIES

This disturbing analysis begins by asking the reader to suspend for a moment the murder of between five and six million Jews. Consider instead the patriotism of German Jews, their immersion in and contributions to German culture, their innumerable services in the professions, most especially in law, medicine, and the academy, to say nothing of their extraordinary and innovative efforts on behalf of the economy. By fully warranting how integrated and successful Jews were in German life, it evident that they were resented as much, if not more, for their virtues as for their shortcomings. Understandably, many Jews were puzzled by the Third Reich, perplexed to the point of failing to appreciate, despite growing, if ambiguous evidence, the murderous depth of its racial anti-Semitism. Many have asked, 'Why did they simply not leave the society which made them anathema?' Adler says, 'The pecuniary motive explains the continuity of Jewish history in Germany.'[3] While generally true, it remains inadequate, especially for the assimilated. A more complex analysis is required. First, most Jews did leave, not only the majority who emigrated, but of those who, over the generations, left Jewry in all but name. These Jews, if proper to so designate them, were Germans in every important respect. For them, 'German-Jew' had little or no meaning. The Nazi claim that they were not and could not be proper citizens, including the narrow legal sense, seemed absurd to these Germans with Jewish backgrounds, who were members of German society in far more profound ways than legal status implied, as their participation in the Great War demonstrated.

As odious as war is, it can test the willingness to sacrifice for one's principles, including loyalty to one's Nation and comrades, which, has often been a down payment in blood for increased equality and participation in the political life of a society.[4] When combat soldiers explain their willingness to risk their lives for an ideal, they must be taken seriously and solemnly. Hear the words of Lt. Fritz Meyer, later killed: 'I am happy to be able to testify in bloody earnest for the truth of idea; the flame of our love for the German people is alive within us and stronger than ever. That the dishonest voices of calumny have, unfortunately, not yet been silenced at home certainly does not discourage us.... What more do they want than our blood? Let them continue their study of racism with the blood shed by our co-religionists. Enemy bullets do not bother with such distinctions.'[5] Note his love for the German people transcends their racism. Listen to Sgt. Henle, also killed: 'Just as I am aware of the great honor of fighting for my dear Fatherland at the front and sharing in the victory, I want also to have a voice later, when it will be used to stand up and fight for the equality of our co-religionists.'[6] Again, note the genuine affection, this time for the Fatherland, and the expectation that it will hear his pleas for his co-religionists. Finally, consider the words of the distinguished Kantian, Hermann Cohen: 'We consider ourselves, as German-Jews, participants in a central cultural power that is called upon to unite peoples in the sense of a Messianic humanity. Thus we reject the view that it is our historic role to undermine peoples and tribes. Whenever there reappears an earnest desire for international understanding and for truly-founded peace among peoples, our example will stand as a model proving German hegemony over all the foundations of the life of the soul and the mind.'[7] Adler concludes 'Despite all the contrary forces, this [Cohen and the front line testimonies] was the degree of the German-Jewish symbiosis of the first part of the twentieth century.'[8] The similarities were not all positive:

It is widely agreed that the mentalities of these two peoples [Germans and Jews] have often converged and interpenetrated in the last two centuries.... Frederick Sieburg, a German cultural historian, described both Germans and Jews as two peoples who are: 'admired and hated...both equally unable to make themselves liked, equally ambivalent between servility and arrogance, equally indispensable as well as troublesome to the world, equally aggressive, equally inclined to self-pity, equally vilified without distinction and admired for their boldness of their thinking; musical, talented for speculative thinking, but hopelessly different in one point: in their attitude toward violence.'[9]

Only by appreciating these widely held sentiments can the reluctance of German-Jews to leave Germany be understood. Leaving aside the unimaginable Final Solution, it simply could not have made sense to these lovers of German culture that they would be murdered by their neighbors. Were they not dedicated patriots, distinguished from other Germans only by religion, a factor of steadily diminishing importance: 'As they became more German, they became more like the Germans in religion as well: this is what had been asked of them. Anything that might set them apart—let it be the Law of Moses—had to be suppressed.'[10] Friedlander adds: 'Special nationality, special food laws, special education—all this had to give way to the full acceptance of the State and the fulfillment of the duties of citizenship—except the faith of Israel and its ritual manifestation.'[11] Have they not proved their devotion on the battlefield? What else could they do? Yet the cry persisted: 'Eliminate Jews!' Surely, Jews were eliminating themselves, as traditionally defined, by means of assimilation, Baptism, intermarriage, and general rejection of traditional Jewry and Judaism. While it is impossible to be precise regarding either the number of assimilated Germans or the degree of their assimilation, Arno Mayer's judgment seems reasonable:

> Only a relatively small but influential group of what might be called 'integral' assimilationists, most of them of great wealth or education, rejected their own cultural and religious past in their bid for complete integration. A much larger number of Jews sought full participation in wider secular society around them without denying their heritage and compromising their identity. These 'limited' assimilationists held fast to their religious and cultural traditions even as they sought to improve their economic opportunities and to encourage their sons to prepare for careers in fields other than petty commerce and manufacture.[12]

Arendt suggests, discounting their religiosity: 'Judaism, and belonging to the Jewish people, degenerated into a simple fact of birth only among assimilated Jewry. Originally it had meant a specific religion, a specific nationality, the sharing of specific memories and specific hopes, and, even among privileged Jews, it meant at least still sharing specific economic advantages.'[13] Stern captures their profound sense of common values:

> Germans and Jews were not opposites alternately attracting or repelling each other.... Necessity had taught Jews the virtue of...efficiency with a special aura... and certainly Germans had long cultivated it. Germans and Jews were a serious, sober, thorough people; they formed close family ties and infused their lives

with a certain ritualized warmth and sentimentality. Educated Germans and Jews shared an extraordinary appreciation for learning: they respected the living scholar and they revered the cultural heritage of the past.[14]

Note that Stern says 'Germans' and 'Jews,' not 'Germans' and 'German-Jews.' From the context, it is clear he means Jews who live in Germany, without suggesting that they were not really Germans. One of the dilemmas of the tragic history of European Jews is the awkwardness of referring to them. If one says 'Jews in Germany,' it suggests a racial divide between Jews and Germans. If one says, 'German-Jew,' then the same risk obtains, perhaps less pejoratively. If one says, 'Germans who happen to have something Jewish about them,' it diminishes Jewish identity, making the attribution sound accidental or otherwise insignificant. My approach has been to avoid 'German-Jew,' except to avoid ambiguity, and use 'Jew,' when the context makes it clear I am referring to Germans, who were also 'Jews' by some definition, that is, Germans who have retained some Jewish heritage.

When the National Socialists took power in 1933, Jewish perception of common values continued to tie them to Germany. One can understand their puzzled responses to racist rhetoric and increasingly anti-Jewish measures. Consider this exchange between those who were considered ineradicably Jewish and a National Socialist. 'We have tried to be the best Germans we can be. We have done everything that has been asked of us and more and preserved despite countless calumnies and humiliations. We agree with Berthold Auerbach when he said: "We rely on the living customs of the nation; we respect German customs and German compassion. I live in the happy and confident conviction that I express the ideas of an entire generation of Jews when I add: put us to the acid test of danger. You will find us clean of the residues of egotism and the indecency of over-refinement. Allow us the Fatherland to which we belong by birth, custom, and love, and we shall gladly lay down our lives and possessions on its altar."[15] To the extent we have succeeded, you seem to resent us all the more. We are perplexed.'

'Perplexed? Of course you are, because you will never understand what it is to be German. A German does not try to be German. He does not say he deserves to be a German. He just is German. Your efforts prove that you are only *ersatz* Germans. Worse, you diminish the importance of being German for the rest of us, making it contingent on worldly success. To be German is to be spiritual. To be German is to be one with the Blood and Soil of Germany.'

'The soil at the Marne made no such distinctions.'

Even without the racist implications of 'Blood and Soil,' this imaginary dialogue indicates the deep and persistent divide between Jews and Gentiles. Rose puts it this way: 'Jewish redemption, in German secular revolutionism, as much as in Medieval Christianity, meant the disappearance of Judaism and the absorption of the Jews into the organic whole of humanity, specifically German humanity. The emotional ideal of the extinction of Judaism constitutes the very essence of revolutionary anti-Semitism.'[16] This formulation exaggerates the twentieth century religiosity of Jews and Gentiles; that is, it assumes that ethnic Germans, including 'secular revolutionists,' shared the anti-Judaism of their forebears and that Jews remained traditional in their outlook. If, however, 'Judaism' can be taken to mean 'Jewish,' then I concur with Rose, who realizes the importance of this distinction, when he writes, citing two revolutionary ideas:

> that the human failing of egoism was embodied for the modern era in the economic system of bourgeois capitalism; and that money was the supreme expression of a self-interest and self-seeking that impeded the final emancipation of humanity and the emergence of a genuinely social new man.... It was in Germany that a specifically Jewish significance was injected into the general idea that humanity was being alienated from its true loving social nature by an egoism that was seen as essentially Jewish, being intrinsic to Jewish national character.... *German revolutionary thinkers of both left and right looked to redeem not just Germans from Judaism, but all mankind from the modern disease of Jewishness.*[17]

He concludes: 'The extraordinary ability of Moses Hess, Spinoza, and Mendelssohn to transcend Judaism would have only served to confirm Herder's suspicion that the eventual assimilation of the Jews into Germanness—into pure humanity—was something that could not take place for a very long time indeed, requiring as it did a feat of genius.'[18]

When the racist determination of Germanness gained credence in the nineteenth century and fulfillment in the Third Reich, many of these distinctions became irrelevant. According to Mayer:

> Heretofore, the defamation of the Jew had been couched in the traditional, essentially abstract language of the theologically based and colored social, economic, and cultural anti-Judaism. After the war the trailblazers of National Socialism inflamed the rhetoric of this *odium theologicum* by using phrases and images drawn from demonology, racial biology, and parasitology. At the same time that they transmuted the vernacular of Jew-baiting, they concretized their attack, holding the Jews responsible for the November revolution, the Munich *Ratterepublic*, the Versailles *Diktat*, and the plague of Bolshevism. The Nazis also denounced the Jews as the mainstay of parasitic capitalism and the masterminds of the modernist subversion of classical culture.[19]

Thus genocide was placed on the menu, awaiting its selection. No matter how assimilated they were, no matter how UnJewish in their appearance, behavior, or religious convictions, Jews remained Jews. Mosse writes: 'As long as racial standards were invoked, the assimilated Jews were made to bear an increasingly difficult burden. They were singled out as arch-fiends, as infiltrators and polluters of the blond Germanic race.'[20] Mosse concedes that many traditional Jews also valued blood ties: 'Purity of blood had become a symbol for the purity of the race and for its vigor. This symbolism was generally pervasive. For example, a little later Martin Buber used the metaphor of blood to strengthen the national feeling of the Jews.... Blood is the root and nourishment of each individual. But for Buber these concepts were metaphors that defined nationality rather than race.'[21] Although understandable, due to the differential power of Germans and Jews, Mosse's qualification is inadequate, confirming Langmuir's central methodological criticism of the historians and theologians who deal with Judaica:

> The implication that Jewish history can be properly understood only from a particular religious perspective brings us to the more basic factor that has made objectivity, as historians use the term, difficult in Jewish historiography. Since Judaism has always been the most essential distinguishing element in Jewish identity, there is an enduring tendency to confuse theological history, the history of a religion, Judaism, and the purely historical investigation of all the activities of those who have been associated with Judaism. The confusion of these three different kinds of inquiry has been aggravated by the extent to which Jewish history has been written by the rabbinate, but it has been aided by the religious commitment of many other Jewish historians.[22]

Political correctness, defined as sympathy for disadvantaged or victimized groups, can be defended on many grounds, but not scholarship. Consider how Mosse apologizes for Hassidic racism: 'To be sure, the Hassidic rabbinical dynasties believed that qualities of leadership were at time transmitted by blood; but this was not held consistently, and in any case no more racist that traditional notions of royal descent.'[23] His standard for the designation of 'racism,' *when applied to Jews* is that it must be 'consistently upheld.' One wonders by whom. Those who avow it or by all Jews? The ambiguity is at best disingenuous. There is no way to avoid the racist implications of having a particular people and only that people, *selected by God as his special beings endowed with a special mission*, regardless of how one defines or values the mission. Every other people are by definition unchosen: rejected, outcasts, enemies of the State, the People, or God, and, therefore, destined to become the eliminated or the annihilated—the progression is short and almost inevitable. It is no cure to say that individual Gentiles might be righteous, anymore that when Goering said, he defined who was a Jew, according to his values, preferences, or prejudices. The belief in the Chosen People also implies that

Yahweh is a racist. That is, notwithstanding universalist claims or purposes of
Judaism, he remains tribal. In the Beit-Hallahmi's words: 'According to Jewish eschatology, human history is a battlefield between good and evil. This
battle will end with the coming of the Messiah, who will bring the course of
history to a stop. This will mean the end of Jewish victimization, revenge on
the Gentiles, Judgment Day for all humans, and universal recognition of God
and His laws.'[24]

Anti-Nazi Germans used the racism inherent in the concept of the Chosen
People against the Nazis: 'Ironically, theologians who opposed Nazism could
often come up with nothing better than the claim that the Nazi emphasis on
salvation through racial election indicated that "Their thinking is completely
Jewish," or "The racial idea is Judaism."'[25] Many Jewish theologians have
taken pains to deny this implication, often without giving up other tribal attributes. When Germans made similar claims regarding Aryans, Mosse makes
all the links, extensions, and implications, without any qualifications. In the
case of Nazi racism, it does not matter, if it were consistently held or not.
Consider how he treats the words of Cardinal Faulhaber:

> We must distinguish between the people of Israel before and after the time
> of Christ. Before the death of Christ during the period between the calling of
> Abraham and the fullness of time, the people of Israel were the vehicle of divine
> revelation.... After the death of Christ, Israel was dismissed from the service of
> revelation.... She repudiated and rejected the Lord's Anointed, had driven Him
> out of the city and nailed Him to the Cross. Then the veil of the temple was rent,
> and with it the Covenant between the Lord and His people. The daughters of
> Zion received a full bill of divorce.... In the second place we must distinguish
> between the Scriptures of the *Old Testament*...and the *Talmudic* writings of
> post-Christian Judaism.... The *Talmudic* writings are the work of man; they
> were not prompted by the spirit of God. It is only the sacred writings of the pre-
> Christian Judaism, not the *Talmud*, which the Church of the *New Testament* has
> accepted as her inheritance.[26]

There is no apology for the Cardinal. His self-rebuking words are allowed
to stand, as religious legitimation for the charge that the Jews were Christ-
killers, rejecters of God, and purveyors of a false holy book, the *Talmud*. To
examine Hassids through a prism of self-serving justification and Faulhaber
through a magnifying glass is simply unfair. Unworthy of a fine historian,
Mosse applies, like countless others, an egregious double standard. A racist
concept is a racist concept no matter who believes it, consistently or not. No
individual or group can be privileged to the degree that they be absolved of
what condemns others, no matter how much they have suffered. As Primo
Levi writes: 'It is naïve, absurd, and historically false to believe that an
infernal system such as National Socialism sanctifies its victims: on the con-

trary, it degrades them, it makes them resemble itself, and this is all the more when they are available, blank, and lacking a political or moral armature.'[27] Victimhood does not sanctify, nor can it allow for double standards. Nor can it reduce the racism inherent in 'Purity of Blood,' by calling it a metaphor.

Jews, perhaps more than any others, should recognize the power of metaphor. Metaphors can shape and drive policy, often injecting its implementers with extraordinary zeal; they cannot be properly dismissed as rhetoric, whatever their basis in fact. Nowhere has this point more catastrophically demonstrated than in the Judeocide. Jews were murdered; this was no metaphor. Part of the reason for the Judeocide, however, was metaphorical: the Jew as archetypal materialist. Jews were murdered to lessen their potential to infect or corrupt Germans. This corruption, though couched in metaphorical terms, was not metaphorical *for the racist anti-Semite*. For other Germans, running the gamut of traditional anti-Judaism and anti-Semitism, Jews corrupted Germans, turning them into bourgeois individualists. The destruction of the Jews, physically and metaphorically, was an effort to dry up this primordial source of corruption. More, much more, was needed, if Germany was to become Aryan. As Gordon puts it: 'It is important to understand that to Hitler, "Jewishness" was not confined to "racial Jews;" non-Jews who sympathized with "Jewish" inventions (democracy, socialism, internationalism, etc. were also classified as Jews...as "spiritual Jews."'[28] While Bauman replaces 'spiritual' with 'conceptual,' the danger for anti-Semites remained the same. '*The conceptual Jew carried a message; alternative to this order here and now is not another order, but chaos and devastation.*'[29] Jewish influence had to be eliminated, an influence which could outlive Jews. Therefore, Germans had to be purified, a process which would persist long after the last Jew was dead. Accordingly, the murder of Jews was the first and easiest stage in a long process. 'Find Jews, kill them.' Much more difficult would be eradication of Jewish values. The Jewish spirit had to be annihilated, a much more profound project than the murder of its biological progenitors. If Jewish values and practices remained, after all Jews vanished, their absence would be meaningless. If the Aryan people were to emerge from the swamp of Jewish values, it was necessary to kill 'the Jew,' who lived in nearly every German.

Similarly, nationality, for many Germans and Jews, could not be dissociated from race. 'In the name of the will of the people, the State was forced to recognize only nationals as citizens, to grant full civil and political rights only to those who belonged to the national community by right of origin and fact of birth.'[30] Without their own Nation-State, how could Jews become citizens? Arendt explains:

> Secularization, therefore, finally produced that paradox, so decisive for the psychology of modern Jews, by which Jewish assimilation—in its liquidation of

national consciousness, its transformation of a national religion into a confessional denomination, and its meeting of the half-hearted and ambiguous demands of State and society by equally ambiguous devices and psychological tricks—engendered a very real Jewish chauvinism, if by chauvinism we understand the perverted nationalism.... From now on, the old religious concept of Chosenness was no longer the essence of Judaism; it became instead the essence of Jewishness.[31]

Hence, the concept of the Jewish, not the Judaic, Nation-State, the point of political Zionism. As there was no way to eradicate Jewishness, even if Judaism disappeared, there was no way to eradicate anti-Semitism. If they were to be protected, if they were to escape their age-old vulnerability to those in power, Jews had to secure their own territory, their own State. Arendt adds: 'Persecution of powerless or power-losing groups...does not spring from human meanness alone. What makes people obey or tolerate real power and, on the other hand, hate people who have wealth without power, is a rational instinct that power has a certain function and is of some general use.... *Only wealth without power or aloofness without a policy are felt to be parasitical, useless, revolting, because such conditions cut all the threads which tie men together.*'[32] The Jewish choice seems to be: become poor or become a political Zionist. Poverty appealed to few Jews, and the Jewish State to only slightly more. Most Jews had their State: Germany. For Gentiles, however, the resentment of Jewish wealth and its negative consequences for community solidarity would prove controlling.

Ignoring the implications of racial anti-Semitism, unable to believe that such a doctrine could defile their beloved Germany, Jews would be overwhelmed by the coming apocalypse. The scorned lovers of Germany would be murdered, demonstrating how hate had become superior to decency in that time and place. Many millions of others were to die in the camps and in the killing fields, many of whom did not share the Jews' elective affinities for Germany. More millions would die on battlefields. Yet the plight of the Jews of Germany seems especially horrific, not because Jewish life is worth more than any other or because genocide is worse than other forms of killing. The Judeocide needs to be highlighted, not because Jews were better than Gypsies, the deformed, the mentally ill, or soldiers, but because their murders demonstrated the catastrophe of race-based nationalism, wielding the resources of the State. More than the power to kill efficiently, cold-bloodedly, the State inculpates its citizens in the murder of their neighbors. By virtue of its capacity to redefine reality by creating and denying facts, it can overcome natural aversions to witnessing, much less inflicting, human suffering, which is, according to Bauman, the hallmark of the modern State. First the relationship of moral standards and the State has to be altered: '*Bureaucracy's double feat is the moralization of technology, coupled with the denial of the moral significance of non-technical issues.* It is the technology of action, not its substance, which is subject to assessment as good or bad, proper or improper, right or wrong.'[33] Once achieved, once in place as the univocal and absolute authority, then all other restraints dissolve: 'The meaning of correction is unambiguous: *the readiness to act against one's own better judgment, and against the voice of one's conscience, is not just the function of authoritative command, but the result of exposure to a single-minded, unequivocal and monopolistic source of authority.*'[34] I am not so sure that this combination of factors suffices for an *extended* series of murders, torture, and other atrocities. I doubt that a mere rational/legal (bureaucratic) State could do this. Neither technology nor its apparatus would be sufficient. Sustained perpetration of inhuman treatment requires a spiritual or idealistic component. To overcome the natural aversion to human suffering, a meaning-conferring and identity-creating Nation-State had to exist, one which provided a sacred canopy devoted to the *Volk* and endowing them with the mission to save European civilization. The Judeocide dwelt in the political theology of the Hitler Movement. And the Hitler Movement dwelt in the Judeocide.

The previous chapter discounted the Hitler Movement's racial anti-Semitism, focusing instead on its spiritual appeal. Here, by granting anti-Semitism its full weight in the Hitler Movement, I argue that the Judeocide was all but inevitable. Conservative German scholarship, to the contrary—Golo Mann, Joachim Fest, and Ernst Nolte and others—tends to discount the philosophical, spiritual, religious or other non-rational factors of the appeal of the Third Reich. While acknowledging that anti-Semitism was a rallying cry for frightened or dispossessed Germans, these scholars argue that anti-Semitism was a marginal factor in the support of the Third Reich, a poor second or third to Hitler's domestic and foreign policy successes. Moreover, they contend that Hitler's successes were necessary to overcome the German *aversion* to anti-Semitism, especially when expressed by lawless groups like the SA.

Within its assumptions, conservative German scholarship has vastly improved its predecessors, making few apologies for Germany's pursuit of its national interests and missing few opportunities to compare it favorably to vindictive British, French, and American practices, to say nothing of Russian barbarism. Burleigh notes that 'Ten times more civilians were killed [in Germany] than the number who perished in London and British provincial cities.'[35] He quotes Bomber Harris, after the gratuitous three day firebombing of defenseless and non-military Dresden in the last weeks of the War: 'I do not personally regard the whole of the remaining cities of Germany as worth the bones of one British grenadier.'[36] The weakness of the conservative approach resides in its assumptions. Too rational, it looks for explanations *only* within the world of facts and values that have objective referents like prosperity or security, notwithstanding the subjective elements of such concepts. Failing to see how deep-seated factors, often irrational, affect public and private behavior, it argues that, for example, German anti-Semitism was less virulent than its French variant, and, therefore, it could not have been a cause of the Judeocide, since it did not happen in France. Or, somewhat modified, it limits anti-Semitism to, for example, the impact of Jews on the economy, particularly finance capitalism, as well as, other sources of societal volatility. In other words, insofar as the Jews were empirically associated with the tribulations of modernity, anti-Semitism *per se* was an insignificant part of National Socialism's appeal. By the same token, to the degree that Jews had links to foreign, anti-German forces, like the French or the Russians, anti-Semitism *per se* was not important. Taking pains to deny the irrational basis of the Hitler Movement, this kind of scholarship denies that anti-Semitism was fundamental to German political theology and, therefore, to an interpretation of the Third Reich. Anti-Semitism, like Hitler and his Movement, was a product of the upheavals of the late nineteenth century and the Defeat in the World War, having no deep roots in German culture or *Weltanschauung*.

This view attacks a straw man: the proposition that anti-Semitism was the sufficient cause of the Judeocide. If French history were like German history, the conservative conflation of French and German anti-Semitism might make sense. In the light of the radically divergent experiences of the Germans and the French for the last thousand years, it is absurd. Racial anti-Semitism did not by itself cause the Judeocide, nor did it drop from the sky. It developed from anti-Judaism, the German defeat in the Investiture Contest, the Reformation, the Defeat in the Great War, the Versailles Treaty, the Weimar Republic, the hyperinflation, and the Great Depression, just to list the principal causes which underlay the coming of the Third Reich. It is true of course that not all of these factors stemmed from anti-Semitism. It is also true that many Germans who were not anti-Semites had reason to support National Socialism and the Hitler Movement. This cannot change the fact that the elimination of Jews, as people and as metaphor, was *Hitler's* principal objective. Only by making Germany *Judenfrei* could the Aryan people develop. Only by making Europe *Judenfrei* could this Aryan Nation fulfill its mission to save European civilization. Hitler could not have created himself or his Movement absent all these other factors. He did not drop from the sky either. Needing the support of a wide cross-section of the population, he appealed to Germans in countless speeches, which elaborated the ideas of *Mein Kampf*. In the final analysis it does not matter that many or most Germans who support the Third Reich were not anti-Semites. They supported their Leader who most certainly was and who proclaimed it often, loud and clear.

Anti-Semitism in all its forms was at the heart of the Hitler Movement. Moreover, its most important form was the least objective. Recall Langmuir's definition: *'Chimerical assertions are propositions that grammatically attribute with certitude to an out-group and all its members characteristics that have never been empirically observed.'*[37] This is much more telling than an indication of paranoid fantasies. Chimerical assertions include fundamentally irrational concepts, like the spirit of Jewry, which are impervious to emendation based on facts or behavior. As much as the Hitler Movement hated Jews and Judaism, it feared metaphorical Jews more, because Jewish values were more difficult to expunge. Without diminishing the importance of Hitler's desire to annihilate human Jews, his purpose was to purge German society from parasitic Jewish influence. Rose makes this point explicitly: 'This dual aspect of Judaism as moral metaphor and social realty was what made it possible for Jewishness to become as central and ubiquitous an obsession in the new secular mythology of political redemption in modern Germany as it had been in the theological universe of Christian Europe.'[38] Nor was the metaphorical Jew a bogy of the Right: 'For Marx successfully replaces the Christian dual meaning of the Jew, as both actual and metaphorical sinfulness, with a new myth that sees Jews simultaneously as real-life agents of egoistic capitalism and as metaphors for the whole sinful civil society.'[39] To deny the power of such irrational factors of the Hitler Movement makes Hitler's support among the educated classes all but inexplicable. In the final analysis, conservative German historians deny the reality of the Hitler Movement, because it was in principle irrational and, therefore, ahistorical; it could not in principle be treated historically. 'The Real is Rational and the Rational is Real,' they seem to say, echoing Hegel.

Yet, they might counter, did I not suspend treatment of anti-Semitism in my discussion of the Hitler Movement? 'Will this chapter not contradict or compromise that analysis?' Not in the least. The previous chapter attempted to explain the Hitler Movement appealed to a wide range of intellectuals who were by no means anti-Semites, at least not of the racist variety. This chapter argues that they were wrong. Their readings simply do not conform to the facts of the Third Reich as they unfolded, nor do they conform to *Mein Kampf* or to the Hitler Movement more generally. It testifies to the appeal of the Third Reich, even after the Judeocide, after its hideous historical expression, that some of these intellectuals, most notably Heidegger, saw the fault in the Third Reich, not in their analyses. In other words, the history of the Third Reich departed from the primordial truth of the Hitler Movement *as they understood it.*[40] The spiritual truth of the Movement was more important than its expression during the Third Reich. 'The Real is spiritual and primordial,' they suggested. If the facts deviated, so much the worse for the facts. When separated from their primordial essence, facts, including the facts of history, are irrational and unreal, mere contingencies, happenstances in Time and Space, 'sound and fury, signifying nothing.'

Perhaps due to an inadequate appreciation of idealist or romantic philosophy, I cannot accept either the 'Hegelian' or the 'Heideggerian' dismissals of the facts of the Third Reich. Nothing is less spiritual or more real than the murder of innocents. No primordial essence, or any other metaphysical construction, should be allowed to contextualize, or otherwise diminish, much less justify, the slaughter of defenseless people. While the vast majority of Hitler's supporters did not approve of the murder of anyone, millions of Germans enthusiastically support the Hitler Movement, including its racial anti-Semitism. And millions more averted their eyes and clouded their minds to its most pernicious elements in order to get on with their lives. They could not have done so without some affinity for many of the tenets of the Hitler Movement, felt perhaps more than articulated. My interpretation will try to account for the reality of the Third Reich in historical, social scientific, theological, and philosophical terms, a reality permeated with racial anti-Semitism.

Allow a brief summary of my analysis so far. Chapter five argued that it was easy for a vast majority of Germans to support the Third Reich for reasons having little to do with anti-Semitism. Hitler's policies were successful beyond all expectations. In six years, after all the travail and discord of the post-war period, Germany recovered. More, it achieved what Germans considered its rightful place as the dominant culture and political force in Europe. What was anti-Semitic rhetoric to that? Was it not simply a sop to the ignorant masses? Was it not necessary to unify the classes, so shamelessly divided by Weimar politics? Was it not a way to increase desperately needed German self-esteem and confidence? Was it no more permanent than the SA, whom Hitler used and dispatched, when they became a threat to stability and to the decent development of German culture? From the perspective of practical politics, anti-Semitism was understood by many as a peripheral issue, a rhetorical device, and little more. Although Jews were subject to boycotts, dismissals, restrictions, and insults, these measures would pass like the SA. Besides, many Germans, including liberals, believed that Jews had become too prominent, too rich, too influential—and all too fast, as Weimar opened the last doors for full Jewish participation: 'From the Jewish viewpoint, the establishment of the Republic was undoubtedly a decisive improvement.... For the first time since Bismarck had cooperated with the Liberals, Jews could play more than a marginal role in politics. Jews held leading positions in both the defeated radical socialist groups and in the parties initially entrusted with the running of the new State.'[41] Jewish participation and influence in Weimar were too much, too soon and, worse, without a definable limit. Moreover, they seemed all too consonant with Jewish calculation and deal-making, which, however unavoidable these traits were in business, corroded German political values. For all these reasons: 'And, of course, although many Jews were fine people,' a German might say, 'were they really German or German enough to be trusted with political power? So, in this sensitive period of the formation of German identity, perhaps Jews should take a back seat for a while, if only to allow Germans to grow in confidence and self-respect.' This reasoning was buttressed by the disproportionate activity of Jews in radical politics. As Gordon writes:

> The stereotype of Jews as opponents of government was in great measure built upon the political activities...of a select group who gained national prominence and visibility, but who unfortunately were far more radical than the general Jewish population whom they were assumed in the main to represent. This was a problem of considerable concern to the conservative and moderate Jewish leadership in prewar years; it became an even greater problem during World War I, the subsequent 'socialist revolution,' and the Weimar Republic because anti-Semites labeled all Jews as socialists and revolutionaries.[42]

This is chapter five's argument. Chapter six shifts the analysis from the *political as policy* to the *political as theology*, as a source of transcendent meaning, as a sacred canopy. With less justification, it ignores the critical concepts of racial anti-Semitism. For just as it would have prevented many German intellectuals from participating in the Hitler Movement, racial anti-Semitism's consideration in that chapter would have impeded understanding why these Germans found so many elective affinities with it. How some of these Germans interpreted the Movement is one thing, however, and quite different from this chapter's argument. This chapter analyzes the Hitler Movement in the fullness of its racial anti-Semitism, that is, how it was actualized in the Third Reich, including the Final Solution. Far from ignoring the role of educated Germans in the Hitler Movement, this analysis explains why they were in many respects its most dedicated and thorough advocates. Understanding the political theology of the Movement, including its efforts to purify German culture, educated Germans, many of them high-ranking SS officers with graduate degrees, zealously implemented homicidal policies in the killing fields of the East and in the concentration camps.

Without its hyperbolic racial anti-Semitism, the Hitler Movement would be inexplicable, lacking its coherent basis. Its principle aim was to create the Aryan people out of the adulterated clay of contemporary Germans. To see this as an unrealizable metaphor or spiritual ideal reduces the Hitler Movement to rhetoric. No one grasps this idea better than Bauman: '*They [Jews] were seen as deserving death (and resented for that reason) because they*

*stood between this one imperfect and tension-ridden reality and the hoped-
for world of tranquil happiness.'* And, 'Their killing was not the work of
destruction, but creation. They were eliminated, so that an objectively better human world—more efficient, more moral, more beautiful—could be
established.'[43] Hitler and his most devoted followers claimed that they were
engaged in bringing about a new and glorious future. This required the sacrifice of the enemies of purity: the Jews. Early in his career Hitler said: 'If
at the beginning of the War and during the War twelve or fifteen thousand
of these Hebrew corrupters of the people had been held under poison gas,
as happened to hundreds of thousands of our very best German workers
in the field, the sacrifice at the front might not have been in vain. On the
contrary: twelve thousand scoundrels eliminated in time might have saved
the lives of a million real Germans, valuable for the future.'[44] Although it
is doubtful that many Germans understood Hitler literally or imagined the
murder of millions, it is difficult to believe that they did not take Hitler seriously, when he pledged to eliminate Jews and Jewish influence from the
Third Reich. Although much easier to credit after the Judeocide, there were
ample contemporary warnings before the Final Solution revealed the Hitler
Movement in all its gruesome horror. There was no way to bring about the
spiritual revitalization of the German people, as Heidegger and many others
believed essential, without eliminating anti-spiritual, anti-German forces:
Jews as metaphors, if not as sacrificial victims. Moreover, this view had
a lengthy pedigree. Consider Kant's description of Jews: 'The [Jews] who
live among us owe their not undeserved reputation for cheating (at least
the majority of them) to their spirit of usury which has possessed them
ever since their exile. Certainly it seems strange to conceive of a Nation
of cheats, but it is just as strange to conceive of a Nation of traders....' [45]
And of Judaism: 'The euthanasia of Judaism is the pure moral religion.'[46]
It is unfair to Kant to read words like 'euthanasia' through the lens of the
Judeocide, yet it is difficult not to take killing, even of an idea, seriously.
Certainly, many Kant scholars, like Fichte, drew explicit racist implications
from this sort of critique: 'Onto his Kantian moralist distaste for Judaism,
Fichte has grafted a French revolutionary moralism that defined the citizen
in terms of revolutionary virtue: only a moral being was capable of being
such a virtuous citizen. Relying on Kant's *a priori* ethical definition of the
Jew as the negation of freedom and morality, Fichte in 1793 constructed a
political definition of the Jew as being inherently unsuitable for citizenship
and civil rights.'[47] Rose concludes: 'In Kant, therefore, we find a collection of potent anti-Jewish concepts: Judaism is an *immoral* and *absolute*
religion; the Jews are an *alien* Nation; the Jews are a Nation of *traders*
devoted to *money*. Unifying all these themes is the central Kantian revo-

lutionary idea of moral freedom that sees Jews as refusing to be free: they chain themselves to an external, irrational Law that reduces them in the end to being slaves of their own unenlightened egoism.'[48]

The consequence of the conviction that Jews have rejected freedom in principle would have devastating modern effects, more powerful than traditional Jew-hatred, because anti-Semitism would seem idealistic, a holy mission: 'The powerful new moralist critique of Judaism nevertheless followed the Statists in rejecting Jew-hatred as Medieval, fanatical, irrational—unenlightened. *Their* modern critique, maintained Kant, Herder, Fiche, and the young Hegel, would be cool and detached from Christian religious superstition: it would be objective and, above all, freedom-seeking. Revolutionary anti-Semitism was thus born of the idealist, revolutionary vision of a newly redeemed, emancipated, free mankind.'[49] By definition these anti-German traits were Jewish, although not confined to ethnic Jews. Without for a moment diminishing the horror of murdering innocent men women and children, expunging the Jewish spirit was a more profound form of genocide. This was the cardinal objective of the Hitler Movement, its *raison d'être*. The Judeocide would have had no meaning for the adherents of the Hitler Movement were it not for their conviction that Jews infected Germans with crass materialism. Otherwise, Mosse asks, 'How could the Jews, with their spirit of usury and love of ostentatious materialism, have gotten the upper hand in Germany? The conclusion was simple and *Volkisch*: the German people must share the guilt for such a state of affairs and consequently must expiate their sin?'[50] Physical Jews had to be killed to enable Germans to rid themselves of their susceptibility to Jewish influences. It was, however, but a first, if decisive, step toward the elimination of the Jewish metaphor. This project became urgent with the increasing pervasiveness of the Jew in every area of European life after the French Revolution.

> In Germany, as in other European countries, the fight for Jewish emancipation was part of the greater conflict between the old feudal powers and the rising middle class. The gains and setbacks for the Jews' struggle for equality run parallel with the fortunes of German liberalism in its fight for democracy and national unification. Paul Massing[51]

EMANCIPATION: A MIXED BLESSING

Despite its celebration of Natural Rights, the French Revolution regarded ambivalently the emancipation of French Jews. In extensive debates in the

National Assembly, Jews and non-Jews expressed misgivings, notwithstanding their support of revolutionary ideals. The perennial question of the Jewish status remained: 'Who were the Jews, a people or individuals, who shared certain attributes, chief of which was Judaism?' Given the individualism entailed in the concept of Natural Rights, the question should have been resolved individually; that is, an individual with Jewish antecedents was, like everyone else, endowed with inalienable Natural Rights. Many Jews accepted this formulation; for those with more conservative or traditional views, identity was a communal or national property. Not a person who happened to have Jewish antecedents, a Jew was a creature of the Covenant, one of God's Chosen People, a member of a Nation created and chosen by God for a special mission. The racist implications of divine election have been often cited by Jews, as well as their critics: 'The notion of race as such, defined as a set of common physical and mental characteristics transmitted within a group by the force of tradition or even in some biological way, had been used by the Jews themselves from Moses Hess to Martin Buber....'[52] No notion of Natural Rights, nor anything else, could change a Jew's identity. By virtue of this conviction, it was virtually impossible to avoid the implication that the Jews were a nation within a nation. Moreover, for non-Jews, especially conservatives and traditional Catholics, Jews were considered different, because they had been designated by God, not as the Chosen, but as the Rejected. Recall Cardinal Faulhaber's words. As a people they had rejected Christ. As a people God rejected them. Individual Jews could be redeemed but only by Baptism, that is, by ceasing to observe Judaism.

Additional consequences for Jews were implied by the *French* Revolution. 'What does it mean to be French?' Again, from a Natural Rights perspective, the answer is relatively simple. Each individual has the right to rule himself (liberty); more generally, groups of rights-bearing individuals have the right of self-rule in an arena of fraternity and equality, providing they did not violate individual rights. All human beings are born with Natural Rights, implying that all tensions between individual rights and civil society would be resolved in favor of this inalienable endowment. Upon reflection, however, the problem of *French* identity remained. 'Is a French person someone who happens to reside within the jurisdiction of the French state?' 'Is he or she otherwise indistinguishable from any other rights-bearing individual?' The answer should have been, 'Yes,' but it was not so, not without major qualification, if not contradiction. According to this line of reasoning, the French Revolution *was French* in two profound senses. First, it was not happenstance that it transpired in France, that it was conceived and made by the French. However universal the rights proclaimed by the Revolution might be, they were proclaimed, recognized, and actualized by Frenchmen. Second, the Revolution *created* the French, that is, French citizens were now *the* French Nation, not only subjects of the French State, or members of an estate or class. Creating meaning and guaranteeing rights, making them politically effective, even if it did not confer them, this identity, in league with political power, created a sacred canopy, especially for those French who did not believe in a personal God. The chief outcome of the Revolution was the French Nation-State. By this reasoning there could be no such thing as a French individual apart from France. Far more than a citizen of a civil society, to be French was to participant in a meaning creating, transcendent national community. To the extent that intense nationalism qualified Natural Rights, it became problematic for Jewish emancipation. For, if the Jews were a Nation, then emancipation would mean that they would constitute a nation within a nation, a circumstance that the newly minted French Nation-State could not countenance. The Nation-State is a jealous god, commanding the total loyalty of its subjects. The majority of the French were too busy with their lives, to be troubled by the tension between Natural Rights and nationalism. Yet the tension remained unresolved, as anti-Semitism persisted, despite the assimilation of most Jews, and found expression in the Dreyfus Affair.

Dreyfus was convicted on flimsy and trumped up evidence, because he seemed to confirm long-standing suspicion of Jewish loyalty. His treason proved that, whatever the loyalty of ordinary Jews to France was, it was foolish to allow a Jew to have access to the nerve center of the army, the General Staff. When the real traitor was discovered, little changed, as the shock wave rapidly dissipated. Never taking foreign criticism seriously, France hardly missed a beat despite the furor. Despite rhetoric about universal rights, Liberty, Equality, and Fraternity applied only to the French and were then subordinated to an ardent nationalism, which did not include Jews, except the most assimilated. Moreover, the French people took pride in the sacred honor of the army (what was evidence to that?) *and* in the zeal of the Dreyfusards. Who but the French could challenge the power of the State in the name of justice? And for a Jew! For Germans, like Jews, including Theodore Herzl, the Dreyfus Affair revealed French hypocrisy regarding Natural Rights. If Jews retained any Jewishness, they could not be French, Natural Rights to the contrary notwithstanding.

For Germans, the French Revolution left a wider array of unresolved issues. German nationalism was far more tenuous and more romantic than the French. Achieving political unification under Prussian leadership only in 1871, many Germans retained provincial political loyalties. More apt to identify themselves as Bavarians, Swabians, or Prussians, German essence was linguistic and cultural, not political. As unification only partially changed these attitudes, German national identity remained problematic. Therefore, it

was entirely understandable that educated elites, disproportionately nationalists, were acutely sensitive to the concept, including its corrosive implication
of a nation within a nation. The Zionist goal of a Jewish Nation-State collided
with the embryonic and incomplete German Nation-State. To be sure, as the
century unfolded, Germans became more secular, while Jewish emancipation
and assimilation accelerated. Nevertheless, the proposition that Jews could
be Germans without qualification was never fully credited by a majority of
Germans, including liberals, like Kant and many others. Katz explains the
complex process of assimilation:

> The root cause of this outbreak of anti-Semitism is illustrated by Theodor Mom-
> msen's reply to Heinrich von Treitschke [1879, after the stock market crash]....
> Mommsen, a staunch and outspoken liberal, conceded that the Jewish commu-
> nity was far too peculiar, ethnically and culturally, to be easily integrated into
> the newly united German Nation.... Mommsen was correct that, even after they
> had been subjected to cultural adaptation, the Jews were distinguishable as a
> separate social group. Mommsen also rightly stated that while liberalism was
> dominant, most of the German public had turned its attention away from the
> signs of internal unity among the Jews. This did not mean that they were satis-
> fied with, or reconciled to, the existence of a separate Jewish community, but
> were quietly hopeful that it might dwindle away...[but] the cultural adaptation
> of the Jewish community never, at any place, led directly to the total absorption
> of that community into the larger society.[53]

The widely held conviction that Jews could never be absorbed into the
Volksgemeinschaft laid the groundwork for intense anti-Semitism, compounded by the difficulties attendant upon the rapid transformation of German economy and society. As fathers and sons of modernity, Jews seemed
responsible for unprecedented dislocations in German society. Capitalism in
particular seemed Jewish. According to Reichmann:

> One need not regard them...as the creators of capitalism, and explain this by
> their religion and early history, in order to fully appreciate their outstanding
> contribution to the development and expansion of capitalistic methods. Their
> very aptitude for a system which has given rise to so much hostility among men
> made it all the more tragic that their emancipation should coincide with, and in-
> deed depend upon, the development of that system. The Jews acted everywhere
> as the pioneers of capitalism. They were not average competitors in that econ-
> omy of which the hallmark was *homo homini lupus*, but they were especially
> able, mobile, and progressive competitors. Untrammeled by the Medieval tradi-
> tion they had not been allowed to share, free from sentimental ties of all kinds
> which continued to restrain their Gentile rivals long after capitalistic views had
> officially prevailed, the Jews applied logically the economic principles which
> were now not only accepted but intrinsically required.[54]

Sombart adds: 'On the one hand, they influenced the outward form of modern capitalism; on the other, they gave expression to its inward spirit.... The Jews contributed no small share in giving to economic relations the international aspect they bear today; in helping the modern State, that framework of capitalism, to become what it is; and lastly, in giving the capitalistic organization its peculiar features, by inventing a good many details of the commercial machinery which moves the business life of today.'[55] As major innovators of capitalism's institutions and procedures, and as its most assiduous exploiters, Jews prospered. The incarnation of capitalism, Jews would be held accountable for the destruction of traditional, largely agrarian, values. In Bauman's words: 'Truly, *the fate of the Jews epitomized the awesome scope of social upheaval and served as a vivid, obtrusive reminder of the erosion of old certainties.*'[56] For Germans, like Heinrich Leo, this process indicated far more than normal societal change: 'The Jewish Nation stands out conspicuously among all other Nations of this world in that it possesses a truly corroding and decomposing mind. In the same way as there exist some fountains that would transmute every object thrown into them into stone, thus the Jews, from the very beginning to this very day, have transmuted everything that fell into the orbit of their spiritual activity into an abstract generality.'[57]

Favoring Jewish emancipation, liberal Germans expected them to become less Jewish and more German. As French nationalism limited French adherence to Natural Rights, German nationalism made minority status intolerable. Identifying the Nation with the *Volk* implied the eradication of *identifiable* Jews in Germany, pressuring Jews to forsake Judaism, even as a private confession. Recall the analysis of the *Merchant of Venice*. Shylock had to convert to Christianity, nothing less would do, because he could not be trusted with a major role in emergent capitalism. No outsider could wield a knife which could cut the financial heart out of Venetian prosperity: 'Become part of the community or die!' Gentle Portia said, in effect: 'Become part of the Belmont or remain pariahs.' As this process unfolded, Jews were expected to normalize their vocations, ceasing to be concentrated in trade and finance, becoming more like Germans:

Marx was one of the first to understand the dynamic and exploitive character of capitalism, but precisely because he denied or denigrated the autonomy of sentiments and misunderstood the force of nationalism, he did not envision the possibility of a strong non-socialist anti-capitalist movement arising; in Germany it played a decisive role. In this uneasy capitalistic, secularizing age, German Jews did superbly well. Nimble and rootless, they seized every possible chance; economic opportunity beckoned for all, often at the price of moving to new and unknown quarters; Jews had little to lose and hence responded to the lure of the new city with untroubled eagerness. Once there, they excelled in certain

traditional functions, quickly adapted to modern needs.... Proportionately they
were richer, better educated, and—at least in some areas—held better positions
than their Christian colleagues and competitors.[58]

The expectation that Jews would avail themselves of broadening vocational
opportunities was not fulfilled:

> By examining the occupational distribution and income of Jews from 1870 to
> 1933, one gains the impression that Jews were more successful in their careers
> and income than were non-Jews.... Jews were never the powerful captains of
> industry...their roles were predominantly those of middlemen, financiers, and
> members of the free professions and cultural fields. Nevertheless, it is clear
> that Jews had an occupational and income distribution different enough from
> that of other Germans to serve as a base upon which gross exaggerations and
> stereotypes could be built.[59]

For compelling reasons, social and economic, Jews remained in trade and
finance: 'Of the fifty-two private banks in Berlin at the beginning of the
nineteenth century, thirty were Jewish owned.... The Jewish economic elite's
particular function during the nineteenth century had been its decisive role
in capital mobilization and concentration through development of the Berlin
stock market, and linkage of the still relatively parochial German economy
with world markets. The centrality of Jewish banking during the Weimar
period did not decrease....'[60] Holborn reminds us: 'Commerce and finance
were still the major pursuit of the mass of German Jews. They were found as
lowly peddlers, as cattle and grain dealers, storekeepers, retail and wholesale
merchants, and finally as bankers. However, the relative influence of the
Jews on finance declined after 1871. None of the big industrial fortunes that
came into being were in Jewish hands, and the modern banks which financed
the German industrialization were not decisively directed by Jewish interests.'[61] When they took on new occupations, they remained associated with
modernity: 'As for the press—excluding the great number of conservative
and specifically Christian newspapers and periodicals—there was, on the
national level, a strong Jewish presence in ownership, editorial responsibility,
and major political and social commentary.'[62] The new phenomenon of mass
media created its own anxieties for the preservation of traditional values.
Ephemeral, irreverent, critical, careless with the facts, and sensational, the
media exemplified all that was corrosive of German values, all that was alien,
all that was Jewish.

Identified not only with economic and social modernization, Jews were
urban. Of course, more and more ethnic Germans were moving to cities to
improve their standard of living, believing that they were driven their by the

changes that naturally urban Jews created. These Germans believed retained agrarian values, grasped all the more desperately and nostalgically for their dissolving reality. This perception was supported by the view that, notwithstanding their residence in villages and towns:

> The Jew has become the urban dweller *comme il faut*. In him we find accumulated and developed to the extreme all the qualities, good and bad, which distinguish the city dweller. Compared to him the Christian is a mere peasant, even the Christian of the city; for he, too, is as a rule the direct or indirect descendant of peasants. What appears to us as the unbridgeable race antagonism between the Aryan and the Semite is in reality nothing but the antagonism between the peasant and the city dweller carried to the extreme.... The anti-Semite...would find typically Jewish the alertness of mind, quickness of motion, facility of language, nervous restlessness, muscular atrophy, and lack of physical prowess which the peasant, half suspiciously, half contemptuously, observes as the characteristic of the urban man.[63]

When they lived in rural areas, it was for urban reasons: to make money, often seen as taking advantage of decent, innocent, and simple rural folk. Hitler seized on this perception, intensifying it with a biological metaphor: 'If the Jew's feelings move in purely material realms, even more so does his thinking and striving.... Everything that prompts man to strive for higher things, whether religion, socialism, democracy, all that is to him only a means to the end of satisfying his craving for money and dominance. The consequences of his activity become the racial tuberculosis of nations.'[64] Unable or unwilling to participate in agrarian life, Jews were its exploiters.

Katz believes, far from normalizing, Jewish occupations became more Jewish. This concentration was sometimes extraordinarily disproportionate, especially in Berlin:

> Even more than before, Jews were now compelled to concentrate both socially and economically. Professions open to them, such as medicine and law, now [nineteenth century] attracted more Jews, not fewer. Moreover, the relative preponderance of Jews in the various branches of the economy and public affairs continued to be active. Jews continued to play a conspicuous role in banking, at the stock exchange, and in management of the press.... For those who regretted the passage of a more restful way of life, or felt economically and otherwise threatened by the new developments, this very process was a thorn in the flesh.[65]

The consequences for anti-Semitism are obvious. Jews became more and more prosperous. According to Gordon: 'By 1929 it was estimated that the per capita income of Jews in Berlin [where more than 30% of Jews resided] was twice that of other Berlin residents.'[66] Moreover, Jews predominated in professions which served Germans when they were ill or otherwise in trouble. While it is reasonable to expect desperate people to be grateful to those who minister to their needs, it is also human for them to resent their vulnerability to strangers. For different reasons, Jewish academic excellence also concerned nationalist Germans. How could true German values be taught to the best students by professors who were not real Germans? An education was far more than skill and knowledge transfer, a process for which Jewish professors were admirably suited. But were not traditional and cultural values another matter? These must not be presented analytically, skeptically or disinterestedly. Did the inculcation of German values not require a passionate German professor? Could any Jewish professor be like Heidegger?

Beyond the normal anxiety regarding change, even when beneficial, when recurring in boom and bust cycles, it unnerves. When the stock market crashed, Germans, new to the institutions of capitalism, suspicious of business, wary of its government's ties to liberal politicians, believed it was a divine judgment. 'The year 1873 is marked in European, and especially German, history as the date of the great bankruptcy, the failure of many financial enterprises established in the preceding years of unprecedented economic boom. The financial debacle ushered in the great depression of the Bismarck years, which lasted with some fluctuations until 1896.'[67] Alien values in the hands of strangers had defeated German values and were in turn defeated by the forces they had unleashed so callously upon Germans. Katz argues that 'It was not the Jews' real or imagined share in bringing about the economic debacle.... It was the conspicuous part they played in economic activity—banking, finance, the stock market—and their rapid rise to economic, social and political prominence.'[68] This is only part of the story, however. At issue was not simply Jewish success; the problem was the infusion of Jewish values, essentially material and individual, into German society. The lesson was plain: curb these forces in the name of traditional values. Save Germans from Jews and save Germans from their susceptibility to Jewish values: become Pure.

Given the pervasive suspicion of Jews, Germans believed the 1873 catastrophe confirmed the Jewish devotion to money:

> Manchesterism is the King Midas doctrine of money. It wants to translate everything into money—the soil, labor and human ability; it glorifies egoism, and rejects all sense of solidarity, humanity and all ethical principles.... Jewry is applied Manchesterism in the extreme. It knows nothing but trade, and of that merely haggling and usury. It does not work but makes others work for it. It haggles and speculates with the manual and mental products of others. Its center is the stock exchanges.... As an alien tribe it fastens itself on the German people and sucks their marrow. The social question is essentially the Jewish question; everything else is a swindle.[69]

No doubt this extreme view was not supported by all Germans, yet in the wake of the crash, many must have held similar views, at least privately. No matter how assimilated a Jew was, no matter how integral his activities were to the economy, no matter how much he had profited, if a choice had to be made between his prosperity and the well-being of Germany, Germany be damned. Therefore, no Jew could be trusted to control the nerve center of the economy: the financial exchanges and the investment banks. Like the French response to Dreyfus, verifiable facts were not dispositive. Whether or not Jewish bankers controlled the economy was beside the point. Banks and exchanges were 'Jewish' in nature, expressing of the Jewish spirit of capitalism, including its sharp practices. According the Graetz:

> To twist a phrase out of its meaning, to use all the tricks of a clever advocate, to play upon words, and to condemn what they did not know...such were the characteristics of the Polish Jew.... Honesty and right-thinking he lost as completely as simplicity and truthfulness. He made himself master of all the gymnastics of the Schools and applied them to obtain advantage over any one less cunning than himself. He took delight in cheating and overreaching, which gave him a sort of joy of victory. But his own people he could not treat in this way: they were as knowing as he. It was the non-Jew who, to his loss, felt the consequences of the *Talmudically* trained mind....[70]

Again, while this depiction may be overstated, it accurately reflected many contemporary German opinions. Arendt offers a more balanced judgment, also going to character: 'It was the lack of "innate personality," the lack of tact, the innate lack of productivity, the innate disposition for trading, etc., which separated the behavior of his Jewish colleague from that of the average businessman.'[71] Talmon accounts for this phenomenon:

> The discomfort experienced by the Jews who had been formally emancipated, but not really admitted into society, did indeed breed traits which it has been only too easy for unfriendly satirists to caricature.... Their common denominator was overreaction. Their perpetual uncertainty about what the tomorrow might bring had for generations driven Jews to amass possessions, and above all money, which could easily be carried from place to place. Their desire to prove their worth to themselves, and still more to others, made many of them over-ambitious, ostentatious and arrogant. Sensing animosity and suspicion, anxious to please and fearful of causing displeasure, some would become too loud and effusive or fawning and furtive.[72]

Whatever the etiology of Jewish values and, however one explains or justifies their behavior in Germany over the centuries, there was no combating the anxiety Germans felt when forces out of their control, seemingly in the hands of deceitful and devious strangers, held their economic security hostage.

While most Germans knew there could be no return to pre-industrial society, they nonetheless believed that capitalism should be restrained by traditional values. As an alien import, a product of the French Revolution's exaltation of materialism and individualism, many Germans believed that the benefits of modernization had to be placed in a more human and humane context, made more German, less French, and less Jewish. Jews had been perceived as the most important and most powerful beneficiaries of the Revolution. Although Jews had little to do with its creation, they, and this seemed typical to many Germans, they took advantage of the work of others. Fueled by the Revolution's values, their incredible prosperity seemed inevitable. And yet they remained a people apart, a position less and less tolerable as nationalist feeling grew on the Continent, despite efforts to block it by Metternich and the Congress of Vienna. According to Katz, 'The designation "nation within a nation," though unfriendly in intention, is factually not incorrect. It was not, in fact, even contested by defenders of the Jewish cause....'[73] Echoing Medieval responses to catastrophe, when German nationalism was confronted with economic disruptions, Jews were blamed. Anti-Semitic parties, explicitly named, came into existence. Although these parties remained small and all but disappeared with economic recovery, the anxiety which helped to create them persisted; so, too, their diagnosis of the problem. Friedlander explains: 'Whereas the French model implied the *construction* of national identity by way of a centralized educational system and other means of socialization …the German model often posited the existence of inherited characteristics belonging to a preexisting organic community.'[74] The modern world was anti-German, because it was too Jewish, because anything Jewish undercut the idea of the *Volksgemeinschaft*. As Mosse writes, 'Not only was the essential nature of the Jews incompatible with the inner character of the German *Volk*, but their national religion made them an irreconcilable foreign element on German soil.'[75]

A catastrophe which devastated all Germans, not just the economically vulnerable, not just those who believed in the Germany of woodland glades and its goblins, the crushing defeat in the Great War made all things non-German criminal. Germans, who supported the Weimar Republic or were otherwise Western, betrayed the Fatherland. Recall Mann's Literary Man. This animus struck Jews with more force, for were they not problematic Germans? Was Germany their *real* Fatherland? 'Yes, some behaved honorably during the War,' one might say, 'but was this not due to a calculation of self-interest rather than bred in Blood and Soil loyalty?' When the Defeat brought economic chaos, 'The [Weimar] government was administering misery instead of relieving it....'[76] For these reasons, anti-Semitism became a rallying cry of the Right. For millions of others, across the political spectrum, its tenets and slogans were reiterated quietly in kitchens, living rooms, and in the lines of misery and despair which traced their way on German streets. The real successes of the Republic seemed too little too late, too much at the sufferance of the Allies, too much the result of Jewish influence, in and out of Germany. Ordinary Germans began to listen to racially phrased counsels of despair. Educated Germans, needing more sophisticated explanations, tended to see Weimar as the logical conclusion of everything that was wrong with the French Revolution. Recall our discussions of Thomas Mann and Heidegger. Although many German intellectuals were by no means racial anti-Semites, their views often gave the racists intellectual legitimacy and a cover of respectability.

The following analysis suggests how easily many of the concerns and themes of German intellectuals flowed into the rhetoric of racial anti-Semitism. The French Revolution, conceived as cause and effect of the Jewification of Europe, debased the agrarian form of life. A new man was needed make Germany whole, a man who would be as confident and effective as Jews, but who would not be corrupted by their materialism. Pure as the humblest peasant, despite his immersion in the modern world, he would transform the world from an arena of sin into a platform for Aryan salvation. The sign of God's favor, Aryan birth would make all Germans equal spiritually, regardless of station. Working in the spiritualized New Order, it would be impossible for a German to exploit a German; the class struggle, becoming absurd. More than the prophet, Hitler became the Leader, the enforcer of the racial structure of the universe, the savior of Germans. By remaining faithful to their essence in Blood and Soil and to the *Fuehrer*, they would make the world *Judenfrei*, creating a garden of Aryan delights.

Felt by many, understood by few, this Aryan Vision was the *raison d'être* of the Hitler Movement, with ominous implications for European Jewry. By adding a biological strain to the anti-Judaism and Jew-hatred of traditional anti-Semites, the ambivalent national identities of Jews and Germans were clarified. Both were racial Nations, mutually antagonistic, locked in a Social Darwinist struggle: Germans, the product of Blood and Soil; Jews, of landlessness, statelessness, materialism and inbreeding. In Hitler's words:

> The Jewish State was never spatially limited in itself, but universally unlimited as to space, though restricted in the sense of embracing but one race. Consequently, this people have always formed a State within States. It is one of the most ingenious tricks that was ever devised, to make this State sail under the flag of religion, thus assuring it the tolerance which the Aryan is always ready to accord a religious creed. For actually the Mosaic religion is nothing other than a doctrine for the preservation of the Jewish race.[77]

Moreover, these conditions made it impossible for Jews to participate in normal human activities. Hitler writes: 'A chosen people does not go into the world to make others work for them, to suck blood. It does not go among the peoples to chase the peasants from the land. It does not go among the peoples to make your fathers poor and drive them to despair. A chosen people does not slay and torture animals to death. A chosen people does not live by the sweat of others. A chosen people joins the ranks of those who live because they work.'[78] Note that Hitler complains about anti-communal, Jewish work, contrasting it with German labor:

> I ask you to bear in mind that we are living in an age which perceives its very essence in work itself; that we wish to build up a State which values work for its own sake and holds the worker in high regard because he is fulfilling a duty to the Nation; a State which aims, by means of its labor service, to educate every-one—even the tender sons of highborn parents—to hold work in high regard and to respect physical labor in the service of the national community.... We want to educate the *Volk* so that it moves away from the insanity of class superiority, of arrogance of rank, and of the delusion that only mental work is of any value; we want the *Volk* to comprehend that every labor which is necessary ennobles the doer, and that there is only one disgrace, and that is to contribute nothing to the maintenance of the *Volk* itself.' [79]

We have already analyzed *Mein Kampf*, perhaps artificially, by excluding most of its racial anti-Semitism. Now is the time to place racial anti-Semitism in its proper context. No candidate for high office has ever made his intentions clearer than Adolf Hitler. In thousands of speeches and less formal presentations, his words reduced themselves to a predominant goal: the enhancement of Germany, culturally, politically, and racially. Although other nationalisms have sometimes sounded a racial or, more often, an ethnic note, Hitler made race purity *the* condition for meeting its other objectives. Without its racist basis, Hitler's other objectives differed little from any other realist approach to foreign policy. He writes: *'Blood sin and desecration of the race are the original sin in this world and the end of a humanity which surrenders to it.'*[80] Again: *'Thus, the highest purpose of a folkish State is concern for the preservation of those original racial elements which bestow culture and cre-ate the beauty and dignity of a higher mankind.'*[81] And again: *'What we must fight for is to safeguard the existence and the reproduction of our race and our people, the sustenance of our children and the purity of our blood, the freedom and independence of the Fatherland, so that our people may mature for the fulfillment of the mission allotted to it by the Creator of the universe.'*[82] The necessity to purify German blood collapses religious and scientific approaches to the Jewish Problem. 'If the worst came to the worst, a splash of

Baptismal water could always save the business and the Jew at the same time. With such superficial motivation, a serious scientific treatment of the whole problem was never achieved....'[83] Moreover, '*by defending myself against the Jew, I am fighting for the work of the Lord*'.[84] Besides, 'without the clearest knowledge of the racial problem and hence of the Jewish problem, there will never be a resurrection of the German Nation.'[85] Although Hitler did not say that Jews would have to be murdered and their influence annihilated, it is difficult to believe he would have countenanced Jewish presence in Germany in any form.

'Elimination' is the word Hitler most often used when he referring to making Germany *Judenfrei*. Before the Final Solution, 'elimination' meant, for National Socialism, the eviction Jews from Germany. In the more religious context of the Hitler Movement, 'elimination' meant the purging of things Jewish from the German Spirit and Blood, the condition for transforming Germans into Aryans. The physical absence of Jews would not suffice in these terms, for their ability to adulterate German blood would remain intact for at least two reasons: first, Germans were already contaminated by Jewish assimilation, intermarriage and Baptism. Secondly, they were infected by Jewish materialism, which he grudgingly respected: 'He admired the Jews. Their racial exclusiveness and purity seemed to him no less admirable than their sense of being a chosen people, their implacability and intelligence. Basically, he regarded them as something akin to negative supermen. Even Germanic Nations or relatively pure racial strains were... inferior to the Jews: "if 5,000 Jews were transported to Sweden, within a short time they would occupy all the leading positions."'[86] So complete has Jewish domination of the world become that it seems invincible, as inevitable and powerful as change itself.

> The Jews, already construed as slimy in religious and class dimensions, were now more than any other category vulnerable to the new tensions and contradictions which the social upheavals of the modernizing revolution could not fail to generate. For most members of society, the advent of modernity meant the destruction of order and security, and once again, the Jews were perceived as standing close to the destructive process. Their own rapid and incomprehensible social advancement and transformation seemed to epitomize the havoc visited by advancing modernity upon everything familiar, habitual and secure.[87]

Only a purified German race, which would involve a long process of Aryanization, could combat this insidious evil. Everywhere a threat, Jewish values harbored by Germans have become the greater danger.

So when Hitler became Chancellor, there was ample reason for concern, not panic. Many Jews left, but many stayed. Moreover, there was reason for optimism, as Rubenstein points out: 'Still, as 1933 drew to a close, even Jewish observers could say that, although many German Jews had lost their economic base for existence, a tolerable Jewish future remained possible in Germany. Coupled with the fact that relatively little legislative action was taken against the Jews in 1934, the purging of the Rohm elements...also portended a moderating climate for Jewish life. Indeed several thousand Jews who had fled Germany returned home in early 1935.'[88] German Jews seemed to say, 'Our love for Germany cannot be denied, because an avowed anti-Semite has become Chancellor. Politicians come and go, as the turbulence of the postwar years has amply demonstrated. Hitler's reign is likely to be shorter than most, since it was an outburst of desperation, not a structural change.'

Perhaps more profound than any assessment of Nazi tactics or their ultimate objectives were the lessons Jews inferred from their long experience in Germany, as Rubenstein writes: 'For the long-standing Jewish strategy of coping with Gentile threats had been that of alleviation and compliance.... When their objective became the Final Solution, alleviation was at best momentary; compliance at worst meant self-destruction.'[89] Their experience prior to the Third Reich enabled Jews to discount Hitler's words and to perceive his inconsistent policies as signs of ambivalence. Hitler's remarkably flexible tactics were the product, on the contrary, of an absolute conviction in his vision of a *Judenfrei* Europe under German domination:

> Christianity regarded all earthly existence as transient, while the Nazis thought in terms of rendering life Eternal through a sort of biological Great Chain of Being. The individual was worth nothing, but the racial collective will live through the aeons. This is what Hitler presumably meant when he said: 'To the Christian doctrine of the infinite significance of the human soul.... I oppose with icy clarity the saving doctrine of the nothingness and insignificance of the individual human being, and of his continued existence in the visible immortality of the Nation.'[90]

In other words, tactics depend on contingencies; Vision is as immortal as the Nation. Blind to this Vision, Jews drew on their experience and relied on the decency of their neighbors. Moreover, the anti-Semitic thuggery of the SA was normal, practically a custom, which the vast majority of Germans found contemptible and which Jews believed they could tolerate. When Hitler purged the SA, murdering its leaders, Jews understandably took solace in the destruction of their principal tormentors. Like other Germans, they welcomed the reassertion of order, *albeit* under dubious law, as Hitler acknowledged: 'I am totally indifferent as to whether a legal clause opposes our actions... during the months when it was about the life or death of the German Nation, it was entirely irrelevant whether other people whined about breaking the law.'[91] Furthermore, Hitler's decisive action seemed to indicate that violent Jew-hatred was no longer acceptable, the realities of governance restraining it further. The State would discipline the mob, as it has always done, preventing Nazi rhetoric from becoming reality. There was little irony in this expectation for assimilated Jews. Germany was their State.

So strong was the Jews' desire to interpret the Third Reich benignly—there could be no more powerful indication of their Germanness—that when significant changes took place, these, too, were interpreted optimistically. For example, when under pressure from the Soviet Union, Eastern Jews fled to Germany, German-Jews, for all their distaste of their coreligionists, thought that their disconcerting arrival might be beneficial. *These* were the Jews the Germans hated, these Jews who were so different from Germans and from us. Gordon writes: 'Immigration of foreign Jews and the high level of mobility among both foreign and German Jews thus fostered the anti-Semites' stereotype of the Jews as an alien and rootless people. Foreign Jews faced particularly difficult problems; they were highly visible because of their distinctive black clothing, sidelocks, yarmulkas, Yiddish speech, Orthodox religious customs, and support for Zionism.'[92] 'Look at them,' one could hear a German Jew saying: 'Could they ever be German, even if they wanted to? Could they ever be like us?' Singly or in their millions, Eastern Jews could never be confused with German Jews. No one was sufficiently foolish to deny all the obvious differences of appearance, culture, language, dress, religious practices, and values. 'Not even the Nazis could deny our value compared to them.' Mayer makes this point bluntly:

By respectively denying and diluting their Jewishness, the integral and limited assimilationists stood apart from the vast majority of the third major component of European Jewry, the *Ostjuden*, who lived in, had come from, or whose families had come from, Eastern Europe.... At the base of European Jewry, the Eastern Jews were by far the most numerous, the poorest, and the most sealed off.... At the time most assimilated and assimilating Jews viewed their unacculturated Eastern coreligionists with a mixture of apprehension, shame, and disdain. On the whole, the former scorned rather than valued the latter's distinctive religious, social and cultural ways. Europeanized Jews disparaged the shtetls and the ghetto-like city districts of Eastern Jews west of the Vistula as stale, oppressive, and dirty, and among themselves referred to their residents as *Polacken, Galizaner, die Frommen,* or the 'others'.... Theirs was a fortress mentality, forged to protect their singular universe from a surrounding world they perceived as immutably hostile. Thus, the Eastern Jews made little effort to breech the invisible walls of isolation and discrimination surrounding them.[93]

Moreover, when the news of the massacre of Jews in Poland reached the West, many Jews discounted it: 'David Cohen, the President of the Jewish Council,

flatly denied its relevance to the prospects of Dutch Jewry: the fact that the
Germans had perpetrated atrocities against Polish Jews was no reason for thinking that they would behave in the same way toward Dutch Jews, firstly because
Germans had always held Polish Jews in disrepute, and secondly because in the
Netherlands, unlike Poland, they had to sit up and take notice of public opinion.'[94] Bauman continues, 'Even if the spokesmen of the established Jewish
community felt compassion for the immigrant Jews rounded up, incarcerated
and deported in front of their eyes, they appealed to community members to
keep calm and refrain from any resistance for the sake of higher values.'[95]

Although unpleasant and racist, this attitude was not unreasonable. It was
fantastic, nonetheless, to believe that racist anti-Semites would care about the
differences between Eastern and German Jews. As many leading Nazis, including Goebbels, Himmler, and Goering often asserted, good Jews were the
greatest danger, because, possessing German virtues and values, they seemed
German. Their integration into German communities, their conviction that
they were Germans, true Germans, would disarm real Germans. Racial
anti-Semitism implies that a Jew is a Jew period. Rhetoric? Of course. This
rhetoric, however, penetrated deep into the strata of the Hitler Movement's
conception of German and Jewish identity. Few Jews seem to have understood the depth of Nazi racism. Not only scientifically dubious and morally
reprehensible, for them, racism was ignorant, uncultured, and fundamentally
anti-German. Jews believed that, far from being *ersatz* Germans, they were
German to the core. Jewish response to the Nuremberg Laws was also indica-
tive, illustrating a propensity to view Hitler as an Austrian upstart.

> The racial legislation consisted of two separate acts. The first specified that only
> 'a citizen...of German or kindred blood' had the capacity and right 'to serve the
> German people and Reich,' and that only such citizens were entitled to exercise
> 'full political rights.' The second prohibited both marriage and extramarital
> sexual relations between Jews and full citizens, and also prohibited Jews from
> employing maidservants of German blood and under forty-five years of age in
> their households.... Except for fanatical proponents of Nazi racial mythology,
> the Nuremberg Laws were not a matter of exceptional interest or concern. Once
> again many Gentiles and Jews were reassured by a seemingly legal handling of
> the 'Jewish question.'[96]

Even the widespread violence and destruction of *Kristallnacht* did little to
change the minds of assimilated Jews: 'After the fact, the terror of Crystal
Night and its immediate sequels was not to make the Jews outcasts in Germany pending their extermination. Rather it was to make Germany *Judenfrei*
by harrying and driving them to flee the country.'[97] Without doubting the Nazis' intention to make Germany *Judenfrei*, Jews, especially those who could

not imagine not being German, tended to draw benign inferences. *Kristall-nacht*, according to Sabini and Silver, was 'a pogrom, an instrument of ter-ror…typical of the long-standing tradition of European anti-Semitism, not the new Nazi order, not the systematic extermination of European Jewry.'[98] As a lapse into thuggery, it would pass. When the War brought forth a harvest of nearly four million Jews, it was too late for reassessments. The twisted road to Auschwitz was becoming straighter.

> [T]he SS planners of the genocide had to steer their way toward that *Endlosung* by guarding the job's independence from the sentiments of the population at large, and thus its immunity to the influence of traditional, spontaneously-formed and communally-sustained attitudes towards their victims. Zygmunt Bauman[99]

INTERMEZZO I

'She was asking again. I don't know what to say.'

'To her or to me?' Can't I ever come home, without being greeted with a problem, he thought?

'To her, of course. She's too smart to be dismissed again.' And so am I, she thought.

'Was it the odor or did she see something?'

'You think I let her near that place? Not only does she have a nose, she has friends. They have seen things….'

'School friends?'

'They tell her things.'

'About which they know nothing.'

'They believe what they see.'

'Why can't parents control their children? I will issue another directive.'

'May we deal with our daughter, not directives?

'You can tell her the truth, if you think she is old enough to understand. The world is filled with vermin and disease. That's what stinks, along with Jews, who don't bathe.'

'Bathe, in those showers? Please be serious.'

'I am trying to ascertain how serious I can be when dealing with an eleven year old.' And, he thought, or with her mother, who refuses to understand the importance and the difficulty of my job.

'Or with your wife?'

'Let's not go through all that again. For God's sake, get me a drink.'

'It's being prepared. Don't you realize she is a decent girl? Do you want her to be indifferent to suffering? She can't stand to kill a fly.'

'Don't confuse sentimentality with decency. Decency is about purity and goodness. She must learn to reflect...'

'No speeches, please. She gets enough of that stuff in school. Now she needs to hear from us. She wants to know what to think.'

'Then tell her the truth.'

'Which is?'

'That her father, as the commander of this area, is engaged in important work, work which will benefit Germans for all time. Tell her we are preparing for the birth of a new world of cleanliness and goodness.'

'Where will these people come from?'

'From the soil, naturally. The Blood and Soil of the Fatherland, purifying and nourishing each other'

'Do you expect her to understand that? It makes little sense to me.'

Which is precisely the trouble, he thought, then said, 'She will not be corrupted by those who doubt the *Fuehrer*.'

'Will she be corrupted by the truth?'

'Of course not.'

'Then I should tell her that we are gassing Jews, including little children like her? And all in the name of an Aryan dream?

'Dream?'

'Perhaps nightmare is better?'

'You had better be careful, Lisette. People have been shot for less.'

'Including the wives of SS majors? The mothers of blue-eyed, blond Aryans?'

'Tell her what you want. My conscience is clear.'

The world of the death camps and the society it engenders reveals the progressively intensifying night side of Judeo-Christian civilization. Civilization means slavery, wars, exploitation, and death camps. It also means medical hygiene, elevated religious ideas, beautiful art, and exquisite music. It is an error to believe that civilization and savage cruelty are antithesis.... In our times the cruelties, like most other aspects of our world, have become far more effectively administered than ever before. They have not and will not cease to exist. Both creation and destruction are inseparable aspects of what we call civilization. Richard Rubenstein[100]

THE FINAL SOLUTION

Before beginning this dreadful account, allow a personal comment. Until the writing of this chapter, after years of research, I expected not have to deal with the Final Solution, except as the logical outcome of the Hitler Movement. Put differently, there was no reason to infuse my analysis with yet another horrific discussion of the concentration camps. Not only has this subject been exhaustively treated in hideous detail by countless writers, an analysis of the camps would have interfered with understanding why so many Germans ignored or tried to ignore them. More than pristine academic values were at stake. According to Fromm: 'To analyze a figure like Hitler with objectivity and without passion is not only dictated by scientific conscience but also because it is the condition of learning an important lesson for the present and the future. Any analysis that would distort Hitler's picture by depriving him of his humanity would only intensify the tendency to be blind to the potential Hitlers unless they wear horns.'[101] Another grisly account of the camps would place horns on all the supporters of the Hitler Movement. Therefore it seemed wise to avoid an analysis of the Final Solution. Writing this book changed my mind. Although the Judeocide was the logical outcome of racial anti-Semitism, the Final Solution was far more than a way to kill millions of people. Not merely a tool, a bureaucratic/technological apparatus for the elimination of unwanted material, the camps, as the most profound expression of the Hitler Movement's political theology, were more than the means of the Final Solution. More than murder factories, they were the proving ground of Aryan values and virtues and would have existed, with or without World War II, in victory or defeat.

Arno Mayer, on the contrary, argues that: 'There is no evidence to support the view that the destruction of the Jews was the primary motive and purpose of Hitler's pursuit of power and the determination to go to war.... Although the anti-Semitism of Hitler and the Nazis was hard-set, it could not have become genocidal without a whole series of enabling and catalyzing contingencies, which ultimately included the opportunistic conquests and irreversible insufficiencies of an ideologically immutable warfare state.'[102] He argues that the Judeocide was due to the impending defeat of Germany by the Soviet Union: 'All in all, the Final Solution may be said to have been forged and consummated in the crucible of the abortive crusading war against Soviet Russia and Judeo-Bolshevism, which in Eastern Europe created the context of extreme cruelty and destruction apart from which the Judeocide would have been unthinkable and impracticable.'[103] In other words, Hitler responded to his defeat by his real enemy, the Bolsheviks, by killing Jews. If one proceeds chronologically, Mayer's interpretation seems cogent. The Final Solution did not take shape as extermination camps, until the debacle of Stalingrad. Therefore, he reasons, the Final Solution was a response [neither an intention nor a goal] to the lost war against the Soviet Union. Mayer's view depends on his opacity to the Hitler Movement as political theology, notwithstanding his references to its religious qualities:

Nationalism became a central tenet of the political faith that was to pit the nascent 'idealistic Reich' against the 'arithmeticians of the present realistic Republic.' Taking the ways of the Catholic Church as his model, Hitler prescribed not only a 'tenacious adherence to dogma' but also an aggressive propagation of the faith, driven by 'fanatical intolerance.' In a distant past, when building 'its own altar,' Christianity did not hesitate to 'destroy the altars of the heathen.' From the expansion of the Christian faith and Church, Hitler claimed to have learned that the drive against an opposing worldview required violence combined with the 'driving power of a basic intellectual conception... and a definitive intellectual conviction.'[104]

He appreciates that: 'by casting the Jews as the principal agents—the "demons"—of economic, social and cultural change, Hitler made them the surrogate victims of his counter-attack against polymorphous modernity, which was his ultimate target. This mutation of unorganized and fitful Judeophobia into political and systematic anti-Semitism went hand in hand with the transformation of the new conservatism into revolutionary counter-revolutionism.'[105] And yet, 'Although anti-Semitism was an essential tenet of the Nazi worldview, it was neither its foundation nor its principal or sole intention.'[106] In brief, he does not warrant the kind of elective affinities intellectuals, like Heidegger, had for the Hitler Movement. As a consequence, like conservative German historians, Mayer relies on 'factual' interpretation of the Third Reich. The Judeocide made little sense, for it expended resources and energy better spent in prosecuting the war. Therefore, Mayer suggests that, if Hitler had defeated the Soviet Union, there would have been no Judeocide. After all, what would have been the purpose of killing valuable assets entirely under the control of the regime? Who throws money away? In other words, the Jews were anything but superfluous.[107]

I have many objections to Mayer's thesis. First, it has little appreciation of the Hitler Movement. Second, it suggests that the Hitler Movement distinguished Bolsheviks from Jews, to the Jews favor, which seems dubious. Third, it denies that Jews could have been considered superfluous because they had value. Can one imagine a victorious Hitler saying, 'We must value Jews because they could be useful to German society?' Bauman cannot and neither can I:

[Unlike normal genocides which aim at beheading the victim group and then enslaving the pacified remnant] enslavement of the Jews was never a Nazi purpose.... The state of affairs the Nazis wished to create was one of total *Entfernung*—an effective removal of the Jews from the life-world of the German race.... Perhaps an anticipated effect of such a 'totalization' of the Jewish problem was the survival of the Jewish communal structure, autonomy and self-government long after similar factors of communal existence came under frontal assault in all occupied Slav lands. This survival meant first and foremost that Jewish traditional elites retained their administrative and spiritual leadership throughout the duration of the Holocaust.[108]

Fourth, it assumes that Hitler was consumed by his efforts to be victorious in Time and Space. This is simply false. Having to be viewed *sub specie aeternitatis*, victories in Time and Space were important, principally because they allowed proto-Aryans to partake of Eternity. Hitler often made this point explicit:

> Because we believe in the Eternity of this Reich, its works must also be Eternal ones, that is…not conceived for the year 1940 and not for the year 2000; rather, they must tower like the cathedrals of our past into the millennia of the future. And if God perhaps makes the poets and singers of today into fighters, he has at any rate given the fighters the architects who will see to it that the success of this struggle finds imperishable corroboration in the documents of a great and unique art. This country must not be a power without culture and must not have strength without beauty.'[109]

Fifth, Mayer assumes that Hitler perceived Jews as a subject people like the Slavs. Even when Hitler had Jews entirely under his control, he treated them differently from other subject peoples. Jews were uniquely victims, not the only ones consigned to death, to be sure, but the only ones for whom, regardless of their behavior, attributes, or virtues, there was no escape. Sixth, Mayer's interpretation portrays National Socialism as anti-modernist. Bauman seems to me indisputable: *'The Holocaust was born and executed in our modern rational society, at the high stage of our civilization and at the peak of human cultural achievement, and for this reason it is a problem of that society, civilization and culture.'*[110] With or without Bolshevism, with or without defeat in the East, Jews were doomed. It was their relation to Bolshevism, as it was their relation to capitalism that was contingent. Jews created Bolshevism and capitalism, verifying their evil *Being*. Therefore, they had to be destroyed.

More than an outcome of racial anti-Semitism, the Final Solution was the spiritual center of the Hitler Movement, not simply its operational headquarters. The eradication of Jews was the first step toward purifying German society. The Judeocide was not sufficient. Jews had to be killed in a way that would prove to the killers that Jews deserved to die because their values, over and above their presence, polluted Germans. The eradication of Jewish Values was the point of the Final Solution. Only by the elimination of everything Jewish, which would require a sustained effort after the last Jew was dead, could Germans transform themselves into Aryans. Only then could they partake of the Eternal. This chapter tries to substantiate this thesis. Our first task is to analyze the taking of human life.

Those who take lives, who see in their ideas a rationalization for mayhem and carnage, are no less taken with ideas than are the life givers. Hence, a culture of life taking no less than life giving is wrapped up with the essential social institutions and cultural agencies of our age. Irving Louis Horowitz[111]

In extreme and intense fashion [Hitler's dictatorship] reflected among other things, the total claim of the modern State, unforeseen levels of state repression and violence, previously unparalleled manipulation of the media to control and mobilize the masses, unprecedented cynicism in international relations, the acute dangers of ultra-nationalism, and the immensely destructive power of ideologies of racial superiority and ultimate consequences of racism, alongside the perverted usage of modern technology and 'social engineering.' Ian Kershaw[112]

TAKING LIFE: EXISTENTIAL PROBLEMS

Without committing to the entirety of his philosophy, much of this section derives from Spinoza. First, all human actions operate under a cloud of ignorance. Although its degree varies widely and significantly, the ethical implication of 'partial knowledge' is that no one can know in principle whether a given act is good or bad, *sub specie aeternitatis*. Only God or Nature 'has' all the facts, past, present and future. The scare quotes will alert the reader to anthropomorphisms which were anathema to Spinoza. God does not possess anything. In a sense God *is* all the facts. Given this understanding, Spinoza's metaphysical determinism is difficult to refute.[113] Yet, due to partial knowledge, humans are 'free' to act (or seem free) no matter how much their actions have been 'caused.' Nevertheless, human beings are existentially 'responsible' for their actions, notwithstanding the absence of Aristotelian choice, fairly or not. Held to be responsible for their actions by their societies, if not themselves. Socially defined criminal acts can therefore be punished without embarrassment, despite metaphysical determinism. One kills a rabid dog, without believing the dog is *guilty* of anything. Nor need anyone believe that it is *ultimately* best to kill the animal. Considered a danger to society, he can be killed in the name of prudence. Implying more than 'life is not fair,' Spinoza believed that concepts like 'fairness' or 'criminal' were social labels derived from prudential concerns, not from 'knowledge' or 'truth.'

Allow an example. No one could have known (or know now) in principle, whether assassinating Hitler, say in 1938, would have been a 'good' thing to do, that is, preferable to any alternative. Unable to make a claim to knowledge or goodness, his assassination would have rested on prudence, nothing more. Besides who imagined that millions of murders would occur? The inability to know in principle should make us hesitant to kill. Yet we in the name of our societies kill, if not routinely, frequently and often without a great deal of reflection, anguished or otherwise. (1) In war strangers kill each other as a matter of duty if not glory. Even in a purely defensive war, the taking of life cannot be entirely attributed to the enemy. All military commanders and their political superiors engage in military triage, making almost continuous assessments regarding how many soldiers will die trying to meet a given objective. In other words, the question is, 'How many soldiers can be "properly assigned" to probable death?' In the best circumstances, the few are sacrificed for the many or for a larger 'good.' William James makes this point with characteristic flair: 'We, the lineal representative of the successful enactors of one scene of slaughter after another, must, whatever more pacific virtues we may also possess, still carry about with us, ready at any moment to burst into flame, the smoldering and sinister traits of character by means of which they lived through so many massacres, harming others, but themselves unharmed.'[114] (2) In virtually all societies, police are entitled to take life to secure the lives and property of the public, as well as, to defend themselves. When imperiled police kill, they are not indicted, if they can show they acted in good faith and in a reasonable manner. Moreover, self-defense allows for the taking of life in general. (3) Many societies employ capital punishment as a criminal sanction in cold blood, that is, without the existential problematics that normally surround police actions. (4) Although the status of a fetus remains controversial, at some point all agree it becomes alive, that is, viable outside the womb. Whatever the justifications, the health of the mother, the prospects for the child, constitutional principles of privacy or equality, and the like, abortion takes life. (5) Furthermore, decisions regarding the relative value of life are routinely determined in every hospital budget. Should we devote more resources to emergency care than to research? Should hospitals have more kidney machines or more cat scans? Every public budget involves these kinds of issues, so does every public policy. Should we spend more money on hospitals or schools, on police or teachers? Should we increase the retirement age to pay for higher education? Should we ration medical resources for people over the age of 80, 90, or 110? Should the rich have unlimited medical services or unlimited use of other scarce commodities? And so on. (6) Let me here deal with some issues of life-taking which may seem trivial. About 30,000 Americans die each year in traffic accidents. Nearly all of them are preventable. Reducing speed limits, making safer cars and roads, and many other policies would undeniably and drastically reduce traffic deaths. To the degree that preventable accidents are not prevented, they are 'allowed,' if only because society had deemed other matters more important than human life, though no one quite puts it this starkly. Moreover, the only serious discussion for limiting the lethality of motor vehicles has centered on the conservation of oil or the protection of the environment. Finally, a word should be said about other preventable deaths due to unhealthy life styles, like smoking, alcoholism, obesity, stressful or dangerous jobs, among others. Clearly lives are 'taken' (or 'given') in the name of dubious pleasures, addictions, or pseudo necessities. In conclusion, while there is much talk about the sanctity of human life, no society considers life an absolute value. Life is one value among others, some which seem significant to many of us, for example, freedom or honor, some of which seem matters of convenience or desire, like driving fast or eating donuts. Before continuing this discussion of the scientifically grounded rationales for taking life, we should deal with the problematics of science and society.

National Socialism is a cool and highly reasoned approach to reality based on the greatest scientific knowledge and it spiritual expression.... Hitler[115]

In line with many advocates of eugenic sterilization and euthanasia...Hitler believed that anyone not fit for life should perish, and that the State should give a helping hand.... [As Hitler said]: 'the bloodiest civil wars have often given rise to a steeled and healthy people, while artificially cultivated states of peace have more than once produced a rottenness that stank to high Heaven.' Michael Burleigh[116]

THE PROBLEMATICS OF SCIENCE AND SOCIETY

First, science cannot *determine* policy scientifically, because the *significance* of science is a political question. Science cannot determine that a hospital is more important than a football stadium. Second, empirical and probabilistic, science is problematic, that is, no scientific finding or premise can be absolutely true. This chapter, however, assumes that well-established science is true enough. In other words, the probabilistic and empirical basis of science will *not* be used to limit its application to policy. Moreover, this chapter uses 'science' to refer to statements about reality, which do not as yet have a scientific basis. For example, it assumes the genetic code has been cracked and that we can 'know' how an individual will turn out within the parameters that public policies normally assume. One purpose is to make the case for the scientifically grounded taking of human life as strong as possible. Another is to move policies for taking life away from the convenience or desire end of the spectrum and toward the self-defense or preservation of society side. Consider some examples which do not have a scientific basis, examples whose likelihood far exceeds the probabilities normally considered appropriate for preventative social action: suppose we could genetically determine, for example: (1) who will be a serial killer; (2) whether a child will live in unendurable pain; (3) whether a child will be severely mentally impaired; (4) whether a child will be unproductive and be a drain on the resources of the society to the point of impairing the chances of survival of 'normal' children; (5) whether a child will develop a disease that will kill thousands before a cure is found. To sum up, in these cases (and others like them) the question is, 'Can society be justified in taking life (or withholding the services necessary to life) of a "defective" child or fetus to further the public good?' The reflexive answer is, 'No,' but can such an irrational response be supported? Or stand unexamined?

Let us revisit the vexed topic of abortion. If one claims an absolute right to life, what about instances when the mother's life is at risk or other instances where one life conflicts with another? If one softens the absolute position by allowing definitions of *human* life to qualify organic existence, more difficult issues arise. Again, let us assume that scientifically demonstrable incurables and unproductive human beings exist. 'Demonstrable' here means 'knowable within the parameters of probability the society has determined is acceptable for the formation of scientifically grounded public policy.' Let me also assume that the 'slippery slope' argument does not apply *within the realm of science*. This means that scientists, acting in their capacity as scientists, will not soften and will not need to soften scientific canons to serve other values, assuming scientists are more pure than they are. Having placed science in the strongest possible position, the inability of science to determine the best policy scientifically remains. A political choice must always be made.

Although for purposes of analysis I have defined away the slippery slope argument within the domain of science, the difficulty persists when non-scientists are tempted, in the name of science, to move beyond the restriction of scientific evidence and verification to deal with cases which address political or social needs. Now we must consider the problematics of the concept of 'society.' As a socially constructed term, 'society' cannot determine policy on an objective basis any more than science can. Unless one vests society with organic properties, it is merely an abstraction which covers the decisions of a small group which impact a large group of people not all of whom are within its jurisdiction. Many social scientists, not properly classified as Nazis, have come close to this organic view. Consider Leslie White: 'Instead of regarding the individual as a First Cause, as a prime mover, as the initiator and determinant of the cultural process, we now see him as a component part, a tiny and relatively insignificant part at that, of a vast socio-cultural system that embraces innumerable individuals at any one time and extends back into the remote past as well....'[117] This 'vast system' has its own logic and justification. The naturalness or the inevitability of human clumping, call it what you will, does not invest the *group* or the *system* with organic, mechanistic, or logical qualities, independent of its members. Policy decisions remain political, whether made by a tyrant, legislature, referendum, or the scientific community. While it is generally better to have as much scientific evidence as possible grounding policy proposals, the danger remains that science will be used to mask fundamentally political decisions.

There is another problem with the socio-political context of science. Powerful or rich societies impact less powerful and less wealthy societies by the very nature of their activities. When it is appreciated that scientific knowledge and its technologies are virtually isomorphic with wealth and power, the problematic of society in a world of Nation-States becomes obvious. For example, suppose that when Nation-State X decides to pursue policies in its national interest members humanely, it exploits its neighbors. This may seem shocking, but it has been the basis of many imperialistic policies and aggressive wars throughout human history. Moreover, such practices have been justified by nearly all Realist Theories, which posit that the Nation-State is responsible its self-preservation, not for anything else. It cannot jeopardize the State's existence in the name of any other value, without violating its reason for being, a principle which has governed international relations for thousands of years. In war, many political and military leaders have said that the life of one of their soldiers is more important than the lives of the enemy, which includes all their women and children. Famously, Himmler made this point: 'If someone comes to me and says: "I can't build an anti-tank ditch with women or children. That is inhuman because they'll die doing it." Then I have to reply: "You are a murderer of your own blood, for it that anti-tank ditch is not built, then German soldiers will die, and these are the sons of German mothers. That is our blood."'[118] Virtually all political leaders, including Roosevelt and Churchill, have abided by this horrific conviction.[119] Whatever rational limitations apply domestically in a scientifically advanced society, they will have no impact internationally. The logic of Hobbes's State of Nature applies among Nation-States: the war of all against all. In these circumstances, science and technology will be employed to kill the enemy. The Third Reich was by no means unique in its use of science to pursue its objectives without mercy or compassion.

If this analysis seems stark and oversimplified, ask yourself what sacrifices would you make to improve the lot of the citizens of other Nations, to say nothing of Nations hostile to your Nation-State? The global warming problem and other environmental issues have foundered on this shoal of self-interest for decades. Nation-States have been willing to spend billions on defense and war and virtually nothing on dealing with their underlying causes in other Nation-States. Twelve billion dollars a month in Iraq was spent for years, without any serious proposal to spending one hundredth of that per year on economic development in poor countries. Americans are not worse than other people. Not to cast aspersions, these prosaic points create a context (not an equivalency) for discussing Nazi justifications for taking life.

No consistent eugenicist can be a *laissez-faire* individualist unless he throws up the game in despair. He must interfere, interfere, interfere!' Sidney Webb[120]

The judge must always bear in mind Hitler's words that 'the right to personal freedom always gives way to the duty of preserving the race.' Hereditary Health Court Judge[121]

NAZI SOLUTIONS: TAKING EUGENICS SERIOUSLY

Almost every treatment of the Third Reich discusses euthanasia and eugenics, if only to prepare for a discussion of the mass murder of Jews and other 'undesirables.' Of course, from the Nazi point of view, the Judeocide was a form of eugenics or, in their terminology, 'racial hygiene.' Accordingly, the Third Reich tried to justify their policies scientifically. Although National Socialists did not succeed regarding racial hygiene, they, nonetheless, believed that their racist policies had a biological basis. Moreover, they knew that the aura of science would help to dull resistance to their race-based anti-Semitism. Discussing euthanasia first is apt for three reasons: these programs antedated the Judeocide, were logically prior to it, and helped prepare for it politically and socially.

The Nazis are often assumed to have been ham-handed thugs, sociopaths, who killed for the joy of it. The difficulty with this assumption is that it cannot account for German debates about their programs dealing with those 'unfitted for life,' debates which took place in many Nation-States, including Britain and the U.S., debates which included well-educated health professionals. Tens of thousands of people were killed in the name of scientifically-grounded public policy.[122] Can rationality provide justification? Anticipating my argument, if one takes the omnicompetent, all-powerful Nation-State as sovereign, as a self-justifying political entity, which must pursue its own interests in a hostile world, there is no way short of war to contest its policies of euthanasia, however repugnant. Not requiring scientifically based policies or rationality, the State's only test is self-preservation, science conferring legitimacy on public policies which otherwise might have been resisted.

While science and its logic may be determinative for scientists and other elites, the masses remain suspicious, fearing that they might be labeled incurable or unproductive. For this reason, scientific arguments targeted German intellectuals, academics, jurists and, above all, the SS, who were responsible for policy implementation. I am not suggesting that science was used *only* as a Machiavellian instrument. Many educated people have believed that science is the sole basis for rational public policies; all else is just politics. Although this conviction may have been particularly strong in Germany, many other European and American elites have shared these views, most of which were effects of the explosion of scientific knowledge in the nineteenth and twentieth centuries. Of course, it takes a leap to move from a generalized respect for science and its applications to programs which take life in its name.

Aware that euthanasia was problematic, the Nazis had to address concerns arising from the still-Christian German society and the normal anxiety of ordinary citizens due to their inability to 'guard the guardians.' Euthanasia began with well publicized easy cases. 'Easy cases' were those which the public would see as properly within the normal categories of taking life as sketched above, without suggesting that the decision to take life could ever be casual. The first category of easy cases took the concept of euthanasia literally, that is, a 'good death' or a death in the interests of the person whose life is taken.[123] An individual may decide that under certain circumstances death was preferable to life. While some might find such decisions immoral or sacrilegious, on what basis can the decision be contested? Difficulties arise when the determination of a life not worth living is made by another, a person who may not have the interests of the 'patient' as a central or determinative factor. When the choice to end life is supported by science, a great deal of the anguish may be removed. Again, this sounds more harsh (or exceptional) than it is. For example, let us suppose that an octogenarian (or pick an age that matters to you) requires a million dollar operation to live for another year or two, the same million dollars that would keep, say, one hundred dialysis patients alive for the same period of time. In a society devoted to private property, it might matter whether the octogenarian could pay the million dollars. Even in this case, would the decision, which skews finite medical resources toward the affluent, be obvious?

More difficulties arise when society determines that some lives are not worth living. Consider, for example, the severely mentally impaired, beginning with those who cannot take basic care of themselves. Should round the clock care for people be provided for those who have never or could ever make a contribution to society, while the needs of the productive are neglected? Remember how viability of a fetus is often determined: can it live on its own? What about those who cannot live on their own in the most elementary senses? What about those who have incurable obsessions for sex with children, due to a scientifically determined defect? What about alcoholics or drug addicts, whose habits drive them to criminal activity? Should society tolerate or support them indefinitely? Should it do so regardless of its opportunity costs? Should it provide the same services during an economic crisis? These questions and many others like them were answered by the Third Reich negatively. I suspect that its answers continue to be whispered by many civilized persons, including liberals. As we have discussed, the role of science in these matters is not and cannot be in principle determinative. Nevertheless, the status of scientific knowledge in modern society is so privileged that scientific support for assessments of incurability, desirability, or cost inevitably plays an important role in public policy formation.

The Nazis believed that Jews were a distinct *anti-Aryan* race. Assuming their sincerity, what can we say about their slaughter of almost six million Jews? Biologically, the concept of race has no scientific grounding.[124] Anthropologically and sociologically, the basis is more valid, that is, there are empirical generalizations, more or less accurate, that applied to European Jews, distinguishing them from non-Jews: 'Anthropologists generally reject the notion that the Jew represents a distinct racial type, but as Horst von Maltitz observed, "it was a fact that the Jews of Germany constituted a group within which, whether as a result of inbreeding or for other reasons, large numbers of a similar type occurred—a type which showed easily recognizable characteristics in physical appearance, voice quality, mentality, behavior, and temperament."'[125] In terms of this discussion, Jews were seen by Nazis as a group of people who produced undesirables, like alcoholics or drug addicts (or dealers) and, especially, sexual predators, who, therefore, threatened German integrity and survival. If this reasoning seems a stretch, what if Jews were terrorists or a group carrying an undetectable deadly virus, would it not have been prudent to eliminate them?

Now a much more problematic set of issues: the elimination of undesirable *groups*. On the one hand, the probabilistic nature of science would seem to apply to groups with more validity than to individuals. It might be accurate to say the average height of a group of humans is five feet eight, without any individual being precisely that tall. It is simply a statistical fallacy, to say nothing of morally reprehensible, to apply a group characteristic to an individual who may not have the characteristic. One might very well think that a group averaging a given height might have more individuals who have that height than a group that averages four feet, but one could not justify punishing the entire group for this propensity. This is the very definition of prejudice. On the other hand, let us assume that we know that a given group of people is statistically likely to carry a deadly virus, but that the virus is undetectable until it is too late to combat it. In other words, by the time the virus becomes detectable, it becomes impervious to treatment, detectability implying death. What then can be done about the group, fully understanding that many individuals in it will not have or develop the virus? This may sound like science fiction, yet its logic is applied routinely by Nation-States, particularly when dealing with terrorists or other deadly enemies. 'We know terrorists inhabit this village. We cannot ascertain or apprehend the individuals, yet an air strike will kill all the terrorists and save countless lives of our citizens. What do you expect us to do, hold a trial?' Did the Nazis believe that the Jews presented this sort of danger to them, a danger scientifically grounded? The short answer was, 'Yes.' For those to whom such claims seemed unfounded, the question became more significant concerning the Jewish metaphor. Suppose 'Jewishness' were a series of characteristics, perhaps as objective as height or as cultural as greed, which threatened the survival of the State, should these threats be tolerated?

More problematic are cases where groups are defined metaphorically. Not only is the group's 'virus' a metaphor, so are its members. 'Jews' in the Third Reich connoted far more than 'Jewish human beings' or, as some Nazis preferred, 'organisms.' Jewishness conveyed a set of concepts which jeopardized the *Volk*: materialism, capitalism, greed, Bolshevism, sexual promiscuity, physical defilement, organic weakness, congenital ugliness, and so on, all of which were 'hereditable' if not 'contagious.' This metaphor had to be annihilated. If Jews were in the building which had to be burned to destroy the threat, so be it. 'Do you expect us to hold a trial?'

Whatever the strengths and capacities of science, it cannot deal with metaphors. Policies concerned with metaphorical Jews required political decisions. While many National Socialists ignored this clear-cut requirement, others, including many scientists, blurred the lines between science and social science, between questions which can be subject to positivistic verification and those which cannot. Taking advantage of the privileged status of scientific knowledge, Nazis elites allowed the 'Law of Race,' including its metaphorical variants, the same status as the Law of Gravity. The true believers of the Hitler Movement went further; the Law of Race was eternally valid, and, hence, beyond all scientific skepticism. In other words, questions of race were subsumed by what Hitler called the Life Philosophy:

> A morality based on the demands of life is unable to set up an unchangeable moral code, because the central flux of life necessitates a progressive internal readjustment. The ethics of the Life-philosophy cannot and will not provide anything but an orientation, an attitude towards these problems. It is of little avail to educate a man according to rigid, preconceived rules; the one important thing is to open his mind and to penetrate every fiber of his being with the current of life. Increase of vitality, that is, the supreme demand of the Life-philosophy.[126]

Mosse appreciates the implications of this outlook for Jews: 'The equation of Aryan with the life force meant that those who opposed Aryanism were indeed people without a soul, cut off from nature and the universe.... The concept of the *Volk* as the mediating organ between the cosmic life force and man could not permit compromise with the forces of darkness.'[127] More precisely, Nazi theorists allowed the appreciation of parasitology to reinforce the social antagonism between the dominant population and a despised minority. While neither the masses nor advocates of the Hitler Movement needed science to support their prejudices, a general respect for scientific authority reduced resistance to the Judeocide.

The West's idea of science was part of a materialist culture long considered superficial by many German thinkers. Consider Martin Heidegger: 'If only our totally superficial culture of today, which loves rapid change, could visualize the future by turning to look more closely at the past! This rage for innovations which collapses foundations, this foolish negligence of the deep spiritual content in life and art, this modern concept of life as a rapid sequence of instant pleasures...so many signs of decadence, a sad denial of health and of the transcendental character of life.'[128] Positivist science, the most antispiritual aspect of materialist society, has been condemned by many German scientists, including Noble prize winners. Allow two quotations to represent the many, first from Philipp Lenard: 'The truth is that which, in our own spirit, corresponds to the reality which is independent of the arbitrariness of our spirit. The truth is not which is verified here or there, but that which must always verify itself because it is derived from a wholly interconnecting reality.' The second from Johannes Stark: 'The spirit of the German enables him to observe things outside himself exactly as they are, without the interpolation of his own ideas and wishes, and his body does not shrink from the effort which the investigation of nature makes of him.... Thus it is understandable that natural science is overwhelmingly a creation of the Nordic-Germanic blood component of the Aryan peoples.'[129] To realize its full potential, science had to be informed by values, for some this implied a sense of Eternal Truth, for others, the *Volksgemeinschaft*. With its methodological discipline removed, science could then serve in good faith both the immediate and the timeless needs of proto-Aryans. Hitler made this point explicitly: 'We will rebuild our *Volk* not according to theories hatched by some alien brain, but according to Eternal laws valid for all time.'[130] Thus, instead of using scientific skepticism to question racial science, they used science conceived as Eternal laws to support racist policies, which culminated in aggressive war and genocide.

By blurring science and social science, by confounding science with morality, by conceiving science as Eternal verities rather than contingent truths, educated Nazis avoided the critical political question: 'Do Jews, conceived organically or metaphorically, present so great a danger to the survival of the

German *Volk* that killing, or otherwise eliminating, them is justified?' My views, based on the concept of Natural Rights, are virtually categorical: a threat to life is *not* sufficient to justify mass executions, whether or not they take place under the color of law. Unless the State adopts Natural Rights premises, or some other extra political absolute, it is virtually unlimited in its quest for self-preservation. Even States with robust constitutions, which presumably limit *raison d'état*, have not found it difficult to ignore, suspend, or otherwise override restrictions to State power. With regard to the taking of life, the continuum runs from 'under no circumstance can the taking of life be justified' to 'the taking of life for amusement or convenience.' In the middle of this continuum, modern States take lives in a multitude of ways, justifiable when the value of life, ostensibly protected by Due Process, conflicts with other values. The issue turns on, what other values? Consider taking life *within* a society or political community. Normally a society, as opposed to an individual acting in an existential situation, cannot kill someone in its jurisdiction without Due Process, a prohibition which depends on many considerations. Notwithstanding that lawyers can dispute any term, for example, 'jurisdiction,' the principle is generally undisputed. Normally, the law applies only to acts, not beliefs or predispositions, not *ex post facto*, and in conformity to 'fairness,' as understood within a given jurisdiction. Having little role beyond forensics, science cannot justify the taking of life *per se* or in concert with a 'greatest good for the greatest number' principle. For simplicity, I ignore those social practices which allow life to be perilous: dangerous traffic, unhealthy food, etc.

What about the taking of life by Nation-States? Justifications for war abound, including aggressive or preemptive wars. In the Total War of the twentieth century, every man, woman, and child has been considered the enemy. Again, science has little role here beyond the technology of applied violence. Recall Bomber Harris's cavalier dismissal of the lives of German civilians. The justification for war usually turns on some notion of the quality of life phrased in nationalistic terms, for example, to protect way of life, freedom, or some national goal. Duty Honor Country.

What about a 'war' *within* society? I do not refer to civil war, as generally understood, but the war against a presumed subversive or anti-social group. Many societies have had such internal 'enemies;' some still do. America has had various Red Scares, in which radicals or Communists have been persecuted and prosecuted for beliefs. The case has often been made, in one form or another, with varying degrees of sophistry, that the Constitution is a 'luxury' or a 'relic' which cannot properly stand in the way of survival. The question—survival as what?—is invariably begged or reduced to physical survival. If, however, survival *as creatures of the Constitution* is meant, no evasions of its provisions can be tolerated. The force of constitutional prohibitions is particularly applicable in cases where life or liberty is jeopardized. Under these circumstances, there can be no 'war' on internal enemies.

How can the persecution of Jews in the Third Reich be understood from these perspectives? Consider a prosaic example: the Nazi response to department stores. If Jews did not invent large-scale retail business, they might as well have. Implying the destruction of less efficient modes of distribution, department stores served many Germans who, nonetheless, were sympathetic to the plight of neighborhood stores. Few of them, however, were willing to pay higher prices to subsidize them. The Nazis, ever sensitive to populist resentment, demonized department stores as an especially pernicious Jewish invention intended to destroy German values. Whether department stores do more harm than good is a political question. It is legitimate to value one group of businessmen over another on socio-political grounds, a process which takes place routinely, even in ostensibly free market, capitalist economies. The Nazis could have outlawed department stores, but did not. They could have outlawed 'Jewish' department stores, but did not. The scare quotes do not indicate the difficulty of defining who is a Jew? They signify the difficulty of defining a '*Jewish department store.*' Is it a store which has good prices? Exceptional merchandise? Serves only Jews? Exploits only Gentiles? Makes exorbitant profits? Especially at Christmas? Is it a store where Jews can express their commercial talents? Their greed? Is it a store which represents the Jewish metaphor?

Dealing with Jewish department stores in characteristic fashion, allowing the stores to perform valued economic functions, while decrying their Jewishness, the Nazis pressured Jews to sell or to take Gentile partners. But difficulties remained, because 'Jewishness' did not necessarily mean ownership; sometimes it meant the effect of the stores, regardless of ownership, on less efficient businesses. When associated with impersonal calculation, efficiency eroded the solidarity of the *Volksgemeinschaft*. As symbols of Jewish materialism, department stores proved that Jews could not coexist with Germans, much less be members of the *Volksgemeinschaft*. Finally, the very success of the department store indicated a way to deal with the Jewish Question. Though insidious and persistent, organic and metaphoric, Jewishness,' could be removed from the stores, allowing its innovations to serve decent Germans.

Not criminalized, Jews, having an evil set of behaviors and influences, were 'enemy combatants.' As such they outside the community of care and, above all, outside the *Volksgemeinschaft*. In Bauman's words, 'To render the humanity of victims invisible, one needs merely to evict them from the universe of obligation.'[131] As obstacles to the objectives of the Nazi State, Jews had to be eliminated *as an ideal*. Consider the words of this *einsatzgruppe*: 'We believed in those times that we had achieved new higher values. It was a matter of struggling against, or rather repressing, the materialism and ego- ism of the individual. That this brought about an inversion of values, that one retreated further from humanism, was by no means clear to me at the time.'[132] Burleigh makes the point in theological terms: 'Justifications for killing defenseless people had reached their apogee with killing described as a by-product of love, in none too subtle perversion of theological sophistries once used to legitimize crusader slaughter of Moslems, Jews and pagans, but blended with the exclusionary nationalism and blood-based racism of the nineteenth and early twentieth century.'[133] While this ideal was never broadly accepted, it was countenanced by a sufficient number of Germans to allow for the murder of millions of Jews. *The Jew as an organic being became one with the Jew as an anti-German metaphor, a 'bacillus' to be annihilated for the sake of the Volk.*

Critical to this process, science, by tracing 'incurables' or 'undesirables' to heredity, allowed Germans to believe taking life was warranted, Nazi science, reinforced by the exigencies of war, trumping traditional, pre-scientific, val- ues. With young, healthy men and women dying in the millions, how could society be expected to expend resources on the severely and incurably dam- aged? Working together science and social science served to dull traditional Christian values regarding human life; life and death were no longer God's dispensations but prerogatives of the *Volk*. Not a concession to partial knowl- edge, probable truth, rationalism, or materialism, the Hitler Movement linked science with Eternal values. Recall Heidegger's conception of Greek science. Unless it were grounded outside of Time and Space, science would be only contingently or empirically true. The world was the 'What Is' by nature, in its transcendental, as well as, temporal moments and comprehensible only by a conception of science which respected its transcendent qualities. The Hitler Movement's purpose required the logical, ruthless, and joyful application of Eternally valid scientific truths. The negative eugenics of Christian human- ism would be replaced by the positive eugenics of the Hitler Movement. Morality, so called, would be replaced by an appreciation of the 'morality' of nature, of nature's dispensations, of nature's preferences for health, beauty, fertility, vigor, courage, and violence. As the transcendental moral core of the Life Philosophy, by living up to its laws, Germans would transcend the limitations, compromises, and impurities of Time and Space, thereby, partak- ing in the Eternal, becoming pure and godlike: Aryan.

What better way to demonstrate the bureaucratic-technological outlook of the officials, who devised and implemented the Final Solution and the programs that led up to it, than the cold-bloodedness of the above analysis?

Whatever the State wanted, it had but to ask its officials to deliver. According to Leo Kuper: 'The sovereign territorial State claims, as an integral part of its sovereignty, the right to commit genocide, or engage in genocidal massacres, against people under its rule, and...the UN, for all practical purposes, defends this right.'[134] To refuse would have been to declare oneself, not simply incompetent, but outcast. Therefore, virtually all German officials, including physicians, applied themselves to the policies of taking life, as they would have to any other objective. Ordinary Germans were more reluctant to grant, at least emotionally, the State this degree of authority, because they were afraid, not only of what they did not understand, but of the possibility that the apparatus of death would be applied to them with the same bureaucratic detachment. So elites considered it wise to shield those unable to understand scientific matters from their realities. Of course, given the scope of the Final Solution, thousands of Germans could not avoid knowing about Auschwitz. Nonetheless, the camps, particularly those dedicated to extermination, like Treblinka, remained veiled, if not invisible, to the millions. Absent a way to convince ordinary Germans that millions of people deemed superfluous or evil had to be killed, secrecy masked the Final Solution. When secrecy was impossible, the Nazis strove to create distance between Germans and their victims.

The very weaknesses of the National Socialist arguments for the elimination of Jews and other undesirables testifies to the inadequacy of accounting for the Final Solution rationally, the means of implementation, horrifyingly so. Understanding the Final Solution implies an appreciation of the Hitler Movement as political theology. Not simply a rationale for the taking of life, the Final Solution differed qualitatively and quantitatively from prior means and venues of killing, including *Einsatzgruppen* operations in the East. As Sofsky writes: 'The setting up of death factories, to which an entire people, from infants to aged, were transported over thousands of kilometers to be obliterated without a trace and exploited as raw material was not just a new mode of murder; it represented a climatic high point of negative history of social power and modern organization.'[135] To understand the Aryan Vision of the Hitler Movement, it is necessary to appreciate the full horror of the camps. However atrocious it may be to sterilize undesirables, however callous it may be to keep the mentally ill in Hellish conditions, however immoral it may be to shoot defenseless men, women and children, similar atrocities have occurred with distressing regularity. Modifying Sofsky, when the murders in the camps occurred directly, efficiently and impersonally, they were extensions of the killing fields, not differing in kind from other mass murders. The path from the train to the showers had its terrors, no doubt, the rushing, the disrobing, the shaving of heads, the packing into the showers, all after a horrific train ride, without adequate food, water, or sanitation facilities. Without minimizing the desperate, panicked torment of the final effort to breathe, as the victims strained toward the ceiling, the immediately killed could have retained a certain dignity. To this degree, for some of the victims, Trunk's interpretation of passivity as defiance might have validity.[136] Without suggesting that the sanitized American television versions of the last moments of the victims are accurate, those immediately selected for death had a chance of retaining some semblance of humanity. Much more rarely was this possible for those for whom death was deferred.

What was much more important than the Final Solution's uniqueness was its effort, largely successful, to drain every last drop of humanity from its victims. The combination of collaboration and humiliation comprised the central importance of the camps. The destruction of Jews *in this way* was intended to validate Hitler's depiction of them, paving the way to Aryan Utopia. First, Jews had to be understood as not only qualitatively different from Germans, but not really human. Secondly, Jews had to be seen clinging to life at all costs, doing anything to survive for one more minute, including betraying other Jews. The abject behavior of Jewish inmates was intended to prove to Germans and Jews that the inmates were unworthy of life, because they were incapable of human decency. The camps existed to deny that Jews were civilized beings, to prove that Jews were abject, cowardly, depraved, and degenerate in their Being, their nature revealed by the process of humiliation and collaboration. Once the truth about Jews became undeniable, Germans could then in good conscience cleanse the world of them, demonstrating in the process their Aryan credentials. It must be understood that the physical, mental, and moral destruction of Jews was a first necessary step on the long road to Eternal harmony, of a world free of Jews and Jewish influence. The metaphorical Jew's capacity to corrupt Germans, their society, and their *Weltanschauung* had to be annihilated as well. Only then could the world be spiritually infused with Aryan values and finally redeemed. Modifying Luther, who had divided the universe into two absolutely different realms, the Spiritual Realm of God and the Material Realm of sinful man, Hitler claimed that the role of the *Volk* was to reconcile the world of Time and Space and Eternity. What Luther had torn asunder, Hitler would heal. What Christ promised in the Kingdom of God, Hitler promised on earth. Not simply glimpsed, Eternity would conquer Time and Space. The chief obstacles to fulfilling this objective were Jews, physical and metaphorical.

Jews...were the very epitome of...strangers—always on the outside even when inside, examining the familiar as if it were a foreign object of study, asking questions no one else asked, questioning the unquestionable and challenging the unchallengeable. Zygmunt Bauman[137]

THE JEWS: THE ANTI-RACE

From the perspective of the Hitler Movement, Jews were an anti-Aryan compound of materialism, greed, individualism, Bolshevism, and anti-German racism. Assuming that a great many Germans subscribed to this portrait does not suffice to make the extermination of Jews comprehensible. As a first step, Jewish existence in Medieval Europe had to be redefined. The epigraph to this section suggests that Jews had a definable status and role as strangers in principle, however irritating. However unjust or dangerous, Medieval Jews were located in Christendom, if only as pariahs. In this light, Luther's desire to make them placeless was far more modern than Medieval, for he demanded conformity, when his times tolerated diversity, however rigidly categorized or ideologically defined. To his mind, one of the many egregious failings of the Roman Church was its failure to convert Jews. What incentives did Jews have to join the worldly Church? And what incentives did the Church have to convert worldly Jews? Accommodating each other over the centuries to mutual advantage, especially financial, there was little reason to change, confirming the corruption of both the Jews and the Church.

Luther attacked the Church, because it falsely valued the world, exactly the sin he imputed to Jews. In Luther's writings, the world was a cess pool, the domain of Satan, depraved, degenerate, and otherwise immersed in sin, having nothing to do with the Spiritual Realm of God and Christ. An absolute faith in Christ required the categorical rejection of the world, except as a place to accept all the degradation it could provide. By accepting God's dispensation and by submitting absolutely to his condemnation of the world, a Christian might, by God's infinite, if arbitrary, Grace, not have his ineradicable sin imputed to him. The Church's failure to redirect its efforts along Lutheran lines confirmed its unbreakable connection to Satan and his world, revealing itself as the anti-Christ. By rejecting his invitation to become true Christians, by rejecting Christ again, to say nothing of Luther's theology, Jews reasserted their worldliness and their service to Satan. To the crime of killing Jesus, they added the felony of denying Luther's doctrine of Christ of the Cross. Having crucified His body, now they crucified His spirit. Moreover, by rejecting the Reformation, Jews, not only lost their Medieval location, but all location, becoming outcasts, in principle, metaphysically.

Since the entire world was outside the Spiritual Realm, what was the significance of the loss of location? Although Luther was far from clear on this question, it seems that Jews, like the world itself, had a role, *albeit* negative, in salvation. By its absolute sinfulness, the world proved to faithful Christians that only the Spiritual Realm had value. Yet they should not ignore the world in the manner of ascetic monks, nor should they ignore Jews, who by their continuing rejection of Christ, must be chastised. Christians must resist sin, however intractable. Pastor Dietrich Bonhoeffer, who was executed by the Nazis for his complicity in the attempt to assassinate Hitler, said: 'The Church of Christ has never lost sight of the thought that the Chosen People, who nailed the Redeemer of the world to the Cross, must bear he course for its action through a long history of suffering.'[138] Bonhoeffer did not literally follow Luther, when he said: '*We are at fault for not slaying them*. Rather we allow them to live freely in our midst despite all their murdering, cursing, blaspheming, lying and defaming….'[139] Nonetheless he believed Jews should suffer for killing Christ.

As Bauman appreciates, a far more damning perception of Jews was necessary to account for the Final Solution. '*They were the opacity of the world fighting for clarity, the ambiguity of the world lusting for certainty.*'[140] Lest this abstract conception fail to reveal its venom, Bauman adds pungently: 'Jews were perceived as a sinister and destructive force, as agents of chaos and disorder; typically, as that glutinous substance which blurs the boundary between things which ought to be kept apart, which renders hierarchical ladders slippery, melts all solids and profanes everything sacred.'[141] If 'glutinous' does not repel, consider this description of the function of Jews in Germany after the French Revolution: 'Whatever remained of the old boundaries [after the collapse of the *ancien regime*] needed desperate defense, and new boundaries had to be built around new identities—this time, however, under conditions of universal movement and accelerating change. Fighting the slime, the archetypal enemy of clarity and security of borderlines and identities, had to be a major instrument in the implementation of both tasks.'[142] Note the connotations of 'slime:' insidious flow, bodily effluents, issue, immersing the clean in the defiled. While there is no need to dwell on the repulsive implications of 'slime,' it is necessary, however, to elucidate one of its most important properties. 'The very fact that the conceptual Jew straddled so many different barricades, built on so many, ostensibly unrelated, front lines, endowed his sliminess with the elsewhere unknown, exorbitant intensity.'[143] Jews could not be located, not because they were invisible, but because they were everywhere. Not merely irritating, repulsive, and corrosive, they threatened to seep across every boundary, physical, social, political and conceptual.

The political implications of these metaphors are not difficult to understand. 'Attachment to the liberal heritage of the Enlightenment supplied an additional element to Jewish "viscosity." Like no other group, the Jews had vested interests in the citizenship that liberalism promoted. In Hannah Arendt's memorable phrase: "In contrast to all other groups, the Jews were defined and the position determined by the body politic. Since, however, this body politic had no other social reality; they were socially speaking in the void.'"[144] Jews were both everywhere and nowhere, anathema to a society that craved definitions, categories and taxonomies. 'Everywhere they served as a constant reminder of the relativity and limits of individual self-identity and communal interest, which the criterion of nationhood was meant to determine with absolute and final authority. Inside every Nation, they were the enemy inside.'[145] More than the presence of Jews disturbed Germans; Jews called into question the German accommodation between self and community. Therefore, despite being the chief beneficiaries and supporters of liberal values in Germany, they *functioned as anti-liberals*, undermining the fragile German attachment to liberal values. Jews exposed the tension that existed between the autonomy of individual Germans, on the one hand, and their emotional immersion in the *Volksgemeinschaft and* the absolute subordination to the omnicompetent State, on the other. This tension would lose none of its force, as Germans shed traditional restraints and communal values. It applied the more, for no one wished to confront their inconsistencies or unprincipled accommodations to reality. The more Germans became liberal, the more they resented the liberalism of Jews, including its negative effect on their own commitment to liberal values. The more Germans remained traditional, the more Jews remained distasteful strangers, falling under Luther's condemnation. The more Jews became liberal, the less German they became. The more Jews remained traditional, the more they became unacceptable. In the context of late nineteenth and early twentieth century Germany, there was no escape from this series of dilemmas.

However obvious, these dilemmas have been difficult for conservative German historians to credit. Consider Nolte:

> For to suppose that Hitler could have provided the Germans with victims in the form of Jehovah's Witnesses or alcoholics instead of Jews as a substitute for the forbidden class warfare is incorrect.... Anti-Semitism is by no means a relic of the Middle Ages or the expression of petit-bourgeois social envy; in an age of the growing awareness of national and social differences it is under certain conditions an element of national consciousness itself. Even liberals, far from being philo-Semitic, were hostile to the idea of Jewish national self-segregation, although, of course, they were also against segregation counter to the will of those concerned as carried out by the proponents of racial anti-Semitism.... It may sound hard, but it remains a fact that German Jewry...faced an inexorable decline after the deceptive upsurge of the first years of its complete emancipation; *it could not escape being crushed between the two extremes which it had itself generated—complete assimilation and Zionism.*[146]

This passage suggests that there was some course of action the Jews could have undertaken and did not, one which would have avoided the 'two extremes.'

Furthermore, it suggests that Zionism, also undefined, was a viable option for Jews in Germany, despite lacking widespread support. If 'Zionism' denotes Jewish identity, then it is hardly an extreme position. If it entailed a Jewish State, then it had little relevance for German-Jews. Just as Nolte overestimates the power of Zionism, he underestimates its extent. Only conservative Jews thought assimilation was an extreme position. For the majority, assimilation seemed natural and desirable, so long as they did not have to deny everything Jewish. Is this the meaning of 'complete'? Nolte situates this instance of blaming the victim in an attack on liberal hypocrisy, he nevertheless suggests that Jews were at fault for not finding a way out of their dilemma. Far from an anti-Semite, he, in his zeal to absolve Germans, nonetheless, has compromised his otherwise astute historical judgment. With the Defeat in the Great War the tensions inherent in liberalism became critical. How would minorities, including Jews, find a place in the parliamentary democracy which seemed to the majority of Germans as a foreign imposition? How would Germans reconcile individual rights with their ideas of community, with the *Volksgemeinschaft?* How could Germans, given their fear of Bolshevism, accommodate themselves to a democratically elected Marxist government? All of these questions and many more would be resolved in favor of the Hitler Movement dooming Jews.

Bauman argues that the modern need for order, all the more urgent with the fall of the *ancien regime*, a need which was met by the rise of a bureaucratic civilization, increased the precariousness of Jews. With the industrial revolution, the rise of science, the development of omnicompetent bureaucracies, and the subordination of all sub-State organizations, the State achieved its modern form, with disastrous consequences for Jews and other human beings. Bauman goes so far as to suggest that the modern State was the major cause of the Final Solution, not simply its condition. He writes: 'The light shed by the Holocaust on our knowledge of bureaucratic rationality is at its most dazzling once we realize the extent to which the *very idea of the Endlosung was an outcome of the bureaucratic culture.'*[147] He retreats from this point by saying: 'This is not to suggest that the incidence of the Holocaust was determined by modern bureaucracy or the culture of instrumental rationality it epitomizes.... I do suggest that the rules the rules of instrumental rationality are singularly incapable of preventing such phenomena; that there is nothing in those rules which disqualifies the Holocaust-style methods of social-engineering as improper or, indeed, the actions they served as irrational.'[148] This qualification seems to contradict the concept of 'outcome.' Can one say that merely because a set of rules [of 'instrumental rationality'] cannot prevent an outcome that, therefore, the context of the rules, 'the bureaucratic culture,' created the outcome? If 'outcome' means a happenstance or otherwise contingent event, rather than something created by the bureaucratic culture, then what is the force of his statement, italicized in the original? If it means something much stronger, like 'created,' then, what is the value of his qualification? The inability of a set of rules to prevent an outcome does not by itself suggest that the outcome is the consequence of the context of those rules. If the statement means that the Final Solution was the outcome of the bureaucratic culture, which includes its decisional rules, then something like 'created' or 'caused' is implied. Otherwise, the proposition becomes, the failure to prevent the outcome allows the outcome, which otherwise what? Therefore, Bauman is stuck with his proposition that the bureaucratic culture caused or, at least, was the major factor in the Final Solution.

Bauman is fond of criticizing gardening, so allow me to put my point in gardening terms. If I fail to prevent the growth of weeds, does this mean the weeds are an outcome of the larger context of the garden or of my failure to apply weed killer? It seems to me that the weeds are the outcome of the context of the garden. There is nothing within the context of the garden to prevent their growth. Rather, the garden provides the conditions for growth of all plants. Only an outside intervention could make the garden less hospitable for particular plants. Bauman, to the contrary, seems hold that unless there be an *internal* weed killer, then weeds would be the necessary outcome of the garden, but not caused by the garden. They are the allowed outcomes of the absence of an *internal* weed killer. Therefore, he seems to argue that the absence of a preventative mechanism *within* the bureaucratic culture, for example, its decisional rules, allowed for the Final Solution but did not cause it. He cautions that bureaucratic culture was a necessary, not a sufficient, condition. When Bauman, however, says the Final Solution was an outcome of bureaucracy, he suggests 'cause,' not a mere condition of a causal chain. I am not criticizing Bauman, to whom I am indebted, for what may be inexact writing. My purpose is to clarify my argument. There is no question that bureaucratic/technological culture informed the character of the Final Solution, as the General Staff informed the character of the War. But to say that the War was an outcome of the General Staff would be an error, although battle plans were. So, too, it is an error to say that the Final Solution was an outcome of German bureaucratic culture, although it might come close to the truth regarding the Great War.

Bauman has an unstated assumption; to wit, that a bureaucratic culture *should* have internal preventative mechanisms which would restrain its application of expertise in certain cases. In other words, bureaucrats would not simply obey the orders of their political superiors. Perhaps bureaucracies should operate in this manner, but none has, as his references to Weber seem to have made clear to him. Existing to obey orders, rebellious bureaucrats will simply be replaced or jailed. Hitler fired scores of high ranking officials, including generals. Bauman suggests that, when confronted by Hitler's vision of a *Judenfrei* Europe, German bureaucrats should have been able to apply decisional rules which would have countermanded or evaded Hitler's commands. By linking bureaucratic culture with civilization, Bauman can say, as *civilized people*, bureaucrats should have stepped outside their roles as technicians and acted *as citizens of the human race*, transcending not only their jobs but their loyalty to the Germany, concluding that their role as bureaucrats morally disarmed them. Therefore, they enabled the Final Solution by failing to prevent it *within the rules of their roles*. Of course, equally, he could say that there was nothing in their loyalty as citizens which prevented the Final Solution. In other words, at some point, one should become a traitor, if one is prevent an immoral outcome. This may be a valid point, however unrealistic it is to expect heroism to be frequent and effective. His reluctance to place the onus on humans, rather than their social context, is due to his desire blame society. Therefore, he does not say, weak human beings in the bureaucracy allowed for the outcome of the Final Solution, but rather that it was an outcome of bureaucratic culture, a culture which is partly defined by its capacity to separate human beings from moral concerns: 'We need to take stock of the evidence that *the civilizing process is...a process of divesting the use and deployment of violence from moral calculus, and of emancipating the desiderata of rationality from interference of ethical norms or moral inhibitions.*'[149] Troubled by the baldness of his assertion that the Holocaust was an outcome of bureaucratic culture, notwithstanding its tendency to separate humans from morality, he immediately eviscerates it, by saying that the failure of decisional rules, not of the human beings who apply the rules, to prevent the Final Solution, allowed it to happen. Bauman performs these gymnastics, because he wants to condemn the entire civilization, that is, the context of rational/legal society, to use Weber's terms. '*The Holocaust was born and executed in our modern rational society, at the high stage of our civilization and at the peak of human cultural achievement, and for this reason it is a problem of that society, civilization and culture.*[150] A fair point, except that civilization is not coterminous with bureaucracy, not yet, at least. He adds, this time dealing with the State:

> *The Holocaust was an outcome of a unique encounter between factors by themselves quite ordinary and common; and that the possibility of such an encounter could be blamed to a very large extent on the emancipation of the political State, with its monopoly of the means of violence and its audacious engineering ambitions, from social control—following the step-by-step dismantling of all non-political power resources and institutions of social self-management.*[151]

To a lesser extent, my objection still obtains. Civilization is not coterminous with the State. The State is a rational/legal, not a moral entity; its role is self-preservation. When it has been liberated or liberates itself from moral or other constraints, it fulfills its nature. All States, left to their own devices, would be authoritarian. The State, like its bureaucratic culture, could not prevent the Final Solution, but that was not its role. Of course, there is no such entity as the State, no disembodied force. It is simply the summation of the decisions made by its human constituents, as they apply their resources to the solution of public problems, as they define them or as are defined by their leaders. To expect it to have internal decisional rules which will veto certain policies on moral grounds is to misunderstand what it is, a category mistake. Humans fail, not social structures. Providing moral frameworks, humans decide whether to enlist the assets of the State to further this goal or that, morally justifiable or not. Even so limited, to focus on the State is misleading. It fails to appreciate that Hitler's Vision, derived from his premise of the sacred German *Volk*, was supported by many Germans. The bureaucracy, an arm of the State, which was in turn subordinated to Hitler's concept of the Nation, was expected to carry out these political/theological policies as technicians, whether bureaucrats agreed with them or not. If they objected to the policies, they should have voiced their views as citizens, failing that, resign their jobs and leave Germany. To reiterate, Bauman's real target is civilization itself, not its instrumentalities, not its human constituents, because it was one of the 'genuine causes' of the Final Solution. '*Confusing heterophobia with racism and the Holocaust-like organized crime is misleading and potentially harmful, as it diverts scrutiny from the genuine causes of the disaster, which are rooted in some aspects of modern mentality and modern social organization....* '[152] Therefore, the Holocaust should not be considered the product of a *defect* of civilization: 'The implication that the perpetrators of the Holocaust were a wound or a malady of our civilization—rather than its horrifying yet legitimate product—results not only in the moral comfort of self-exculpation, but also in the threat of moral and political disarmament.'[153] But again, he makes the inability to prevent an immoral outcome a kind of veiled cause: '*Civilization proved incapable of guaranteeing the moral use of the awesome powers it brought into being.*'[154] Notwithstanding my agreement with much of Bauman's analysis, a better way to account for the Final Solution would be to see it as a consequence of a Vision of a purified Aryan Utopia, which, once accepted, ordained its means. Nothing in the structure of implementation, the bureaucracy, could have been or should have been expected to destroy the Vision. All the rational/legal resources of the modern State, including the bureaucratic culture, were thus enlisted in the pursuit of the Vision. The real question is how did this Vision come to be accepted? That is the question this book tries to answer.

In a similar manner, Bauman deals with the issue of German guilt: 'The exercise in focusing on the *Germanness* of the crime...is an exercise in exonerating everyone else, and particularly *everything* else.'[155] I realize that exonerating non-Germans may be the purpose of focusing on the Germanness of the crime, a process Bauman avoids. Is it not reasonable to ask, why did Hitler's Vision take such a hold? Was there something particularly German embedded in the factors leading to Hitler's ascension to power? The purpose of these questions is not to condemn or exonerate anyone. Dealing with these questions seems essential, if one is to understand the most distressing catastrophe of our times and perhaps in all history. Of course, one can go up the ladder of abstraction and say something to this effect: a defeated Nation, desperate for self-respect, feeling betrayed, will look for a charismatic Leader who will deliver them from the wilderness, by providing them with hope. Twentieth century Germans were in this situation. Charismatic Hitler came to power, and history unfolded accordingly. There is little to object to in this sort of analysis as a framework. It is not, however, an explanation. It leaves too many questions unanswered. Why this Vision? Why this Leader? Why were the Jews scapegoats? And on and on. I don't see how it is possible to deny the Germanness of the Third Reich and, therefore, the Final Solution. This is not to say, as some have, that there is something defective in Germans, something that other Europeans do not have. I cannot explain here what comprises the Germanness of the Third Reich. There have been a multitude of factors spread out over a thousand years of German history which help provide some answers. Each of the preceding chapters has tried to illuminate various factors in this complex explanation. I am not saying the Final Solution happened in Germany, therefore, it was German. While a similar genocide could have happened elsewhere, this particular genocide happened in Germany, for reasons deep in European history. While this analysis neither exonerates nor condemns, it is important to deal with the facts, under the assumption of human responsibility. We may be as determined as Spinoza believed. There may be no free will. Yet we can hold ourselves and other human beings responsible, despite our imperfections and limitations, even though we do not have all the facts and the wisdom necessary to evaluate them. To suggest that the Judeocide was the outcome of civilization erodes the idea of human responsibility for civilization and its outcomes. Bauman and I come together, in the final analysis: '*The inhuman world created by a homicidal tyranny dehumanized its victims and those who passively watched the victimization by pressing both to use the logic of self-preservation as absolution for moral insensitivity and inaction.* No one can be proclaimed guilty for the sheer fact of breaking down under such pressure. Yet no one can be excused from moral self-deprecation for such surrender.'[156]

There is perhaps a moral and psychological element explaining why most of the victims went quietly and passively to their death: a possible refusal to show the murderers any panic or hysteria that might have given additional pleasure to the sadists among them. The victims preferred dying with dignity and with scorn to the killers. The Jews might also have actually wondered whether it was worth fighting for one's life in a world where the human beast could rule undisturbed amid the passive silence of the entire civilized world. Isaiah Trunk[157]

INTERMEZZO II

'But the risk!'

'Of what? Dying ten minutes sooner or later?'

'Life is life,' the old man said. 'It is not ours to question or to forfeit.'

'The Germans don't seem so squeamish. Besides, life as what? We are already dead. We wait to be buried.'

'There are always survivors. The Allies are coming, Russians, Americans. We must retain hope.'

'Spare me your crap about the remnant. A remnant of *muselmanner*, in spirit if not body.'

'Life, life is life…'

'So all is to be endured?'

'It's God's Will.'

'Some God! The God of Jew Hatred. The God of Jew Humiliation. Have we been chosen for that? Did we bargain for that in the Covenant?'

'One does not negotiate with God. The Covenant was God's way to choose us—for whatever He might send us.'

'The one time Jews failed to negotiate and look where it got us.'

'Don't blaspheme.'

'Blaspheming a God that wants Germans to kill us is an obligation.'

'We do not know what God wants or intends. We must…'

'Yes, accept in good faith. Trust in God. Make His face to shine unto us. God help me!'

'Faith always appears ridiculous to unbelievers.'

'What would it take to prove to you that we are rejected by God, your conception of God, that is?'

'Nothing could do that.'

'I see.'

'No, you don't. To be Chosen is to be rejected, in your terms, that is. God has asked us to reject the easy path, the pagan ways of our enemies. God has asked us to reject what he has always found hateful: lust, greed, envy, murder, idolatry. You know the list. The *Torah*. The Commandments. In this sense we are the Rejected People, because we are expected to reject the devices and desires of an apostate world. We were chosen to reject sin by obeying the Law.'

'Did He have to immerse us in a cess pool to get us to reject sin? Can we find the Law under all the shit?'

'Job's questions rudely put.'

'The answers he got stink more than the shit.'

'By the canons of reason, of course. That is the point. God is God. He is not to be questioned but obeyed.'

'The only gods here wear SS uniforms,' the young man said, ending the futile exchange. The next day a *Kapo* beat him to death for failing to carry out an order, as the old man watched and prayed.

[SS militiaman to prisoners:] 'However this war may end, we have won the war against you; none of you will be left to bear witness, but even if someone were to survive, the world will not believe him.' Primo Levi[158]

ULTIMATE CONTEMPT:
HUMILIATION AND COLLABORATION

By 'Final Solution' I do not refer to the decision, including its implementation, to kill Jews. The *Einsatzgruppen* did this on the Eastern Front. Far more than Judeocide, the Final Solution comprised the *entire* experience of the camps. It entailed the deferred killing of Jews, their survival for a time, paid for with collaboration and humiliation. The Final Solution implied that the murder of Jews by Jews was more important than their murder by Gentiles. Jewish participation in the entire apparatus of the camps, an acceptance of a process of absolute humiliation and an eradication of their last vestiges of human feeling were their most important features. My emphasis on degradation is not intended merely to illustrate the capacity for human beings to descend into a pit in the name of survival. The larger point is that, unless the full and gruesome experience of the camps is comprehended, the Final Solution will remain inexplicable. It is important to know *why* the Germans employed the Final Solution, a 'why' embedded in the process of humiliation and collaboration more than a bullet in the head or an expeditious death in gas chambers. The Final Solution's murder and humiliation of Jews was done *for* Germans. It must be seen, therefore, from the German perspective. This re-visioning of the Final Solution has been impeded by many well-meaning attempts to present sanitized versions of life in the camps, allegories of good and evil, where the Jews met their fate with grace and dignity. 'Pleasantly resonant with public mythology, it can shake the public out of its indifference to human tragedy, but hardly out of its complacency—like the American soap opera dubbed *Holocaust*, which showed well-bred and well-behaved doctors and their families (just like your Brooklyn neighbors), upright, dignified, and morally unscathed, marched to the gas chambers by the revolting Nazi degenerates aided by uncouth and blood-thirsty Slav peasants.'[159] It is significant that Rubenstein uses 'honor' only when referring to Jewish resistance, when survival had to be foresworn. [160] Resistance was a message sent by Jews to Jews and to Germans. It said, 'We remain human.' Levi writes: 'We are not yet animals, we will not be animals as long as we try to resist.'[161] A resister might have said, 'We are honorable beings. Nothing Germans can do to us removes our essential and irreducible humanity, except abject acceptance of their view of us.' Sensing this, the SS reacted harshly to any assertion of humanity by Jews. An escape attempt was particularly egregious: 'If he was tracked down and captured alive, he was invariably punished with death, but his hanging was preceded by a ceremony…of an unheard of ferocity, an occasion for the imaginative cruelty of the SS to run amok.'[162] It was precisely this claim to humanity that the Final Solution intended to destroy. For the same reason, suicide attempts were punished with the utmost severity. Levi explains, 'Suicide is an act of a man and not of an animal. It is a mediated act, a noninstinctive, unnatural choice, and in the Lager there were few opportunities to choose: people lived precisely like enslaved animals that sometimes let themselves die but do not kill themselves.'[163] It was a message to Jews that you are not human. Shylock's great speech, 'Do we not bleed?' was but a veneer, yet another sham, another duplicity. The Final Solution was intended to send messages from Jews to Jews. Levi testifies: 'There is not a prisoner who does not remember his amazement at the time: the first threats, the first insults, the first blows came not from the SS but from other prisoners, from colleagues, from those mysterious personages who nevertheless wore the same striped tunic that they, the new arrivals, had just put on.'[164] The Jewish message seemed to be: 'There is no depth to which we will not descend to live one more minute. We have always been degraded. It has always been the price of our survival. That is why we hold each other in contempt, why we hate ourselves.' As a consequence, the Germans gave Jewish collaborators remarkable leeway in the handling of other Jews. '[The *Kapos*] were free to commit the worst atrocities on their subjects as punishment for any transgression, or even without any motive whatsoever: until the end of 1943, it was not unusual for a prisoner to be beaten to death by a *Kapo* without the latter having to fear any sanctions.'[165] Regarding those detailed to perform acts like disentangling and searching corpses and other defiled acts, Levi writes: 'The Special Squads were made up largely of Jews. In a certain sense this is not surprising, since the Lager's main purpose was to destroy Jews…. From another point of view, one is stunned by the paroxysm of perfidy and hatred: it must be the Jews who put the Jews into the ovens; it must be shown that the Jews, the subrace, the submen, bow to any humiliation, even to destroying themselves.'[166]

Perhaps the most remarkable and depressing consequence of the Final Solution was not that it occasionally failed to send and receive these messages, but how often it succeeded. Therein may lie its enduring lessons. It is important to live and to die with dignity and honor. There is more to death than dying. Are we not all under a death sentence? Do we not derive morality from our mortality? And, thereby, our honor and dignity? With regard to Jews, the Third Reich's answer to these questions was, 'No.' The purpose of the humiliation and collaboration regime of the camps was to validate this answer to Jews *and* Germans. First, consider collaboration. According to Bauman: 'The memorable verdict of Hannah Arendt—that were it not for the deeds of the Jewish collaborators, and for the zeal of the *Judenrate*, the number of victims would have been considerably reduced—would seem not to be able to bear close scrutiny.'[167] Whether more or less Jews would have been killed without the role of collaborators is an empirical question that can never be answered. Bauman concludes: 'To some remarkable extent, *the Jews were part of that social arrangement which was to destroy them.* They provided a vital link in the chain of coordinated actions; their own actions were an indispensable part of the total operation and a crucial condition of its success.'[168] There are additional significant issues relating to collaboration, which the provocative Arendt raised. While she was not the first to discuss Jewish collaboration in the ghettos and camps, her prominence as a leading political theorist made her difficult to ignore or dismiss. Gentiles have tended to read her analysis, like any other work of political theory. Many Jews, in and out of academe, however, have vilified her, sending her hate letters. This rage cannot be accounted for by the facts of collaboration. It resides in her explanation, which links collaboration to the structure and texture of European Jewish society. We have already glimpsed some of its pernicious effects, when we discussed how Eastern Jews were viewed by Jews in Germany. While accepting that collaboration by Jewish elites was a rational response to an impossible situation, she adds that it was self-serving. Moreover, and worse, collaboration was a predictable outcome of Jewish society, one which has always sacrificed ordinary Jews to the interests of their betters. Although Jewish social structure did not cause the Final Solution, it facilitated it, giving it much of its character and largely accounting for the complicity Jewish elites in the destruction of ordinary Jews: 'Thus a perfect harmony of interests was established between the powerful Jews and the State. Rich Jews wanted and obtained control over their fellow Jews and segregation from non-Jewish society; the State could combine a policy of benevolence toward rich Jews with legal discrimination against the Jewish intelligentsia and furtherance of social segregation, as expressed in the conservative theory of the Christian essence of the State.'[169] The implication of this striving had pernicious effect on ordinary Jews:

> The Jewish notables wanted to dominate the Jewish people and therefore had
> no desire to leave it, while it was characteristic of Jewish intellectuals that they

wanted to leave their people and be admitted into society; they both shared the same feeling that they were exceptions, a feeling perfectly in harmony with the judgment of their environment. The 'exception Jews' of wealth felt like exceptions from the common destiny of the Jewish people and were recognized by the governments as exceptionally useful; the 'exception Jews' of education felt themselves exceptions from the Jewish people and also exceptional human beings, and were recognized as such by society.... Conforming to a society which discriminated against 'ordinary' Jews and in which, at the same time, it was generally easier for an educated Jew to be admitted to fashionable circles than for a non-Jew of similar condition, Jews had to differentiate themselves clearly from the 'Jew in general,' and just as clearly to indicate they were Jews; under no circumstances were they simply allowed to disappear among their neighbors.[170]

She indicts the *Judenrate*: 'What was morally so disastrous in the acceptance of these privileged categories was that everyone who demanded to have an "exception" made in his case implicitly recognized the rule, but this point, apparently, was never grasped by these "good men," Jewish and Gentile, who busied themselves about all those "special cases" for which preferential treatment could be asked.... As though...it went without saying that a famous Jews had more right to stay alive than an ordinary one.'[171]

Perhaps now my cold-blooded analysis of taking life can be put to use, for it mirrors precisely the concerns of the *Judenrate*: 'Chief Gens declared: "With a hundred victims, I save a thousand people. With a thousand, I save ten thousand."'[172] Does not this proposition make sense, at least some of the time and in some instances? Relocate those questions and that mode of analysis in Auschwitz and then evaluate, or better, try to understand the predicament of the *Judenrate*. Were their actions justifiable? Do they have a reasonable basis? The answer could be, 'Yes.' The rationality of their actions is central to Bauman's interpretation of the Judeocide, the reason he condemns modern civilization. The outlook and the terminology of bureaucratic civilization enabled Germans to place Jews outside the community of care. It enabled the moral *Judenrate* to do the same to ordinary Jews.

As we have already suggested, Bauman's remedy, pluralist democracy, is inadequate in the context of the very power State and its civilization he so brilliantly dissects. Democracy provides an irrational element in the political forum. The people feel and emote; they do not think. Bauman, however, asks them to do more. More than doubtful, experience seems to show that it is far more likely that the power State can employ the irrationality of the masses to extend and deepen its reach. No one is more willing to grant absolute power than the ignorant, the desperate, and the fearful. No one is more unlikely to resist extreme actions, including genocide, if undertaken in their behalf. So long as fear remains the principal ally of the power State, democratic infusions reinforce its absolute sovereignty.

There is no better indicator of the modern State's attitude toward its constituents than it policies regarding violence and weapons. Bauman amplifies Weber's famous definition of the State as that institution that has a 'monopoly of legitimate coercion.' Moreover, it has become a hallmark of civilization to eschew violence in all its forms, save in some instances of self-defense: '*The Holocaust was an outcome of a unique encounter between factors by themselves quite ordinary and common; and that the possibility of such an encounter could be blamed to a very large extent on the emancipation of the political State, with its monopoly of the means of violence and its audacious engineering ambitions, from social control—following the step-by-step dismantling of all non-political power resources and institutions of social self-management.*'[173] Bauman suggests that disarmed people are a morally disadvantaged: 'Pacification of daily life means at the same time its defenselessness. By agreeing, or being forced to renounce the use of physical force in their reciprocal relations, members of modern society disarm themselves in front of the unknown and normally invisible, yet potentially sinister and always formidable managers of coercion.'[174] The French sociologist, Georges Sorel makes the point bluntly: 'There are so many legal precautions against violence, and our upbringing is directed towards weakening our tendencies toward violence, that we are instinctively inclined to think that any act of violence is a return to barbarism.'[175]

Another critic of modernity, Ortega Y Gasset, seems to have anticipated Bauman's general critique: 'Under the name first of *raison*, then of enlightenment, and finally of culture, a radical prevarication of terms and the most indiscreet deification of intelligence were affected. Among the majority of almost all thinkers of the period, especially among the Germans... *culture*, *thought*, came to fill the vacant office of a God who had been put to flight.'[176] More than God has been evicted. So, too, have been the courage to resist and the self-respect and honor entailed in resistance: 'Death is certain, there is no escaping it! Yet it is clear that the expression invites us to choose *between* the wall *and* the sword. Terrifying and proud privilege that man at times enjoys and suffers under—the choosing the pattern of his own death: death of a coward or death of a hero, an ugly or a beautiful death.'[177] More important than making the courageous choice is the choice itself: 'It is the objects and events in its environment which govern the animal's life, which pull and push it about like a marionette. It does not rule its life, does not live from *itself*, but is always intent on what is happening outside it, on all that it *other* than itself.'[178] This passage precisely recalls Levi's description of life in the camps. It also counters Trunk's interpretation of the passive acceptance of death and reveals the importance of Arendt's critique of collaboration. Trying to escape, fighting back, or any other sort of resistance, not only complicates the enemy's tasks, it asserts the humanity of the resisters. Deaths are not equal; how one dies can make all the difference. One can die like a human being, taking to the sword, or one can cringe against the wall, like a trapped animal. Apart from notions of courage, however admirable, passivity demands explanation, part of which must deal with the historic relations of Jews with the ruling classes.

While all citizens must trust the State with their physical preservation, Jewish dependence on political elites has been more profound. Were not Jewish notables correct, when they trusted more in reason and expertise, that is, the hallmarks of the modern State, than in the inchoate feelings of ordinary Jews, to say nothing of Gentile masses? Did they not, especially rabbis, hold the community together in the face of powerful disintegrative forces? Did they not avoid the shoals of powerlessness by their ability to accommodate Gentile rulers? Were not the *Judenrate* correct when they collaborated with the SS, saving what they could, preserving what was precious by spending what was not? Was their appraisal of Hitler as the irrational Leader of the masses, the incarnation of evil and chaos, incorrect? Were not the SS, by contrast, educated and reasonable? Remember, we must apply the rules appropriate to the Final Solution, not those of a vanished world.

The title of this chapter derives from the analysis of this section. Existence in the camps was comprised of a *danse macabre* comprising the SS and their non-German associates, including Jewish collaborators, and ordinary Jewish prisoners. It was a dance in four parts, each partner with two steps. For Germans, Step One was the assertion of their status as supermen; Step Two, the assertion of the depravity of Jews. For Jews, Step One was the assertion of the bestiality of Germans and, to a lesser degree, their Jewish accomplices; Step Two, the assertion of Jewish humanity, despite their hideous conditions. Each part of the dance required a response from the partner. Keeping the dance metaphor in mind, I believe many of the anomalies of the camps will dissolve, for example, executing SS officers for killing Jews. Rubenstein believes that 'One of the most bizarre aspects of the mass killings was that it was possible for an SS officer to be charged, convicted, and executed for the unauthorized murder of individual Jews....'[179] This policy was anything but bizarre to anyone familiar with life in the military. Medals are awarded for killing authorized enemies, while soldiers can be prosecuted for violence against civilians. Moreover, it is misleading to apply standards which apply outside the camps to life inside them. In this instance, it was critical for the SS to maintain its moral superiority over the Jews. This could not be done, if the SS acted like common criminals. Although there were many abuses, Himmler expected scrupulous behavior, which would reflect their spiritual mission, under the guidance of the *Fuehrer*: 'Mere links in big biological time or cosmic space, the SS had been granted a one-off opportunity to save future generations of their Nation and race from chaos, subversion and oblivion, for the concept of race meant that one day the SS would be generalized beyond national borders. The murderers had a mission, whose accomplishment would justify any human cost.... "When you see our *Fuehrer*, it is like being in a dream; you forget everything around you, it is as if God has come to you.'"[180] Coupled with the divine aspirations of the SS and the Hitler Movement was the need to prove that Jews were *unwertes Leben*. Hence the furious reaction of the SS and their accomplices to any assertion of humanity by Jews.

Realizing the danger of decency, Himmler tried to create emotional and physical distance between the SS and the Jews. Whenever the inmates resisted, punishment was swift, severe, and theatrical. No mere bullet would suffice. A message had to be sent. As an inappropriate and fraudulent assertion of humanity, resistance and the honor associated with courageous behavior had to be ruthlessly eliminated. This applied equally to suicide. There would be no Jewish Ajaxs. Friendships and other acts of solidarity were severely punished, because human decency undermined the *raison d'être* of the camps: that is, to demonstrate that Jews were only interested in personal survival, no matter what degradation it entailed, no matter how many betrayals of other Jews were implied. 'See,' the Germans would say, 'they cannot even be friends. How could they be members of the *Volksgemeinschaft?* The most basic human attributes are alien to them; therefore, they cannot be human.'

It is now necessary to put the concept of distance in the context of humiliation and collaboration *per se*. As many studies have shown and first hand testimonies have confirmed, it is far easier for a normal human being to shoot someone than to stab him and far more easy to bomb him than to shoot him. The farther away the killer is from the blood, guts, and agony of his victim the better. In other words, the purpose of killing, even in war, rarely suffices to overcome the repugnance to witness, much less participate in, killing. Hardened troops on the Eastern Front had difficulty killing defenseless Jews; unable to see their faces, they often personalized the backs of their necks. The Final Solution had to overcome human reluctance to participate in human suffering. To this degree Bauman is correct, when he cites the bureaucratic culture as a significant factor in the Final Solution. A distanced way to kill millions is necessary, when to kill thousands, traditional methods suffice, modernity supplying the way. The Final Solution was more than technology, narrowly conceived, more than Zyklon B, and more than gas chambers. As Bauman argues, the bureaucratic/technological culture enabled Germans to place Jews outside the community of concern, making them a problem, a question to be answered, in Weber's classic phrase, 'without fear or favor.' More, however, was necessary than the distance created by expertise and its mindset. The regime of humiliation and collaboration provided the last key to how so many ordinary Germans could have withstood the strain of murdering innocent men, women, and children.

In its simplest sense, Jewish collaboration allowed Germans to supervise the process of killing and incinerating Jews. After selection at the depot, the entire process was operated by 'Functionary Jews.' Bauman explains, quoting John Lachs: 'without first hand acquaintance with his actions, even the best of humans moves in a moral vacuum; the abstract recognition of evil is neither a reliable guide nor an adequate motive.... We shall not be surprised at the immense and largely unintentional cruelty of men of good will....'[181] Physical separation was reinforced by creating an emotional space between the Germans and their victims and their collaborators. Who but Jews would treat their own like this, proving they were *unwertes Leben*? Moreover, the passivity of the victims confirmed the Nazi stereotype that Jews were a species without honor, vermin in a not very convincing human disguise. The final piece to the process of distancing involved the deferred victims, Jews who were selected for gassing but not yet. In addition to the physical and emotional deprivation entailed in the camps, the SS added doses of gratuitous humiliation. For example, eating utensils were not supplied the victims. So they had to lap up their food like animals. This was not due to the absence of utensils: 'When the camp at Auschwitz was liberated...we,' Levi says, 'found tens of thousands of spoons.... So it was not a matter of thrift but a precise intent to humiliate.'[182] Similarly women prisoners were allocated one bowl with which to eat, to wash and to urinate at night. '"Considering you were going to kill them all...what was the point of the humiliations, the cruelties?" the writer asked Stangl...and he replies: "To condition those who were to be the material executors for the operations. To make it possible for them to do what they were doing." In other words, before dying, the victim must be degraded, so that the murderer will be less burdened by guilt.'[183]

Under the circumstances, given the context of a war of annihilation and the long troubled history of Jews in Germany, the Defeat in the Great War and its aftermath, it should not surprise anyone that Germans were willing to kill their enemies, including noncombatants. Nor should it surprise that SS contingents were willing to murder their ideological and racial enemies. More than killing factories, the camps were ideological institutes, whose curriculum proved that Jews were not really human and, therefore, were unworthy of life and that those who were worthy of life must prove themselves by making the world *Judenfrei*. The practices of the camps were lessons which would convince the most reluctant learner. What kind of human would collaborate with their sworn enemies? What kind of human, one already condemned, would allow him or herself to be humiliated? What kind of human would betray comrades? The answers to all these questions were that Jews were not human at all. It is certain that many Germans, including members of the SS, could not quite accept the idea that Jews were parasites. Many of these, perhaps a majority, acted out of a profound sense of duty and loyalty to Germany, rather than a belief in the Aryan Vision. Yet, even for these Germans, doing their duty might have seemed less odious and more necessary due to the abject and degrading behavior of Jews.

The purpose of the camps was fulfilled by two means: immediate selection for gassing and deferred selection, accompanied with humiliation and torment. Not merely an outcome of the Final Solution, more than a major reason for its successful implementation, the camps were part of the process by which the means fused with the end, the technique with the Vision. At all events, it is important to realize that the camps were central to the mission of the Third Reich and to the Vision of the Hitler Movement. They manifested Hitler's political theology in its most dramatic and horrific terms. By cleansing Europe of its diseased organisms, Germans would become Aryans, thereby, realizing in Time and Space their role as Europe's saviors, partaking in Eternal Harmony. It is difficult to believe all this happened. Who believes that the slaughter of millions of people, whatever their perceived defects, would purify anyone, much less please any God worth worshipping? Who can believe that anyone can glimpse Eternity standing on a pile of corpses? It seems undeniable that millions of Germans, among them some of the best educated, did believe in something like this. I can come to no other conclusion.

NOTES

1. Rubenstein, Richard L. & Roth, John K.: *Approaches to Auschwitz*, Atlanta, 1987, p. 167.

2. Friedlander, Saul: *Nazi Germany and the Jews*, Harper Collins, NY, 1997, p. 116.

3. Adler, H.G.: *The Jews in Germany: From the Enlightenment to National Socialism*, Notre Dame, London, 1969, p. 2.

4. Both Aristotle and Machiavelli praise citizen-soldiers; only Aristotle notices the link between their service and a demand for political participation.

5. Adler, *op.cit.*, p. 115.

6. *Ibid.*

7. *Ibid.*, p. 117.

8. *Ibid.*, p. 118.

9. Fischer, Klaus: *Nazi Germany: a New History,* Continuum, NY, 2003, p. 29.

10. Quoted in Adler, *op. cit,* p. 50.

11. *Ibid.*, p. 51.

12. Mayer, Arno, *op. cit.*, p. 41.

13. Arendt, Hannah: *The Origins of Totalitarianism*, World, NY, 1958, p. 73.

14. Stern, F.: *Gold and Iron: Bismarck, Bleichroder and the Building of the German Empire*, Vintage, N.Y., 1979, p. 471.

15. Adler, *op. cit.*, p. 56.

16. Rose, Paul Lawrence: *Revolutionary Anti-Semitism in Germany*, Princeton, 1990, p. 28.

17. *Ibid.*, pp. 44–5, emphasis supplied.

18. *Ibid.*, p. 197.

19. Mayer, *op. cit.*, p. 92.

20. Mosse, George: *The Crisis of German Ideology*, Grosset & Dunlap, NY, 1964, p. 140.

21. Mosse, G.: *Towards the Final Solution*, Madison, 1985, p. 104.

22. Langmuir, Gavin: *Toward a Definition of Anti-Semitism*, Berkeley, 1990, p. 51.

23. Mosse, *Final, op. cit.*, p. 122.

24. Beit-Hallahmi, B.: *Original Sins*, Olive Branch, NY, 1993, p. 7.

25. Burleigh, *op. cit.*, p. 259.

26. Mosse, George: *Nazi Culture: Intellectual, Cultural and Social Life in the Third Reich*, translated by Salvator Attanasio and others, Grosset & Dunlap, NY, 1966, p. 258.

27. Levi, Primo: *The Drowned and the Saved*, translated by Raymond Rosenthal, Summit, NY, 1986, p. 40. I shall depend on Levi later in my analysis of the Final Solution.

28. Gordon, Sarah: *Hitler, Germans and the Jewish Question*, Princeton, 1984, p. 92.

29. Bauman, Zygmunt: *Modernity and the Judeocide*, NY, 1991, 39, original emphasis.

30. Arendt, *op. cit.*, p. 230.

31. *Ibid.*, p. 74.

32. *Ibid.*, p. 5, emphasis supplied.

33. Bauman, *op. cit.*, p. 160, original emphasis.

34. *Ibid.*, p. 165, original emphasis.

35. Burleigh, *op. cit.*, p. 761.

36. *Ibid.*, p. 781. The list of gratuitous murders by the Allies is virtually without limits: Hiroshima, Hamburg, Berlin and on and on. Many Germans and Japanese felt absolved for their many crimes by this retribution.

37. Langmuir, *op. cit.*, p. 328, original emphasis.

38. Rose, *op. cit.*, p. 132.

39. *Ibid.*, p. 302.

40. Not limited to the political right, this distinction has been made by Marxist scholars in the wake of the dissolution of the Soviet Union, claiming that it had nothing to do with Communism.

41. Katz, *Prejudice, op. cit.*, p. 312.

42. Gordon, *op. cit.*, p. 22.

43. Bauman, *op, cit.*, pp. 76 & 92, respectively, original emphasis.

44. Quoted in Burleigh, *op. cit.*, p. 100.

45. Quoted in Rose, *op. cit.*, p. 94.

46. Quoted in *ibid.*, p. 96.

47. *Ibid*, p. 121.

48. *Ibid.*, p. 97, original emphasis.

49. *Ibid.*, p. 93, original emphasis.

50. Mosse, *Crisis, op. cit.*, p. 49.

51. Massing, Paul: *Rehearsal for Destruction*, Harper, NY, 1949, p. 3.

52. Friedlander, *Nazi, op. cit.*, p. 118.

53. Katz, *op. cit.*, p. 258.

54. Reichmann, Eva: *Hostages of Civilization*, Beacon, Boston, 1951, p. 72.

55. Sombart, Werner: *The Jews and Modern Capitalism*, translated by M. Epstein, New Brunswick, 1982, p. 21.

56. Bauman, *op. cit.*, p. 45, original emphasis.

57. Quoted in *ibid.*, p. 53.

58. Stern, Fritz: *Dreams and Delusions*, Knopf, NY, 1987, p. 104.

59. Gordon, *op. cit.*, p. 16.

60. Friedlander, *Nazi, op. cit.*, p. 77–8.

61. Holborn, Hajo: *A History of Modern Germany, 1840–1945*, Princeton, 1969, p. 279.

62. Friedlander, *op. cit.*, p. 79.

63. Quoting Kautsky, Massing, *op. cit.*, p. 162.

64. Quoted in Fest, *op. cit.*, p. 115.

65. Katz, *Prejudice, op. cit.*, p. 303.

66. Gordon, *op. cit.*, p. 15.

67. Katz, *Prejudice, op.cit.*, p. 247.

68. *Ibid.*, p. 251.

69. Massing, *op. cit.*, p. 11, quoting one Glagau.

70. Quoted in Sombart, *op. cit.*, p. 246. Although Graetz was writing of Polish Jews, there can be little doubt that he believed that much of his analysis would have applied to Jews in Germany, perhaps not so crudely.

71. Arendt, *op. cit.*, p. 169.

72. Talmon, J.L.: *The Myth of the Nation and the Vision of Revolution*, Berkeley, 1980, p. 188.

73. Katz, *Prejudice, op. cit.*, p. 109.

74. Friedlander, *Nazi, op. cit.*, p. 85.

75. Mosse, *Crisis, op. cit.*, p. 38.

76. Fest, *op. cit.*, p. 314.

77. Hitler, *op. cit.*, p. 150.

78. Quoted in Hilberg, Raul: *The Destruction of the European Jews*, NY, 1985, p. 20.

79. Quoted in Burleigh, *op. cit.*, p. 240.

80. Hitler, *op. cit.*, p. 249, original emphasis.

81. *Ibid.*, p. 394, original emphasis.

82. *Ibid.*, p. 214, original emphasis.

83. *Ibid.*, p. 120.

84. *Ibid.*, p. 65, original emphasis.

85. *Ibid.*, p. 339.

86. Hitler quoted by Fest, *op. cit.*, p. 533.

87. Bauman, *op. cit.*, p. 45.

88. Rubenstein, *op. cit.*, p. 112.

89. *Ibid.*, p. 171.

90. Burleigh, *op. cit.*, p. 256.

91. Quoted in *ibid.*, p. 192.

92. Gordon, *op. cit.*, pp. 9–10.

93. Mayer, *op. cit.*, pp. 41–2.

94. Bauman, *op. cit.*, p. 132.

95. *Ibid.*, p. 133.

96. Mayer, *op. cit.*, pp. 149–50.

97. *Ibid.*, p. 10.

98. Quoted by Bauman, *op. cit.*, p. 74.

99. *Ibid.*, p. 185.

100. Quoted by Bauman, *op. cit.*, p. 9.

101. Fromm, Erich: *The Anatomy of Human Destructiveness,* Holt, Rinehart, NY, 1973, p. 433.

102. Mayer, *op. cit.*, p. 113.

103. *Ibid.*, p. 314.

104. *Ibid.*, p. 98.

105. *Ibid.*, p. 94.

106. *Ibid.*, p. 90.

107. The term, 'superfluous' conforms to Rubenstein's usage. *Op. cit.*, p. 30.

108. Bauman, *op. cit.*, p. 120.

109. Fest, *op. cit.*, p. 527.

110. Bauman, *op. cit.*, p.x.

111. Horowitz, I.L.: *Taking Lives,* New Brunswick, 1997, p. 209. I thought of the title 'Taking Lives' before I began my systematic research, before, that is, I became aware of Professor Horowitz's book. There is more than coincidence in this—although what to call it escapes me. Professor Horowitz taught my first course in sociology, more years ago than either of us likes to remember. I must add that his chapter 13, 'Exclusivity and Inclusivity of Collective Death,' is among the very best treatments of this extremely difficult and emotional subject.

112. Kershaw, Ian: *Hitler: 1889–1936: Hubris*, Norton, NY, 1998, p.xix.

113. Determinism became a pejorative term in the twentieth century and remains so for those who fear that, even as a metaphysical concept, it will undermine human responsibility and morality. It is the basis of one of the four fears which swirl around the concept of human nature. According to Pinker: 'If people are the products of biology, free will would be a myth and we could no longer hold people responsible for their actions.' Pinker, Stephen: *The Blank Slate: the Modern Denial of Human Nature,* Penguin, NY, 2002, p. 139.

114. Quoted by Pinker, *op. cit.*, p. 56.

115. Quoted in Burleigh, *op. cit.*, p. 13.

116. *Ibid.*, p. 99.

117. Quoted in Pinker, *op. cit.*, p. 26.

118. Quoted in Burleigh, op. cit., p. 660.

119. For those who doubt this judgment, see Baker, Nicholson: *Human Smoke, the Beginnings of World War II and the End of Civilization*, Simon & Shuster, NY, 2008.

120. *Ibid.*, p. 346.

121. Quoted in *ibid.*, pp. 357–8.

122. It is difficult to get a precise number of those killed under the policies of euthanasia. A reasonable estimate is about 100,000. According to Burleigh, 'Graphs showed how the deaths of 70,273 people [mostly mentally ill] achieved so far [1941] would have saved a projected 885,439,800 RM by 1951....' *Ibid.*, p. 404. Note how easily the medical justifications become economic, especially in war.

123. 1933 Law for the Prevention of Hereditarily Diseased Progeny:] the law specified... congenital feeblemindedness, schizophrenia, manic-depressive illness, epilepsy, Huntington's chorea, hereditary blindness and deafness, and severe physical malformation. *Ibid.*, p. 354.

124. For a demolition of the biological concept of race, see Lebarre, Weston: *The Human Animal*, Chicago, 1954.

125. Fischer, *op. cit.*, p. 32.

126. Quoted in Burleigh, *op. cit.*, p. 254.

127. Mosse, *Final, op. cit.*, p. 99.

128. Quoted in Farias, *op. cit.*, p. 32.

129. Quoted in Mosse, *Culture, op. cit.*, pp. 203 & 205.

130. Quoted in Burleigh, *op. cit.*, p. 152.

131. Bauman, *op. cit.*, p. 27.

132. Quoted in Burleigh, *op.cit.*, p. 614.

133. *Ibid.*, p. 661.

134. Quoted in Bauman, *op. cit.*, pp. 11–2.

135. Sofsky, Wolfgang: *The Order of Terror: the Concentration Camp*, translated by William Templar, Princeton, 1996, p. 12.

136. There will be more references to Trunk below.

137. Bauman, *op. cit.,* p. 53.

138. Quoted in Rubenstein, *op. cit.*, p. 208.

139. Quoted by *ibid.*, p. 58, emphasis supplied.

140. *Ibid.*, p. 56, original emphasis.

141. *Ibid.*, p. 50.

142. *Ibid.*, p. 40.

143. *Ibid.*

144. *Ibid.*, p. 50.

145. *Ibid.*, p. 52.

146. Nolte, Ernst: *Three Faces of Fascism*, translated by Leila Vennewitz, Mentor, NY, 1963, 1969, pp. 480–1, emphasis supplied.

147. Bauman, *op. cit.*, p. 15, original emphasis.

148. *Ibid.*, pp. 17–8.

149. *Ibid.*, p. 28.

150. *Ibid.*, p.x, original emphasis.

151. *Ibid.*, p.xiii.

152. *Ibid.*, p. 81, original emphasis.

153. *Ibid.*, p.xii.

154. *Ibid.*, p. 121, original emphasis.

155. *Ibid.*, p.xii.

156. Bauman, *op. cit.*, p. 205, original emphasis.

157. Quoted in Rubenstein, *op. cit.*, p. 174.

158. Levi, *op. cit.*, p. 11.

159. Mayer, *op. cit.,* p.ix.

160. Rubenstein, *op. cit.*, p. 175.

161. Levi, *op. cit.*, p. 111.

162. *Ibid.*, p. 155.

163. *Ibid.*, p. 76.

164. *Ibid.*, p. 20.

165. *Ibid.*, p. 46.

166. *Ibid.*, p. 52.

167. Bauman, *op. cit.*, p. 117.

168. *Ibid.*, p. 122, original emphasis.

169. Arendt, *op.cit.*, p. 33.

170. *Ibid.*, pp. 64–5.

171. Quoted in Bauman, *op.cit.*, p. 131.

172. *Ibid.*, p. 134.

173. *Ibid.*, p.*xiii*, original emphasis.

174. *Ibid.*, p. 107.

175. Sorel, Georges: *Reflections on Violence,* translated by T.E. Hulme, NY, 1961, p. 181.

176. Ortega Y Gasset, *op. cit.*, p. 30.

177. *Ibid.*, p. 45.

178. *Ibid.*, p. 17.

179. Rubenstein, *op. cit.*, p. 136.

180. Burleigh, *op. cit.*, p. 196.

181. Bauman, *op. cit.*, p. 25.

182. Levi, *op. cit.*, p. 114.

183. *Ibid.*, pp. 125–6.

Bibliography

Abulafia, David. *Frederick II: a Medieval Emperor*, Oxford, NY, 1988.

Ackerman, Robert John. *Nietzsche: a Frenzied Look*, Amherst, 1990.

Adler, H.G. *The Jews in Germany: from the Enlightenment to National Socialism*, London, 1969.

Allison, David B., editor. *The New Nietzsche: Contemporary Styles of Interpretation*, NY, 1977.

Armstrong, Karen. *A History of God*, Ballantine, NY, 1993.

Arendt, Hannah. *Eichmann in Jerusalem*, Viking, NY, 1963.

———. *The Origins of Totalitarianism*, World, NY, 1958.

Augustine, St. *City of God*, translated by Gerald Walsh *et al*, Doubleday, NY, 1958.

Bach, H.I. *The German Jew: a Synthesis of Judaism and Western Civilization, 1730–1930,* Oxford, NY, 1984.

Baeck, Leo. *The People of Israel,* translated by Albert Friedlander, Holt, NY, 1964.

———. *Judaism and Christianity,* translated by Walter Kaufmann, Philadelphia, 1958.

Bainton, Roland. *The Reformation of the Sixteenth Century*, Beacon, Boston, 1952.

Baker, Nicolson. *Human Smoke, the Beginnings of World War II and the End of Civilization*, Simon & Schuster, NY, 2008.

Barraclough, G. *the Origins of Modern Germany*, Capricorn, 1963.

———. *The Medieval Papacy,* Norton, NY, 1979.

Beit-Hallahmi, B. *Original Sins*, Olive Branch, NY, 1993.

Barnard, Chester. *The Functions of the Executive*, Harvard, Cambridge, 1938, 1968.

Baron, Salo. *A Social and Religious History of the Jews,* Vol.I, Philadelphia, 1937, 1952.

Bauman, Zygmunt. *Modernity and the Holocaust*, Cornell, NY, 1991.

Bendix, Reinhard. *Kings or People: Power and the Mandate to Rule*, California, Berkeley, 1978.

Berdyaev, N. *The Origin of Russian Communism*, translated by R. M. French, Ann Arbor, 1937, 1960.

Berger, Peter, L. *The Sacred Canopy, Elements of a Sociological Theory of Religion*, NY, 1969.

Berlin, Isaiah. *Two Concepts of Liberty*, Oxford, 1970.

Bialas, Wolfgang & Rabinbach, Anson. *Nazi Germany and the Humanities*, Oxford, 2007.

Black, Antony. *Political Thought in Europe: 1250–1450*, Cambridge, 1992.

Bloch, Marc. *Feudal Society: The Growth of Ties of Dependence*, Vol. I, translated by L.A. Manyon, Chicago, 1961.

Boehmer, Heinrich. *Luther and the Reformation,* translated by E.S.G. Potter, Dial, NY, 1930.

———. *Martin Luther: Road to the Reformation*, translated by J. Doberstein & T. Tappert, Meridan, NY, 1957.

Bornkamm, Gunther. *Paul*, translated D.M. Stalker, Harper & Row, NY, 1972.

Bracher, Karl D. *The Age of Ideologies*, translated by Ewald Osers, St. Martin's, NY, 1984.

———. *The German Dictatorship,* translated by Jean Steinberg, Penguin, Middlesex, 1970.

Broszat, Martin. *German National Socialism,* Clio, Santa Barbara, 1966.

Browning, Christopher R. *Ordinary Men: Reserve Battalion 101 and the Final Solution in Poland*, Harper, NY, 1992.

Buber, Martin. *Moses and the Revelation of the Covenant*, Harper, NY, 1946.

———. *The Prophetic Faith*, Harper, NY, 1949.

Bull, Hedley. *The Challenge of the Third Reich,* Oxford, 1986.

Bullock, Alan. *Hitler: A Study in Tyranny*, Harper, NY, 1960, Bantam, NY, 1961.

Bultmann, Rudolf. *History and Eschatology*, Harper, NY, 1957.

———. *Jesus and the Word*, Scribners, NY, 1926.

———. *Primitive Christianity*, translated by R.H. Fuller, Fortress Press, Philadelphia, 1980.

Burleigh, Michael. *The Third Reich: a New History,* Macmillan, NY, 2000.

Calleo, David. *The German Problem Reconsidered*, Cambridge, NY, 1978.

Cameron, Euan. *The European Reformation*, Oxford, 1991.

Cantor, Norman. *The Civilization of the Middle Ages*, Harper, NY, 1993.

Cassirer, Ernst. *The Myth of the State*, Yale, New Haven, 1946.

Chabod, Federico. *Machiavelli and the Renaissance*, Harper, NY, 1965.

Cheyney, Edward. *The Dawn of a New Era: 1250–1453*, Harper, NY, 1936.

Cobban, Alfred. *The Nations-State and National Self-Determination*, Collins, London, 1969.

Cohn, Norman. *Cosmos, Chaos, and the World to Come: the Ancient Roots of Apocalyptic Faith,* Yale, New Haven, 1993.

———. *The Pursuit of the Millennium*, Oxford, NY, 1970.

———. *Warrant for Genocide*, Harper & Row, NY, 1966.

Cranz, Edward, F. *An Essay on the Development of Luther's thought on Justice, Law, and Society*, Harvard, Cambridge, 1959.

Craig, Gordon A. *Politics and Culture in Modern Germany*, Palo Alto, 1981–98.

Dahrendorf, Ralf. *Society and Democracy in Germany,* Doubleday, NY, 1969.

Davies, W.D. *Christian Origins and Judaism*, Westminster, Philadelphia, 1962.

Dawkins, Richard. *The God Delusion*, Houghton-Mifflin, Boston, 2006.

DeCasseres, A. *Spinoza: Liberator of God and Man*, NY, 1932.

Deleuze, Gilles. *Nietzsche and Philosophy,* translated by Hugh Tomlinson, Columbia, NY, 1962.

DeMolen, Richard L. *One Thousand Years: Western Europe in the Middle Ages,* Boston, 1974.

D'Entreves, A.P. *The Notion of the State*, Oxford, 1967.

Donagan, Alan. *Spinoza*, Chicago, 1988.

Dunham, Barrows. *Heroes and Heretics*, Knopf, NY, 1963.

Eckart, Dietrich. *Bolshevism from Moses to Lenin, A Dialogue Between Hitler and Me*, translated by William L. Pierce, National Vanguard Books, 1924, 1966.

Elias, Norbert. *Power and Civility*, translated by Edmund Jephcott, Pantheon, NY, 1939, 1982.

Ellis, Peter, editor, *Seven Pauline Letters*, Collegeville, Minnesota, 1982.

Erikson, Erik. *Young Man Luther*, Norton, NY, 1958.

Ericksen, Robert P. *Theologians Under Hitler: Gerhard Kittel, Paul Althaus, and Emanuel Hirsch*, Yale, New Haven, 1985.

Eyck, Erich. *A History of the Weimar Republic*, Vol. I., translated by Harlan P. Hanson & Robert Waite, Harvard, Cambridge, 1962.

Fackenheim, Emil. *The Religious Dimensions in Hegel's Thought*, Beacon Press, Boston, 1970.

Farias, Victor. *Heidegger and Nazism,* edited by Joseph Margolis & Tom Rockmore, translated by Gabriel Ricci, Philadelphia, 1989.

Ferry, Luc & Renaut, Alain. *Heidegger and Modernity*, translated by Franklin Philip, Chicago, 1990.

Fest, Joachim. *Hitler*, translated by Richard & Clara Winston, Harcourt, NY, 1974.

Fichte, Johann Gottlieb. *Addresses to the German Nation*, translated by R.F. Jones, Westport, 1979.

Fingarette, Herbert. *The Self in Transformation*, Harper, NY, 1963.

Finkelstein, Norman. *The Holocaust Industry*, NY, 2003.

Fischer, Klaus. *Nazi Germany: a New History.* Continuum, NY, 2003.

Freud, S. *Future of an Illusion*: Doubleday, translated by James Strachey, NY, 1964.

Friedlander, Saul. *Nazi Germany and the Jews*, Harper Collins, NY, 1997.

———. *Reflections on Nazism,* Harper, NY, 1982.

Fritzsche, Peter. *Nietzsche and the Death of God,* St Martins, Boston, 2007.

Fromm, Erich. *The Anatomy of Human Destructiveness,* Holt, Rinehart, NY, 1973.

Fuhrmann, Horst. *Germany in the High Middle Ages, c.1050–1200*, translated by Timothy Reuter, Cambridge, 1986.

Gager, John. *The Origins of Anti-Semitism*, Oxford, NY, 1985.

George, Stefan. *The Works of Stefan George Rendered into English*, by Olga Marx & Ernst Moritz, 2nd edition, Chapel Hill, 1974.

Gierke, Otto. *Political Theories of the Middle Age*, translated by F.W. Maitland, Boston, 1958.

Glaser, Hermann. editor, *The German Mind of the Nineteenth Century,* Continuum, NY, 1981.

Goldhagen, Daniel J. *Hitler's Willing Executioners,* Knopf, NY, 1996.

Gordon, Sarah. *Hitler, Germans and the Jewish Question,* Princeton, 1984.

Grayzel, Solomon. *Church and Jews in the Thirteenth Century,* Philadelphia, 1933.

Grunfeld, Frederic. *The Hitler File,* Random House, NY, 1974.

Guignebert, Charles. *The Early History of Christianity,* Thwayne, NY, 1927.

Haas, Ernst. *Beyond the Nation-State: Functionalism and International Organization,* Palo Alto, 1964.

———. *Nationalism, Liberalism and Progress, Vol.I,* Ithaca, 1997.

———. *Nationalism, Liberalism and Progress: the Dismal State of New Nations, Vol. II,* Ithaca, 2000.

Hallett, H.F. *Creation, Emanation, Salvation: a Spinozistic Study,* the Hague, 1962.

Hamerow, Theodore. *Restoration, Revolution, Reaction,* Princeton, 1958.

Harbison, E. Harris. *The Age of Reformation,* Ithaca, 1955.

Heer, Friedrich. *The Intellectual History of Europe,* translated by Jonathan Steinberg, World, NY, 1953.

———. *The Medieval World: Europe 110–1350,* translated by Janet Sondheimer, NY, 1998.

Hegel, Friedrich. *On Christianity,* translated by T.M. Knox, Harper, NY, 1948.

———. *Three Essays,* translated by Peter Fuss & John Dobbins, Notre Dame, Indiana, 1984.

Heidegger, Martin. *Being and Time,* translated by John Macquarrie & Edward Robinson, Harper, NY, 1962.

———. *The End of Philosophy,* translated by Joan Stambaugh, Harper, NY, 2003.

———. *The Question Concerning Technology,* translated by William Lovitt, Harper, NY, 1977.

———. *Poetry, Language, Thought,* translated by Albert Hofstadter, NY, 1975.

Heine, Heinrich. *Religion and Philosophy in Germany: A Fragment,* translated by John Snodgrass, NY, 1986.

Herder, J.G., *Herder on Social and Political Culture,* translated and edited by F.M. Barnard, Cambridge, 1969.

Hertzberg, Arthur. *The French Enlightenment and the Jews,* Columbia, NY, 1968.

Hertz, Frederick. *The Development of the German Public Mind,* Allen & Utwin, London, 1962 Vol. I.

———. *Nationality in History and Politics,* Humanities, NY, 1943, 1950.

Heschel, Abraham. *The Prophets,* Vol. I&II, Harper, NY, 1962.

Hess, Jonathan. *German Jews and the Claims of Modernity,* Yale, New Haven, 2002.

Hilberg, Raul. *The Destruction of the European Jews,* Holmes & Meier, NY, 1961.

Hillgruber, Andreas. *Germany and the Two World Wars,* translated by William Kirby, Harvard, Cambridge, 1967, 1981.

Hitler, Adolf. *Hitler's Secret Book,* translated by Savatore Attanasio, 1962, 1986.

———. *Mein Kampf,* translated by Ralph Manheim, Houghton-Mifflin, Boston, 1925, 1971.

Holborn, Hajo. *A History of Modern Germany: the Reformation,* Knopf, NY, 1964.

——. *A History of Modern Germany: 1648–1840*, Knopf, NY, 1964.

——. *A History of Modern Germany, 1840–1945*, Princeton, 1969.

Holmes, George, editor. *The Oxford History of Medieval Europe*, Oxford, NY, 1992.

Horowitz, I.L. *Taking Lives,* New Brunswick, 1997.

Huizinga, J. *The Waning of the Middle Ages*, Doubleday, NY, 1954.

Isaacs, Jules. *Has Anti-Semitism Roots in Christianity?* translated by Dorothy & James Parkes, NY, 1961.

——. *The Teaching of Contempt*, McGraw Hill, NY, 1965.

Israel, Jonathan. *European Jewry in the Age of Mercantilism,* Oxford, 1969, 1989.

Jackel, Eberhard. *Hitler's Weltanschauung: a Blueprint for Power*, translated by Herbert Arnold, Wesleyan, Middletown, 1972.

Jaspers, Karl. *Nietzsche,* translated by Charles Wallraff & Frederick Schmitz, Tucson, 1965.

——. *The Question of German Guilt*, translated by E. B. Ashton, Dial, NY, 1947.

Joachim, Harold. *A Study of the Ethics of Spinoza*, NY, 1964.

Jung, C.G. *Civilization in Transition*, 2d edition, translated by R.F.C. Hull, Princeton, 1975.

Kahler, Erich. *The Germans,* Princeton, 1974.

——. *The Jews Among the Nations*, Ungar, NY, 1967.

Kantorowitz, Ernst. *The King's Two Bodies: a Study in Medieval Political Theology,* Princeton, 1957.

Katz, Jacob. *Out of the Ghetto: The Social Background of Jewish Emancipation, 1770–1870,* Schocken, NY, 1978.

——. *Tradition and Crisis: Jewish Society at the End of the Middle Ages*, Schocken, NY, 1993.

——. *From Prejudice to Destruction: Anti-Semitism, 1700–1933*, Harvard, Cambridge, 1980 Kaufmann, Walter. *Nietzsche, Philosopher, Psychologist, Antichrist*, Vintage, NY, 3d. ed., 1968.

Kautsky, Karl. *The Foundations of Christianity: Studies in Christian Origins*, translated by Henry F. Mins, International, NY, 1925.

Kelly, George, A. *Idealism, Politics and History, Sources of Hegelian Thought*, Cambridge, 1969.

Kern, Fritz. *Kingship and the Law in the Middle Ages,* translated by S.B. Chrimes, Harper, NY, 1914, 1970.

Kershaw, Ian. *Hitler: 1889–1936: Hubris*, Norton, NY, 1998.

——. *Hitler: 1936–45: Nemesis*, Norton, NY, 2000.

Kertzer, David. The *Popes Against the Jews,* Knopf, NY, 2001.

Kerenyi, C. *Religion of Greeks and Romans*, Dutton, NY, 1962.

Keynes, John Maynard. *The Economic Consequences of the Peace,* Dover, NY, 1920, 2004.

Kisch, Guido. *The Jews of Medieval Germany*, Chicago, 1949.

Klemperer, Victor. *I Will Bear Witness*, translated by Martin Chalmers, Random House, NY, 1998.

Kohler, Joachim. *Wagner's Hitler,* translated by Ronald Taylor, Polity, Cambridge, 2000.

Kohn, Hans. *The Mind of Germany*, Scribner's, NY, 1960.

Krausnick, Helmut. *Anatomy of the SS State,* Walker, NY, 1965.

Krell, D. & Wood, D. *Exceedingly Nietzsche,* Routledge, London, 1988.

Krieger, Leonard. *The German Idea of Freedom*, Chicago, 1957.

Lane, B.M. & Rupp, L. J. *Nazi Ideology before 1933: Documentation,* Austin, 1978.

Lang, Berel. *Heidegger's Silence*, Cornell, Ithaca, 1996.

Langmuir, Gavin. *Toward a Definition of Anti-Semitism,* Berkeley, 1990.

Lea, Henry, Charles. *A History of the Inquisition in Spain*, Macmillan, NY, 1906.

Le Barre, Weston. *The Ghost Dance: the Origins of Religion*, Dell, NY, 1972.

———. *The Human Animal*, Chicago, 1954.

Levi, Primo. *The Drowned and the Saved,* translated by Raymond Rosenthal, Summit, NY, 1986.

Levy, Richard S. *The Downfall of Anti-Semitic Parties in Imperial Germany*, Yale, New Haven, 1975.

Lewis, Ewart. *Medieval Political Ideas*, Knopf, NY, 1954.

Low, Alfred. *Jews in the Eyes of the Germans,* Philadelphia, 1979.

Lowenthal, Marvin. *The Jews of Germany: a Story of Sixteen Centuries*, Philadelphia, 1936.

Lowith, Karl. *From Hegel to Nietzsche: the Revolution in Nineteenth Century Thought,* translated by David Green, Doubleday, NY, 1941, 1967.

———, *Martin Heidegger and European Nihilism,* Richard Wolin editor, translated by Gary Steiner, Columbia, NY, 1984, 1995.

———, *Meaning in History*, Chicago, 1949.

Luther, Martin. *Commentary on the Epistle to the Romans*, Grand Rapids, 1954.

———. *Table Talk*, translated by William Hazlitt, Gainseville, 2004.

———. *Three Treatises*, translated by various, Fortress, Philadelphia, 1970.

Lyotard, Jean-Francois. *Heidegger and the Jews*, translated by A. Michel, and M. Roberts, Minneapolis, 1990.

MacKinnon, James. *Luther and the Reformation, Vol.1*, Russell & Russell, NY, 1962.

Mann, Golo. *The History of Germany Since 1789,* translated by Marian Jackson, NY, 1968.

Mann, Thomas. *The Coming Victory of Democracy*, Chicago, 1938.

———. *Doctor Faustus*, translated by H.T. Lowe-Porter, Knopf, NY, 1948.

———. *Reflections of a Non-Political Man*, translated by Walter Morris, NY, 1918, 1983.

———. *Three Essays*, translated by H.T. Lowe-Porter, Knopf, NY, 1918, 1991.

Maritain, Jacques. *Three Reformers: Luther, Descartes, Rousseau,* London, 1928, 1970.

Marx, Karl. *A World Without Jews*, translated by Dagobert Runes, Philosophical Library, NY, 1959.

Mayer, Arno. *Why Did the Heaves Not Darken? The Final Solution in History*, NY, 1988.

McKeon, Richard. *The Philosophy of Spinoza: the Unity of his Thought*, NY, 1928.

Mearsheimer, John. *The Tragedy of Great Power Politics*, Norton, NY, 2003.

Meeks, Wayne, editor. *The Writings of St Paul*, Norton, NY, 1972.

Meinecke, Friedrich. *the German Catastrophe*, translated by Sidney Fay, Beacon, Boston, 1950.

———. *Machiavellianism: The Doctrine of Raison D'état and its Place in Modern History*, translated by Douglas Scott, London, 1957.

Mendelssohn, Moses. *Jerusalem*, translated by Alfred Josper, Shocken, NY, 1969.

Meyer, B.F. *Aims of Jesus*, London, 1979.

Meyer, Michael. *German Political Pressure and Jewish Religious Response in the Nineteenth Century*, NY, 1981.

Mitcherlich, Alexander. *Society Without the Father*, Harcourt, NY, 1969.

Mitzman, A. *Iron Cage*, Knopf, NY, 1970.

Montefiore, Claude. *the Jewish People*, Arno, 1914, 1973.

———. 'Nation or Religious Community?' *The Jewish Quarterly Review, Vol. 12*, Jan., 1900, pp. 177–94.

———. *The Old Testament and After*, Macmillan, London, 1923.

Moss, H.St.L.B. *the Birth of the Middle Ages*, Oxford, 1964.

Mosse, George. *The Crisis of German Ideology*, Grosset & Dunlap, NY, 1964.

———. *Fallen Soldiers*, Oxford, 1990.

———. *Germans and Jews*, Grosset & Dunlap, NY, 1971.

———. *The Image of Man*, Oxford, NY, 1996.

———. *Nazi Culture: Intellectual, Cultural and Social Life in the Third Reich*, Grosset & Dunlap, NY, 1966.

Nehemas, Alexander. *Nietzsche: Life as Literature*, Harvard, Cambridge, 1985.

Neske, G. & Kettering, E. *Martin Heidegger and National Socialism*, Paragon, NY, 1990.

Neumann, Franz. *Behemoth: The Structure and Practice of National Socialism*, Harper, NY, 1942, 1966.

———. *The Democratic and the Authoritarian State*, London, 1957.

Nietzsche, Friedrich. *Beyond Good and Evil*, translated Marianne Cowan, Chicago, 1955.

———. *The Gay Science*, translated by Walter Kaufmann, NY, 1974.

———. *Nietzsche and the Death of God: Selected Writings*, Peter Fritzsche, editor and translator, Boston, 2007.

———. *A Nietzsche Reader*, selected and translated by R.J. Hollingdale, London, 2003.

———. *Twilight of the Idols and the Anti-Christ*, translated by R.J. Hollingdale, London, 1990.

———. *The Birth of Tragedy*, translated by Francis Golfing, Doubleday, NY, 1956.

———. *On the Genealogy of Morals*, translated by Kaufmann & Hollingdale, NY, 1967.

———. *The Gay Science*, translated by Walter Kaufmann, NY, 1974.

———. *Thus Spoke Zarathustra*, translated by R. J. Hollingdale, London, 1961.

———. *The Nietzsche Reader*, edited by Pearson, K. & Large, D., Blackwell, Oxford, 2006.

———. *The Will to Power*, translated by W. Kaufmann & R.J. Hollingdale, NY, 1967.

Noakes, J. & Pridham, G. *Nazism: 1919–1945*, Shocken, NY, 1983.

Nock, Arthur Darby. *St Paul*, Harper, NY, 1938.

Nolte, Ernst. *Three Faces of Fascism*, translated by Leila Vennewitz, Mentor, NY, 1963, 1969.

Norton, Robert E. *Secret Germany: Stefan George and His Circle*, Ithaca, 2002.

Novick, Peter. *The Holocaust in American Life*, Houghton-Mifflin, Boston, 1999.

Ortega Y Gasset, Jose. *Man and People,* translated by Willard Trask, Norton, NY, 1957.

Otto, Walter. *Dionysus: Myth and Cult*, translated by Robert Palmer, Bloomington, 1965.

Parkes, James. *The Jew in the Medieval Community*, 2d, Hermon, NY, 1976.

———. *The Conflict of the Church and the Synagogue*, Atheneum, NY, 1969.

———. *Judaism and Christianity*, Chicago, 1948.

Peterson, Edward. *The Limits of Hitler's Power*, Princeton, 1969.

Peukert, Detlev. *Inside Nazi Germany: Conformity, Opposition and Racism in Everyday Life*, translated by Richard Deveson, New Haven, 1982.

Pirenne, Henri. *A History of Europe: From the End of the Roman World in the West to the Beginnings of the Western States,* Vol. I, translated by Bernard Miall, Doubleday, NY, 1956

Pflanze, Otto. *Bismarck and the Development of Germany,* Princeton, 1963.

Pinker, Steven. *The Blank Slate, the Modern Denial of Human Nature*, Viking, 2002.

Pocock, J.G.A. *The Machiavellian Moment*, Princeton, 1975.

Pollock, Frederick. *Spinoza: His Life and Philosophy*, NY, 1966.

Pulzer, Peter. *Jews and the German State,* Blackwell, Cambridge, 1992.

Rauschning, Herman. *The Revolution of Nihilism,* translated by E. W. Dickies, NY, 1939.

Reitlinger, Gerald. *The Final Solution,* 2d edition, Valentine, Mitchell, London, 1961.

Rhodes, James M. *The Hitler Movement*, Hoover, Stanford, 1980.

Rhodes, Richard. *Masters of Death: the SS and the Invention of the Holocaust*, NY, 2002.

Ritter, Gerhard. *Luther: His Life and Work*, Harper & Row, NY, 1959.

Rockmore, Tom & Margolis, Joseph, editors. *The Heidegger Case on Philosophy and Politics*, Philadelphia, 1992.

Roth, Cecil. *History of the Jews in Venice*, Schocken, NY, 1930, 1975.

Rose, Paul Lawrence. *Revolutionary Anti-Semitism in Germany,* Princeton, 1990.

———. *Wagner: Race and Revolution,* Yale, New Haven, 1992.

Rosenberg, Hans. *Bureaucracy, Aristocracy and Autocracy: the Prussian Experience,* Cambridge, 1958.

Rubenstein, Richard L. *After Auschwitz, Radical Theology and Contemporary Judaism*, NY, 1966.

——— & Roth, John K. *Approaches to Auschwitz*, Knox, Atlanta, 1987.

Russell, Jeffrey Burton. *Witchcraft in the Middle Ages*, Cornell, Ithaca, 1972.

Shapiro, Michael. *Language and Politics,* NY, 1984.

Salomon, Ernst von. *The Answers*, translated by Constantine Fitzgibbon, Putnam, London, 1954.

Samuel, Maurice. *The Great Hatred*, Knopf, NY, 1940.

Sander, E.P. *Paul, the Law, and the Jewish People,* Philadelphia, 1983.

Sadler, M.F. *Commentary on Romans,* London, 1898.

Sandmel, Samuel. *The Hebrew Scriptures,* Oxford, 1963, 1978.

———. *The Genius of Paul,* Farrar Strauss, NY, 1958.

Schleunes, Karl. *The Twisted Road to Auschwitz,* Chicago, 1970.

Schoenbaum, D. *Hitler's Social Revolution: Class and Status in Nazi Germany,* Doubleday, NY, 1966.

Schoeps, H.J. *The Jewish-Christian Argument,* translated by David Green, Holt, NY, 1963.

Schorske, Carl. *German Social Democracy,* Wiley, NY, 1955.

Schurer, Emil. *The Literature of the Jewish People in the Time of Jesus,* Schocken, NY, 1972.

Shahak, Israel. *Jewish History, Jewish Religion,* London, 1994.

——— and Mezvinsky, N. *Jewish Fundamentalism in Israel,* London, 1999.

Skinner, Quentin. *The Foundations of Modern Political Thought, Vol. II,* NY, 1978.

Smith, Preserved. *Reformation in Europe,* Collier, NY, 1962.

Sombart, Werner. *The Jews and Modern Capitalism,* translated by M. Epstein, New Brunswick, 1982.

Sorel, Georges. *Reflections on Violence,* translated by T.E. Hulme, Collier, NY, 1961.

Speer, Albert. *Inside the Third Reich,* translated Richard and Clara Winston, NY, 1970.

———. *Spandau: the Secret Diaries,* translated by Richard & Clara Winston, Macmillan, NY.

Spengler, Oswald. *The Decline of the West,* translated by Charles Francis Atkinson, Oxford, NY, 1918, 1991.

Spinoza, Benedict de. *Ethics,* edited by James Gutmann, translated by William Hale White & A.H. Stirling, NY, 1949.

———. *Works of Spinoza,* translated by R.H.M. Elwes, NY, 1951.

Southern, R.W. *Western Society and the Church in the Middle Ages,* Michigan, 1970.

———. *The Making of the Middle Ages,* New Haven, 1953.

Stace, W.T. *The Philosophy of Hegel,* Dover, London, 1955.

Steigmann-Gall, Richard. *the Holy Reich: Nazi Conceptions of Christianity, 1919–45,* Cambridge, London, 2003.

Steiner, Jean-Francois. *Treblinka,* Simon & Schuster, NY, 1967.

Steiner, George. *The Portage to San Cristobal of A.H.,* Chicago, 1971, 1999.

Stern, Fritz. *Dreams and Delusions,* Knopf, N.Y., 1987.

———. *Gold and Iron,* Knopf, NY, 1977.

———. *Einstein's German World,* Princeton, 1999.

———. *The Politics of Cultural Despair,* Berkeley, 1974.

———. *A Study of Nietzsche,* Cambridge, 1979.

———. *Ernst Junger,* Yale, New Haven, 1953.

Stern, J.P. *The Fuehrer and the People,* Berkeley, 1975.

Strauss, L. & Cropsey P. *History of Political Philosophy,* 3d edition, Chicago, 1987.

Strayer, Joseph. *Medieval Origins of the Modern State,* Princeton, NJ, 1970.

Talmon, J.L. *The Myth of the Nation and the Vision of Revolution,* Berkeley, 1980.

Taylor, A.J.P. *The Course of German History*, Capricorn, NY, 1946, 1962.

Tcherikover, Victor. *Hellenistic Civilization and the Jews,* translated by S. Applebaum, Atheneum, NY, 1959, 1970.

Tellenbach, Gerd. *The Church in Western Europe from the Tenth to the Early Twelfth Century,* translated by Timothy Reuter, Cambridge, 1993.

Thiele, Leslie Paul. *Friedrich Nietzsche and the Politics of the Soul. A Study of Heroic Individualism,* Princeton, 1990.

Toland, John. *Adolf Hitler*, Doubleday, NY, 1976.

Trachtenberg, Joshua. *The Devil and the Jews*, Jewish Publication Society, Philadelphia, 1983.

Treitschke, Heinrich von. *Politics*, translated by Blance Dugdale & Torben de Bille, Harcourt, NY, 1963, 1916

Valentin, Veit. *The German People*, translated by Olga Marx, Knopf, NY, 1952.

Vermes, Geza. *Jesus and the World of Judaism*, London, 1983.

Vital, David. *A People Apart: the Jews in Europe 1789–1939*. Oxford, 1999.

Waite, Robert. *The Psychopathic God: Adolf Hitler*, NY, 1977.

Weber, Max. On Law in Economy and Society, translated by Edward Shils & Max Rheinstein, NY, 1954.

———. *The Protestant Ethic and the Spirit of Capitalism*, translated by Talcott Parsons, Scribner's, NY, 1958

———. *Sociology of Religion*, translated by Ephraim Fishoff, Boston, 1963.

———. *The Theory of Social and Economic Organization,* translated by A.M. Henderson & Talcott Parsons, Free Press, NY, 1947.

Weiss, Johannes. *Earliest Christianity*, Vol. I, translated by F. Grant et.al., Harper, NY, 1959.

———. *Paul and Jesus*, Harper, NY, 1909.

Weiss, John. *Ideology of Death*, Dee, Chicago, 1996.

Wilks, Michael. *The Problem of Sovereignty in the Later Middle Ages*, Cambridge, 1964.

Wolin, Richard. editor, *The Heidegger Controversy*, MIT, Cambridge, 1993.

Wolin, Sheldon. *Politics and Vision*, Little Brown, Boston, 1960.

Yovel, Y. *Spinoza and Other Heretics*, Princeton, 1989.

Subject Index

317

Index of Names

CPSIA information can be obtained at www.ICGtesting.com
Printed in the USA
BVOW011942081211

277876BV00001B/2/P